Marines under Armor

MARINES
UNDER ARMOR
The Marine Corps and the
Armored Fighting Vehicle, 1916–2000

KENNETH W. ESTES

Naval Institute Press
Annapolis, Maryland

Naval Institute Press
291 Wood Road
Annapolis, MD 21402

Library of Congress Cataloging-in-Publication Data

Estes, Kenneth W.
    Marines under armor : the Marine Corps and the armored fighting vehicle, 1916–2000 / Kenneth W. Estes.
        p. cm.
    Includes bibliographical references and index.
    ISBN 1-55750-237-4 (alk. paper)
    1. United States. Marine Corps—Armored troops—History—20th century. 2. Armored vehicles, Military—United States—History—20th century. I. Title.
VE23.E88 2000
359.9'683'09730904—dc21   00-29212

Printed in the United States of America on acid-free paper ♾
07 06 05 04 03 02 01 00   9 8 7 6 5 4 3 2
First printing

For Geneviève

Contents

Preface

The morning of 16 June 1944, Maj. Robert Neiman signaled to his fourteen Sherman tank crews to start their engines. The twenty-eight General Motors diesels throbbed in response. His C Company, 4th Tank Battalion, spread out in a shallow V formation and passed through the lines of the 23d Marine Regiment, then facing across the waist of the island of Saipan. Ahead lay the best defenses yet offered by the Japanese army, and Neiman knew that the success of the offensive lay in his own hands. But he knew also the mettle of his men; he had personally selected them and their officers, and had personally directed the preparation of his machines, the twin-diesel M4A2 medium tanks with which his company had been equipped since the previous November. Now he had to close with the enemy, some 2,000 yards beyond over open terrain, impossible for the infantry to cross. There the entrenched Japanese troops stood ready to die at their guns, if necessary. The division had promised artillery support for the attack, but the guns remained silent. The essential coordination had fallen through again, as remained customary for the war.

But attacking was Bob Neiman's specialty, and he proved it that day as he led his tanks against the Japanese lines. His command tank received a heavy shell hit, knocking out its electrical system even as it careened toward the Japanese lines. He quickly waved over an alternate vehicle and continued the attack. "Boom!" A mine canceled that effort and he jumped into a third tank, one from his nearest platoon, and continued to direct the advance. The tanks proceeded into the position, destroyed all the Japanese weapons emplacements, and savaged the enemy infantry until the men of the 23d Marines arrived. As the marines mopped up the outmatched enemy, they could see the water's edge of the east coast. The island had been crossed, and they were winning.

That day, when Bob Neiman won his Navy Cross medal on Saipan, fairly illustrated the distance covered by the men and machines of the Marine Corps fighting-vehicle units since their commandant had ordered them into existence less than a decade before. In fact, only three years earlier, Second Lieutenant Neiman, fresh out of his platoon leader class, had taken his first tank-driving lesson with 1st Lt. Bruce Mattson in number eight of the Corps's "fleet" of ten tanks. The tank slipped

from a Quantico hilltop and rolled sideways down the hill after running one track up on a stump. At the bottom, the tank lay on its side.
Mattson was knocked out, and Neiman revived him and led the way out
of the hatch as the tank caught fire. Unwittingly, Neiman had that day
contributed both to the first Marine Corps tank loss and the demise of
the independent procurement of tanks by his Corps. Yet, in 1944, the
Marine Corps operated diesel tanks banned from overseas service by
the U.S. Army, and the army operated some of the amphibian tanks
ordered originally for Marine Corps use. These and other interesting
anomalies characterized the introduction of the armored fighting vehicle into the U.S. Marines.

The coming of the Second World War brought a new look and maturity to the U.S. Marine Corps, achieved in an astoundingly short time,
much like the other U.S. forces. The incorporation of modern weaponry,
like the armored fighting vehicle, into that service forms a small but crucial part of that greater story. But the acquisition and use of armored
fighting vehicles over the course of several generations by the Marine
Corps also illustrates to some extent the characteristics of both the
Corps as a military institution of the United States and the men who
have thus far guided its development.

This is a story of men, machines, and mission. It is, almost regret-
tably, not a history of combat operations, for that would require yet
another book. It is, rather, a study of how the U.S. Marine Corps came
to acquire the armored fighting vehicle—why, how, what, from where
and when, and what it tried to do with it. In doing so, we learn much
about the institutional workings of the U.S. Marines as a military organization.

This book treats the planning, acquisition, and employment of
armored fighting vehicles, chiefly tanks, amphibian tractors, and
armored cars, by the Corps. I explore the concepts and plans that led to
the fielding of these weapons systems, the doctrines and tactics
intended for them, and how the Corps used them in combat operations
of the Fleet Marine Force during its twentieth-century conflicts. I cover
the combat operations in sufficient detail to describe how armored fighting vehicles were used or to what extent. The idea is to identify trends,
not to analyze battles or present a primer on Marine Corps history and
lore. Apart from the story of men and machines, the nature of the
Marine Corps as a military institution reveals itself. The reader will see
it as a fairly closed system of institutional goals and values, with doubtful feedback and analysis loops, seldom extending to foreign practices,

open to exogenous variables, such as army procurement practices, and well ridden with cults of personality. These points have been covered before by such historians of the Marine Corps as Allan R. Millett, but never in such a microcosm.

Unlike the British army, the Marine Corps has never had a regimental system, replete with its traditions, customs, and regimental histories. That being said, I offer what follows to my fellow armored vehicle unit comrades as a hopefully worthy substitute for a regimental history.

Acknowledgments

My continuing interest in history grew under the guidance of the late Professor William H. Russell, my mentor during my undergraduate years (and later) at the U.S. Naval Academy. Professors Theodore Ropp and Irving B. Holley improved the vigor and scope of my contemplation at Duke University, and George O. Kent and James A. Harris of the University of Maryland sharpened my discourse while guiding my doctoral studies there.

This study owes much to the pathfinding work of Arthur E. Burns III, who wrote an excellent student paper at the Marine Corps Command and Staff College on Marine Corps tank units through 1945 and discussed his work with me while we attended a short course together at Fort Knox in 1979. Col. Robert C. McInteer, USMC, served as my military mentor and allowed me to broaden my abilities as an officer and tanker. Brig. Gen. Edwin H. Simmons, USMC (Ret.), as Director of the Marine Corps History and Museums Division, encouraged me over many years to contemplate and attempt this project, and Dr. Allan R. Millett caused me to begin work with his enthusiastic endorsement for a related work.

I have received considerable support from individuals and institutions over the years of research and preparation of this work. Lt. Gen. Martin R. Steele, as Assistant Chief of Staff for Plans Policy and Operations (retired June 1999), and our senior USMC tank officer, sponsored my renewed security clearance and access to classified documents stored at Suitland, Maryland, and still under the control of Headquarters, U.S. Marine Corps. Brig. Gen. James M. Feigley, Commanding General, Marine Corps Systems Command, and his staff furnished much information on the contemporary armor programs. The most essential services of the National Archives and Records Administration were rendered in particular by Barry Zerby and Trevor Plante of the Military Records sections and Michael Waesche, custodian of the classified files at Suitland. At the USMC Historical Center, Washington, D.C., I received expert assistance from Danny A. Crawford, Robert V. Aquilina, Lena M. Kaljot, Evelyn A. Englander, and Frederick J. Graboske.

Donald Gagnon, friend, tanker, secretary, and newsletter editor of the Marine Corps Tankers' Association, gave generously of his time and material and introduced me expertly to the members most likely to have the background I sought. My loyal Lieutenants of Marines (now lieutenant colonels), Dennis Beal and Jeffrey Wilkinson, assisted me at every turn with contacts, insights, and contemporary updates, including at last a chance to drive the M1A1 tank.

Variously, the following wrote, read, and helped me refine various concepts: Nicholas Andreacchio, Jack Atwater, Edward L. Bale Jr., Donald Beal, Dave Beeman, James C. Bradford, Michael F. Campbell, Roger G. Charles, Victor Croizat, James R. Davis, Helmuts A. Feifs, Andrew Findlayson, Philip Gioia, John E. Greenwood, Gerald W. Hodum, George F. Hofmann, Thomas Hoysa, E. C. Kiesling, Francis T. Klabough, Brig. Gen. James N. Mattis, Lt. Gen. Louis B. Metzger, Robert M. Neiman, Dan Shepetis, Annette E. Trampenau, and George F. Tubley. My acquisitions editors at the Naval Institute Press, Thomas Cutler and Mark Gatlin, guided my efforts to publish, and Therese Boyd and Kimberley A. VanDerveer performed great feats of salvage to render my manuscript into a more logical and readable work. Many others willingly gave me time in interviews (see bibliography), letters, and telephone calls. The errors remaining after all this collaboration solely accrue to me.

Portions of chapters 6–9 appeared previously in my two chapters published in George F. Hofmann and Donn A. Starry, ed., *From Camp Colt to Desert Storm: A History of U.S. Armored Forces* (Lexington: University of Kentucky Press, 1999). All photographs are courtesy of the USMC, unless otherwise noted.

Abbreviations

AA	Antiaircraft
AAAV	Advanced amphibious assault vehicle
AAV	Assault amphibious vehicle
Amphib	Amphibious
Amtrac	Amphibious tractor (*see* LVT)
AP	Armor-piercing (ammunition)
APC	Armored personnel carrier; or armor-piercing, capped (ammunition)
AT	Antitank
BLT	Battalion landing team
Bn	Battalion
BuAero	Navy Bureau of Aeronautics
BuOrd	Navy Bureau of Ordnance
BuSup	Navy Bureau of Supply
C/S	Chief of staff
CC	Command chronology
CINCAF	Commander in Chief, Asiatic Fleet
CMC	Commandant of the Marine Corps
CO	Commanding officer
Co	Company
CTL	Combat tank, light
CTM	Combat tank, medium
POA-CWS-H1/H5	Chemical Warfare Service, Pacific Ocean Area, model H1 or H5 (flamethrower tank)
DMZ	Demilitarized zone
FLEX	Fleet exercise
FMC	Food Machinery Company (later Corporation)
FMFM	Fleet Marine Force manual
FY	Fiscal year
GMC	Gun, mount, carriage
HEAT	High explosive, antitank (ammunition)
HQ, HQMC	Headquarters; Headquarters, Marine Corps
LAI	Light armored infantry
LANT	Atlantic
LAR	Light armored reconnaissance
LAV	Light armored vehicle
LCM	Landing craft, mechanized
LFB	Landing force bulletin
LSD	Landing ship, dock
LSM	Landing ship, medium

LST	Landing ship, tank
LVA	Landing vehicle, assault
LVT	Landing vehicle, tracked. Suffixes: (*A*), armored; *C,* command; *E,* engineer; *H,* howitzer; *P,* personnel; *R,* recovery.
LVX	Landing vehicle, experimental
M-H	Marmon-Herrington Co., Inc.
MCDEC	Marine Corps Development and Education Center
MCEB	Marine Corps Equipment Board
MEB (MAB)	Marine Expeditionary (later Amphibious) Brigade
MEF (MAF)	Marine Expeditionary (later Amphibious) Force
MEU (MAU)	Marine Expeditionary (later Amphibious) Unit
MPS	Maritime prepositioning ship(s)
MPWS	Mobile protected weapons system
MTO	Motor transport officer
NBC	Nuclear, biological, and chemical
NKPA	North Korean People's Army
Ontos	M50 antitank vehicle (1956)
Ops	Operations
Ord	Ordnance
P&P	Plans and Policy Department, HQMC ("Pots & Pans")
PAC	Pacific
QM, QMMC	Quartermaster; quartermaster of the Marine Corps
RefSect	Reference Section, History and Museums Division, HQMC
RPG	Rocket-propelled grenade (antitank rocket launcher)
SecNav	Secretary of the Navy
SecWar	Secretary of War
SOP	Standing operating procedure
Spl	Special
TACOM	Tank and Automotive Command (U.S. Army)
Tk	Tank
TkSect	Tank Section, Ground Combat Weapons Branch, Marine Corps Systems Command, Quantico, Va.
TOW	Tube-launched, optically directed, wire-guided (antitank missile)
Trng	Training
Trp	Troop(s)
UN	United Nations
VC	Viet Cong
VT	Variable time (proximity fuzed) (ammunition)

Marines under Armor

Chapter 1   **Ideas and Experiments, 1916–1935**

Purchase of two experimental armored cars. Returned, approved for purchase from the Armor Motor Car company.
—Assistant Secretary of the Navy Franklin D. Roosevelt (1916)

The tank platoon, as other outfits, saw no service and in operations of this nature it is believed that they are unnecessary. It would be much better to have a mobile blockhouse trailer which would be better suited to perform duty assigned to a tank platoon.
—Maj. Gen. Smedley D. Butler (1928)

On the eve of the Great War, the U.S. Marine Corps, 18,000 strong on paper, continued to render useful service in a variety of ways as the naval infantry of the U.S. Navy. From its traditional origins as ships' police and landing party, the Corps had taken on expeditionary duties overseas in American colonies and protectorates and served in American wars of intervention either alongside the army, as in the Mexican War, or with the fleet in an emerging base seizure doctrine demonstrated at Guantanamo, Cuba, in 1898. Not yet a separate service, the Corps had achieved considerable autonomy in a Department of the Navy full of autonomous fiefdoms only loosely administered by the secretary of the Navy.

The expansion of the Marine Corps for World War I did not alter its character or doctrine. The acid test of combat against a first-class continental opponent proved an expensive lesson in aspects of modern warfare only tangentially approached by marines in the past. But because the war was fought on land primarily by infantry-artillery armies, at walking pace with only limited assistance from machine weapons like the airplane and the tank, the structures of the battalions of the 4th and 5th Marine Brigades required little change. The officers and men assigned to the front simply "grew up" through training with the U.S. and French armies and on-the-job experience. One easily forgets that most of the expanded Corps of 75,000 found themselves on duty afloat or with the other brigades and lesser units in Philadelphia,

Cuba, Dominica, and on the Mexican border. Other than combat experience with the enemy, perhaps the most significant outcome of the war for the Marine Corps proved to be an increasing unease between the Corps and the U.S. Army, which began to regard each other with increasing suspicion in the ensuing decades. With the return to peacetime strength at 20,000 and going down, the Marine Corps's experience of the Great War seemed destined for the classroom and library.[1]

World War I saw much use of science and engineering in the search for victory, and the Marine Corps took the opportunity to experiment with many new weapons and items of equipment of possible use for its far-flung forces. The tank emerged relatively late in the war and American use depended upon shared knowledge and equipment loaned from the French and British allies. However, the armored car was available locally and combined the recognized utility of the machine gun with the American fascination with all things automotive. Thus, the earliest Marine Corps experiment with armored vehicles came in the summer of 1916 when the quartermaster of the Marine Corps secured funds for two armored cars for experimental use. The quartermaster's letter noted that the army had two prototypes under consideration, had shipped them to the Mexican border for trials with the expeditionary force there, and contemplated the eventual purchase of fifty of them. Capt. Andrew B. Drum (1883–1955) of the Advanced Base Force, Philadelphia, conducted tests in August of a car provided by the Armor Motor Car Company (AMC) of Detroit. These included small boat compatibility checks, which involved loading and unloading successfully from a 40-foot motor sailing launch using improvised ramps placed over the stern. In October Assistant Secretary of the Navy Franklin D. Roosevelt approved the purchase of two cars from the AMC for a cost not to exceed $5,500 each.[2]

Drum then formed the Armored Car Squadron, Headquarters, First Regiment, at Philadelphia with a few drivers and mechanics, adding more cars until a total of eight were on hand. Neither he nor the headquarters staff ever advanced any concept for their operation, and no evident doctrine emerged, but the assignment of the unit to the First Regiment indicated that the armored cars would serve in the defense of advanced naval bases. Later use focused on mobile patrolling as the primary mission for the armored car. Thus the employment of the first armored vehicles in the Marine Corps remained a technical expedient, with training simply gained on the job using random skills present in the troops.

The three-man AMC cars, each built on a King touring car chassis powered by an eight-cylinder motor, featured three removable quarter-inch armor sections, capable of resisting .30-caliber service ammunition at 100 yards. A revolving turret, mounting a one-pound automatic gun (37mm), sat well to the rear of the four-wheeler. Although featured in several public demonstrations, the Armored Car Squadron, like its parent regiment, never went to war and disbanded on 4 May 1921 at Quantico, Virginia. Five of the cars served later in Haiti with the 2d Marine Regiment but the few roads afforded little tactical use for them and they returned to Quantico in a heavily used condition in 1927.[3]

The first experience with such improvised equipment could hardly have inspired much confidence. Drum's report of 1919 cast serious doubts upon the design. Seven of the eight were still in commission, and five of them were put through testing. The performance was not all that good, stemming from the car's poor transmission and weak engine and a lack of personnel skilled enough to keep cars in running order. Only well-trained drivers could operate the cars. Drum recommended complete overhaul of six cars, with the other two retained as spares. The one-pounder gun worked well and he recommended many engineering changes for the naval base shops to undertake. He also suggested substitution of a White truck chassis for the King body.[4]

A depot report of 1933 assessed the condition of a King car:[5]

Armored car no 728 is a combination of a 1917 King frame, 1917 Cadillac motor, GMC [General Motors Company] steering gear, White truck axles. It is equipped with solid tires mounted on wood wheels. In this vehicle the steering gear is too short and the steering wheel rubs side armor. In fact, the wheel comes to drivers' knees. The floor is made of ¾" lumber. The steering gear is very light. The springs are weak. The frame has been straightened, has been drilled for two steering gear locations, and is very weak. The side armor had to be cut away in order to clear drag rod of steering gear. The front wheels are out of true due to the hubs being slightly offset. [Parts were mostly dated 1917, impossible to replace.] At present the vehicle can be operated, but, is absolutely unsafe at any speed exceeding 8 miles per hour, due to weak steering linkage, shimmy, and poor brakes.

The armored cars remained in storage at the Philadelphia supply depot well into the 1930s. Few options for development of such vehicles remained during the Great Depression for a declining Corps. A single White armored car was purchased in 1927, probably in response to requests for them by the China garrisons, and a few sets of armor remained in storage after disposal of the King cars was authorized in 1934. By 1938, when the 4th Marines (regiments, usually infantry, are thus referred to in Marine Corps jargon) in China requested support of the Commander, Asiatic Fleet in obtaining armored cars, the response of Headquarters, Marine Corps (HQMC) was a terse telegram, "No armored cars available in Marine Corps and no funds available for their purchase."[6]

The early armored cars offered little capability for the new challenges studied by the Marine Corps in the 1920s. Despite competing schools of thought on the future roles and missions of the Corps, the new commandant of the Marine Corps, Maj. Gen. John Archer Lejeune, steered it inexorably into amphibious warfare as an adjunct to naval campaigns in the Pacific and Caribbean. The navy's focus upon Japan as the likely future opponent led the Corps to embrace almost single-mindedly the planning, organization, and doctrine necessary to undertake its portion of the Great Pacific War two decades hence. Lejeune in 1923 approved the crucial study *Advance Base Operations in Micronesia* as the main Marine Corps operations plan. Written by the mercurial Lt. Col. Earl H. "Pete" Ellis (1880–1923), it postulated the seizure and defense of the Japanese-held Marshall Island archipelago in support of the U.S. Navy's strategic advance across the Pacific. Ellis detailed the organization, equipment, and tactics required for the offensive and defensive forces involved, two distinct types of units. Among the various weapons and units he listed, no mention of tanks appears, probably because the ships and craft required to land them had not been conceived, let alone tested and produced. However, when the operating forces of the Corps began to plan practice landings and devise tactical doctrine to deal with the types of fixed and mobile beach defenses discussed by Ellis, they perforce chose to include light tanks among the desired hardware, in both defensive and offensive forces.[7]

Thus, the genesis of tanks in the Marine Corps lay in the decision to accept the mission of forcible entry against beaches defended by a determined and well-armed enemy at the center of a naval campaign, which would at the same time require other Marine Corps units to defend islands and coastlines against similar all-out assault. Given the knowledge of modern warfare gained by Marine Corps officers in the Great War and the observation gained of tank employment by other land forces there, the choice of the armored fighting vehicle remained an obvious one. Tanks would support the advance and defense of infantry just as they and other weapons had been employed in the 1918 offensive in Western Europe.[8]

Secretary of the Navy Edwin Denby made a tentative proposal to the secretary of war in March of 1922 to train some marines for this future requirement:[9]

> 29 March 1922
> Sir:—
> *If it can be done without inconvenience, I would very much appreciate permission being granted to the Major General Commandant of the Marine Corps to detail a limited number of officers and enlisted men as students in the Tank School, Camp Meade, Md.*
>
> *At the present time it is hoped that one (1) second lieutenant and five (5) enlisted men may be detailed to take the officer's course and enlisted men's basic course respectively.*
>
> *In all probability the Marine Corps would not be able to maintain students at the school as a regular proposition, but it would be of much benefit if a limited number of students from the Marine Corps could be detailed to the school from time to time until a small nucleus of officers and men is built up who could be adequately instructed in the subjects taught at the Tank School.*

A light-tank platoon was hastily assembled at Quantico in late 1923 for testing in the navy's Winter Maneuvers of 1924. Using an organizational table approved in October, the light-tank platoon, Marine Corps Expeditionary Force, formed at Quantico on 5 December 1923, with a strength of two officers, twenty-two men, and three M1917 six-ton tanks, borrowed on verbal agreement from the army. Under command of 1st Lt. Charles S. Finch (1896–1956), a 1919 Naval Academy graduate, the platoon embarked USS *Chaumont* on 3 January 1924 and headed for Culebra Island.

The two-man M1917 tank, a domestic license-built version of the French Renault FT17, carried either a short-barrel M1916 37mm gun or the Browning .30-caliber M1919 machine gun. The army had over 900 on hand after the war, far in excess of requirements and already rather obsolete. As a training and orientation machine, however, the M1917 would prove simple to operate and maintain for the novice crews.

After unloading pierside at Culebra, the platoon joined the defending Marine Corps Expeditionary Force. The ensuing mock battle proved a debacle for the attackers, hobbled by inadequate boats, transports, communications, and unwieldy equipment. An interesting sidelight was the surprise appearance of a new creation of J. Walter Christie, the innovative designer of tractors and fighting vehicles who influenced tank design considerably in the 1930s. His "amphibian tank" was really a 75mm assault gun on a convertible wheel-track suspension, with a large buoyant hull. General Lejeune and his commander at Quantico, Brig. Gen. Smedley D. Butler, had accepted Christie's offer of a free loan for the maneuvers and arranged passage from New York on board the battleship *Wyoming* just in time for the landing at Culebra. Sailors craned the "tank" onto a submarine for the final launch into the sea and the vehicle indeed churned around the transport area, but the crew declined to attempt to cross the surfline. So the opportunity for a tank battle during the exercise faded, as did any further hopes for Christie and his tank. The M1917s ashore did not even enter the fray, being relegated to a counterattack role not needed in the end.[10]

The light-tank platoon continued to develop after returning to Quantico from the Culebra maneuvers. It participated in annual land maneuvers of the Marine Corps Expeditionary Force, but took part in no more landing exercises. More personnel and tanks swelled its ranks, and a formal loan agreement with the army brought more vehicles into the unit.[11]

NAVY DEPARTMENT
295296   April 1925

From: The Secretary of the Navy.
To: The Secretary of War.
Subject: Loan of Tanks to the Marine Corps.
References: [omitted]

Will you please direct the Chief of Ordnance, U.S. Army, to furnish the Marine Corps, as a loan, the following mentioned equipment, which it is understood is available in excess of immediate requirements of the Army, delivery thereof to be made to the Depot Quartermaster, Marine Barracks, Quantico, Va., viz:

Item No.
1.	4	Tanks, 6-ton, Model 1917, complete with Browning tank machine gun, caliber .30, model 1919.
2.	2	Tanks, 6-ton, Model 1917, complete with 37-mm. Guns, Model 1916.

The above mentioned equipment is required in the training of marines in the use thereof, but in view of the depleted condition of the current appropriations for the Marine Corps, will you please direct that trans-

*fer of such equipment be made without expense to the Marine Corps
except for handling, transportation, etc. The tanks referred to will be
kept in repair by the Marine Corps and returned to the Army upon
demand in the condition in which they are received.*

*Shipment should be made by freight on unrouted Government bill of
lading, all charges incident to handling, transportation, etc., to be paid
by the Marine Corps out of appropriation "General Expenses, Marine
Corps, 1925," and it is requested that a memorandum copy of such bill
of lading be forwarded from the shipping point direct to the
Quartermaster, U.S. Marine Corps, Navy Department, Washington, D.C.
at time shipment is made.*

In all, the Corps acquired eight M1917 six-tonners during the 1920s
(one of the early loan vehicles apparently returned to army custody),
enabling the platoon to keep five vehicles on line, despite the frequent
overhaul requirements. Because of the detailing of its troops to mail
guard duty in 1926–27, however, the platoon had to be reassembled for
the greatest challenge of its curious life, the China expedition.

On 3 February 1927 the bulk of the 4th Marines sailed on USS
Chaumont for Shanghai to add American presence to the growing international forces arrayed there in the midst of the Chinese civil war and
evident threats to the center of international trade and settlement in
China. The need for additional units, which would garrison Tientsin
and guard the international community in Peking, if necessary, led to
the decision to expand the expedition to brigade size, commanded by
General Butler, adding artillery and aircraft as well. The decision to
reinforce the brigade with tanks came not from the desire of local commanders but rather from the lack of any other suitable materiel. A few
weeks earlier, the Expeditionary Force staff had asked headquarters if
any armored cars might be available for China duty. Inevitably, the reply
closed off any hopes: there were none in the country; commercial cars,
such as bank armored cars, were not suitable; and the headquarters officers rated the King cars in Haiti as unreliable and unsuitable. But the
issue would not die. On 27 April a telegram arrived at Headquarters
from the Commander, Asiatic Fleet, relaying Butler's personal request
for immediate shipment of six Christie light tanks or armored cars with
short wheelbase. Since no Christies had been procured after their poor
performance at Culebra in 1924, and employing the five King cars from
Haiti remained an unsatisfactory solution, the decision was made to
send the light-tank platoon to China.[12]

The platoon gained new life and energy. A more senior commander,
Capt. Nathan E. Landon, a former marine gunner commissioned in

1917, assumed command of the platoon, mustering then two officers, thirty enlisted men, and five tanks for the 6 April departure by train for the West Coast. On the seventeenth, they embarked SS *President Grant* for passage to Olongopo, Philippines, from which they and other reinforcements shipped out in navy vessels for Tientsin. At this point, the platoon relaxed into garrison life, seeing lots of "exotic" life, but no combat in a "show of force." Under the watchful eye of future commandant Maj. A. Archer Vandegrift, the brigade operations and training officer, the light-tank platoon conducted its training regime:

> Light Tank Platoon: (a) Drills and instructions will include, in addition to infantry drill: Nomenclature and care of the Tank. Instruction in driving tanks. School of the Tank. Tank signals and visual signals. Nomenclature and care of the Machine gun and 37mm. gun. (b) Field training will include: March and march discipline. Maneuvering and tactics of tanks, both on the offensive and defensive. Tanks as movable pill boxes in street fighting and mob control.[13]

By late 1928, the show was over, as General Butler's final report would demonstrate:

> The tank platoon, as other outfits, saw no service and in operations of this nature it is believed that they are unnecessary. It would be much better to have a mobile blockhouse trailer which would be better suited to perform duty assigned to a tank platoon. The tank platoon as a unit was excellent; its material, even though old, was always in excellent condition and it never failed to function in all drills and maneuvers.[14]

As the deployment began to wind down, the tank platoon shipped out with other units on 25 September 1928 for the United States. Upon arrival in San Diego, 31 October 1928, the platoon shipped its vehicles and disbanded on 10 November. The tanks never saw further use and all eight were declared excess property for disposal in 1935.[15]

The light-tank platoon probably fell victim to further personnel cuts endured by the Marine Corps, as it shrank from 17,586 to 15,355 men under the Hoover administration.[16] Lacking funds as well for further exercises, the Corps continued the study of amphibious operations. A *Tentative Manual for Landing Operations* emerged from this effort in 1934, establishing the need for units of infantry, light artillery, tanks, and engineers trained to land from navy shipping in landing craft under the support of air and naval gunfire. At the end of 1933, the Fleet Marine Force (FMF) replaced the old Expeditionary Force as more evidence that the Corps would focus on amphibious operations and base defense for the fleet as a matter of policy. Although only a few thousand marines could be assigned to the FMF, planning began for the organization, equipment, and doctrine that would support a wartime force of 25,000 men, consisting chiefly of a brigade of all arms on each coast and companion air groups and specialized defense battalions. The new mission orientation assisted the Corps in gaining new authorization and funding for 19,367 men by 1939, of which fewer than half mustered with the FMF.[17] The resumption of fleet exercises in 1934 revealed the same difficulties as their predecessors, and the development of suitable landing craft for personnel and heavy equipment would be the most elusive of the problems perceived at the time.[18]

The *Tentative Manual for Landing Operations* underscored the utility of tanks in the future operations of the FMF and called for their landing early in the assault. However, "the difficulties of transport and movement from ship-to-shore indicate that only light tanks can be used in the landing operation. These can be land tanks or amphibious tanks." Now the light-tank category was the only one in which the army had state-of-the-art development, not only testing high-speed Christie tanks, but also developing excellent radial engines, transmissions, volute spring suspensions, and rubber-block track, all of which would contribute to the next war's designs. However, the army light-tank models had already reached the ten-ton level by the mid-1930s, and navy cargo-handling gear available on most ships imposed a five-ton limit. Thus, the Corps would have to pursue an independent development for a *very* light tank.[19]

The Marine Corps budgeting for the FMF initially permitted only the Quantico-based 1st Brigade to be outfitted in the first three years, and the West Coast 2d Brigade, based at San Diego, would remain with only an infantry regiment on hand. Only a single tank company was programmed in the 1934 planning, therefore, with fifteen tanks. The tank envisioned at that time was a three-tonner, carrying a 1.1-inch automatic gun, or a 37mm cannon, plus .30-caliber machine guns, armored to resist small arms and .50-caliber rounds, and capable of 25–30 MPH speed. Of course no such vehicles had yet been developed, and these initial specifications had a certain aspect of fantasy (i.e., a 37mm gun on a three-ton chassis, with such protection as specified). However, the staff at this point specifically ruled out amphibious tanks for the Corps, as these could not handle open seas expected three to six miles offshore. Instead, navy lighters would be procured, which they hoped would be capable of 13 knots, fitted with bow ramps and three pairs of .30-caliber machine guns. Alas, such landing craft remained at the same level of fantasy as the light but well-armed tank.[20]

Rapid decisions in wake of the formation of the FMF continued toward the creation of a Marine Corps tank arm in 1935. Even though no tanks were on hand, beyond the old M1917s in storage, the commandant obtained army approval for a Marine Corps officer to attend the tank course, now taught at the Infantry School, Fort Benning. Headquarters sent orders to Capt. Hartnoll J. Withers (1903–83), a 1926 graduate of the Naval Academy who had enlisted in the Corps in 1920. Experienced from duty in Nicaragua and Haiti, he had just completed sea duty on the cruiser USS *Chicago*. His crucial contributions to the Marine Corps tank arm would qualify him in every sense as a pioneer in the field.[21]

Finally, on 29 November 1935, the commandant, Maj. Gen. John H. Russell, directed his quartermaster to "initiate steps for the procurement of five (5) light fighting tanks, in accordance with the enclosed specifications, from funds now available at the [Navy] Bureau of Ordnance." The Marine Corps had fully accepted the tank as an essential element of its doctrine.[22]

Chapter 2   **Early Rearmament, 1935–1940**

Why the hell do we have to have a five ton tank with a fifteen ton boom. Why don't you increase the weight of the tank to seven tons?

—Lemuel C. Shepherd Jr. (1938)

Going It Alone: The "Light Fighting Tank"

The characteristics specified for the Marine Corps "light fighting tank" amounted to seven pages of legal-sized, single-spaced text, not counting testing criteria. These summarized not only the normal criteria for a complicated mechanical piece of equipment, but also the emerging concept perceived by marines at the time. They wanted a machine that would accompany the infantry ashore in some numbers and enable their amphibious assault to overcome beach defenses and prevail against determined enemies. The concept for employment seldom advanced beyond that vague and typically understated role. Doctrine for the use of armored vehicles remained in the distant future, for the practitioners of amphibious warfare to determine, mostly in the field.

By 1940, for example, the newest doctrinal manual published by the Marine Corps simply stated:

When strong opposition to the initial landings is expected or encountered, the employment of tanks will be a material aid and will reduce the number of casualties. Tanks are particularly valuable in assaulting towns and villages, and in controlling the inhabitants of an occupied hostile city.

Armored cars can be employed to patrol the streets of occupied cities and to maintain liaison with outlying garrisons. With suitable motorized infantry escorts, they are effective in dispersing the hostile forces encountered in the early phases of the occupation.

Except for the fact that tanks and armored cars can be used more freely in small wars due to the lack of effective opposition, their tactics will be basically the same as in a major war. As the hostile forces withdraw into the more remote parts of the country, where the terrain is generally unsuited for mechanized units, their usefulness in the field will rapidly disappear.[1]

Apart from the usual contracting language specifying the format of the proposals and bids to be made by industry, the Marine Corps set the following requirements for a suitable tank.[2]

1. Medium weight (not over 9,500 pounds) and two-man crew
2. Rubber-faced track to prevent damage to ship decks
3. Use of commercial components where feasible
4. Delivery of pilot vehicle six months after contracting
5. Refurbishment of pilot vehicle to new condition after testing
6. Track removal and replacement in 30 minutes
7. Readily accessible engine, with a clutch comparable to standard motor vehicle; steering levers operable by not over 10 pounds pressure
8. Hand brake
9. Twelve-volt electrical system of 450-watt capacity, 35-ampere maximum current.
10. Two headlights and a taillight, removable for combat
11. One siren, one air horn
12. Maximum dimensions: 140-inch length, 76-inch width, 65-inch height (ground clearance 12 inches)
13. Maximum silence of operation to support landing parties
14. Performance:
    Speed: 30 MPH maximum, 20 MPH sustained.
    Range: 125 miles in 10 hours
    Turning: 18-foot diameter
    Ford 40 inches of water
    Cross 50-inch trench, climb 22-inch, drop 48-inch vertical obstacle
15. Armament:
    Two .30-caliber and one .50-caliber machine gun with 2,000 and 500 rounds, respectively, of ammunition, or
    Two .30-caliber and one 37mm gun with 2,000 and 100 rounds of ammunition.
    Flexible mounts providing 20-degree traverse and elevation, 10-degree depression for machine guns, 16 elevation, 10 traverse, and 5 depression for 37mm gun.
16. Armor protection:
    Front and turret: One-half inch
    Rear and side: 7/16 inch (side plates above track as turret plates)
    Top and bottom: One-quarter inch

The requirements proved highly optimistic for a combat vehicle on a mere 9,500-pound weight regime, and the resulting vehicle would provide endless headaches for the Corps, earning little benefit for the "lightness" it provided.

Although various firms and the army's Ordnance Department received tenders for offer, the eventual successful bidder, the Marmon-Herrington Company of Indianapolis, was already demonstrating its candidate vehicle at Quantico on 6 December, barely a week after the commandant ordered the quartermaster to begin procurement actions. It would seem clear that there had been some contact already with the Marmon-Herrington Company, which was marketing its "light tractor tank" as a commercial venture. Regardless of the anticipated results of this collaboration, obtaining the specified performance would prove a tough engineering challenge. Their 1935 CTL-1 (Combat Tank, Light) competed for a Persian army contract for a vehicle obviously destined for constabulary or police functions, not modern combat. Armed with a single machine gun, fitted with quarter-inch armor and weighing 8,975 pounds, it did demonstrate an impressive speed of 30 MPH using a V-12 Lincoln engine of 110 hp. The second vehicle, CTL-2, increased the armor to three-eighths of an inch and weighed 9,565 pounds. There seemed to be some hope, therefore, that the company could build the "Marine Tank" to its desired specifications.[3]

The Marmon-Herrington CTL-3 contracted for that December was a turretless, two-man tank employing the Lincoln V-12 engine and rubber-band track over a quadruple bogie-wheel suspension to move at a maximum speed of 33 MPH. Equipped with dual driving controls, it carried three ball mounts in the hull front for the intended weapons. It reflected a good deal of Marmon-Herrington's experience with truck manufacture (including many novel four-wheel-drive designs) as well as the firm's understandably limited experience with armored-vehicle design and production. For instance, the CTL-3 used a truck-type air-boosted track locking system for steering. The tankers found it too weak and vulnerable to breakdown and requested a redesign that would incorporate a conventional controlled differential steering. The truck-type differential in the CTL was not handling the stresses generated by pivoting, compared to the lesser requirement of compensating for torque differences when a truck makes a normal turn. The company responded that the truck parts enabled the CTL to stay below the five-ton weight limit and that no other design would work, nor could a controlled differential simply be dropped into the present design.[4]

Fresh out of the Fort Benning tank course, newly promoted Major Hartnoll Withers moved to the Marmon-Herrington factory as the inspector and began to familiarize himself with the CTL-3 pilot vehicle then being assembled. As the designated liaison between the factory and government, he drew much on his technical education and demonstrated a true aptitude for things mechanical and especially automotive. He received the government-provided weapons for the CTL-3: a 37mm M1916 cannon, a .50- and two .30-caliber machine guns, and a .45-caliber submachine gun. He conferred with the engineers over vehicle design and relayed the concerns of the Marine Corps Equipment Board (MCEB), formed in 1935 at Quantico to coordinate the requirements and procurement of needed FMF equipment. Withers tended to exhort more from the company than his charter provided. The Quantico board advised:

> In regard to the comment on steering drums . . . it should be understood that the contractor is not constructing a pilot model to be changed as seen fit during construction. The contractor is building a tank to conform to specifications already laid down and agreed to and which must pass agreed upon tests. The contractor, so long as he fulfills these requirements, cannot be expected to undertake any added expense concerning matters that are not required by these specifications unless he desires to undertake such expense for his own ultimate gain in improving the tank.[5]

Despite some reservations voiced by the marines, the pilot CTL-3 managed to pass its tests and the navy contracting office accepted it on 5 June and ordered the remainder of the contract executed. As a separate matter the army proving ground at Aberdeen certified the quarter-inch armor plates of the CTL-3.[6]

Withers now began to divide his time between Indianapolis and Quantico as time approached to activate the tank company. The five CTL-3s arrived at Quantico on 22 February 1937, all equipped with machine guns. Not surprisingly, no CTL-3 ever carried a 37mm cannon, and the obsolete model M1916 originally envisioned would have produced little result of tactical value. Withers formally activated the 1st Tank Company, 1st Marine Brigade, on 1 March 1937, although it remained in equipment and personnel a mere platoon for a considerable time. Headquarters authorized the installation of one radio, a navy-type RU, by the platoon for evaluation. That summer, two more officers joined the company from the Fort Benning tank course, First Lieutenants Robert L. Denig Jr. and Hector de Zayas, both 1932 Naval Academy graduates and experienced infantry officers. Withers turned over command of the company to de Zayas in October and returned to the Marmon-Herrington plant as the inspector. The latter then prepared the company to take its five CTL-3s to the Caribbean for Fleet

Exercise #4 (FLEX4). The result improved greatly on the clumsy attempts in 1924 to employ the Christie floating tank and the M1917s ashore at Culebra.[7]

Only one prototype navy landing craft served the force, so the landing at Culebra Island proved an administrative matter of shuttling the five Marmon-Herringtons ashore. However, the platoon moved aggressively against the defenses and routed the reserve as it arrived in trucks on the mock battlefield. A second landing exercise, conducted at nearby Vieques Island, saw the tank platoon split to support both sides of the exercise. The landing force's tank lighter transported its tank to the beach with the initial assault wave and it was credited with the neutralization and destruction of beach defenses in support of the assaulting infantry. The rest of the platoon, ashore with the defenders, later made a spirited counterattack, routing a company on foot and placing the entire landing in jeopardy. All concerned agreed that the tanks demonstrated great possibilities and that they could contribute mightily to every phase of the missions tested in FLEX4.

Lieutenant de Zayas remained critical of the CTL-3 performance, however, and his reports characterized the tank as unreliable and underpowered for cross-country maneuvering. Predictably, the two-man crew had difficulties handling three machine guns as well as their other crew duties. The lack of a turret left the vehicle vulnerable on the sides and rear. The company commander also noted that since the navy was able to lift the 21-ton tank lighter from the transport and place it in the sea, a heavier tank ought to be considered for landing force use, especially some of the newer light tanks then entering service with the army.[8]

These and other criticisms of the CTL-3 tank scarcely interrupted the acquisitions plan, though, as the Corps had already contracted for a second platoon of tanks with the Marmon-Herrington Company on 14 September. Engineering changes in this production run aimed at correcting design weaknesses but not the basic arrangements of the CTL-3. A Hercules engine and a strengthened suspension proved to be the major improvements. These tanks would be designated CTL-3A. Headquarters designated 1st Lieutenant Denig as the second platoon commander.[9]

Upon its return from FLEX4, the company turned to needed repairs and overhauls of their already well-worn machines. Among the growing list of defects were some serious trends: broken drive shafts, failed differentials, and cracked armor plates. For its part, the Marmon-Herrington

Company shipped three differentials and six drive shafts to Quantico at its own expense, requesting that the parts from two deadlined tanks and an additional set from one other be returned to the factory for engineering analysis. Earlier failures had already prompted the company to recommend increasing the allowable weight of the CTL-3 series to 10,900 pounds, to permit the use of more robust parts and components. The commandant did not approve this weight change until 20 May 1938, in midst of the construction of the second platoon vehicles, which would suffer severe teething problems. Rather defensively, the Marmon-Herrington engineers claimed that several components showed signs of overstress due to excessive speed or lack of proper lubrication. This set the stage for the next two years of a rivalry between the tankers, ever anxious to point out flaws in the CTL-3 design, and the plant representatives, consistently alleging abuse by the crews.[10]

Reassessing the Program

The ultimate issue of what type tanks would equip the FMF fell to the MCEB to decide. At the end of 1937, the members saw no need to alter the existing plan, despite the diverse opinions already surfacing on the CTL-3 design. In its status report of that month, the board opined:

> 1. *TANKS.* Last February the Marine Corps purchased a number of light tanks which were designed exclusively for Marine Corps use and built by the Marmon-Herrington Company of Indianapolis. The particular distinguishing feature of this tank is its comparative lightness, being limited by specifications to not over five (5) tons weight which is considered to be the limit for handling by ordinary cargo carriers without special equipment. In order to stay within this weight requirement it was necessary to sacrifice to some degree features which would otherwise be desirable in a military tank.
>
> The tanks have been in the possession of the First Tank Company, F.M.F., since date of delivery and have seen considerable service since that time, participating in various combat exercises and maneuvers held by the First Marine Brigade. Although being far from perfect at the present time it is believed that with the continued cooperation of the manufacturer and the continued valuable suggestions of the personnel of the Tank Company we will have a valuable weapon that is particularly adapted to Marine Corps requirements, which no other tank now in existence meets.
>
> Additional tanks are now in the process of manufacture which it is believed will have considerable improvements over the present model.

The Board has no reason to believe that these will be perfect either, as tanks are essentially mechanical monstrosities which contain within themselves many diametrically opposed features. The history of tank development since the World War indicates that it is largely a process of "trial and error" and fraught with considerable expense.[11]

The board's optimistic forecast proved more than the pilot CTL-3A could achieve. With Major Withers playing a strict martinet role in liaison at the Indianapolis plant, the difficulties of the "improved" tank threatened the continuation of the contract relationship between company and Corps. The pilot model CTL-3A repeatedly failed its trials. The Marmon-Herrington engineers and management insisted that nothing failed that would not be rectified by refurbishing the pilot tank or minor redesign. They stipulated that the pilot proved a distinct improvement over the CTL-3. The tank committee of the board, led by Lt. Col. Lemuel C. Shepherd Jr., remained adamant. The failures to them seemed decisive, such as the shearing off of a road wheel after 121 miles on a road march, and so forth. The board moved on 1 September 1938 to terminate the contract, citing road wheels and suspension defects as cause, but allowed one last test to prove whether the defects could in fact be rectified. Major Withers held a minority view that objected to even this pause before full termination. Perhaps he saw this moment as a chance for the Marine Corps to free itself of the Marmon-Herrington problem forever. The company appealed to the commandant, in the form of a personal letter from the company president, for a repeat of the acceptance trial. Still convinced in the need for the lightest of all tanks, the commandant, Maj. Gen. Thomas Holcomb, urged the navy contracting authorities to grant the request. At this juncture, the commandant reasoned that, although final rejection of the pilot model tank would be justified under contract terms, the Marine Corps urgently needed the tanks and considered that "the failure of the pilot tank in the first test was apparently due to minor maladjustments which might occur in any newly built machine and . . . would not affect the value of the tanks for use by the Marine Corps."

On 20 September, the Bureau of Supply notified the Marmon-Herrington Company of a third test series, agreeing to accept the tank as deliverable if it met the specifications.[12]

The Corps replaced Major Withers as plant inspector on 6 October with 1st Lieutenant Denig, sending the former to sea duty as commander of the Marine Detachment, USS *Tennessee*. This removed the principal bureaucratic obstacle to continuing development of the CTL-series tanks, but left the demanding Major Withers professionally healthy and able to return to the tank arm, which he would do in a few years. The evident mutual distrust between the officer and the firm would emerge later, however.

In November the crucial retrial of the CTL-3A was conducted, at the expense of the contractor. On 25 November the commandant notified the Bureau of Supply that he approved the recommendation of the board to accept the tank, despite being 390 pounds overweight and failing to climb a 22-inch vertical concrete step (it did climb 18 inches). On 23 December the Marmon-Herrington Company received its contract for the five CTL-3A tanks. The crisis was past and the Corps would continue to receive its "light fighting tanks."[13]

The second platoon of tanks, all CTL-3A "improved" light tanks, entered Marine Corps service on 16 June 1939, over two years after the 1st Tank Company, FMF, stood up and just under four years since Commandant Russell had ordered the initial procurement. But the tortuous establishment of the new armored fighting vehicle arm was only half over.[14]

Lt. Col. Lemuel C. Shepherd Jr., a veteran infantry officer who would go on to be one of the Corps's most revered commanders, had already begun to take steps to correct evident deficiencies in the tank program, both in concept and execution. His influence prompted the board to begin work on changing the commandant's policy, as the president of the board reported:

> 1. At the last meeting of the Marine Corps Equipment Board on 15 September, 1938, the subject of combat tanks for the Marine Corps was again fully discussed.
>
> The report of the Board which conducted the acceptance tests of the pilot model now under construction was read by Lieutenant Colonel Shepherd, Senior Member of the Committee on Tanks. As a result of the defects and failures noted in this report the Board is convinced that adequate performance and fire power cannot be obtained in any tank with the weight limitations of our present model tank. The fire power of the present model has already been reduced to two (2) .30 caliber guns [the .50 was deleted from the specifications on 20 June 1938] in spite of an increased allowance of 1000 pounds in weight and it is doubtful whether radio apparatus can be installed due to the lack of space in the drivers compartment.
>
> 2. In all the many discussions of tanks and their use in the Marine Corps in which this Board has participated in the past year the pre-

sumption exists that the five (5) ton weight limitation was imposed because this was the maximum lifting capacity of the ship's cargo hoisting gear. This presumption can not be correct if it is contemplated landing tanks in tank lighters which weigh over twenty-one (21) tons and the further fact that an increased allowance of 1000 pounds was granted for the present model bringing the weight up to 11,000 pounds. It is therefore requested as a necessary basis for making recommendation for future tanks, that definite information be furnished the Board in this respect. The Board fully concurs in the opinion of many well-advised officers of the Marine Corps that all of our equipment should be as light as possible consistent with adequate performance and will continue to keep this factor in mind, but it has been clearly demonstrated that the present weight limitation is a serious handicap to the manufacturer and that in order to obtain better performance and greater effective fire power the weight of our tanks will continue to increase. This may eventually eliminate any advantage of the Marine Corps tank over the Army tank.

3. As regards the Army tanks, either the M2A2 light tank or the M-1 combat car; two (2) principal arguments have been advanced against its adoption: (a) That it is too heavy and (b) that procurement of it in a national emergency is doubtful. No authority for these opinions has come before the Board. It is therefore requested that the Board be advised on these particular questions:

a. Can the Navy handle a ten (10) ton Army tank on transports in the ship to shore movement? It would appear that this is the only place where the weight of the tank is a serious consideration.

b. Since the matter of procurement in time of national emergency is something which can not be accurately foretold, either as regards our own tank or the Army tank, information is requested as to whether the Army can furnish us now with Army tanks in the same amounts as our plans contemplate for procurement of Marine Corps Tanks.

4. While the Army tanks mentioned above are not generally conceded to be perfect, the Board believes that in their present status they are superior in performance and fire power to ours as was shown by actual demonstration at this Post. If the matter of weight and procurement can be satisfactorily determined it is recommended that the Marine Corps purchase either one (1) M2A2 light tank or one (1) M-1 combat car of the latest model from the Army for use during Fleet Landing Exercise No. 5 so that it can be tried out under landing conditions. The purchase is recommended rather than a loan for the reason that it is considered highly desirable that our own personnel operate the tank under these conditions.

Drawings of the new tank lighter furnished the Board indicate that its load capacity is sufficient to carry the Army tank and the dimensions of the well are adequate to contain it.[15]

Shepherd would later relate how he accosted the Marine Corps staff:

All of a sudden, it struck me, why who in the hell said it had to be five tons. I went to headquarters, G-3 section, I said, "who wrote these specifications." Well, I won't mention his name. I had previously made investigations that the booms on the transports, at least one or two of them were fifteen ton booms. I said, "why the hell do we have to have a five ton tank with a fifteen ton boom. Why don't you increase the weight of the tank to seven tons?" We can make a good tank weighing seven tons, but we can't get it down to five.[16]

The reply of the commandant's staff demonstrated the extent to which they still believed in the separate Marine Corps Tank concept. On 19 October their reply arrived and it agreed with the board's interpretation of the true capacities of navy cargo-handling and landing-craft equipment, and further agreed that the army could supply the numbers of light tanks envisioned for the FMF. However, the staff still held to the unique requirements that they had conceived:

It is considered most essential that all materiel employed in the landing against opposition and especially that required during the early phases of such operation be kept at a minimum weight and size consistent with the ability to perform the task assigned. While heavier equipment may be landed under favorable conditions, Marine Corps equipment must be designed to permit its landing when conditions are unfavorable. The condition of the sea, of the shore-line, and the possible lack of special materiel such as tank lighters must be considered. The characteristics hitherto required of the Marine Corps tanks limited their weight and size in order to obtain a vehicle that could be handled and landed under unfavorable conditions and by the use of the materiel at hand such as 50' motor sailers or by such improvisations as the lashing of a float between two 40' motor sailers. Furthermore, it is not believed desirable to incorporate added weight in the Marine Corps tank in order to provide for long trips overland inasmuch as it has been designed primarily for use in a beach head of comparatively small area and for a limited advance inland. The continuation of this policy in the Marine Corps is deemed mandatory for the accomplishment of its assigned mission.

The Marine Corps has under procurement five (5) tanks which are expected to prove superior to those now on hand. It is considered advisable to thoroughly test these new tanks before initiating procurement of a tank radically different in characteristics.

In view of the above, the recommendation for the procurement at this time of an Army Light tank, for test, is not approved.[17]

The MCEB had already looked at the current light tanks being readied for service with the army. The evident preference of the headquarters staff for a specially designed "Marine Corps Tank" that would best serve the roles and missions of the FMF paled before the demonstrations conducted at Quantico. These factors became clear long before the "improved" CTL-3A tank was failing its pilot tests. The army drove an M2A2 light tank and an M1 combat car (also a light tank, but so designated for the cavalry branch) from Aberdeen Proving Ground to Quantico in April for a demonstration, covering the 110 miles without incident. On 14 April the two tanks maneuvered for the MCEB and other interested observers over varied terrain, accompanied by two CTL-3s of the 1st Tank Company for comparison. All tanks boarded and unloaded from the standard tank and artillery lighter without difficulty. One CTL-3 promptly fell out of the test with a broken differential while exiting the riverfront. On the trail to the field, the second CTL fell out with a thrown track, returning later to the tank park. The army tanks then forded streams, negotiated hills and ravines, toppled three- to four-inch oak trees, and climbed three-foot-high mud embankments along the creeks. The board minutes recorded that the army tank, although too heavy, proved superior in all performance areas to the CTL design.[18]

The pressure on the board mounted in 1939, for the requirements of the two-brigade FMF had to be met shortly as the manpower soon to be available allowed the FMF to fill its ranks. As planned in 1936, each brigade's tank company would have fifteen tanks each, later raised to eighteen with a three-tank headquarters element added. Yet only one five-tank platoon had been ordered in each succeeding year. Costing some $19,000 each, with armament, the light tanks would remain precious and scarce commodities in the FMF inventory for the foreseeable future. The Marmon-Herrington "Marine Tank" was continuing to develop, but the army tank program, based upon key engineering developments accomplished in the 1930s, was progressing at astounding speed. Navy landing craft already existed in prototype and planning that foresaw the handling of tanks in the 20-ton range. The original

concepts of conducting amphibious landings on a narrow band of shore-
line with infantry backed by a selection of support troops also developed
into a much more complex and sophisticated amphibious doctrine.[19]

Some interest had continued since the 1920s in wheeled scout and
armored cars as well, although no definite plans for units had yet
emerged from the planned expansion of the Marine Corps. The quartermaster department of the Corps experimented with "cross-country
cars," equipped sometimes with a pintle-mounted .30-caliber machine
gun and with racks for rifles or submachine guns. Frequently the depot
fitted some light armor on these civilian vehicles, particularly around
the gas tanks. The quartermaster bought some 6.5-ton chassis for the
summer 1931 maneuvers and proposed vehicles for certain organizations of the expeditionary force which might require them for security
patrols, artillery observation, and scouting. In 1937 the quartermaster
decided to procure four-wheel-drive stationwagons from the Marmon-
Herrington Company for use as the cross-country car. The field reports
did not encourage further efforts. The Marmon-Herrington cars produced complaints in the field, although several different types appeared
at the 1939 FLEX6 as reconnaissance cars in the one-half- to two-ton
range. In the end, the equipment board judged them interesting but of
questionable value as substitutes for light tanks.[20]

The beginning of the end of the problem-plagued Marmon-Herrington
probably came with the discovery that the CTL-3 series even lacked the
minimum specified level of protection. The tankers of the 1st Tank
Company remained ever eager to advertise new weaknesses and failures. Lieutenant de Zayas reported at the end of December 1938 that
tests with only .22-caliber ammunition had produced bullet splash
through the vision ports and engine louvers. The mission of the CTL-3
on the beach was to destroy machine-gun nests and other field fortifications in support of the assaulting infantry. Now it appeared that the
drivers and the engine radiators and fuel lines might be vulnerable to
small arms fire. With Lieutenant Colonel Shepherd already searching
for justification to move the headquarters staff off their policy regarding the Marine Tank, this was just the proof needed. The company participated in Fleet Exercise 5 (FLEX5), still with its single platoon, during January and February of 1939. Tactically, the tanks performed well
again, with offloading aided by a second prototype tank lighter. But the
complaints of the mechanical performance of the CTL-3 began to read
like a diatribe. Operating only 100 miles per vehicle over the fifty days
of deployment, the CTL-3s experienced 107 failures requiring action by

mechanics. Crews complained of structural weakness and a tendency to throw track at any time. The brigade commander seconded the tankers' complaints, stating that the tank was now required to perform inland missions in addition to clearing the beach.[21]

The long-awaited second platoon of CTL-3A tanks arrived, as stated above, in July 1939. Colonel Shepherd had already seized the opportunity in May, however, to write yet another letter to the commandant, via the president of the MCEB, Brig. Gen. Emile P. Moses, urging the abandonment of the Marine Tank policy in favor of standard army machines:

> *It is the opinion of this [tank and motor transport] committee that any future tanks procured by the Marine Corps be purchased from the Army. The funds available to the [Army] Ordnance Corps for research, development and test, and their resources for production, are far superior to the mediocre facilities and limited funds of the Marine Corps for development of a special type vehicle manufactured by a civilian concern. Although the characteristics of the Army tank may not be ideal for landing operations, their many excellent features and assurity of procurement make their adoption by the Marine Corps desirable.[22]*

Shepherd went on to recommend new specifications for a light-combat tank initially drawn up by Captain Denig, now the liaison officer at the Marmon-Herrington plant. These notes specifically argued for a three- to four-man crew, turreted armament of up to 37mm size, periscope viewing ports, and armor protection against more powerful antiaircraft weapons likely to be encountered. Appending a photograph of an Italian M11 tank as an example of tanks generally available and suitable for Marine Corps use (published in the 28 May issue of the *New York Times*), Shepherd's report condemned by implication the Marmon-Herrington design and the Marine Tank policy.

This time the appeal stuck, for perhaps the evidence had become too overwhelming. The staff memo to the commandant proposed a moratorium on any new tank purchases until the 1941 procurement plan. Noting that the second platoon of Marmon-Herringtons shortly would reach Quantico in August and no maneuvers would be held until the following winter, the Plans and Policy Division staff recommended spending the funds on new antiaircraft weapons and deferring future tank acquisition pending the testing of new tanks, with more funds anticipated in 1941. The staff evaluated the bullet-splash problem of the CTL-3 as proof that it was vulnerable to .30-caliber and larger weapons.[23]

The 1st Tank Company, now commanded by Capt. Charles G. Meints and executive officer 1st Lt. William R. Collins, both graduates of the 1938–39 tank course at Fort Benning, participated in FLEX6. They took both platoons of CTL-3 and -3A tanks, as well as a single army light tank, the new M2A4. Both officers and five enlisted men had become familiar with the tank at Aberdeen Proving Ground. The beginning of the European war enhanced the seriousness but not the size of the January–February 1940 exercise, which served mostly for the testing of newer navy landing craft. The M2A4 showed that it could operate from these landing craft quite well, although the suspension system proved vulnerable to saltwater, causing some consternation among the tankers. The newer model CTL-3A handled much better when fitted with its new 10.5-inch band track, proving that the Marmon-Herrington engineers could improve as well.[24]

Commandant Holcomb wanted to wait no further in building up that tank company, for the Marine Corps budget swelled with each congressional debate over defense readiness and the necessary expansion of the forces in 1940. He instructed the president of the Marine Corps Equipment Board that experience already indicated the need for improvements to light tanks since the last procurement. Anticipating funds for eighteen to twenty new tanks, he requested specifications for these tanks by mid-April.[25]

On 3 April 1940 the MCEB sat in full-day session to determine the future of the Marine Corps's tank program. In addition to the board, commanders of the schools and 1st Marine Brigade and their key officers appeared to give advice on the best courses of action to adopt. The MCEB had determined, on a tentative basis, that an increase of vehicle weight to 18,000 pounds was advisable. But the president of the board wanted the key FMF commanders to make their feelings a matter of record, perhaps because of the tortuous development that the initial Marine Tank program had followed. That record reads as much as an iconography of future Corps leadership as it does a testimonial on tank policy.

Brig. Gen. Holland M. Smith desired improvements in firepower and mobility, but also great handiness in ship-to-shore movement. He therefore opposed acquisition of an army tank, preferring to land two marine tanks for each army tank that could be carried in the 45- and 50-foot lighters. As a consequence of the six-ton target weight, he accepted the fact of the marine tank being unprotected in its rear, but noted that the second set of CTL vehicles had demonstrated superiority to the first one and that further improvement could be expected. He liked the concept of the turreted tank, but sensed that such a vehicle would be too large to permit loading two per lighter.

Col. Julian C. Smith found the present tank too underarmed and preferred one carrying the 37mm gun in a turret. He acknowledged that such a tank would take the entire capacity of the planned landing craft.

Col. Charles D. Barrett saw the tank as a machine-gun killer on the beach, armed primarily with the .30-caliber machine gun. But he preferred a turret-mounted armament. Since a turreted tank would be larger and heavier, he advocated a mix of turretless and turreted tanks, especially in the interim period while the specific value of turreted tanks might be assessed.

Col. Archie F. Howard advocated a simple design able to crush barbed wire obstacles and combat .30-caliber machine guns on the beach. He believed that the present marine tank could be improved mechanically and, when that was done, it would provide all desired capabilities, except for all-round fire.

Lt. Col. Graves B. Erskine moved for the adoption of a medium tank armored against .50-caliber fire even if it would be less maneuverable than a light tank.

Brig. Gen. Philip H. Torrey stated that the Corps expected too much performance from such a small vehicle as the present design and that if it was required to have a lightweight tank, some degree of firepower would have to be sacrificed.

1st Lt. William R. Collins advocated adoption of a diesel engine with its greatly reduced fire hazard, with additional advantage of high torque output at low speeds. He stated that the driver should have fixed machine guns under his control as a flexible mount proved inoperable while driving.

Master T.Sgt. C. E. Anderson stated that he had considerable experience with the army light tank and the operation of turret weapons in general. He advocated its adoption for Marine Corps use because of its superior power, ruggedness, and trench-crossing ability. He admitted that the present tank, when made mechanically sound, could render good service, especially when fitted with a controlled differential, improved track, and modified suspension, as well as redesigning the vision ports of the crew.

The board then held a trial vote, including the testifying nonmembers as well as members; however, three of the former declined to participate. The three candidate vehicles were:

1.Improved CTL-3 series tank, maximum weight 12,500 pounds, less armament

2.Turreted tank, maximum weight 18,000 pounds, less armament

3.U.S. Army light tank, weight 24–25,000 pounds.

The assembled group cast two votes for tank number 1, five for number 2, and six for number 3. There were then nine votes cast for a combination of ten number 1 and five number 2 tanks. The minutes noted, curiously, that colonels and generals tended to vote for the present type tank, mechanically improved, while officers more junior voted for turreted tanks. After dismissing the nonmembers, the MCEB voted to procure both the present type tank and the turreted tank in proportion of 2 to 1, respectively. The present type tank was to be improved in armor, suspension, and gun mountings, and both vehicles were to use controlled differentials.[26]

Within the week, headquarters briefed the commandant on the board's recommendation. With about $660,000 available in the current year's budget, the board advocated buying improved Marmon-Herrington 12,500-pound tanks and a new, three-man turreted tank of 18,000 pounds. The operational concept provided for using the smaller tank for clearing the immediate beach area in an assault, with the heavier, more capable tank used for operations inland. General Holcomb signed the order that day.[27]

Thus, in the spring of 1940, the Marine Corps reassessed its tank program, after years of struggling with the limitations of the "light fighting tank" first proposed in 1935 and produced as the CTL-3 series. Despite the clearest of warnings from early tank operators like Major Withers and the incisive recommendations of Colonel Shepherd, the board sought a compromise by gambling on the further improvements of the Marmon-Herrington tanks, backed up by the adoption of an enlarged, turreted tank of nine tons, not yet designed. A plurality of the test vote on 3 April had advocated changing to the army's light tank, and the board had rather obviously recoiled from such an "incorrect" policy running counter to the previous written guidance of the commandant and opinions of senior commanders such as Holland M. Smith, commander of the 1st Marine Brigade. Meanwhile the world war approached, and the United States began its earnest preparations for defense and intervention. Congress voted increased taxes in June 1940 and approved the "two-ocean" navy building program the following month. In the ensuing expansion, the quibbling represented by the equipment board would be swept away by the stark realities of wartime pressures.

Chapter 3

Preparing for War, 1940–1942

> These tanks do not hold up under the strain of field conditions and are constantly breaking down during field training exercises. There have been on the average of five tanks a day on the deadline due to these necessary repairs.
>
> —Capt. Gardelle Lewis (1942)

Early Planning and Trends for War

In its final year and a half of peace, the Marine Corps would grow not only in structure but in mission. Already in July of 1940 the Joint War Planning Committee Board planned the use of the 1st Marine Brigade to seize the Vichy-French island of Martinique.[1]

The Corps thus was thrust into the same two-ocean war as the navy, having thought mostly of Pacific campaigns for the FMF this far in its existence. Navy war planning now called for an FMF consisting of two complete divisions, several defense battalions, and two aircraft wings. The staff at Headquarters, Marine Corps began to envision three divisions as a wartime strength.[2]

Yet the entire armored fighting vehicle strength of the Corps that same July consisted of the three officers and forty-six enlisted men of the 1st Tank Company, 1st Marine Brigade, and their ten CTL-3 series tankettes. The West Coast brigade still had no tank company, yet the planning now focused on expanding these brigades to division strength. Clearly, the fledgling tank arm of the Marine Corps would have to accelerate its growth from the platoon-a-year rate it had experienced.

The April decision by the MCEB to recommend the procurement of both improved CTL-3s and a new turreted tank produced fast action after General Holcomb's approval. The board provided more detailed specifications and the commandant ordered the quartermaster on 19 April to buy both types of tanks as soon as bids had been received. He also ordered the modernization of the original platoon of CTL-3s to the new standard. The commandant later explained to the navy's ordnance chief that the cost of rebuilding them was high but that scrapping them early would not help the current problem.[3]

Events moved far too rapidly for normal peacetime planning, however. As the Battle of France ensued in Europe and the British army retreated from the continent of Europe, the commandant received a disturbing memo from his chief planner, Charles D. Barrett, a brigadier general and the chief architect of the 1930s amphibious doctrine. Barrett sounded a new urgency for the tank program. Noting that the Corps had ten Marmon-Herrington tanks in hand, twenty more on order, and a further five of the new nine-tonners on order, Barrett asserted that more urgent measures now became necessary.

> Several factors have recently arisen which materially affect the policy of the Marine Corps with respect to tanks. First. The present war has demonstrated the great effectiveness of tanks, and the relative numbers of tanks to other arms has been greater than formerly thought desirable. Second . . . it seems probable that in a number of cases, that the FMF could land without opposition and would then be called upon to defend a relatively large area. In this event a fast striking force would constitute the best defense. Third. The possibility of being ordered on operations before new tanks can be built has been increased. In this case, Army tanks actually on hand would constitute the only supply. It is believed that Army tanks could be secured if the emergency were sufficiently great.[4]

General Barrett recommended the immediate acquisition by transfer of five army light tanks, sending two to each brigade for training, and keeping a fifth tank as a spare, all to facilitate training on the new machines. Commandant Holcomb approved the memo and the conversion to the army's light-tank fleet began to develop. Even if the Marmon-Herrington tanks, both turreted and tankette type, had developed into successful vehicles, the quantities required for the rapid expansion of the FMF would have never arrived in time. Moreover, the Marine Corps leadership now faced the imminent prospect of combat operations if hostilities began against Germany. Even the more passive strategic notions of hemispheric defense held the prospect of action against the Vichy French forces in the Caribbean. A proposed landing in the Azores, it was feared, could bring U.S. forces into direct conflict with the German army, flushed with its successes against the best armies of Europe. Far from the island and atoll naval war prophesied by Pete Ellis, the Marine Corps could find itself in combat in the European *Blitzkrieg*.

The MCEB now seconded General Barrett's suggestion and recommended procurement of army light tanks for the East and West Coast brigades as soon as possible. The tank companies assigned to those

brigades would be required before any tank previously recommended
by the board could be developed. On 8 July 1940 the secretary of the
Navy formally requested thirty-six army light tanks from the secretary
of the Army. He urgently asked for crew training and five training tanks,
as well as delivery estimates for the other thirty-one. The letter specified the new M3 light tank as particularly desired, but indicated that
the M2A4 would be acceptable. The Marine Corps also preferred diesel
engines for its tanks but accepted the gasoline engines if more available.
Actually, talk of the M3 tank proved premature, as series production
did not begin until March 1941. The M2A4, however, gave excellent
service and would serve in the first campaigns of the Marine Corps.[5]

The M2A4, developed during 1938–39 with heavier armor and
greater armament than previous light tanks to satisfy the demands of
the infantry branch, introduced a two-man manual turret, fitted with a
37mm antitank gun and a coaxial .30-caliber machine gun. An additional .30-caliber topped the turret in an antiaircraft mount. In the bow
of the hull, the driver could fire two .30-caliber machine guns mounted
in fixed sponson mounts while driving. The assistant driver, operating
dual controls to the right of the driver, also handled a ball-mounted
.30-caliber. With riveted armor of one-inch thickness, the tank resisted
all light weapons and weighed over 11.5 tons empty and almost 13 tons
loaded. Its Continental W670 air-cooled radial engine (developed from
an aircraft engine) developed 262 hp and drove the tank to speeds governed to 36 MPH with a five-speed manual transmission. A robust bogie-
wheel volute spring suspension and linked rubber-bushed track blocks
represented years of sound engineering and enabled this and most other
American tanks to maneuver at high speeds across broken terrain with
great confidence.[6]

After years of experiment and frustration, the 1st Tank Company
now swelled with new men and tanks. Captain Meints visited Aberdeen
Proving Ground in August and sent ten crewmen to the Fort Benning
course in the M2A4. Headquarters ordered five of these men to the 2d
Brigade at San Diego as part of its new tank company. The M2A4s
arrived at 1st Tank Company at the end of September. The company
still had its ten CTL-3As and their crews, and therefore began to
embark on 10 October for Guantanamo, Cuba, and FLEX7, considerably overstrength.[7]

The new tank companies formed officially on 1 November 1940.
Captain Meints and 102 of his men formed the 3d Tank Company in the
1st Brigade, taking all eighteen of the new M2A4s and leaving the 1st

Company and Capt. Henry W. Buse its old Marmon-Herringtons. On the West Coast, Capt. Jesse S. Cook Jr. and executive officer 1st Lt. Alexander B. Swecensky stood up the 4th Tank Company with its newly arrived M2A4s. The lack of tanks and personnel prevented the forming of an additional company with 2d Brigade for the time being, and no 2d Tank Company ever formed.[8]

FLEX7 proved routine, as only a few transports had been added to the forces available the previous year. But General Smith praised the performance of the M2A4, stating that it was satisfactory in all assigned missions and found it in every respect superior to the Marmon-Herrington CTL-3A. He recorded no difficulties in handling the tank from the 40- and 45-foot tank lighters furnished by the navy. Contrary to his testimony to the MCEB the previous April, Smith recommended that no more Marmon-Herringtons be procured until that company had produced a vehicle of comparable quality.[9]

Separate companies of Marmon-Herringtons and M2A4s seemed to be the Marine Corps's plan for the time being, however, and radios and other supporting equipment for both were ordered in November for the thirty-six delivered army light tanks, thirty-seven more expected to be ordered, and the twenty Marmon-Herrington tanks under construction and expected in the following April. With two full divisions being assembled from the two brigades, a battalion of light tanks for each would require many more vehicles.[10]

While FLEX7 was playing out the growing pains of amphibious warfare, the East and West Coast brigades officially expanded to division-size organizations on 1 February 1941. As new regiments of infantry and artillery formed and the expansion of tank and engineer companies to battalions ensued, the Marmon-Herrington companies found themselves shunted to the division special troops as scout companies, leaving the M2A4-equipped 3d and 4th Tank Companies to form with the new battalions. The 1st Division commander redesignated the 1st Scout Company on 1 March, and on the sixteenth of that month the 2d Scout Company formed in 2d Marine Division, with Capt. Bennet G. Powers commanding and 2d Lt. Richard K. Schmidt the platoon leader. The latter would have been the 2d Tank Company, FMF, in numerical sequence, but the decision to form scout companies from the Marmon-Herrington tank companies had superseded that action. Both companies operated the Marmon-Herrington turretless tanks, CTL-3 (2d Scout Company receiving the rebuilt CTL-3M tanks originally numbered T-1 through T-5), and later added fourteen four-wheel M3A1 armored scout cars. These scout companies evolved strangely and remained almost orphans in the division structure. Obviously intended for some form of European-style mechanized warfare, the scout company eventually consisted of three scout platoons with scout cars, a single Marmon-Herrington light-tank platoon and a motorcycle platoon of twenty-four Harley-Davidson WLA motorcycles. The scout cars also went to defense battalions, artillery, and other organizations needing such mechanized equipment.[11]

The 1st Scout Company, 1st Marine Division, remained part of Division Special Troops, but in 2d Marine Division the 2d Scout Company formed with the 2d Tank Battalion's headquarters when that unit was organized. As scout cars arrived in early 1942, the companies retained a single platoon of CTL-3M tanks. However, when the Marine Corps returned to a Pacific war orientation, the scout cars, hundreds of which had been ordered, looked comparatively useless. At the end of 1942, the commandant ordered the M3A1 scout-car program canceled, with the quarter-ton jeep designated as the replacement scout vehicle. He also decided that the scout companies would routinely form with Division Special Troops and not be part of the tank battalions in the future. Although some interest was shown in the army's six-wheel armored car project, the T-24, no further procurements of this type equipment occurred. The divisions found space on board for shipping already scarce in the Pacific and the M3A1 cars became early losses in the thinning out of unnecessary equipment.[12]

Another casualty of the return of the Marine Corps to its Pacific war orientation was the tank destroyer. A popular army program intended to release tanks for offensive roles on the battlefield, the tank destroyer concept called for placing large-caliber antitank guns on lightly armored carriages, which were to be moved quickly to any sector threatened by enemy tanks. In the Marine Corps employment of the tank destroyer, each division special troops echelon was to have a battery of these weapons, and each infantry regiment a platoon, and for two complete corps antitank battalions each of three batteries were planned. In the end only the halftrack-mounted 75mm cannon reached the field in the marine division. This was the M3 GMC (gun, mount, carriage), armed with surplus M1897 guns, the famous "French 75" of World War I fame. The Corps initially ordered only thirty M3s of the sixty desired in January of 1942, because only thirty of the M1897 guns were on hand. The new army M5 75mm motor carriage then became the approved replacement as the Marine Corps standard "heavy self-propelled anti-tank weapon." However, the army canceled the M5 program and none of its other tank destroyers seemed to be light enough for amphibious landings. The shortage for three marine divisions and two antitank battalions totaled 87 tank destroyers. Belatedly, headquarters ordered 219 more M3 carriages with guns and ammunition from the army in the fall of 1942.[13]

On 1 September 1942 the first of these corps-level reinforcing antitank battalions, 2d Antitank Battalion, stood up at Camp Elliott, the San Diego FMF training base. Apparently unimpressed with his prospects, the battalion commander and future three-star general Lt. Col. James Snedeker transferred on the seventh to the 3d Marine Division, leaving three captains in charge as the battalion trained and shipped out to New Zealand, unloading at Wellington on 12 March 1943 as part of the I Amphibious Corps. Arriving at Nouméa on 4 December 1943 with 21 officers and 367 men, the battalion was disbanded ignominiously on the seventeenth and its personnel assigned to units already on that rear-area island.[14]

The M3 GMC batteries of the division special weapons battalions (antiaircraft and antitank weapons) and the separate defense battalions occasionally served as assault guns alone or with the tanks, but generally they functioned as self-propelled artillery during the Pacific war. The infantry regiment also had a pair of M3 GMCs in its antitank company. The few opportunities for tank destroyer employment in the island campaign proved extremely fleeting and no doctrine or experience emerged from this brief dalliance with the weapon. By the end of the war, these units would operate M7B1 self-propelled artillery howitzers.

Among the numerous military fads and inventions that punctuate the early phases of this war, the salient success story for the United States and the Marine Corps together was the amphibian tractor. It remains a well-known and often-told story that we might only review in outline here, as it has its origins not in the search for armored fighting vehicles, but as part of the eternal search for landing equipment for the FMF. Donald Roebling, a Florida engineer and inventor, built his "alligator" amphibious tractor in 1935 as a swamp-crossing rescue vehicle in the wake of a destructive series of hurricanes in the Okeechobee region. Successive modifications had produced an 8,700-pound tractor, built of aluminum, capable of 18–20 MPH on land and, in the water, a creditable 8.6 MPH using its tracks with an ingenious curved cleat design that functioned with a paddlewheel effect in the water. An article in Life magazine interested several senior navy and Marine Corps officers, and the MCEB dispatched its recording secretary to consult with Roebling at his Clearwater, Florida, shop.

Roebling put the vehicle through its paces, and a report with accompanying movie film impressed the board. In May 1938 the commandant asked the navy to procure a pilot model for testing, leading to its use in FLEX5. Without forthcoming navy funds, the Marine Corps officers were forced to persuade the inventor to design and fabricate a pilot model military amphibian, which he accomplished in May 1940. In contrast to the usual fate of tracked vehicle design, the "Alligator" lost weight through successive redesigns, and the new model, measuring 20 by 8 feet and weighing 7,700 pounds, could carry a 7,000-pound payload in the water at 8–10 MPH, in an open sea way, through reefs and surf. It drew only three feet of water and remained afloat even with its cargo bay filled with water. Thanks to the "limited national emergency" state of 1940, the navy could fund more work. Roebling brought yet another version, with a more powerful engine, to Quantico in November for testing and demonstration. The new Alligator later performed in FLEX7. Perhaps indicating its importance, Brigadier General Smith assigned his own aide-de-camp and logistics officer, Capt. Victor H. Krulak, to run the test vehicle throughout the exercise, providing the first troop test results from the FMF.[15]

The Quantico demonstration had already impressed the navy sufficiently, however. The MCEB championed the vehicle, establishing a "restricted" classification on all correspondence dealing with the tractor in September 1940. On the seventeenth, the quartermaster requested procurement of ten Roebling tractors at a total cost of $160,000. After the Quantico demonstration of November the navy contracted with Roebling for those ten plus another 100 tractors, with the proviso that the production models be built from steel instead of aluminum. Roebling then turned to the Food Machinery Corporation of nearby Dunedin, Florida, for redesign and production assistance and the first production vehicle, designated LVT1 (landing vehicle, tracked) rolled off the assembly line in July 1941.[16]

At this point, however, the amphibian tractor, or "amtrac," represented a logistics, not a fighting vehicle. The quartermaster of the Marine Corps summarized, "it is understood that the Amphibian 'Alligator' Tractor is not intended for use as an offensive weapon but rather as an amphibious vehicle for the rapid & expeditious transfer of supplies from ship to combat units ashore during a landing attack." The good intentions of the planners would not survive the exigencies of combat, however, and the LVTs would be thrust into combat roles the likes of which could not be imagined by them or the Roebling design team. Amphibious characteristics notwithstanding, the Alligator remained a very primitive tracked vehicle. Woefully underpowered with its 150-hp Hercules engine, the all-steel LVT1 weighed 22,000 pounds full and carried a 4,500-pound cargo no faster than 12 MPH on land with its rigid suspension consisting of track rollers moving over steel channels fixed to the hull sponsons. The maximum hull thickness of 3/16-inch soft steel provided virtually no protection from small arms or artillery shell fragments. But it did provide waterborne mobility unattained with conventional landing craft. Suspension and engine defects demanded a major overhaul every 100 hours of operation, and training time would be limited severely as a consequence.[17]

During his redesign of the LVT1, Donald Roebling already thought of an armored fighting vehicle based upon the Alligator. Initial sketches completed in January 1940 produced no initial interest, but once production of the cargo-carrying amtrac began, the Corps began to see a role for an armored amphibian fighting vehicle. Headquarters determined the original armament for the cargo-carrying amtrac as one .50- and three .30-caliber machine guns, but most of these vehicles operated with fewer guns. But the need for increased firepower at the beach assault point had long been recognized by the doctrine manuals. The commander of the amtrac school established at Dunedin for drivers and mechanics began to function as a liaison officer for further developments. The commandant authorized Roebling's request for a light-tank turret for development of the armored amphibian on 3 November 1941. A 37mm turret from the M3 light tank and mockups of the new Marmon-Herrington turret would be provided as examples of the armament desired for the amphibian "tank," armored against .50-caliber fire and capable of overcoming typical beach defenses as they were thought to be at the time.[18]

Equipping the Fleet Marine Force

For the time being, therefore, only the light tank would serve as the fighting vehicle of the Corps. Forming the two new battalions took all of 1941, from the formation of the 3d and 4th Tank Companies on each coast in November 1940 to the final activation of the 1st and 2d Tank Battalions in November and December of 1941, respectively. The supply of army M3 tanks, successors to the M2A4, determined the schedule for filling out the larger units. Pres. Franklin Roosevelt undoubtedly helped the situation for the marine tankers when he determined in 1941 the priorities of issue of scarce materiel would favor the FMF, which would likely see action outside the United States before any stateside army units. The army chief of staff saw no good from this, saying, "my main battle is equipping the Marines. Whether we have anything left after the British and Marines get theirs, I do not know."[19]

In February headquarters ordered another thirty-four M2A4 light tanks, sufficient for the next two light-tank companies, but was advised by the army that none would be available as the M3 had already gone into production. This was the next order subsequent to the forming of 3d and 4th Tank Companies, so the total number of M2A4s acquired by the Corps remained just the thirty-six vehicles ordered in the summer of 1940. Only 365 of these tanks were produced by the army between May 1940 and March 1941. But they were well engineered for the period and presented the FMF with their first truly capable machines.[20]

The light tank M3 corrected weaknesses in the M2A4 with increased frontal armor for the hull (from 1.0 to 1.5–1.75 inches) and turret (from 1 to 1.5-inch gun shield). With an improved rear idler wheel, the M3 increased its ground contact area, reducing ground pressure despite its 14-ton weight. The chief changes would come in the turret, which used the ubiquitous 37mm antitank gun, mounted as in the M2A4 with limited traverse and elevation moved by the gunner in a yoke mounting, and manual traverse for full 360-degree turret rotation. Late-production M3s had a 37mm gun with a modified breechblock that ejected the spent cartridge upon the recoil of the firing, remaining open for the next round to be loaded. Initially, a small cupola with vision ports topped the M3 turret, but it disappeared in later turrets, which also employed more welding in place of riveting. Later a power traverse turret with a turret basket and two-inch gun shield armor would appear in the M3A1 version. A vertical gyrostabilizer unit was added to production vehicles, but would prove tricky to use. This last version continued in production until February of 1943.[21]

Two production lines turned out M3s with successive modifications with either gasoline or diesel engines through August of 1942, further complicating the uniformity of supply. The army developed the Guiberson T-1020 diesel during the 1930s and it gave a mixed performance, depending very much on the user's sympathies. Its high compression demanded the use of starter cartridges, but it offered increased economy and reduced danger of fire. The Guiberson engine fell out of production after a 1942 decision reversal by the Army Armored Force to no longer advocate diesel engines for combat vehicles. In fact, a later decision by the army to deploy no diesel-powered vehicles outside the

United States made more of these available to the Marine Corps than might otherwise have been the case.[22]

With such a variety of light tanks of the same nominal mark being produced, the novice tankers of the two marine divisions encountered much more heartache than they might have expected. The M2A4s had already required modifications to the suspension to prevent their freezing up under saltwater immersion. Now an array of M3 tanks began to flow through the quartermaster channels to the East and West Coast bases.

The commandant ordered another thirty-nine M3 tanks in March 1941, thus completing the requirement for the first two tank battalions, which were to operate three companies of light tanks and a fourth of Marmon-Herringtons. We will remember that the MCEB had conceived of an improved CTL-3 and a larger, turreted tank, to be procured on a 2 : 1 ratio. The new turretless CTL-6 passed inspection at the Marmon-Herrington plant in May, along with the rebuilt original CTL-3, now called CTL-3M. Curiously, the same armament of three machine guns, all .30-caliber, was retained in separate ball mountings for the two-man crew to operate. The new three-man turreted tank, called the CTM-3TBD, carried two .50-caliber machine guns in the turret, also retained the three machine guns in the front hull, and, surprisingly, sported the diesel engine so strongly commended to the MCEB by 1st Lt. William R. Collins. The new tanks proved to be overweight by 1,870 (CTL-6) and 2,680 (CTM-3TBD) pounds, but with more urgency in the procurement process there was no more quibbling at this point. The CTM-3TBD turret with a dual machine-gun mounting was not liked, however, and the inspectors recommended a single gun mounting for the future. The suspensions of the new tanks now resembled the M2A4 and used a redesigned steel-linked track.[23]

But new misgivings began to surface over the Marmon-Herrington tanks. One of the CTL-3As of 1st Scout Company's tank platoon, named *Maria* (the five tanks took names of the Dionne quintuplets), had rolled down a hill with its two lieutenants aboard, one of whom was the tank platoon commander giving instructions to one of the newly reported company officers at Quantico. The officers managed to exit the vehicle, but the engine caught fire from spilled gasoline. The CO_2-type fire extinguisher system of the tank could not smother the fire of an overturned tank and the vehicle became a total loss. The resulting investigation concluded that all the Marmon-Herrington tanks would need modified extinguisher systems, as well as modifications to the fuel tanks to prevent such spills in the future.[24]

The first M3s arrived at their 1st and 2d Marine Division destinations during October. The divisions began to activate additional tank companies for their tank battalions. Already, the 3d Tank Company had been designated A Company, 1st Tank Battalion, and 4th Tank Company had become A Company, 2d Tank Battalion, on 1 May 1941. The latter, still commanded by Major Cook, then deployed with the 1st Provisional Marine Brigade organized around the 6th Marines to garrison Iceland in July. The first of November saw the B companies of each battalion activated and the 1st Tank Battalion activated its headquarters under Major Meints as well. On 20 December the 2d Tank Battalion activated its headquarters under Major Withers, newly returned from sea duty, and additional companies formed in succeeding months.[25]

This rather haphazard organization of tank battalions by accretion of troops and tanks contributed to the low level of preparation of the units. Only the A companies had operated with their M2A4s for any length of time. Although the M3 represented minimal change, a large number of untrained officers and men now joined the expanding battalions. The new tanks arrived in various states of packup, with few spares and manuals and no parts lists. Captain Swecensky wrote directly to the quartermaster of the Marine Corps on 12 November, requesting blueprints and standard nomenclature listings for the M3 and blueprints and operator's manuals for the W670 engine. He lamented, "at present, this organization [B Company, 2d Tank Battalion] possesses no spare parts and has no suitable reference from which to order same." Lacking any such materials at hand, the quartermasters immediately requested four sets of blueprints, parts, and price lists from the army chief of ordnance. The new companies and battalions sent officers and men to the Army Armor School at Fort Knox as they could be spared, in order to develop a cadre of personnel trained to handle the new equipment and procedures. Officers also attended the 1st Army maneuvers in Louisiana to gain tactical insights for the future. Much had to be improvised, and when Captain Denig's B Company, 2d Tank Battalion, detached for duty in January 1942, with the 2d Marine Brigade guarding Samoa, they only managed to test-fire their 37mm guns for the first time while on the road to San Diego.[26]

Robert Denig's first report on service with the first tank unit in the field in the Pacific contained stern warnings for the headquarters staff that summer. Eventually sent to Wallis Island in a French island group north of Samoa, Denig saw little that could be considered conventional in the beach defenses, as they were backed by impassable hills, making the usual tank counterattack almost infeasible. The humidity reached extremes, and trafficability on the island remained poor except on gravel roads that might not survive enemy shelling. Maintenance problems continued to pose serious difficulties, as too few men and too little time remained for 100-hour checks, repairs, and overhauls. The gasoline storage remained suspect, with corrosion present in the cans, and the ammunition had to be inspected and repacked. Only the assignment of some aviation mechanics by a sympathetic commander had reduced the general burdens of operating the tanks in the island paradise.[27]

The eventual solution to the training problem came with the establishment of a Marine Corps tank school on the West Coast. William R. Collins (1913–91), who was Meints's executive officer at 1st Tank Company and advised the MCEB in 1940, was now a major and, like Hartnoll Withers, returned fresh from sea duty to the rapidly expanding FMF. In July 1942 Collins formed the Tank School, FMF Training Center, Camp Elliott. For the next two years, he and his instructor staff would train marines to operate and maintain the various tanks and variants. Camp Elliott had already expanded with the purchase of more land for training, and Collins and the tankers of the battalions forming at Camp Elliott worked to build a camp and training facilities at "Jacques' Farm" at the same time that they struggled to devise a training program for the new vehicles and weapons. "Rip" Collins, a 1935 Georgetown University graduate, led the tank school through all its stages of evolution, retraining the school and students in each new vehicle and new tactical concept emerging from the war, and assisted in the formation of each of the tank battalions forming at Jacques' Farm. He would later take command of the last battalion to form there, lead it into the Pacific war, and become the first active-duty general from the ranks of the World War II tank unit commanders.[28]

No relief came in the unending change of type, model, and series of vehicles acquired by the Marine Corps in World War II, however. No sooner had marine tankers become familiar with the early gas and diesel versions of the M3 light tank when a new version arrived at East and West Coast camps. The army had decided to install power turret traverse in the M3 series and the turret "basket" already proven beneficial in British designs. The basket was a turret floor hung under the turret ring, permitting the turret occupants to remain oriented with the gun and mount at all times. The use of welding would increase in this M3A1 design and a simple periscope replaced the commander's cupola. So far so good, but the army decided to modify the M3 production with some of these "improvements" while the retooling to M3A1 production took place simultaneously. This action resulted in the delivery of many M3 "hybrid" tanks at the end of the M3 production run, fitted with the new flat-top turret and gun mount but without power traverse and basket. But the mount designed for the missing power traverse also lacked the 20-degree gimballed movement formerly used by the gunner to lay on target. The tank commander-loader handled the manual traverse but had no gunner's sight, while the gunner had elevation but no final traverse control. These M3 Hybrid tanks, including the usual proportion fitted with diesel engines, were shipped to Marine Corps bases at the same time that the M3A1 production began to arrive, producing howls of protest from the already harassed tankers. Dubbed "flat-tops," the Hybrids were condemned as unfit for combat and useless even for training. Apparently, similar tanks went to the British army as part of scheduled Lend-Lease shipments. Their ordnance shops in the field changed the manual traverse to the gunner's position to solve the immediate problem, but the Corps, of course, lacked any such field capability in 1942.[29]

Major Withers best summarized the dilemma facing the nascent battalion commanders in his letter of 11 September 1942 to the commandant. He assailed the supply deficiencies resulting from the admixture of tanks and the deployment of units with army tanks and two types of Marmon-Herrington tanks. These included tanks delivered without radios, special tools, starter cartridges, firing linkages, and periscopes. Correcting these deficiencies demanded spares, time, and skilled mechanics, all of which proved scarce or, at times, nonexistent.

> At present, the Marine Corps seems to have the following types of tanks in the Pacific, several types of which belong to one unit: M2A4 gasoline, M3 gasoline hightop, M3 diesel hightop, modernized engine, M3 diesel hightop, engines not modernized, M3 hybrids, diesel and probably gas. Soon additional types will be added: M3A1, M3A3, M5 gas and diesel.

He noted that the Amphibious Corps headquarters still had the fifty-one M3 Hybrids, but they were unfit for combat. He recommended that the Marine Corps only procure the army light, medium, or heavy tank that came from standard procurement, with gasoline engines. He said that Washington needed a regulating supply organization, with subsidiary organizations also needed on the East and West Coasts, which would ensure uniformity of issue, recordkeeping, support, data on enemy tanks, and advance information on new U.S. tanks.[30]

Withers's confidence in the army procurement system may have been misplaced. Of course, he was in no position to know that many of the production changes and shortages fell totally beyond the control of the Marine Corps officers engaged in the procurement of the myriad materiel required for the marine units, whose number and requirements varied greatly from month to month. Lesser priority army units received M3 tanks at the same time without armament, so strained was the production system of 1942. Marines at Camp Elliott and the new FMF bases at Camp Lejeune, North Carolina, and Camp Pendleton, California, could not be aware of the rather skilled handling by the planners and quartermasters of the gigantic difficulties of filling out the two prewar divisions as well as the four more in the process of creation. Such efforts extended also to the four aircraft wings, separate squadrons and battalions, and the two amphibious corps headquarters, support, and reinforcing units all planned for the wartime Marine Corps. Among the bureaucratic heroes of the Washington front stands the figure of Lt. Col. John D. Blanchard (1901–54). A 1925 Naval Academy graduate who earned a Navy Cross in 1929 in Haiti, Blanchard headed the Ordnance Section under the quartermaster of the Marine Corps. His good judgment and tireless efforts sorted out most of the problems that befell the FMF commands and he averted many others through his sound management of naval and military procurement channels.

Lieutenant Colonel Blanchard's 31 August report to the quartermaster gave keen insight to the flap resulting from the delivery of unserviceable tanks to the 2d Tank Battalion that month. The tanks were unserviceable because of the new deliveries of the "flat-top turret" good for either the M3 or M3A1 in current use. However, the turret was not power-traversed, lacked periscopes, and dispensed with the gunner yoke for 37mm gun, and required hand firing of the coax machine gun. Fifty-one of these bad tanks were on hand, albeit new deliveries, of the seventy-five total in the San Diego area. Immediate overseas deployments required exactly forty-eight tanks, leaving the command short twenty-four. Blanchard had already arranged for the army to turn over twenty-four tanks from local forces by the following week. In retrospect, on the tank problem and the resulting exchanges of correspondence, Blanchard noted with some prescience that even the Marine Corps tank personnel were not completely capable of inspecting and evaluating materiel; hence experts from the army would be required until a Marine Corps expertise evolved.[31]

The quartermasters had already had some experience with Maj. "Barney" Withers and his 2d Tank Battalion. The files of the quarter-

master of the Marine Corps contain the interesting story of the first tank
to be cannibalized in the Marine Corps. Tankers, like other operators of
motorized equipment, have been "brought up" in the hoary traditions
that promise a slow death by torture as appropriate for anyone caught
cannibalizing their valuable fighting vehicles. But in the pioneering
days of tanks, perhaps like aviation (with its proverbial "hangar
queens"), that concept was not yet established.

On 28 February 1942 Withers wrote to the quartermaster, requesting the rebuilding of one tank, light, M3, USMC number 1507. He reported it to consist of only a bare hull and turret, as the rest of the tank
had been stripped for parts in Company B. On 28 March Lieutenant
Colonel Blanchard acknowledged receipt of the battalion commander's
letter, continuing tersely, "this office has no record of any authority having been given for such action. Please furnish information regarding the
circumstances making it necessary to strip this tank." Withers made no
attempt to fashion a lawyer-like answer. His letter of 2 April responded,
"The subject tank had been partially stripped of parts to keep other
tanks in Company B running. When B Company joined the 2d Marine
Brigade and prepared to sail, expected parts for it [the company] did
not arrive and at the last moment, rather than leave without parts, I
authorized stripping the remaining parts from the subject tank."

Blanchard must have had sympathy that month for a battalion commander desperate to prepare green troops and new equipment for the
Pacific war, for the response of headquarters was to send a 7 May letter
to the army's chief of ordnance requesting the rebuilding of one tank at
the Benicia Arsenal, near Vallejo, California. On 20 May the Quartermaster Department's letter to Major Withers was more conciliatory in
tone, asking for a list of items remaining as well as parts required in order
to determine the practicality of rebuilding tank no. 1507.

But Barney Withers proved himself ever a resourceful man, one who
would go on to command an infantry regiment on Iwo Jima, among his
many Marine Corps tanker "firsts." His response on 14 July was to
"request permission for the battalion to rebuild the tank using parts on
hand. The Ordnance Company at Camp Callan has requested participation for training. It is not considered practical to furnish a list of the
parts required to rebuild this tank as the list would involve all items
in the SNL less those few large items listed in the 2d Tank Battalion
28 February letter."

The final note sounded in this story was penciled by a sergeant in the
headquarters ordnance section: "Lt. Col Blanchard: They have the parts

OH [on hand] and I'm getting more sets of parts. It's OK. Sgt Doble."
Scrawled in red by the ever-patient Blanchard: "tell them OK JDB."[32]

Blanchard's staff handled many more details of armored fighting
vehicle procurement than the turret problems on the light-tank series.
In addition to the light tank, they studied the new army medium-tank
development, the amtrac engineering and production, and the ongo-
ing armored scout car and tank destroyer, the latter two disappearing
in 1943 to be replaced by demands for flamethrower vehicles, fording
equipment, and upgrades and new designs of all kinds. Moreover, in
light of the fall of Wake Island to Japanese assault earlier in the war,
headquarters ordered the provision of tank platoons for the existing and
planned defense battalions that would garrison islands held by and
recaptured in future campaigns.

The quartermaster had ordered 367 M3 tanks at a cost of $11.795 mil-
lion in February 1942, a number seemingly sufficient to refit all tank
units then planned and existing. Priorities then had to be set for the
allocation of the new tanks to each division and unit. Then, as the tank
mix problem began to develop from the army procurement sources, the
quartermasters requested plans and specifications from the army for the
various models to better follow these developments. They ordered a few
more M3 gasoline tanks (60) in August as the "flat-top" complaints
arrived, but then a giant order for 735 light tanks (for $25.725M) of the
"latest type" went to the army, signaling the decision to refit the FMF
in its entirety with the latest light tank, to include combat-loss replacements. Also on that date, 13 August, the quartermaster ordered 375
medium tanks, also of the "latest type," from the army, as headquarters now intended to form a corps tank battalion of mediums for each
of the two planned amphibious corps, to be used as reinforcing units in
the upcoming amphibious campaigns.[33]

That decision to standardize also sounded the death knell of the
Marmon-Herrington tank, which continued to draw fire from the FMF
tankers throughout 1942. After modifications to prevent further accidental fires had been completed at the plant, headquarters had shipped
the CTL-6s and the turreted CTM-3TBDs to the two divisions in February and March. The 1st Marine Division received the five turreted
tanks and eight of the lighter models and the remaining twelve CTL-6s
were delivered to the 2d Marine Division. Each divisional scout company already operated four or five CTL-3 series tankettes, and the new
shipments filled each tank battalion's fourth light-tank company. The
mixed joy of receiving these tanks was not long in surfacing. The 2d Tank

Battalion reported defects in the CTL-6 tanks in a letter of 20 April, after only 400 miles of operation, presumably cumulative. We will remember that little love was lost between Major Withers and the Marmon-Herrington Company and a series of letters crossed accusations of poor design with negligent operation by the tankers and so forth. A team of engineers sent by the Hercules Motors Corporation judged the tanks to have been run at excessive engine speed and recommended more careful operation. But the battalion commanders had apparently convinced their division commanders of the futility of operating the Marmon-Herringtons in combat, and the tanks were taken out of the battalions in May and June on the West and East Coasts.[34]

The Marmon-Herringtons did not yet leave service however, and the corps commanders formed the 1st and 2d Separate Tank Companies on the East and West Coasts to man the Marmon-Herringtons. Capt. Robert Bruce Mattson, commanding the 1st Company, was the lieutenant platoon commander who had rolled the CTL-3A down a Quantico hill the previous year, which thus became the first USMC tank loss. He wasted little time contemplating this new situation and attached to the newly formed 3d Marine Regiment, a component of the future 3d Marine Division. On the West Coast, however, Capt. Gardelle Lewis fumed over his new charge, writing the commander of the 22d Marines:

> 1. It has been the practice of this Company since it was organized on the 14th of May, 1942, to note the unsatisfactory performance of the Marmon-Herrington light tanks (CTL-3 six [actually five] ton and CTL-6 nine [six] ton). The following are the more prevalent mechanical failures that have been consistently occurring:
> (a) Defective timing gears
> (b) Leaking water pumps
> (c) Broken axles
> (d) Weak volute springs
> (e) Defective ignition systems
> (f) Overheating of motors.
> These tanks do not hold up under the strain of field conditions and are constantly breaking down during field training exercises. There have been on the average five tanks a day on the deadline due to these necessary repairs.
> It has been found in only a few cases that the personnel of this organization were at fault when these failures occurred. All are experienced in their duties and have been indoctrinated in tank operation and care.

The majority of these tanks are practically new but still present the problems of the older ones. Care has been exercised to insure the proper breaking in of the new tanks.

The combat missions are very limited due to a minimum of armor, armament and speed. The armament would be of little effect against other tanks in combat.

It is recommended that the Marmon-Herrington tanks now on hand be kept at the Fleet Marine Force Training Center for purposes of instruction of future tank personnel and that this organization be equipped with the 13½ ton light tanks now employed by the Marine Corps.[35]

Lewis's arguments convinced the staffs of the 22d Marines and the Amphibious Corps that they had a poor machine on their hands, but headquarters remained adamant that the company would deploy with the Marmon-Herringtons to Samoa with the 22d Marines to reinforce the garrison there. However, headquarters promised to fit the CTL tanks with engine governors and to refit with M3 tanks as part of the normal refurbishment cycle.[36]

Captain Mattson's 1st Separate Tank Company also embarked with its regiment, the 3d Marines, for Samoa at the end of August. The new regiments and tank companies would replace the 7th and 8th Marines with their respective C Company, 1st Tank Battalion, and B Company, 2d Tank Battalion attachments, and allow those units to return to their parent organizations and combat operations. The 1st Separate Tank Company continued on to Uvea Island, in the Wallis island group, closest to the Japanese direction of advance in the South Pacific, and there relieved B Company, attached to the 8th Defense Battalion, Wallis Island Defense Force. The 2d Company remained in British Samoa with the 22d Marines, joined by personnel of the tank platoon, 1st Scout Company. Thus, almost the entire USMC Marmon-Herrington tank inventory served its last days in support of the Samoa garrisons.[37]

The deployment to Samoa ended the active service of the Marmon-Herrington tanks in the Marine Corps. The separate tank companies operated them there until returning to the United States with their regiments in March 1943. The tankers of the Wallis Island Defense Forces left most of their tanks behind, dug-in as pillboxes, a practice followed as well by the M3 tank platoon of the 8th Defense Battalion, until that platoon disbanded later in 1943. These Marmon-Herringtons were left undoubtedly for the defense battalions to use in Samoa, but none ever entered combat with U.S. forces. Ironically, the Dutch East Indies government had purchased large numbers of other versions of the various

Marmon-Herrington tanks and a few made it to Java in time to fight there. The majority of the Dutch vehicles ended up in Australian and U.S. Army hands as orphans. The army used a few in Alaskan garrisons and distributed some to countries like Cuba, Ecuador, Mexico, and Guatemala.[38]

After making the huge August order for tanks, the Ordnance Section conducted a Corps-wide inventory in September of the tanks on hand and distributed the serviceable tanks to the units most in need, retaining the deficient flat-tops and many of the diesel M3s for units still in training or not yet scheduled for deployment. Lieutenant Colonel Blanchard arranged a further transfer of eighty-one M3A1s from the army to fill out immediate needs. The quartermasters then made their plans for the distribution of new tanks on 25 September. The M2A4s and Marmon-Herringtons would be replaced, nine defense battalions would receive eight tanks each, and the 3d Tank Battalion outfitted. They notified the army that only M3A1 through -A3 models would be acceptable. By 13 November the cumulative deliveries of army tanks to the Marine Corps totaled:

- 36   M2A4 [in the two A companies, 1st and 2d Tank Battalions]
- 73   M3 gasoline
- 175   M3 diesel
- 375   M3A1 gasoline (of 508 allocated).

The army by now had shipped so many tanks to the Marine Corps that the depot commander in San Francisco complained to the quartermaster that he had 107 M3A1 tanks on hand, with neither the personnel nor shop facilities to handle, process, repair, and adjust them. He requested that future shipments go via the nearest army tank depot for servicing, then be sealed for export shipment. Radios also became a problem, and many M3A1 tanks apparently received some of the 329 British army no. 19 radio sets ordered as substitutes for the aircraft model RU. Some of these had instructions in Russian, so confused were the supply channels dealing with various Lend-Lease transfers.[39]

The 3d Tank Battalion formed up in a very dispersed manner, reflecting the way that the Corps formed the 3d Marine Division, and later the 4th Marine Division. Perhaps because of a shortage of staff and training areas, the three infantry regiments formed and trained independently at the East and West Coast bases, with tank companies forming with them. Thus the B and C companies, 3d Tank Battalion, formed with the 21st and 23d Marines in July at New River Training Center (later Camp

Lejeune). There, the 1st Separate Tank Company had already joined the independently formed 3d Marines and supported its training. On the West Coast, the rest of the 3d Division formed on 1 September, and on the sixteenth the 3d Tank Battalion formed at Camp Elliott with its headquarters, A, D, and E (Scout) companies. Hartnoll Withers, newly promoted to lieutenant colonel (as was Charles Meints in 1st Tank Battalion) took command with his executive officer, Maj. Bennet Powers, leaving the 2d Tank Battalion in the hands of Maj. Alex Swecensky. Most of the officers and many of the enlisted men came from the 2d Tank Battalion, further complicating the training and preparation of the latter for its deployment overseas. When the East Coast companies left to form with the division in November, further tank training on the East Coast came to an end. As a further complication, the 3d Marine Division later took as one of its infantry regiments the 3d Marines, leaving the 23d Marines to form with the 4th Marine Division. Accordingly, the new C Company, 3d Tank Battalion, came in the form of the redesignated 1st Separate Tank Company.[40]

The three tank battalions formed by late 1942 also took charge of the training and maintenance of the separate tank platoons of any nearby defense battalion, which sorely lacked the necessary parts and tool sets for tank maintenance. Each division also mustered an amtrac battalion of headquarters and three amtrac companies, considered part of the divisional Service Troops. The three-division amphibious force foreseen in the war planning had finally emerged from an often-chaotic sequence of events, in which the formation of tank units suffered no less than with other units. For the new tank and amtrac battalions, enormous shortfalls still existed in trained personnel, tactical and maintenance publications, parts, and services, but the desired organizational structure had been achieved. Moreover, elements of the tank and amtrac force already had entered combat, in an obscure corner of the Southwest Pacific, where U.S. forces struggled ashore in the appropriately nicknamed "Operation Shoestring." Marine Corps armored vehicles received their baptism of fire that August, at Tulagi and Guadalcanal.[41]

Chapter 4

Going to War, 1942–1943

> We watched these awful machines as they plunged across the
> spit and into the edge of the grove. It was fascinating to see
> them bustling amongst the trees, pivoting, turning, spitting
> sheets of yellow flame.
> —Richard Tregasis (1942)

Early Testing

The 1st Marine Division had sailed from North Carolina to New Zealand,
less the 7th Marines, already tapped for the Samoa defense forces. Major
Meints and the men of the 1st Tank Battalion began to unload at
Wellington from transports in July 1942 and made an administrative
camp at Petone Beach, New Zealand. Maj. Gen. A. Archer Vandegrift, the
1st Marine Division commander, anticipated a training period of several
months to bring the division into fighting trim, after which it and the 2d
Marine Division of the new I Marine Amphibious Corps would likely see
action in the various Allied offensives projected for 1943. Now, however,
a limited offensive was already in the planning stage as the division
crossed the Pacific in various convoys. The alarming spread of Japanese
detachments south and east of Rabaul threatened the vital sea lanes supporting Australia and the bases from which the Southwest Pacific
Command wished to launch its campaign to recover the Philippines.
Pacific Fleet forces would land units of the 1st Marine Division in the
Guadalcanal-Tulagi area to take the nearest Japanese advance air and sea-
plane bases and block any further advance. The islands thus seized would
later serve as jumping-off bases for the planned reduction of Japanese
positions at Rabaul and the northern coast of New Guinea.

Shipping and reinforcements in theater proved scarce for Operation
Watchtower, the official name of the amphibious landing, and the 2d
Marines with attached supporting companies were added via direct sailing from Camp Elliott in the United States. The shipping shortages and
hurried reloading at Wellington contributed to a disheartening rehearsal
landing exercise in the Fiji Islands, after which the task forces headed for
the objective area. Only companies A and B of 1st Tank Battalion and

Company C of 2d Tank Battalion (with the 2d Marines) would go with the assault troops, and the headquarters of the 1st Tank Battalion remained at Petone Beach, with its D Company. Vandegrift left most of his motor transport behind as well, but took all of the 130 LVT1 tractors of 1st Amtrac Battalion, reinforced with A Company, 2d Amtrac Battalion.

Intelligence of the area of operations remained scarce, both in terms of enemy strength and the beaches and terrain to be encountered. Vandegrift's troops thrust ashore at Guadalcanal a few miles from his airfield objective with about two-thirds of his force on 7 August. The remainder of his force had begun landing at five different points an hour earlier across the sound at Tulagi. Although companies A and B, 1st Tank Battalion, landed on the seventh, they encountered no opposition and merely accompanied the infantry as they carefully picked their way across the Tenaru River to set up a defensive perimeter around the Lunga Point airfield. The tanks generally remained scattered around the airfield for security and available for counterattacks as part of the division reserve as the operation developed.

Around Tulagi, however, terrain prevented much use of Capt. Thomas Culhane's C Company, 2d Tank Battalion. A single tank landed on hilly Tulagi Island and then threw its track. Little Tanambogo Island proved such a hornet's nest of resistance, though, that the landing failed and a second attempt had to be made on the second day of the landing. Two M3 tanks, led by 2d Lt. Robert J. Sweeney, landed from 45-foot tank lighters in advance of I Company, 3d Battalion, 2d Marines. Each tank worked along one side of the hilltop islet. Lieutenant Sweeney was killed by small-arms fire and the tank was disabled, but it continued to cover the advancing infantry. The other tank continued ahead of the infantry against a pillbox and was swarmed over by Japanese defenders. They disabled the tank's tracks with an iron bar and set it on fire with fuel-soaked rags. The marine tank crew fought hand to hand until their infantry finally closed the distance and secured the area. Two of the crew died and two others suffered severe wounds. But forty-two dead Japanese ringed the tank.[1]

Tank-infantry cooperation seemed nonexistent at this point, but the existing doctrine for tank employment as evolved in the 1930s had only called for tanks to clear the beach of enemy emplacements. Little thought had been given to the precise techniques the troops would employ. Moreover, the troops had received little training. Col. Clifton Cates, commanding the 1st Marines, said his troops "had less than three months of battalion training. . . . Not once have we had a regimental problem, much less training with planes, tanks, and other units."[2]

The LVTs worked well in their supply and transport role, even lending a bit of machine-gun fire to the fray on the Tulagi side. Truck shortages required the amtrackers to pull artillery pieces and perform much inland transport. Given the rudimentary state of their design, it was only a matter of time before the rollertrack and groove suspensions began to give out under continuous operation in salt and sand. Maintenance support for this battalion had largely been neglected in the original table of organization; it was treated more like that of a transportation unit than a tank battalion. As the vehicles became unusable, the troops of 1st Amtrac Battalion occupied defensive positions on the beach and later augmented the ground crews servicing the aircraft based at Henderson Field.[3]

The 1st Marine Division soon found itself stranded in a precarious foothold on Guadalcanal. The defeat of Allied cruisers at the Battle of Savo Island and continuing air raids caused the navy to pull back its partly unloaded transports. Most of the supplies and tanks (the fifteen undamaged vehicles of Culhane's Company C), amtracs, and other equipment, as well as over a thousand troops stranded with them, headed back to port on board the ships.

For the remainder of General Vandegrift's fight for Guadalcanal, the troops ashore fought off repeated Japanese attacks while Allied air and naval forces gradually wrested control of the area in a series of deadly naval engagements. The marines generally fared better in the defense than the offense, burdened by the need to preserve Henderson Field at all costs. The tanks guarded the airfield as mobile pillboxes, but did see some action in small numbers. At the first major engagement, the Battle of the Tenaru, on 21 August, Colonel Cates's 1st Marines routed the Ichiki Detachment, when the latter brazenly attacked the perimeter defenses from the east. At the end of the battle Vandegrift ordered a tank attack, and a platoon of M2A4 tanks from A Company charged across the river's estuary into a tree grove to annihilate the remnants with 37mm canister and machine-gun fire before nightfall. Attacking again without infantry support, two tanks were disabled, but the crews withdrew under covering fire of their platoon mates. We can thank Richard Tregasis for one of the most florid observations of tank action in the campaign:

> We watched these awful machines as they plunged across the spit and into the edge of the grove. It was fascinating to see them bustling amongst the trees, pivoting, turning, spitting sheets of yellow flame. It was like a comedy of toys, something unbelievable, to see them knocking over palm

trees which fell slowly, flushing the running figures of men from under-
neath their treads, following and firing at the fugitives. It was unbelievable to see men falling and being killed so close, to see the explosions of
Jap grenades and mortars, black fountains and showers of dirt near the
tanks, and see the flashes of explosions under their very treads.[4]

A counterattack involved tanks of B Company on 14 September, in the
aftermath of the epic fight for Edson's Ridge. The commander of 3d
Battalion, 1st Marines, continued to exchange fire with an estimated
battalion across the Ilu River plain from his positions east of Edson's
Ridge. The call went out for tanks, and after a quick reconnaissance six
M3s attacked the enemy lines, shrouded by jungle fringe. In this instance,
enemy antitank guns knocked out two tanks, another rolled over a rise
only to plunge 30 feet into the Tenaru River, a fourth also took hits from
an antitank gun, and a fifth tank had a track shot out as it approached
this last gun, forcing the crew to abandon the tank. Only one tank thus
returned to friendly lines. One officer and thirteen men died in this
action; B Company had suffered a startling reverse.[5]

Army troops began to relieve the 1st Marine Division in December,
and the worn-out and malaria-ridden troops sailed for Australia and a
long period of refit and recovery. Elements of the 2d Marine Division
remained in action with the army's XIV Corps, which continued to pressure the Japanese forces until their withdrawal in February 1943. The
Guadalcanal and Tulagi actions demonstrated that the light tanks had
clear vulnerabilities in close action against the enemy and could not
maneuver or see well in a jungle environment. They had, however, executed the landing doctrine of 1936–38, as presented in deliberations
of the MCEB: landing and taking out beach defenses, then supporting
further advances inland. Defensively, the tanks had constituted a counterattack force, as prescribed for base defense forces in the prewar exercises in the Caribbean. These did not occur frequently, however, since
the infantry held their lines well, and the few Japanese tanks used in
the Guadalcanal campaign had been readily handled by the antitank
guns of the division. The problem of tank-infantry cooperation had not
been examined before the war, and was now found totally wanting. For
all the criticism of the light tank, the tanks could not operate reason-
ably well without infantry support in the confined terrain over which
the 1st Marine Division had fought.

Neither the jungle nor the Japanese soldiers would disappear soon.
Ironically, the continuing operations in the Solomon Islands saw the

tank platoons of a few defense battalions beginning the long and arduous process of developing tank-infantry tactics and equipment. The drive through the Central Solomons fell to the army to execute, as the 2d Marine Division prepared for action in the Central Pacific. However, the Marine Corps defense battalions in the theater continued to provide antiaircraft and coastal defense functions for most island battles. Most defense battalions had an organic tank platoon, each of eight tanks, during 1942 and 1943, and in the Central Solomons these gave yeoman support to the largely army forces fighting in the thick jungle trails against Japanese detachments defending roadblocks and bunker complexes.[6]

The planned offensive in the New Georgia island group to take Munda airfield included a planned assault by infantry with the tank platoon of the 9th Defense Battalion, commanded by 1st Lt. Robert Blake. But the army forces first had to be reinforced to break through the unexpectedly difficult terrain and Japanese field fortifications on the approaches to Munda. First action for Lieutenant Blake's tankers came on 15 July, supporting the 173d Infantry near Laiana. Tanks engaged several bunkers, although the infantry found it hard to accompany them through the enemy fire. Alternating canister with high-explosive 37mm ammunition allowed the tanks to strip away the concealing vegetation and fire into the bunker embrasures. The next day the Japanese infantry responded with close assaults against the M3A1 tanks, using hand grenades, but only producing slight damage. Continuing with better infantry support, Lieutenant Blake provided five tanks, operating under the agreement that thirty men accompany each machine. The Japanese infantry defended with a flamethrower, which fortunately did not light, and grenades, knocking a hole in one tank, but the bunkers fell to the assault. The next action, on 24 July, found the tanks assisting the 172d and 103d Infantry. One tank fell out with too many hits on its gunner's periscope, and two others were hobbled by poor fuel. The strongpoint had to be bypassed, but it later took seven days to mop up with tanks and two battalions of infantry. The tired tankers could not know that their lives remained less complicated when a reinforcement by sea for the Japanese was knocked out on 22 July by airstrike, sending twenty-two Japanese army tanks to the bottom. The final assault on Munda began on the twenty-fifth, with the tank platoon spearheading a flanking attack by the 172d infantry. On the twenty-sixth another tank platoon arrived from 10th Defense Battalion (six tanks), and the tanks and portable flamethrowers cracked a bunker line (fourteen pillboxes fell to the tank-infantry teams). Three tanks were lost as the infantry found themselves hard-pressed to support the tanks under heavy fire and the tanks had to defend themselves. On the twenty-seventh, the marine tankers encountered their first antitank gun with disastrous results. One of the 9th Defense Battalion tanks supporting the 43d Division was hit by an AT gun, backed into a second machine, and then a third tank was hit. Then Japanese infantry hit the other two with close assaults, using magnetic mines and grenades. All these vehicles managed to return to friendly lines, but the 9th Defense Battalion platoon remained out of action (three other tanks remained under repair). On the twenty-eighth four tanks of the 10th Defense Battalion attacked with 3d Battalion, 103d Infantry, along the coastline, using the best tank-infantry cooperation yet seen in the campaign. They chalked up a 500-yard advance, even against antitank fire, but the terrain was flat and more open along the shoreline. On 1 August the troops reached the edge of Munda field. The Japanese fell back for a last-ditch stand on the opposing high ground. Reinforcement arrived on 3 August in the form of the 11th Defense Battalion tank platoon, and the two remaining tank platoons roamed the airfield at will, shooting up defenses. On the fifth, as a lone tank from 9th Defense Battalion rejoined the team, the airfield was declared secure.

The army did not forget their marine tank support, and when the 43d Division got into trouble on nearby Arundel Island, with Japanese reinforcements arriving, they called once again for their firemen. The 9th, 10th, and 11th Defense Battalion platoons, mustering thirteen tanks, arrived via LCM landing craft on 16 September. Their attack on the seventeenth took the Japanese troops by surprise, advancing 500 yards with infantry support. The next day, two tanks were nailed by 37mm antitank guns as they attempted a repeat performance, but their crews escaped under infantry covering fire. On 19 September, the nine tanks still running attacked in two lines followed by the infantrymen, blasting with canister and machine-gun fire to clear the way. The Japanese army chose to evacuate the next night. Vella Lavella Island came next in the chain, and the 4th Defense Battalion arrived to support the New Zealand troops given the assault mission, but the tanks saw no action.

These offensive actions garnered much operational experience for the marine tankers. They learned about operating light tanks in the jungle and coordinated tank-infantry tactics, as well as a few technical innovations that would become commonplace in the Pacific war. The troops rigged field telephones on the rear of their tanks to improve communications with the infantry, since the tank radios did not net with those carried by the infantry. Often torn off by movements or fire, the phones nevertheless gave some useful service. The tankers also tried to mount the infantry flamethrower on the tank, using the bow machine gun as a brace for the flame gun. These improvisations proved less than successful, but indicated technical improvements that had to be developed. They also signaled the never-ending interest among the tankers to tinker with their machines. On a very small scale, the Marine Corps tank arm was proving its worth.[7]

The Marine Corps tankers of the 1st and 2d Tank Battalions and the separate companies and platoons assigned to Samoan defense forces operated with the prewar equipment, tactics, and techniques. If these had proven inadequate for the tasks at hand, that experience remained no different than most other military organizations when first encountering the novelties of combat in 1942–43. Their tracked vehicle brethren of the amtrac battalions also found the predictable limitations and teething problems of their equipment and organization. The question was, what would the Marine Corps do with the armored fighting vehicle based upon the combat experiences of the Solomons and the defense of island naval bases to date?

First Improvements

After a year at war, the industrial capacity of the United States began to deliver the quantities of equipment first designed in the limited preparedness phase after the European war began in 1939. The FMF of 1943, expanding to four divisions and aircraft wings and two amphibious corps headquarters, would find itself incomparably better equipped for the Pacific counteroffensives being planned by the Joint Chiefs of Staff. The companies of the 4th Tank Battalion being prepared on East and West Coast bases in 1943 would receive the new 16.5-ton M5A1 light tank, an evolution of the M3A1, fitted with twin Cadillac V-8 gasoline engines and a hydromatic transmission, which combined to make the tank roomier and much less demanding to drive and maneuver. The M5 series took advantage of the latest welding techniques, had better sloping and shaping of its still thin armor, and had the important addition of a belly escape hatch just behind the assistant driver's position. The earlier tank battalions would receive the M5 in retrofit after the Solomons campaign concluded.[8]

Wartime also brought the American medium tank abreast of light-tank development, and the M4 Sherman series entered production in February of 1942. The Marine Corps necessarily took a serious look at

its potential tactical value. Navy landing craft of the LCM-3 type now
in production had been designed to carry this 33-ton vehicle, but the
evident difficulties of loading the tank into a landing craft using cargo
booms from a transport in a seaway seemed daunting at best. The light
tanks were handier and could be loaded from any cargo hatch. However,
the firepower available from the M4 Sherman 75mm cannon seemed
highly attractive. Remembering how the MCEB had opted for a larger,
turreted version of the Marmon-Herrington to better support inland
operations after the CTL types had participated in the beach assault,
planners now designed a corps medium-tank battalion for just such a
mission. After a beachhead had been secured by the assault troops, the
new beaching ships, the landing ship, tank (LST) and landing ship,
medium (LSM), could land the M4 medium tank directly over the
beach, and the medium-tank companies could then support and reinforce the light-tank battalions of the marine divisions. Since two amphibious corps would be created for the Pacific war, two corps medium-tank
battalions, each of four (later reduced to three) companies with fourteen
tanks each would be necessary. Note that headquarters determined all
these measures before any reports of combat operations in the Southwest Pacific could have been reviewed.

The army reluctantly agreed to provide these tanks, and in October
1942 released the first six M4A4 medium tanks to the Marine Corps.
The quartermasters requested they be sent to San Diego, and the army
offered another sixteen M4A4s in November. There was little time to
spare if the tanks were to contribute to the next series of operations
planned for the Pacific war, so the quartermasters issued the mediums
simultaneously to the cadre of the 1st Corps Medium Tank Battalion
and the FMF Training Command, Camp Elliott. Lt. Col. Bennet G. Powers
formally activated the battalion on 18 January 1943 with a headquarters and four tank companies, all commanded initially by second lieutenants. Powers and many of his personnel came from the 3d Tank
Battalion, itself organized only four months earlier, plus some new
drafts from the training center. Their limited experience would be chal-
lenged by the new machines.[9]

The initial problem was that there was not *one* new M4 medium tank
in the offing for these Marine Corps tankers, but *four* different models,
each with sharply differing engine installations. The used M4A4s received from the army had been built with a novel five-bank Chrysler gasoline engine, conceived when both tank and aircraft radial-engine production lagged behind the vehicle orders. In essence, five six-cylinder

in-line engines had been combined into a single power package, the "A57," requiring careful synchronization of carburation, clutch, and ignition components. There were five carburetors, five water pumps (later reduced to one), five sets of pulleys, and so forth, but the resulting design package allowed engine, radiator, and fan to be dismounted together in a single operation. The M4A2 came with twin General Motors two-cycle, six-cylinder diesels. They had separate throttle and clutch linkages, which frustrated maintenance, but, oddly enough, permitted operation on a single engine in the event of a failure of the other. The M4A1 had the original Wright Whirlwind nine-cylinder radial R-975 chosen for medium tanks in 1939, which proved as simple to maintain as the Continental W670 radial in the light tanks. However, growing medium-tank weight left the M4A1 badly underpowered. The later-production M4A3 tank, however, used the Ford GAA V-8 liquid-cooled engine, developed in late 1941 and standardized for tank use in 1943. After the bugs had been worked out, the GAA emerged as the best performing tank engine in terms of compactness, horsepower-to-weight, and total output.[10]

Lieutenant Colonel Collins, commanding the Tank Battalion School at Jacques' Farm, first took notice of the problems of training and operating the M4-series tanks. Before receiving a single Sherman tank, he relayed information he had garnered from the army's desert training center to headquarters in November. Collins recommended taking only the M4A3 and not accepting any of the -A4s, relegating the -A1 as second best, followed by the twin-diesel -A2 models. By mid-December Collins had become more vehement, protesting the acquisition of the twin-diesel tank, citing difficulties in synchronizing engines, weaknesses in the clutches, and an overall bad reputation from the army in the desert training center. At this point, he advocated no procurement of the M4A2, and use of the -A3, -A1, or -A4, in order of preference. He complained separately to a friend at headquarters, "From all that I can gather the M4A2 is a stinker which is probably the reason why the Army is so liberal with them. . . . You could probably find out if the dope that I have on the M4A2 is correct, and if it is, do the Marine Corps a service by stopping their procurement."[11]

Opinions on the most suitable tanks, though, would vary greatly in and out of the tanker community in the Corps throughout the war. As an unknown Plans and Policy staff officer penciled on Collins's official protest letter, "1st Med. Bn. has the M4A2 now and Maj [Lt. Col.] Powers has not made any [such] comment." The planners in Washington had already immersed themselves in the politics and technical details of this most ambitious tank program entered to date by the Marine Corps. Attending the 28 November International Tank Committee meeting at the War Department, the planners in Washington learned that production of the M4A1 and -A3 would go on a priority to the British and the army, with the British forced to take some -A4s as well. Other -A4s would be used as training vehicles in the United States. An earlier protocol had slated the twin-diesel M4A2 for the Russians, who would take no other version in their Lend-Lease allocation. The Marine Corps found that they could get the M4A2 earlier than any other model amid all this competition and recommended the procurement of 112 tanks, plus 56 replacement tanks in order to meet the initial requirement for the two corps medium-tank battalions scheduled for standing up in January and March. Lieutenant Colonel Blanchard noted to his quartermasters a few days before the 1st Corps Medium Tank Battalion activated:

> 22 M4A4 at TC-SD [Training Command, San Diego]. 168 M4A2 ordered to SD for 1st/2d TkBns (med) [one of few references to the number of medium-tank battalions planned], 40 actually arrived. 168 M4A2 allocation proposed for March. Deliver by priority rating. Do not believe M4A1 or M4A3 will be available by March or April. Since initial issue to 1st and 2d battalions will not all require replacement at same time, seems impractical to switch to new model, even if available. Model was changed from M4A4 to M4A2. British have committed to accepting ALL M4A4 tanks produced. They consider them combat-worthy.[12]

The usual struggle began anew for the medium-tank trainees at Jacques' Farm with unfamiliar vehicles, lack of tools, parts, and manuals. They alone would bear the initial burdens as the second corps medium-tank battalion was canceled, probably because planners realized the unlikely chance that both amphibious corps would be in action at the same time. Instead, the quartermasters would issue the new M4s to the division tank battalions over the next year, sufficient in number to equip one tank company of the four with the more powerful tank. In this way, all the battalions would refit and form with M5 light and M4A2 mediums by early 1944.[13]

The 1st Corps Medium Tank Battalion had only six months to prepare for deployment to the South Pacific. Alone of the seven tank battalions created for the war, the 1st seems to have been star-crossed from its birth. The commander, Ben Powers, singularly lacked the iron-willed discipline to mold the motley gangs of men culled from all over the San Diego FMF into a well-functioning organization. Issued a double-quota of M4A2 tanks because the sister 2d Corps Tank Battalion never formed, the tankers trained and operated in the Camp Pendleton training areas, then "left town," deploying to Nouméa, New Caledonia, and leaving the worst Shermans behind for the garrison quartermasters to gather and dispose. No other tank battalions then operated the M4-series vehicles, and so the custody and care of these orphaned tanks was left to property control quartermasters. As luck would have it, the M4A2s then required an urgent modification that could only be performed by depot-level maintenance, so the tanks had to be rounded up from scattered locations around Camp Pendleton tank lots and shipped to the army's Benicia Arsenal for the work. The army's complaints and reports about the condition of the vehicles proved very embarrassing for the Marine Corps. The army's Munitions Assignment Committee had allocated a total of 162 tanks, valued each at $63,397 without parts and tools, from the December production as a special measure in response to the Corps's urgent request for medium tanks.[14]

The commander of the San Diego FMF command, Maj. Gen. Clayton Vogle, bore the brunt of the responsibility and reported the matter formally to the commandant in October. Continuing investigations by Vogle's staff and Lieutenant Colonel Blanchard of the headquarters ordnance section turned up more unhappy news, such that the commandant then requested a formal judge advocate general (JAG) investigation from the secretary of the Navy. The resulting investigation, although it might make a Marine Corps veteran wince, gives us as good a picture of the trials and tribulations of forming up these large and highly technical units as we shall ever have. Certainly, the division tank battalions operated under equal pressure of time and task, and may have suffered some of the same ills that befell the 1st Corps Tank Battalion. The amphibian tractor and armored amphibian battalions also stood up very quickly and found themselves shipping off for remote island campaigns with little knowledge of their equipment or of each other.[15]

The JAG investigation turned in on 31 December 1943 by Col. Frank Whitehead reported his findings of fact and conclusions, as well as forwarding the transcripts of witnesses interviewed, including Lieutenant Colonel Powers, two company commanders, the maintenance officer, and a few enlisted men. In Whitehead's opinion:

> The damage sustained by the group of sixty-eight (68) medium tanks turned in by the First Corps Medium Tank Battalion on July 20, 1943, can be attributed to inexperienced personnel; mechanical deficiencies

inherent in a new product; lack of tools, accessories, parts and repair facilities; lack of discipline; and finally, to vandalism during the period July 20, 1943, on which date the tanks were taken over by a detail from the Base Depot, San Diego, and August 10, 1943, on which date the last tanks were shipped out of the area.

A large percentage of the personnel of the Battalion received their training in the operation and maintenance of medium tanks at the expense of the vehicles, rather than through preliminary instruction designed to prepare the personnel for their duty with the particular tank with which they were equipped.

The tanks . . . developed many defects which could not be remedied with the equipment and facilities available to the battalion.

During the first three (3) months of the training period the Battalion was not provided with equipment, facilities, tools or parts in quantities sufficient for proper maintenance and repair of the vehicles in use. Under these conditions, required parts were removed from vehicles not in use to replace broken parts on operating tanks.

The sixty-eight (68) Medium tanks, M4A2 . . . were, when turned over to a representative of the Base Depot, San Diego, in a poor state of repair and police, several of the tanks were in an inoperable condition, three could not be towed due to missing tracks, and clocks and other instruments were missing from approximately one-half the vehicles.

On several occasions during the period [after the battalion's departure] prowlers were driven from the area and on one occasion a total of seventeen (17) locks were twisted off as many tanks during one night. The discipline of the First Corps, Medium Tank Battalion, was not of the best and this lack of discipline was reflected in the condition of the tanks.

The testimony of Lieutenant Colonel Powers revealed the salient problems the new unit had to endure in its formation.

Q[uestion]. How many tanks were operated during the training period?
A[nswer]. We used 84 tanks, sir. There are 84 tanks in a medium tank battalion. We were actually responsible for 150 tanks, which included the 84 which belonged to us. Eighteen tanks were sent to Jacques' farm [the Tank School]. We had sixty-six extra tanks which were being held for the Second Corps Tank Battalion, which was supposed to have been formed in February. We did not operate the tanks which belonged to the Second Corps Tank Battalion at all. But ten or twelve men were sent up from Jacques' Farm for the express purpose of guarding the tanks and maintaining them. These men did nothing but work on the 66 tanks that were for the Second Battalion.

Q. You had the custody of them and you saw that the men took care of these tanks?

A. That is right, sir. We had two officers and 35 men to start with and from those 35 men, I think that there were only about two that had seen a medium tank before. We had to operate our own tanks which numbered about 87. I gave each company three extra ones when we began to get over strength. We sent men to schools at different places. About 75% of my organization had to be put through various schools of some sort. We sent men to Ft. Knox at every opportunity. I requested that we be allowed to send officers too. It took about four months for these people to get back. In the meantime we made out as best as we could, holding our own school, and so forth and so on. I was told to make out a three month training schedule. In making out this training schedule it was impossible to be ready for combat in three months, as it took twelve weeks to teach nomenclature of the tank and of different tools, as it stated in the manual. Somehow or other we rushed it through. In operating these tanks, we had to build our own maintenance shed, and make up most of our heavy tools. After many requests we finally got cement to put down on the floor of our shed, so that we could run the tanks under the shed for repairs. We actually didn't get any tank tools until we arrived here. In spite of the many requests which I had put in, which I had sent to various officers at Headquarters, and various other officials, which I have on file. The maintenance officer which I had and did have until about 1½ months ago [Capt. Charles A. Dunmore], was probably one of the best maintenance officers in the armed forces. I say that because he not only knows what he is supposed to do, but also knows what he is doing. He had enough initiative to go out and do things right, against heavy odds.

During the six or seven months of out training we had no tank tools at all. The spare parts for the tank didn't arrive for about two or three months. We had one hell of a time. The first tanks we had came from some Army arsenal, I don't know just where. They were, in many respects, lacking combat qualifications. All together there were about 27 modifications to be made on the tanks before we could use them, after they came off the line. These tanks were kept in operation throughout, without the proper tools and for a long time without parts. We finally got a ¼ set or it may have been a ½ set. We received compliments from many concerns on the maintenance of our tanks.

It finally got so bad toward the end of the period, that we had to strip parts from the Second Battalion tanks in order to keep our own tanks running. At that time we knew that none of these tanks were going into combat. I wrote a letter requesting authority from the Commandant to strip these extra tanks. This letter went up to the San Diego Area and was not forwarded to the Commandant, but came back approved. I have that letter now, sir. We had to take several things from those extra tanks, including some bogie wheels. We were given tires to put on our [own] bogie wheels, but we had not tools with which to do it with, so we had to use some from the extra tanks.

We made arrangements to send some of the tanks, from the Second Battalion tanks, to the Army for over-hauling if necessary, and for modification. Three or four of those needed over-hauling. Several Army officers came down to see us about them. The Army said nothing about the tanks which we had stripped, because we left before anything happened. We left 67 tanks there.

After we received the new tanks [exchanged for the older ones needing the depot modifications], we had to unload them ourselves. I then had to give each tank commander two tanks, one a combat tank and one a training tank. The tank commander was a Private First Class or a Corporal, and was in charge of two tanks, each valued at $75,000. I wouldn't let them operate the new tanks, we wanted to get them well equipped. While we equipped the new tanks for combat we used the old tanks for training purposes. Then, at the word "go," they locked up the old tank and opened up the new one. I was told by Colonel Blanchard to swap the .30 caliber gun [in the turret hatch antiaircraft mount] on the new tank for the .50 caliber on the old tank. We made the change, welding the .50 caliber guns on the new tanks, we also had to remove some fittings from the old tank, to go with the guns in the new tank. This modification was made just two or three days prior to the first organization moving out. At the same time we were turning over the old tanks to the Base Depot. After that I do not know what happened to them. We moved to [Camp] Elliott for some little time before moving out aboard ship. I do not know what was done about the tanks after that.

Q. What was the condition of the 100 tanks turned back to the Army [under the modification program]?

A. These tanks were not run at all, except from the flat car to the parking area, and they were turned over [i.e., engines started for upkeep] every week.

Q. Was it from those tanks that you got your spare parts?

A. Yes sir. Colonel Blanchard was out a few times, and he said it was the only thing to do, that cannibalism was sometimes necessary.

Q. It isn't clear to me, Colonel, how you came into possession of the 168 tanks?

A. There was no one else who knew anything about them. We took the responsibility for the unloading of them, it was the only thing to do, I had responsibility for lots of things that I wasn't ordered to do. It was forced on me. As a matter of fact, we never received any Marine Corps orders to send tanks to the Army for modification or anything, sir. We received only a few memos, some Army memorandums on the subject.

Q. Was it necessary to strip any of these old tanks in order to provide spare parts and tools for the new tanks?

A. I think that in some cases they found shortages in the new tanks, one or two tools or some minor things. In order to equip the new tanks it is quite possible that they might have taken enough of the old tanks to make sure that the new tanks were ready for combat. Since everyone realized that the old tanks were not going into combat, in fact we had heard that they were not even going to be used for training purposes any more. It was quite possible. Some of the equipment was on back order, and that just about means that we wouldn't get them.

One has to sympathize with Lieutenant Colonel Powers, even given the often self-contradictory nature of his testimony, for the personally overwhelming forces he seemed to be facing. His maintenance officer, Captain Dunmore, had to respond to the investigation by deposition. In his deposition Dunmore claimed that the battalion had operated only the assigned tanks and that even less advantage had been taken with the older machines than Lieutenant Colonel Powers had already admitted. Several points raised by Dunmore add eloquently to our understanding of the frequently chaotic method in which the tank battalions formed:

> The great difficulty that we have had to overcome in all tank units is the undue amount of work required in training green men assigned to us with very little mechanical aptitude, background or experience. Because of the fact that these men had not received adequate instruction, we were forced to use our equipment in educating them. It is easy to see such a procedure is unduly hard on mechanized equipment of any type.
>
> It was very difficult to establish responsibility for the proper maintenance of the equipment of this battalion in the days of its early training; there were only three (3) officers and very few men who knew the first principles. Constant shifting of the personnel of tank crews made necessary by original shortage of men and later organization of all crews, and lack of trained maintenance personnel and trained officers.

Regarding the officers we received at the time the battalion was activated, I might say that mostly they were green second lieutenants. These officers had had no experience in handling men. They had no tank experience other than that received at the tank school which was both incorrect (wrong equipment) and insufficient. We were forced to use these men as company commanders. We had no trained or experienced executive or operations and training officers and we were forced to carry out our training programs under these conditions for about eight or ten weeks. As a result of the incorrect and insufficient training at the tank school, the men were not impressed with the importance of clutch synchronization peculiar to the M4A2 tank. We saw tank after tank deadlined with burned out clutches. The men made available to us who were graduates of the Army tank maintenance courses were well trained maintenance men. However, you must remember that they joined us late in our training program beginning in June, I think. We needed them at the beginning much more than we needed them at the end. All of our troubles with the maintaining of our tanks occurred not at the end of our training program but in the first two or three months.

Dunmore's diatribe against the prevailing conditions continued with background on the previous experiences he had as maintenance officer of the 2d and 3d Tank Battalions:

[In the 2d Tank Battalion] we not only were trying to form maintenance sections for the tank companies in this battalion but also were called upon to supply maintenance men for tank platoons assigned to defense battalions. We were sometimes allowed as little as ten days in which to train mechanics for assignment to such platoons although at the same time men were being sent to Fort Knox for two to three months to acquire such training. In order that you may understand the type of equipment with which tank units have been equipped, I would like to tell you that the 2d [Separate] Tank Company under command of Capt. Lewis actually towed some of their tanks to the dock to embark for duty in the theater of operations. These tanks were obsolete, worn out and entirely unfit even for training purposes, never mind combat.

In the 3d Tank Battalion, we again saw during the training period no parts, no tools and green men. This organization had to build its own camp on training time, had no shop facilities and absolutely operated on open conditions from practically its activation. . . . The tools and parts arrived when the battalion was boxing and crating for embarkation overseas. . . .

In the First Corps (Medium) Tank Battalion, our tank maintenance tools were received by us 10 days after arrival in the South Pacific. . . . The selection of tools was very impractical and they evidently had been supplied to the Marine Corps by the Army and . . . based upon Army Echelon repair policies. We cannot take the Army's recommendation for the solution to our maintenance problems inasmuch as we do not operate as does the Army with a deep supply zone in rear of the combat zone.

Other records, not considered by the investigation, had come to the attention of headquarters officers reviewing the case and cast further doubt on the way the battalion had functioned. For instance, the battalion quartermaster's inventory of 21 July 1943 showed that the battalion had no accurate records of receipts and expenditures of material. A report by a civilian employed by Army Ordnance proved particularly damning of the battalion's leadership and discipline:

During some of my recent travels on the west coast, I was privileged to spend some of my time in a camp with a newly organized Medium Tank Battalion. Both officers and men were a friendly crowd and made my stay very pleasant. As the battalion was preparing to break camp and leave for active service in a foreign theater, the men were winding up their affairs and having their last fling at social life before leaving.

Living and working with the men over a period of 7 to 10 days impressed me with their lack of experience and training in mechanical work and the use of mechanized equipment. The officers were mostly young and fresh out of college, very eager to get into the fighting but in my opinion very much unprepared for it, being more interested in social activities and the sowing of a few wild oats. One of the most dangerous explosives known can be made from liquor and mechanized equipment and this situation should be avoided as much as possible. I was annoyed by the looseness of control and lack of authority exercised over the soldiers [marines] by the officers who were very seldom with the troops at all. A large number of the officers and men were on leave which may have made the situation appear worse than it really was. These troops were about to go into battle with highly mechanized equipment but knew very little about its maintenance, and although now equipped with brand new tanks, would soon be faced with preventative maintenance problems which would require experienced direction.

As camp was broken up and the vehicles and troops began moving out, I wondered just how they would fare when they arrived at their destination, and wished that they had with them at least a few tough commissioned officers with mechanized equipment experience and some old line type hardboiled sergeants, that knew how to crack the whip when necessary. These were the finest American men and Military equipment in the world BUT —[16]

There is also a 4 November report to the commandant by Lieutenant Colonel Blanchard, with background plus observations from his own trips to the West Coast and on the investigation. According to Blanchard's report, the battalion was authorized twenty-eight officers, four warrant officers, and 648 enlisted men, with a tank inventory of fifty-six M4A2 tanks, plus twenty-seven as replacements. The personnel strength was 55 percent on 30 January, 85 percent on 17 February, 91 percent on 3 March, and 114 percent on 14 March, and remained overstrength until its departure in July. Personnel transferred from the tank school into the battalion included fifteen lieutenants and 450 enlisted men. Eleven officers were graduates of the tank maintenance course at Fort Knox, but one recalls Captain Dunmore's comment that they had learned the wrong model tank there. Lieutenant Colonel Powers had finished the advanced tactical course at Fort Knox as well as the infantry course at Fort Benning. Blanchard noted the swap-out of the 168 tanks to catch up with all recent modifications, with 100 new tanks delivered by 22 June. The battalion had received eighty-four of these new tanks directly (sixteen for the training command). From Blanchard's view, blame would fall in equal shares among the battalion commander, base support, and headquarters for various defects in provisioning, training, and operations.[17]

With those intimate views of the trials and perils of standing up a tank battalion from scratch, we can better understand the difficulty of introducing new weapons in military organizations and then to a campaign. Other problems remained to be solved, for headquarters only learned of the availability of fording material for the new M4 and M5 tanks in April 1943. The normal wading ability of a light or medium tank ranged from only 36 to 40 inches, and that applied to smooth inland water, not rolling Pacific Ocean surf. With special waterproofing materials and tubing for the engine intake and exhaust, the chances of the tanks coming ashore from their landing craft measurably improved. But how soon could these kits be procured and how would they be sent to battalions already en route to the South Pacific?[18]

Headquarters also solved a surprise problem with radios in 1943. Since the first light tanks entered service in the late 1930s the Marine

Corps had equipped them with aircraft radios, the ubiquitous model GF/RU. When the 1st Marine Division left Guadalcanal, however, they requested the model NO as a new radio. This was the first indication to the staff that the radios in the tanks were not completely satisfactory. They did not buy the model NO as it did not meet Marine Corps standards and was not under procurement by the navy either. The solution came in the new Army Signal Corps's radios, models SCR-508A and 528A (equal except the SCR-508A had two receivers to permit listening on separate nets). All tanks received these radios by mid-year. These sets still did not network with the radios of the infantry, however, and cumbersome liaison arrangements had to be arranged to permit simple passing of messages between units.[19]

As the tank forces of the Marine Corps began to evolve in doctrine, equipment, and organization, a parallel effort was taken for the amphibian tractor, in somewhat belated fashion. Here, of course, the Marine Corps continued on its own, with no massive army procurement and industrial management for worldwide and international distribution. The need for improvements on the immature LVT1 "Alligator" led to a redesign effort both by FMC Company, in charge of production on East and West Coast plants, as well as the Borg-Warner Company, which was invited by the navy to compete in the new effort. The track and suspension system invited early reappraisals, of course. The use of roller-track running over a rail gave way to a more conventional suspension system of small road wheels mounted on torsilastic (rubber mountings providing torsion) arms. The light-tank radial engine, transmission, and final drive replaced the Hercules engine of the Alligator vehicle. FMC's improved version won the contract for the successor vehicle, designated LVT2 and called the "Water Buffalo." However, Borg-Warner's successful integration of the 37mm M3A1 light-tank turret was adopted for the amphibious tank version, dubbed an armored amphibian. The resulting LVT(A)1 had only quarter-inch hull armor and half-inch cab protection, so it barely lived up to its billing. The LVT2 design also provided for bolt-on armor protection for the cab. There was also limited production (450 vehicles) of an armored cargo carrier for the army, called LVT(A)2. This vehicle had the armor and driver periscopes of the gun version but alone of the "(A)" versions retained its cargo compartment and carried no turret. Production of the LVT1 Alligator continued into 1943 for a total of 1,225 vehicles. The LVT2 production began then, producing another 2,963 units of this improved but essentially first-generation vehicle.[20]

FMC and Borg-Warner tested their armored amphibian prototypes in May and June 1942. The Marine Corps planned on production beginning in January 1943, with 300 units to be delivered by June. Headquarters ordered the preparation of extensive training facilities in the Camp Pendleton property, purchased in 1942 to permit large-scale amphibious training and tactical training. With the first two battalions scheduled to stand up there, extensive planning estimated the shop, storage, housing, launching ramps, and classroom facilities that would eventually become Camp Del Mar. In the end, production lagged and only in August 1943 did Maj. Louis Metzger formally activate the 1st Armored Amphibian Battalion. Metzger, one of Denig's platoon leaders in B Company, 2d Tank Battalion, on Samoa, had returned to the United States to attend Fort Knox and join the Tank School staff at Jacques' Farm. The assault mission of the armored amphibian units clearly indicated that tank officers would be most suited. The final production of 509 armored amphibians outfitted the three Marine Corps armored amphibian battalions as well as several more placed in service by the army.[21]

The true second-generation amtrac came from the Marine Corps request for a cargo ramp, similar to the contemporary landing craft, which would enable cargo and troops to load and exit rapidly. Both Borg-Warner and FMC produced new designs, with FMC placing the engine in the front of the LVT4 vehicle and fitting a stern ramp. Borg-Warner opted for a more radical design, fitting the twin Cadillac engines of the M5 light tank into the sides of its LVT3 and integrating the rest of the drive train, including the automatic transmission, to gain a much larger cargo area than with the front- or rear-engine designs. Both of the improved vehicles could carry artillery pieces or a jeep in the expanded cargo bays, adding much to their utility. Production of the LVT4 went forward without a hitch in December 1943, generating 8,348 units. Borg-Warner encountered production difficulties with the LVT3, dubbed the "Bushmaster," which delayed their start until 1944, but eventually turned out 2,962 of these advanced vehicles.[22]

FMC then produced the equivalent armored amphibian of the second generation by mounting the army's M8 self-propelled 75mm howitzer turret on an LVT(A)1 hull. The resulting LVT(A)4 went into production in early 1944 until 1,890 vehicles had been built; another 269 LVT(A)5 vehicles were added in 1945, fitted with gyrostabilizers and power traverse not initially available on the M8 turret design.[23]

As much as the vehicles matured, however, the amphibian tractor remained a supply vehicle and landing craft, and only the armored amphibian was considered to be a combat vehicle. Fitted with its tank turret and light-tank armament, the LVT(A)1 was expected to clear the beach in the standard light-tank role established in prewar thinking, until the tank units could be unloaded from landing craft and reinforce the attack. From the time that the improved LVT2s and the first armored amphibians rolled off the assembly lines, the doctrine for their employment continued unchanged since Guadalcanal, with what was hoped were better machines and more skilled troops becoming available. The changed circumstances of the Pacific war had yet to dawn on the rapidly expanding FMF.

That suited the Marine Corps units still working up the Solomons chain in support of Gen. Douglas MacArthur's war in the Southwest Pacific. The landings by the 3d Marine Division on Bougainville ended Pacific Ocean Area (Adm. Chester Nimitz's command) participation in the isolation of the Japanese strategic position of Rabaul. The landing resembled Guadalcanal at the outset, for the planners deliberately chose to land at a relatively undefended part of the island. However, instead of wresting an airfield from the enemy in a prolonged struggle, the landing force would simply fan out and secure a perimeter permitting airfields to be built by the navy construction battalions. The 1 November landing at Cape Torokina saw the 9th Marines landing unopposed over the northern tier of beaches, but the 3d Marines and an attached raider battalion uncovered some dug-in infantry and an artillery piece on the cape itself, which almost broke up the landing on the extreme right of the division zone. Quick work by infantry trained in the bunker-busting tactics developed after the New Georgia experiences eliminated enemy resistance by the next day. Curiously, this action tested the M3 GMC tank destroyers of the infantry regiments in close support of infantry, rather than the M3A1 tanks of the 3d Tank Battalion, which landed later only in part and took no part in clearing the beach.

This last operation of an all–light tank battalion featured only limited action because of the jungle vegetation and severe mud encountered during the campaign. The tanks operated on the narrow coastal strip and, with increasing difficulty, inland on a few trails. B Company of the 1st Corps Medium Tank Battalion was assigned to the operation as reinforcement, but remained behind on Guadalcanal because of lack of shipping. The M3A1 tanks (mostly from B Company, with a platoon each from A and C companies) first fought in support of infantry attacks against a mixed Japanese battalion that conducted a counterlanding just northwest of the division perimeter on 7 November. Just as in New Georgia, the 37mm gun and machine-gun armament blew away the vegetation covering the Japanese positions and then destroyed enemy emplacements with direct fire. But only tank sections or platoons could be brought into action and the tank companies simply provided direct support to the infantry regiments the few times required as the perimeter was expanded. The heaviest fighting had to be born by the infantry, with tanks occasionally used in a secondary role, mainly in reinforcing the perimeter lines.[24]

Amtracs performed essential work through harsh surf conditions and in the difficult terrain across crowded beaches. Their routine tasks included towing and positioning artillery, bringing in supplies, and (later) running them out to forward positions on the growing perimeter. Despite intolerable maintenance conditions, the LVT1s proved their worth as they crossed swamps and traversed muddy trails, often the sole transportation available for the frontline troops.

After the last Marine Corps forces withdrew from Bougainville in June of 1944, the curtain closed on the Solomons campaign, leaving only the 1st Marine Division attached to General MacArthur's forces and slated for the invasion of western New Britain. In Melbourne the tankers of A Company turned in their well-worn M2A4 light tanks and received Army M4A1 mediums in preparation for the new operation. The other two tank companies drew new Army M5A1 light tanks at the same time. Divided into three combat teams, the division trained in the broken countryside around Melbourne during the summer and then moved to eastern New Guinea staging camps in September 1943. Amphibious training ensued, until on 26 December the division landed from the motley collection of landing ships, landing craft, and destroyer transports that constituted MacArthur's "navy." The operation essentially became an unopposed shore-to-shore landing instead of an amphibious operation, which would become typical for the army forces employed in MacArthur's Southwest Pacific Command. The 1st Tank Battalion, less Company B, supported the 5th and 7th Marine regiments as they expanded the beachhead surrounding the Cape Gloucester airfields, which required overcoming enemy resistance, torrential rains, and difficult terrain. No enemy opposed the landings, but resistance grew as the landing forces expanded their perimeters and moved over trails to take the targeted airfields. As usual, the light tanks proved difficult to use in heavy vegetation and their weapons did not penetrate the log and sand bunkers discovered by the advancing troops. The Sherman tanks of A Company found themselves called upon repeatedly to spearhead the infantry movements. Tanks were used mostly in sections of two and three, supported in each case by a platoon of infantry. The medium tanks proved their worth both in breaking through the jungle undergrowth and in destroying the bunkers with their 75mm cannon. Frequently the engineers had to carve a corduroy road through the jungle to enable the Shermans to close the enemy, as at the Battle for Suicide Creek. The Japanese had few antitank guns, never larger than 37mm, and employed no armor of their own. Tanks continued in action in small units throughout the campaign. An interesting innovation saw tanks placed in landing craft as makeshift gunboats covering the initial landing. The navy also employed patrols of these craft against the otherwise better-armed landing craft of the Japanese army still plying the waters around New Britain.[25]

Company B of the 1st Tank Battalion had been left behind in the New Guinea staging base because of the limited terrain available for employment in the 1st Marine Division operation. It landed later at Arawe, across New Britain from the Marine Corps zone, with army troops on 12 January 1944. In support of the 158th Infantry Regiment, the company split into platoons, leading infantry companies into a typical thousand-yard attack on 16 January. Using the close-support techniques practiced by the 1st Marine Division, a rifle squad protected each tank in the advance. Although the advance succeeded, it proved once again that the light tank could not handle the main attack mission very well. They had difficulty pushing through undergrowth and felling trees. The 37mm gun lacked explosive power and tankers fired machine guns and canister to overwhelm the defenses with volume of fire. Two tanks broke down in inaccessible spots and had to be destroyed to prevent enemy use. During the single day's attack, the company fired 283 rounds of 37mm canister, 68 of high explosive, and 36 more of armor-piercing ammunition. The tanks also used up approximately 38,000 rounds of .30-caliber machine-gun ammunition. Here at Arawe, tankers again experimented with the infantry flamethrower mounted next to the assistant driver's position, using it on the seventeenth in mop-up operations. The tanks had again proved essential for offensive operations in close terrain, but the light tank simply failed to measure up to the real needs of the troops. During the withdrawal of the 1st Marine Division from New Britain in April–May, the army made one last use of the Marine Corps tank support, landing A Company at Tanahmerah Bay near

Hollandia on 22 April. They could advance no farther because of adjacent mountains and swamps, and were returned to the division once shipping became free.[26]

Into the Cauldron

These later landings in the Solomons and New Britain by the 1st and 3d Marine Divisions demonstrated the value of the new style of close-support tank-infantry teams as well as the continuing exploitation of the LVT as a logistics carrier over the beaches and in marginal terrain inland. They remained, however, almost unopposed landings, which only later demonstrated the marginal value of the standard light tank as an infantry-support combat vehicle. For Marine Corps tank and LVT units, as for the rest of the FMF, the real changes in doctrine and equipment would come out of the close encounter with disaster that the 2d Marine Division would find at Tarawa. The fighting for that coral atoll set the standard required for the rest of the Pacific war and the many challenges that remained. With their participation in Operation Galvanic, the seizure of bases in the Gilbert Islands, the Central Pacific drive began for the FMF forces.

Marines held little doubt that a real fight awaited them on Betio, the major island of the Tarawa atoll. Japanese defenses stood out in the aerial photographs and few of the commanders believed that the air and naval bombardments would eliminate enough of them to permit an easy landing. In fact, the threat of the major-caliber guns to the transports contributed to the decision to assault the island across beaches inside the lagoon, from transports anchored outside the atoll, thus requiring the landing craft and LVTs to cover a record 10 miles from ship to shore. Unlike in previous landings, the landing force had to cross 600–800 yards of reefs before coming ashore against a sea wall and the surviving enemy and his weapons.[27]

The 2d Amtrac Battalion still operated seventy-five LVT1 Alligators, as usual in need of overhaul after their use during the division's actions on Guadalcanal. A further fifty LVT2 Water Buffaloes reinforced Maj. Henry C. Drewes's battalion, but these could only arrive at the island at the last minute, transported by LSTs from California. Drewes already had his men hard at work installing bolt-on armor and an additional machine-gun mount on the cabs of the LVT1s, but fewer improvements could be made to the late-arriving Water Buffaloes. The long waterborne approach and the assault landing through surf and over reefs would prove the mettle of the LVTs. The division staff dedicated eighty-four of these vehicles to landing the first waves of assault infantry, fearing that the reefs would hold up the landing craft. A logistics vehicle would thus become a combat infantry carrier, with eighteen to twenty troops in each, a role until now denied by all planners and tacticians since the MCEB had first laid eyes on the LVT.[28]

With the armored amphibians just arriving on the West Coast for the new battalions, none would be ready for the 20 November 1943 assault on Betio. But a company of the 1st Corps Medium Tank Battalion reinforced the division. The newest class of the specialized amphibious ships entering navy service provided the key to using the M4 medium tank in the amphibious assault. The landing ship, dock (LSD), served as a mobile dry dock, carrying LCM-3 landing craft and their preloaded cargos of tanks, artillery, or other equipment, ready to disgorge over its stern gate once the well deck flooded using the ships' internal ballast tanks. The first of these ships, USS *Ashland,* arrived in the South Pacific in time to load the fourteen M4A2 mediums of 1st Lt. Edward L. Bale's C Company for the assault. Bale would take the M4 tank into combat for the first time with the marines. These would be the only tanks immediately available to the landing force, as the M3A1s of the 2d Tank Battalion remained stowed in the holds of the various transports now heading toward the objective area.

The epic struggle of the 2d Marine Division to take Betio from its determined Japanese naval infantry garrison provided costly lessons that would greatly improve the rest of the Pacific war for the Marine Corps and navy.

The Japanese defenders saw the strange landing craft rise over the reef barrier and advance toward the lagoon-side beaches. They held their fire until the LVTs came within 150 yards of the beach, then opened up with 37mm and 75mm guns as well as the rest of their infantry weapons. The LVTs responded with their machine guns and continued to the beaches, a few even passing over the seawall. Although the LVTs delivered most of their infantrymen to the beaches, they suffered considerable damage and not a few total losses. Many of the tractors not destroyed by direct hits (eight of the initial effort) sank on return runs from flooding through numerous bullet and shrapnel holes in their hulls. Maj. Henry G. Lawrence Jr., the executive officer of the amtrac battalion, approached the beach,

> personally leading the center group of amphibian tractors in the initial landing, [he] directed his own tractor over barbed wire and other beach obstacles in the face of intense antiboat and machine gunfire, thereby

enabling subsequent waves to land successfully and, when his driver was killed, unhesitatingly took the drivers seat and made four trips to the beach with urgently needed supplies and men. With his tractor finally disabled and his Battalion Commander reported killed, he promptly reboarded a landing boat and reorganized the remaining vehicles for continued action. Throughout the following three days, he worked tirelessly to direct the landing and delivering of supplies to the front line troops although three of his drivers were killed and he, himself, was twice hit by shrapnel while attempting to get ashore in tractors.[29]

Japanese cannon, mortars, and small-arms fire shattered the infantry units that waded ashore from their landing craft stuck on the edges of the reefs at a freak low tide. These craft had followed the initial waves of amtracs, and the sheer volume of fire on the isolated infantry on the beaches prevented their tactical movement into the island's interior. Losses to the amtracs and their crews mounted. Major Drewes and many other amtrackers died in their mined and shot-up vehicles, and the battalion suffered 323 casualties among its 500 men. After three days of action, only nineteen LVT1 and sixteen LVT2 vehicles remained in action. As the senior surviving officer, Major Lawrence said later, "Ah really don't know what to tell y'all except that we went from shit troops to shock troops in a helluva hurry!"[30]

The Sherman tanks did not come ashore as scheduled in the fifth wave of the landing, as the control craft circled beyond the reef, under enemy fire, before giving orders to the LCMs to discharge their tanks directly onto the reef. Lieutenant Bale led his headquarters tanks and a four-tank platoon on the right side of the beach, while the other eight tanks aimed for the shipping channel and the left-side beach. Liaison scouts from the company attempted to guide Bale's tanks through the water to land, but one of the eight other vehicles plunged into a hole, taking the crew with it. As Bale's six tanks approached the beach, he saw that it was crowded with troops, including many dead and wounded lying directly in his path. Instead of driving over them, he turned back into the water and waded farther around to the right. Japanese fire killed the trailing platoon leader, and the four leaderless tanks fell into shell holes. By moving to the right Bale inadvertently joining the orphaned pocket of infantry gathered together by Maj. Michael Ryan on the point known as the Parrot's Beak. Bale's tank, *Cecilia,* dueled with a Japanese Type 95 light tank. Bale lost his main gun to a chance hit before destroying the Type 95, the first enemy tank to fall to Marine Corps tank fire.

His other surviving Sherman, named *China Gal,* would remain in action for the entire battle, next to the machine gun–armed *Cecilia.*

The seven M4s reaching the left side of the beach went into action unsupported and blind, drawing much of the fire of those Japanese weapons able to bear upon the lagoon side of the island. The 2d Marine Division had yet to develop close support by infantry as a tactic, and Bale's tankers had never worked with the division at all. The radios, of course, only served to communicate among the tanks and could not net with the infantry sets. The Shermans moved over the seawall and began to take out the bunkers they could identify. Two fell into shell holes, two were knocked out by Japanese guns, and yet another was destroyed by a navy dive-bomber responding to the threat of several Japanese tanks still moving on the island. A Japanese infantry attack with mines knocked out yet another, and the surviving tank limped back to the beach on fire, wading into the sea to douse the flames. The troop commander ashore, Col. David M. Shoup, radioed the discouraging message, "tanks no good," and called for his regiment's M3 GMC tank destroyers to land, but neither of these lasted long enough to make a dent in the enemy positions.

Hunkering down for the night defense, the infantry commanders made good on some of their bad experiences, and the second day's action saw close infantry support for *Colorado* on the center beach, and for *China Gal* on the western end of the island. Both Bale and 2d Lt. Louis Largey of *Colorado* spent much time overnight with their respective infantry formations to coordinate the effort. Both tanks supported the drive of their respective infantry to clear the western end and surge across the airfield, dividing the island in two. The infantry accompanied the tanks, firing on and around them as they advanced to kill each pillbox encountered, sometimes mounting an infantryman behind the turret to shout directions down to the hardworking crews. Miraculously, the two tanks stayed in action for the rest of the battle, returning frequently to the beach to reload ammunition. No tank ammunition came ashore, but howitzer ammunition fit the gun and more ammunition was scrounged from disabled Shermans on the third day.

The 2d Tank Battalion fared little better in the assault. Their commander, Lt. Col. Alexander Swecensky, fell severely wounded and his operations officer died when a shell hit his LVT offshore. A platoon of C Company attempting to follow the Shermans of Lieutenant Largey into the shipping channel had four of its landing craft sunk from under them. The light tanks of B Company did not come ashore until late on the second day of the battle, and most of C Company landed on the third day. Most of the light tanks lay at the bottom of holds stuffed with various supplies still undeliverable to the hostile shore. Each platoon rode a different transport, and loading the tanks by cargo boom into the bobbing LCMs imposed the usual problems.

As the remaining battalions of the 2d Marine Division began to turn the tide of battle on Betio, the light tanks attempted to support the advance, with C Company, 2d Tank Battalion, operating at times with the two intact M4A2s. Once again, the 37mm cannon revealed its short-comings even when the tankers bravely drove up to the very embrasures of the Japanese emplacements to fire. One light tank served as a radio vehicle for the battalion commander at the division command post, try-ing to maintain tank-infantry liaison. But close cooperation between tanks and infantry still depended on visual signals and mounting an infantryman high and exposed on the vehicle. At least with the M3A1 tanks ashore, they could be used to support the two mediums, "clean-ing" them with canister and machine-gun fire of the Japanese infantry-men who continually tried to stop them with close assaults. The tanks moved like a bunch of baby chicks surrounding the mother hen. After the marines destroyed a counterattack on the third night, resistance slackened perceptibly and the island officially became "secured" on 23 November. Only eight of the 2,571 Japanese naval infantry survived this fierce battle, a difficult harbinger of things to come.[31]

Lessons from Tarawa and the Gilbert Islands campaign filled the reports of navy and Marine Corps commanders at all levels. For the armored vehicle units, these remained relatively clear and succinct. The amtrac now became an assault vehicle, absolutely necessary for attack-ing further atolls in the future. The light tank had to go and the medium tank became absolutely necessary, with the additional requirement for deepwater fording equipment still not in the hands of the units. Cooperation with the infantry remained a sore point and both the tank-infantry telephone and better tactical training became mandatory. All the commanders demanded flame weapons of all kinds, including ones mounted on the tank and LVT. The vehicles themselves needed in-creased firepower and armor. More tanks in the assault required more dedicated landing craft and LSD-type ships. The officers surveying the shattered defenses of Tarawa cringed at the discovery of hundreds of mines not yet laid on the lagoon approaches, which had received the last priority for the garrison's work effort. Unbelievable as it seemed, things could have been worse. The Japanese surely would make improvements to their defense schemes based upon their own lessons drawn from the battle. The amphibious art simply had to improve or the war would seemingly last forever.

Improved weapons and material and new units already being prepared would answer many of the problems uncovered at Tarawa. But we can see now that the prewar concept of the amphibious landing, and its requirements for armored fighting vehicles, had reached the limits of usefulness. Merely landing light tanks from landing craft after the infantry waves in order to knock out some machine-gun nests and then assist in the general advance inland scarcely reflected the problems now known to exist. Enemy beach defenses included thick log or concrete pillboxes and high-velocity cannon as well as numerous heavy and light machine guns, fronted by mines and obstacles, all inconceivable to the early planners of the 1920s and 1930s. The tough construction, effective siting, and camouflage of the defenses made them all but impervious to air and naval bombardment. Defeating such an enemy array required larger, more powerful machines, linked by effective communications and tactics to the infantry, engineers, and fire support all now required to work as a team to overcome the defenses. Further inland, any advance would bring the landing force in contact with additional belts of fortifications, artillery concentrations, and counterattack by enemy tanks and infantry.

The revamped armored fighting vehicle units of the Marine Corps, as with the rest of the landing forces, would fight the rest of the Pacific war with much improved prospects for success. Incorporating the lessons of Tarawa and the Southwest Pacific campaign would bring huge dividends to the troops of the III and V Amphibious Corps, already preparing for the epic battles of 1944.

Chapter 5

Armored Victory, 1943–1945

> If any one supporting arm can be singled out as having con-
> tributed more than any others during the progress of the cam-
> paign, the tank would certainly be selected.
> —Maj. Gen. Lemuel C. Shepherd Jr. (1945)

Applying the Lessons
The rest of the Central Pacific drive would see the new tank and amtrac
battalions in action. The decision to field the M4 Sherman tank as a new
standard issue interrupted the wholesale procurement of M5A1 light
tanks, and only the 4th Tank Battalion received an initial issue of the
latter. Proper deepwater fording kits and waterproofing materials ensured the safe and rapid landing of all new tanks, now able to ford seven
feet of water. In tandem with the Sherman tank issue, the commandant
approved a new battalion organization for April 1944 with fewer men
and all medium tanks. The medium-tank company would have only fifteen tanks, using three platoons of four each, and the battalion would
field only three medium-tank companies, with a battalion commander's
tank bringing the total to forty-six. The old scout company finally
reverted permanently to the division headquarters, dismounted except
for jeeps. This decision reflected the commandant's desire to reduce the
personnel strength of the division, which had swelled by 2,700 men
since 1941, but with some doubts "whether a commensurate increase
in overall effectiveness has been obtained." He also sought further
reductions in the numbers of tank companies and the antitank units of
the division, but these possibilities proved illusory. At the same time
the number of men necessary for corps reinforcing troops had soared,
especially with the administrative transfer of all amtrac and the new
armored amphibian battalions to the amphibious corps headquarters,
along with new battalions of artillery and engineers now thought necessary for the continuing campaigns.[1]

The 4th Tank and 4th Amphibian Tractor Battalions formed with
companies attached to the infantry regiments of the division on East

and West Coast bases, as had been the case with the 3d Marine Division the previous year. The regiments remained apart for at least six months before the division finally united at Camp Pendleton in September 1943. The 12 May activation of the 4th Tank Battalion belied the fact that its companies remained scattered to the winds. Even the D (Scout) Company formed as separate platoons under the regimental tank companies. With the gathering of all the tank units by July under command of Maj. Richard K. Schmidt at Camp Pendleton, training improved. The nearby Tank Battalion School at Jacques' Farm provided trained replacements and instructors. Training by the division in the new assault tactics included much emphasis on reducing field fortifications and tank-infantry cooperation. Live-fire exercises included the movement of light tanks directly through an artillery air-burst barrage, a demonstration effort unfortunately never achieved in combat. Although it opened many officers' eyes to the tactical possibilities, effecting such coordination in combat conditions proved too difficult. Finally, the issue of new M4A2 mediums to C Company, 4th Tank Battalion, improved the firepower of the unit considerably. For the moment, though, the battalion would operate both light and medium tanks until further deliveries came to the Corps.[2]

The preparation of the 4th Amtrac Battalion progressed less smoothly, because the experiences at Tarawa demonstrated that more amtracs would be required for future amphibious assaults. Accordingly, Maj. Victor Croizat had to split his 4th Amtrac Battalion to form and take command of its "clone," the 10th, on 5 December 1943, which further had to spin off A Company, 11th Amphibian Tractor Battalion. Considering the newness of the 4th Division, its separated origins, and the embarkation for the Marshalls campaign in January 1944, one can see readily that the LVT officers and men scarcely had time to form ranks and issue supplies, let alone train for their dangerous mission.[3]

As the division loaded ships in early January to participate in Operation Flintlock in the Marshall Islands, hopes of avoiding another Tarawa hinged partly on the employment of the 1st Armored Amphibian Battalion and its 75 LVT(A)1 tractors. Maj. Louis Metzger, a 1939 Stanford graduate and yet another veteran of Capt. Bob Denig's B Company, 2d Tank Battalion, commanded and trained this new unit in its baptism of fire and for a total of 25 months in the war. These vehicles composed the first landing wave under revised doctrine, leading the assault and firing the 37mm and .30-caliber weapons, while swimming into the beaches to suppress the enemy, after the air and naval bom-

bardment had to be lifted. As the succeeding waves of troop-carrying
LVT2s passed through the wave of armored amphibians to unload on
the beach, the LVT(A)1 units would render fire support for the troops
until the tanks could land and take up that mission.

So far so good. The 4th Marine Division plan for the assault on the
linked islands of Roi-Namur, in the Kwajalein atoll, demanded much
from its rather inexperienced troops, however. On D-day, part of the
division's amtracs and armored amphibians would assault no fewer
than six nearby islets to place artillery and secure the approaches to
Roi-Namur. Then, on D+1, the entire array of amtracs and landing craft
would land the 23d and 24th Marines on Roi and Namur, respectively.
Strangely, the 4th Division plan assigned the complicated effort of day
one with its required recovery and maintenance period before attacking Namur on day two to the greener 10th Amtrac Battalion, formed a
mere month before the departure from the United States. The inevitable
problems and confusion of landing various contingents on the outer
islets, then returning to the mother-ship LSTs, which were also manned
by green crews and officers, frequently after dark, placed severe demands
on the troops prior to the next days' maximum effort. Fortunately, resistance on these islets proved light and the daily bombardments smoth-
ered the defenses of the Roi-Namur main objective.[4]

Because of the previous days' efforts, the 24th Marines assaulted
Namur late the morning of 1 February in ragged fashion with only 62
of the 110 assigned LVT2 tractors, plus some amtracs and landing craft
rounded up at the last minute. But attack they did, landing without difficulty on the island. The armored amphibians could not cross a tank
ditch and dense foliage separating the beach from the island's interior.
Accordingly, they supported by fire from the water's edge. Quite the
opposite occurred on Roi, however. That island consisted of an airfield
of three runways and taxi strips, almost devoid of any cover or obstacles. Here, the 23d Marines landed in good order, using the fresh LVTs
of the 4th Amtrac Battalion, reinforced only minutes later by the M4A2
Shermans of C Company, 4th Tank Battalion. Capt. Robert M. Neiman,
a 1939 University of Maryland graduate and seasoned tanker, found Roi
much to his liking. Seeing the few visible emplacements knocked out
and a vast flat, open area in front of him, he launched his vehicles across
the island from the initial regimental pause line, preferring to overrun
any enemy antitank defenses before they could lay sights on his lined-
up tanks. The armored amphibians and not a few infantrymen went
along as well and supported the advance of the tanks. Horrified at such

initiative, the regimental and division commanders reined the tanks and troops back for a second, more dignified effort. The enemy remained in shock after the initial tank-infantry storming of the island and could barely resist the more formal attack, scheduled for 1515. The troops conquered the island a second time and commanders declared it secure at 1805.[5]

Securing Namur required more vigorous efforts, however, for here the terrain and surviving enemy favored a stronger defense. The light tanks of B Company began to land in the 24th Marines' zone an hour after Captain Neiman's Shermans had landed on Roi. Some of the M5A1s bogged in sand and shell holes, but others succeeded in reaching the infantry on their initial pause line. Undergrowth and rubble concealed many of the surviving pillboxes, hindering both the advance and mopping up of the zones already covered. The advance continued and the light tanks advanced, supported closely by infantry squads. The Japanese attempted to swarm the light tanks with grenades and mines whenever possible but in all but one case the accompanying infantry and tanks swept them away with fire. That exception proved fatal for the tank of B Company's Capt. James L. Denig, as he led his headquarters section forward to replace a platoon pulled back for rearming. Attacking into the underbrush, Denig's tank veered out of line after striking a log and stopped, only to be attacked by a squad of Japanese. A grenade passed into the turret through the signal port, left open inadvertently, killing Denig and his gunner and setting the tank on fire.

Gen. Harry Schmidt, the division commander, ordered a reserve battalion and Captain Neiman's mediums over to Namur to reinforce. That night, while the 24th Marines resisted Japanese infiltration efforts, the C Company crews, now far from their own ammunition dump, transferred their remaining fuel and ammunition to one of the platoons for the next day's operation. That platoon moved into the lines just in time to assist in shattering the Japanese main counterattack. The following day the entire medium-tank company supported the attack of the reinforced 24th Marines until they secured the island that afternoon.[6]

The seizure of Roi-Namur confirmed the reforms of amphibious doctrine and organization undertaken before and after Tarawa, although the latter had presented significantly tougher defenses at the outset. More and better amtracs, supported by armored amphibians and followed immediately by medium tanks, could put the assaulting infantry ashore and spearhead their drive through any defensive barrier seen to date. The follow-on landing at Eniwetok on 18–22 February used the V

Amphibious Corps reserve. This consisted of the 22d Marines and its 2d Separate Tank Company, last seen on Samoa, with the latter now refitted with M4A2s. The tactical situation repeated itself, and the tank-infantry team overran the three-island atoll in as many days. As at Tarawa, a company of Japanese Type 95 tanks fought the defenders both from dug-in positions and in counterattack, so the welcome additional weight of the 2d Separate Tank Company's 75mm cannon made the fight a one-sided affair.[7]

As would happen so many times in the Pacific war, no sooner had the U.S. Marine Corps oriented to a new set of operational challenges than the situation changed. From attacking isolated Japanese garrisons in coral atolls, the III and V Amphibious Corps now turned to confronting large units of the Japanese army, defending large Pacific islands presenting all possible variations of terrain. The Marianas formed the inner-island defense barrier of Japanese strategy for the Pacific war, and a decisive battle fought on land, at sea, and in the air would settle the fate of the Empire. Although U.S. Navy submarine and air interdiction delayed Japanese reinforcements and key fortification materials from reaching the islands in the early part of 1944, the garrisons already in place boasted reinforcing artillery, tank, and other arms, including more of the naval infantry that had defended Tarawa so tenaciously. The U.S. invasion force, the largest yet assembled in the Pacific, would target three large islands for Operation Forager: Saipan and nearby Tinian in the northern archipelago, and Guam in the south. The V Amphibious Corps, using the 2d and 4th Marine Divisions and in reserve the 27th Infantry Division of the army, planned to take Saipan first, then turn on nearby Tinian. The III Amphibious Corps (formerly the I Marine Amphibious Corps of the Solomons campaign), would land on Guam with the 3d Marine Division, the 1st Provisional Marine Brigade (4th and 22d Marines), and the 77th Infantry Division, held initially at Hawaii, in reserve.

The now-veteran Marine Corps units readied new equipment and rehearsed the latest tactical procedures for this decisive engagement. The second-generation LVT4 formed over one-third of the amtrac strength fielded by the 2d, 3d, 4th, 5th, and 10th Amphibian Tractor Battalions, as well as three army amtrac battalions. The new armored amphibian, LVT(A)4, with its 75mm short howitzer, saw its debut with the 2d Armored Amphibian Battalion and part of the army's 708th Amphibian Tank Battalion. The 1st Armored Amphibian Battalion continued operating its older model LVT(A)1, with its obsolete 37mm guns.[8]

The tank battalions had refitted completely with M4A2 Shermans, albeit on the reduced forty-six-tank organization. The 1st Corps Medium Tank Battalion now lacked a role and therefore disbanded on 15 February, its companies distributed to the divisional battalions. Some of the older M3A1s had been modified with an infantry-type flame-thrower fitted in the bow gunner's position, duplicating the improvisations begun in the Solomons the previous year. In addition, the Corps had requested twenty-four of the army's depot-converted light flame-thrower tanks, the "Satan." This conversion mounted a Canadian Ronson flamethrower in the M3A1 turret, with 170 gallons of thickened flame fuel, projected by compressed carbon dioxide to a range of 60–80 yards for up to two minutes of use. The 2d and 4th Tank Battalions each received a dozen of these vehicles, formed with some M5A1s into improvised D companies in each, but also took a few of their locally converted M3A1 flame tanks to Saipan. Of course, the Satan retained the weak armor of the base vehicle and the flame equipment limited the turret traverse to 10 degrees left and 80 degrees right of center.[9]

The marine tankers had seen the prowess with which the Japanese infantry pressed their close assaults against their tanks, using grenades and antitank mines. The latter posed a threat to medium-tank armor, which presented 2 to 3 inches of thickness frontally, but had only 1.5-inch side armor (including along the fuel tank) and 1 inch on the turret roof. As in the case of their army brethren in Europe, the crews strapped on extra sections of steel track to the front and sides of their M4s. Protection for the turret roof and crew hatches frequently took the form of nails welded to the tanks, points up. Sandbags placed on the engine tops protected against satchel charges and thrown mines. In C Company, 4th Tank Battalion, Captain Neiman's energetic carpenters and welders mounted "cages" of heavy mesh, rising two inches over the hatches, preventing any direct contact with these vulnerable points by hand-placed explosives. On the sides, sections of channel-iron, strung through with reinforcing bars, supported wood planking, 2 x 12 inches wide, hung four inches outward from the hull. These became forms for a four-inch thickness of concrete poured between planks and hull. Replacing sections blown away in combat only required more lumber and concrete, readily available from navy construction battalions. The wood prevented use of magnetic mines and the concrete proved immune to the antitank guns of the Japanese. The only hitch in the local improvisation came when the company dozer tank was so modified that its weight threatened to sink the standard landing craft. It took a long time for the company first sergeant to remove the concrete with a pneumatic hammer![10]

The assault landing on Saipan, 15 June 1944, called for the infantry of the leading waves to debouch from the LSTs (34 in number) in their amtracs, escorted by the armored amphibians on each flank, following navy gunboats, and head for the beach, climbing over coral reefs 1,000 to 1,500 yards offshore. Putting the armored amphibians on the flank of the troop carriers allowed all the LVTs to use their weapons on the run into the beach. The V Amphibious Corps attack plan called for the armored amphibians to lead the troop-carrying LVTs a mile inland to the pause line, a mechanized thrust calculated to bypass enemy resistance and avoid any clustering on the narrow beaches. The 2d Division commanders rejected this scheme because of evident problems with terrain inland and opted to dismount at the water's edge, while the armored amphibians pinned down defenders a short distance inland. The 4th Division, viewing the aerial photographs, attempted the mechanized attack.

Tanks of the 2d and 4th Tank Battalions followed the 719 LVTs and unloaded at various distances from the beach, as their LCMs touched down on the reefs. The landing plan required several of the LVTs to link with the tanks and guide them off their LCMs, across the reefs and thereby avoiding crevices or holes that could swamp them. The noise and confusion of battle made this measure impossible to execute, and several tanks of the 4th Tank Battalion hit bottom. All of C Company made it ashore, the amazing Major Neiman having detailed some of his headquarters personnel to swim ahead of the tanks, unrolling toilet-paper rolls to mark the safer route. He received further assistance from a boatload of navy assault swimmers, returning to the ships, who pointed out where the reef contained the fewest underwater obstacles.[11]

The advancing infantry of the 4th Marine Division found the going very rough toward the pause line. Two groups of the 23d Marines used the only dirt roads to penetrate to the line, but the remainder of the forces encountered swamps and steep inclines in the terrain inland. The advanced outposts had to fall back at nightfall. An enemy counterattack hit the extreme right of the beachhead, causing a momentary problem for 1st Battalion, 25th Marines, but the infantrymen repelled the attack, assisted by a few tanks. The troops continued on foot, reaching much of the pause line by that evening. The enemy's counterattack of the first night fell mostly upon the 6th Marines of the 2d Marine Division. Japanese naval infantry and a few amphibious tankettes attacked on the extreme left, while another group of naval infantry and tanks, joined by a Japanese army light-tank company and infantry battalion, attacked in the early morning. These made no progress against the fire of infantry and 2d Tank Battalion Shermans, aided by naval starshell illumination. Some 700 Japanese troops and two dozen tanks fell before their lines.[12]

Opinions varied on how well the 4th Marine Division mechanized amphibious attack might have fared. The commander of the 24th Marines stated later, "Several LVT(2)s did reach the 0-1 [pause] line but the majority failed to go inland beyond 75–100 yards. Responsibility for the failure of the LVTs to reach the 0-1 line was due to the fact that the LVT(A)s refused to lead the way as originally scheduled and ordered." Yet, the commander of the 1st Battalion, 24th Marines affirmed that "[o]n five different days LVT(A)'s reinforced our tanks in the attack in our sector. Though they received many casualties they were very aggressive and their fire power very effective. All LVT(A)s were armed with 37's, no 75's were available." In the main, it seems that the armored amphibians, mostly of the army's 708th Amphibian Tank Battalion then supporting the 4th Division, may have suffered rough handling from the Japanese weapons, with their thin armor and large target area when out of water. The army unit lost thirty of sixty-eight armored amphibians at Saipan and Tinian.[13]

The Japanese attacks on the first night of the landing turned out to be merely a probing action. The all-out counterattack came the next night, including the largest Japanese tank attack faced in the Pacific war. Approximately forty-four tanks, mostly mediums, some armed with 47mm cannon, rolled toward the lines of the 2d Marine Division facing the dominant terrain of Mount Tapochau. Following them came about 500 men of an infantry regiment, hell-bent to drive a wedge into the American lines until reaching the beach, less than a mile away. However, air reconnaissance had spotted a few tanks during the day and engine sounds filled the early hours of the evening. The marines stood ready, although the night tactics of the enemy allowed them to come uncomfortably close. The Japanese tanks roared out of the darkness, but ran into "a madhouse of noise, tracers, and flashing lights. As tanks were hit and set afire, they silhouetted other tanks coming out of the flickering shadows to the front or already on top of the [rifle] squads." From 0345 until 0700 on the seventeenth, the landing force flayed the Japanese with tank, bazooka, antitank gun, artillery, and naval gunfire. Only twelve Japanese tanks survived the battle. Not a single U.S. tank from A Company, 2d Tank Battalion, fell out of action, but the infantry took almost a hundred casualties and the artillery suffered some losses in counterbattery duels with the large and varied Japanese artillery park. The surviving Japanese tanks reappeared later in the advance to the north, falling to the guns of C Company, 2d Tank Battalion, and to army light tanks.[14]

For the rest of the campaign, no doubt existed about the outcome. Both the 2d and 4th Marine Divisions had practiced tank-infantry attacks to the utmost. The troops trusted the tank far more than the artillery as a supporting weapon, since the latter could occasionally fire on their own positions. The tanks never posed such a friendly-fire problem. Hundreds and, occasionally, thousands of yards of defended terrain fell to the tank-infantry teams, generally operating on a ratio of one tank company, with a few flamethrower tanks added, for each regiment. Only in the central part of Saipan, with its mountainous terrain, did the infantry not receive the full measure of tank support and that is where the main attrition occurred. Death Valley, Purple Heart Ridge, and other deadly ground claimed many casualties, and the tank units could rarely struggle up a few bulldozed paths on occasion to render support. After the assault battalions passed this gut-wrenching episode of conquering the center portion of Saipan, the mopping up resumed, with the island declared secure on 9 July.

V Corps artillery had already bombarded the next objective, in concert with the array of ships available to the amphibious task force. Tinian, a relatively flat island, crowded with cane fields, remained for the two marine divisions to conquer. Under perfect, almost laboratory-like conditions, the amphibious assault fed first the 4th Marine Division, reinforced with the tanks and artillery of the 2d Marine Division, across narrow beaches on 24 July into a suitable beachhead line. The Japanese counterattack was broken the very night of the landing, the lone Japanese light-tank company and its accompanying infantry washing up in total futility against the firepower of the well-prepared marines. Marine tanks could contribute little to the carnage, as the line infantry poured .50-caliber machine gun, bazooka, 37mm, and 75mm fire into the Type 95 light tanks, followed by the rapidly diminishing lines of infantry. The next day the 2d Marine Division could land with impunity, and then the two divisions rolled across the island, alternating main attacks through the cane fields with infantry racing to keep up with the tank companies in the lead. Only the mined areas of the southern portion of the island presented true obstacles before the enemy resistance fell and the corps commander declared the island secure on 1 August. For the tank troops, enjoying really favorable tank terrain for once, the only novelty proved to be an unpleasant encounter with a fortified 47mm antitank gun, the Type 1 high-velocity cannon, which penetrated the armor of two Shermans several times before they could blind it with smoke shells and maneuver for a killing shot.[15]

The parallel assault on Guam began a few days before the V Corps hit Tinian. Here the landing force benefited from the delay imposed while the 5th Fleet fought off the Japanese navy in the Battle of the Philippine Sea. Better reconnaissance information and aerial photography reached the units. A thirteen-day naval and air bombardment, longest of the Pacific war, softened the island's defenses before Maj. Gen. Roy Geiger's III Amphibious Corps began their storm landing. The 3d Marine Division combined with the 1st Provisional Marine Brigade for the assault. The latter unit later formed the 6th (and last) Marine Division, after the interservice opposition to Marine Corps expansion had been settled in Washington. Lemuel C. Shepherd, the early advocate of the "Army type tank" in the MCEB meetings at the end of the 1930s, was now a brigadier general and commanded the brigade as he would the 6th Division. Shepherd's two infantry regiments, the 4th and 22d Marines, each had organic tank companies. The 2d Separate Tank Company still accompanied the 22d Marines. The 4th Marines Tank Company (sometimes erroneously called the 4th Separate Tank Company), formerly A Company, 3d Tank Battalion, had been formed for the regiment in March 1944 for its landing at Emirau Island, located north of Rabaul, which turned out to be unopposed.[16]

Three times the size of Saipan, with more mountains, caves, and jungle growth, Guam presented a dangerous proposition. Older Marine Corps officers knew it well, however, not only from its former status as a "post of the Corps" but also as the subject of numerous map exercises in their prewar Quantico schools. The Japanese garrison proved smaller than that of Saipan, but equally well equipped. The navy and Marine Corps forces staged the now-textbook landing on 21 July 1944. Major Metzger's 73 armored amphibians led the 373 amtracs of the 3d, 4th, and 11th Amtrac Battalions over the 500 yards of reef against the battered and disoriented defenders, north and south of the large Orote Point, which would keep the two forces separated by five miles for a few dangerous days. As at Saipan, the landing plan called for the troops to ride their amtracs 1,000 yards to the pause line, but enemy fire, obstacles, and terrain prevented their advancing more than 200 to 500 yards while mounted. The use of amtracs to guide tanks over the reef did succeed this time, though, and the 3d Tank Battalion landed all of its tanks between 30 and 90 minutes after the leading amtracs had touched sand. In the brigade's sector, surf conditions imposed more delays on the regimental tank companies, but all tanks deployed ashore by noon. The ensuing advance carried the assault troops up to a mile inland the first day, after which preparations began to receive the typical Japanese night counterattack.[17]

The main counterattack fell upon the 4th Marines, and the M4A2 tanks of that regiment's tank company killed four accompanying Type 95 tanks. A fifth one was shot up the next day at an amazing 1,840 yards' distance, certainly a record engagement range for the Pacific war tankers. The advance of the division and brigade continued daily against the Japanese defenders, using tank-infantry tactics whenever the terrain permitted. The armored amphibians had to fill in for tanks when otherwise engaged or rearming, and they guarded the beach flanks of the landing force as well. The 2d Separate Tank Company destroyed five more Type 95 tanks opposing the 22d Marines' advance on 24 July and three more fell to navy aircraft attacks. The piecemeal counterattacks of the Japanese whittled down their strength for no apparent gain.[18]

The Japanese commander on Guam thus decided to throw his best effort at the landing force on the night of 25–26 July, mostly against the lines of the 3d Marine Division and its 3d Tank Battalion. This time the Japanese tanks lost their way on the trails and did not join the attack, leaving the American tankers free to demolish the attacking infantry. The Japanese damaged only one tank in the attack. Fortuitous tank-infantry attacks the previous day into the Japanese assembly areas had hurt the Japanese forces even before they launched this largest attack.[19]

The clearing of Guam took twenty days, in which the tanks frequently provided the firepower necessary to demolish the defensive positions and caves that would have added many days and casualties to the operation. General Shepherd even called for additional platoons of tanks from the army's 77th Division, added to the III Amphibious Corps after the main landings had occurred. Tank dozers and bulldozers cut new roads where necessary to bring tanks and other weapons to bear on the enemy. Both the 77th Division and the 3d Marine Division tried to employ an armored reconnaissance in force when terrain permitted. Lieutenant Colonel Withers organized and led one such armored column the afternoon of 3 August. Withers took his command section and A Company tanks, a halftrack, and four jeeps from the divisional reconnaissance company and mounted an infantry company of the 21st

Marines in trucks, along with a mine-clearing detachment. Hitting Japanese lines along a jungle trail, the column took fire from both sides and had to fight its way out in a two-hour engagement, leaving behind the halftrack and one truck, and bringing back fifteen casualties. The division did not repeat the experience.[20]

Instead, dogged attacks along the narrow trails leading to the north coast of Guam completed the occupation of the island by 11 August. One last series of actions showed that the Japanese tanks still had fight in them. The surviving Type 97 mediums and a few Type 95s had withdrawn to the last northeastern enclave at Tarague. Early in the morning of 6 August, two mediums and a platoon of infantry attacked down a trail into the lines of the 77th Infantry, killing fifteen and wounding forty-six U.S. soldiers before withdrawing intact. Later that day, an advancing tank-infantry patrol of the 9th Marines encountered a roadblock, from which a Japanese tank scored three hits on an M4A2 before being knocked out. Then, the night of 9 August, it was the turn of the 2d Battalion, 3d Marines, to receive a tank-infantry attack, as it moved down a trail typically inadequate to support the American medium tanks. The marines scattered the Japanese infantry with their fire, but could not make their rain-soaked bazookas and rifle grenades work. They retreated ignominiously into the jungle from the three Japanese Type 97s and withdrew through the jungle to another battalion's position. Amazingly, the battalion took no casualties. By noon the next day, bulldozers had cut a tank trail and the Shermans moved up with 3d Battalion, 3d Marines, to counterattack. Nearby, the 9th Marines eliminated another light tank roadblock. The morning of 10 August the 2d Battalion, 3d Marines, took its revenge, attacking with tank support into the Japanese tank bivouac. The accompanying M4A2s destroyed two Type 97s but found the remaining seven Japanese mediums abandoned for lack of fuel or spares. Effective Japanese resistance had ceased.[21]

The Marine Corps FMF reached its maturity with the Marianas campaign. The marines and the U.S. Navy had achieved almost all the desired improvements in doctrine and equipment for the amphibious landing. The armored amphibian and the less armored cargo amphibious tractor, especially the new LVT4 series, proved reliable and effective in the assault and in supporting the operations inland with fire support and the transportation of key supplies from ship to shore. The tank battalions and separate tank companies proved the value of the M4A2 in combat and the value of the new levels of teamwork now established with the infantry. The aggressive use of tanks by the enemy had made no impact on the landings, for the M4A2 tanks remained impervious to all but lucky hits by the Japanese 37mm gun, and the American tankers encountered few of the more effective 47mm high-velocity cannon. The close assaults so bravely pressed by the desperate Japanese infantrymen almost always failed, either from the toughness of the tanks and field-improvised additional armor or the vigilance of the accompanying infantrymen. The flame tanks, both the Satan and the improvised M3A1 modifications, saw action mostly in mopping up, escorted by two or more gun tanks. They remained in reserve until lucrative targets appeared: caves, pillboxes, or packets of personnel. Still, the 4th Tank Battalion rated the light flamethrower tanks unsatisfactory. The M3A1 tank lacked protection and its radios proved impossible to maintain or repair. The Ronson turret of the Satan demanded too much of its operators and the lack of real napalm mixture left it with too little range. The poor mechanical installation of the Ronson also impressed no one. The FMF needed to either develop a medium flamethrower tank or abandon the project. Ammunition consumption reported by the 4th Tank Battalion on Saipan alone illustrated the effort by the tanks to support their infantry regiments: The six M3A1 and forty-two M4A2 tanks operating there had fired 1,500 rounds of 37mm, 8,400 of 75mm, and 4.5 million rounds of .30-caliber ammunition. The after-action reports of the 3d Marine Division and 1st Brigade unanimously praised the medium tank as the best weapon against enemy emplacements. The 75mm gun had reliably eliminated all types of field and permanent fortifications. The 3d Tank Battalion reported good use of flamethrower tanks, but also disliked the improvised infantry flamethrower mount in the light tank.[22]

The Final Formula for Victory
In the aftermath of the Marianas, the tank, amtrac, and armored amphibian battalions received new vehicles to replace their battered machines. The 37mm tank cannon all but disappeared from the FMF, as the tank battalions discarded the last of the light tanks and new production LVT(A)4 vehicles reached the armored amphibian battalions. Unfortunately, these arrived too late to completely outfit the new 3d Armored Amphibian Battalion, which sailed for Peleliu with twenty-four of the older LVT(A)1 vehicles. The amtrac battalions received new production LVT2 and LVT4 vehicles in a 1 : 2 ratio in 1944, and converted to all second-generation amtracs during 1945.[23]

Refurbishing the tank battalions turned out to be a bigger problem for the harassed quartermasters. Already in March 1944, Maj. Gen. Gerald C.

Thomas, director of Plans and Policies, warned the commandant, Lieutenant General Vandegrift, that the M4A2 medium tank's days were numbered. Only the Marine Corps and the Red Army used the diesel-powered Sherman tank, and the army had standardized the M4A3, with its gasoline-fueled Ford GAA engine, for its own mass production. Only this latter tank received the latest design improvements and field modifications from the army ordnance system. Moreover, by abandoning the light tank, the Marine Corps's required medium-tank inventory now exceeded 500 vehicles, counting training and replacement stocks. To make things worse, the army now intended to up-gun the M4A3 with the high-velocity 76mm tank cannon, needed for combat in Europe against the better-armored German tanks. The changes in the production line, scheduled to take place on 1 July, threatened the Marine Corps tank fleet as well as the ammunition supply so laboriously built up in the Pacific theater. The Marine Corps had no interest in the upgunned Sherman, as the 75mm cannon performed all that was expected of it. Thomas recommended ordering no more diesel Shermans and accelerating the acquisition of the latest M4A3 models to equip the new 5th Tank Battalion and refurbish the remaining tank battalions with the last of the 75mm production line. Vandegrift agreed, ordering replacement of all the diesel M4A2s with the gasoline-engine medium tank.[24]

The cries of protest arrived right away from the veteran battalions. The reaction of Maj. Richard Schmidt and his 4th Tank Battalion staff proved typical. His letter, written after the Tinian operation had concluded, related how he had seen so many gasoline-engine vehicles, the LVTs, self-propelled artillery, and army light and medium tanks blow up and burn, while his diesel M4A2s survived repeated hits and penetrations without catching fire.[25]

> On at least three different occasions on Saipan, tanks of Company "C" were partially damaged when magnetic mines exploded over the engine compartments. In each instance the result was one engine destroyed and several fuel lines shattered with fuel blown over the hot engines. But on neither of these occasions did a tank catch fire. Never was a vehicle destroyed or a crew lost. And always the damaged tank was able to return to safety powered by its one good engine. On Jig plus 8 on Tinian, a tank of Company "A" was damaged when a magnetic mine exploded on top of the left fuel tank. A huge hole was blown in the fuel tank and diesel oil was scattered over the hot engines. Of course the contents of the left fuel tank were lost, but there was no fire, the driver of the vehicle merely switched to the right fuel tank and the tank remained in action for the

balance of the operation. . . . On Jig plus 7 on Tinian, another tank of Company "C" had its left side penetrated by a base detonating armor piercing projectile fired from a 47mm antitank gun. This was the same type of projectile that the undersigned saw set an army gasoline powered tank and several gasoline powered LVTA's on fire. This projectile entered the left fuel tank and caused all of the fuel to rapidly run out of the tank. However, as in the other instances, the vehicle did not burn, but fuel was merely drawn from the right fuel tank instead of the left and the vehicle remained in action.

Schmidt argued not only that the twin-engine feature of the M4A2 had repeatedly brought damaged tanks and their crew back to safety, but also that he considered the gasoline tank engine more temperamental, requiring more maintenance, and more failure-prone because of its sensitive ignition system. The diesel tank reliably had operated for two days of operations without refueling.

Nothing could alter the facts on the homefront, however, and only the 1st Tank Battalion, then on its way to Peleliu, escaped the eventual fate of the other battalions. But the problem then grew worse, in the opinion of many. Six months after his first warning on tank production, General Thomas advised the commandant of another army change in the tank program. In 1945 the army intended to replace the M4 with the new T26 medium tank, with its 90mm gun, as the standard production tank. M4A3 production would continue, but only with the new 105mm howitzer turret, intended as a close-support tank for infantry. Should the Marine Corps desire more M4A3s in 1945, it would have to accept 105mm gun tanks or obtain special procurement of 75mm tanks, a responsibility that no one with procurement experience wanted the Corps to undertake.[26]

The commandant's field inspection in the Pacific conducted after Guam had fallen to the III Amphibious Corps revealed that the opinions among six divisions remained divided. Retaining the 75mm cannon made better use of training and experience and the ammunition offered higher muzzle velocity for accuracy and armor penetration as well as easier handling in the turret (18.5 vs. 42 pounds weight). Points in favor of the 105mm including its adherence to the army standard, the availability of the ammunition from the artillery stocks, the triple weight of the explosive filler, and the increased variety of ammunition, including high-explosive antitank (HEAT, a shaped charge), smoke, and white phosphorous munitions. On the other hand, tankers found to their shock that the early production models with the 105mm had no power traverse or gyrostabilizer. Nevertheless, the evident realities caused Vandegrift to order the shift to the 105mm gun tank in 1945.

The commandant's letter to the field at the end of October detailed some of the difficulties he faced. In response to the pleas to continue use of the twin-diesel tank, he sympathized: "The fact that diesel affords a superior source of power for tanks is well recognized." But, he asserted, the Marine Corps could not justify separate production lines in the U.S. war industry. Furthermore, deviation from the army standards would result in lack of maintenance and technical support. The conversion to gasoline tanks remained firm.[27]

At the Tank School at Jacques' Farm Lieutenant Colonel Collins organized the new 5th Tank Battalion, with the now-standard three tank companies, in March of 1944. This unit received the first Marine Corps M4A3s and departed the United States with the 5th Marine Division in the fall, the last of the tank battalions to form in the United States. The 6th Tank Battalion formed on Guadalcanal on 1 October, combining the tank companies of the veteran 4th and 22d Marine Regiments with that of the last regiment to be formed in the United States, the 29th Marines. Lieutenant Colonel Denig took command, with Maj. Harry T. Milne his executive officer. This organization completed the final arrangement of tank units in the World War II Marine Corps, all six battalions having three medium-tank companies, and no separate tank companies or platoons remained in the FMF.[28]

With the last battalions departing the United States in 1944, the tank and amtrac schools served only for replacement training. Their headquarters moved with the Training Command, San Diego Area, from Camp Elliott to new facilities on board Camp Pendleton. The amtrac schools had consolidated at Camp Pendleton in early 1944. The LVT maintenance courses continued as an exception at the original amtrac school site at Dunedin, Florida. Specialty courses evolved as the burden of forming the new battalions eased. A tank-dozer course began in April 1944 and the school inaugurated a tank platoon-leader course of seventy days and 700 hours instruction on 27 September 1944. The school began work on its armored amphibian gunnery course for the LVT(A)4 in June of 1944. The commandant approved a tank NCO refresher course on 12 April 1945, paralleling an earlier order for the amtrac NCOs. The gunnery curriculum changed from 75mm to 105mm in June 1945, and the Corps had by this point achieved virtual independence from army schools for its fighting vehicle troops.[29]

Before the new tank and amtrac battalions faced the ultimate climactic battles of the war, however, the veteran 1st Tank and 1st Amtrac Battalions would land with the 1st Marine Division at Peleliu, reinforced by the new 3d Armored Amphibian Battalion and the still-forming 6th and 8th Amtrac battalions. This fiercely contested battle, beginning on 15 September, presaged the violence of the 1945 island battles but also contained some parallels with the preceding actions. Once again, amtrac battalions were rushed into action with green commanders and crews. Shipping shortages caused the tank battalion to leave sixteen tanks behind. As experienced as the 1st Marine Division was, it had yet to make an opposed landing and, in retrospect, its training and planning failed to meet the new standards already demonstrated in the Marianas operation.[30]

After hiding from the typical three-day naval bombardment, the Japanese defenders came alive upon the approach of amtracs, armored amphibians, and tanks of the 1st Division. The Japanese now knew that they had to stop the medium tanks and these drew much fire. Almost all the tanks received hits, but only three fell disabled out of the drive to the beach, guided by assigned amtracs. The tanks passed ashore in only 30 minutes, but twenty-eight amtracs remained on the reef knocked out, so severe was the defenders' fire. The thirty tanks of 1st Tank Battalion proved too few in number to support the many groups of assault troops landing at several sites. Too many Japanese emplacements had survived and now hammered the troops dispersed across the beaches. The armored amphibians, many armed with only the 37mm gun, dueled bravely with the Japanese as the tanks rolled ashore to reinforce. Slowly the tank-infantry teams edged forward, reducing the defenses, pillbox by pillbox. At about 1630, too late to save his beach defenses, the Japanese commander launched his fifteen Type 95 light tanks against the 1st and 5th Marines on the edge of the island's airfield. The Japanese tanks gave it their best effort, racing ahead of their infantry to close the distance quickly, with many infantrymen riding the wildly plunging vehicles. The 1st Tank Battalion's crews responded in kind, some hurrying back from rearming at the beach. They proved more than enough to stop the Japanese attack. Platoons of tanks engaged the enemy formation, and infantry turned bazookas, 37mm antitank guns, and .50-caliber machine guns, all lethal against the Type 95, against the oncoming tide. Even a navy dive-bomber chanced overhead, adding a 500-pound bomb to the fracas. The tankers switched from armor-piercing to high-explosive ammunition as they saw their solid shot passing all the way through the light tanks. Amazingly, the speed alone of the onslaught carried several surviving tanks into the artillery in the rear, before they could be shot up and destroyed.[31]

The apparent victory did not mollify the strong-willed commander of the tank battalion, though. Lt. Col. Arthur J. Stuart, the last of Bob Denig's lieutenants from B Company on Samoa to take command of a battalion, did not hesitate to call attention to the defects evident in this battle in perhaps controversial tones. In his later assessment of the Battle for Peleliu for the official histories, he criticized landing-force planning for tank employment, and remarked that the destruction of the Japanese army's tank-infantry counterattack left "no grounds for smugness in regard to our antitank prowess. Had the Japanese possessed modern tanks instead of tankettes and had they attacked in greater numbers the situation would have been critical."[32]

Several more surprises awaited the assault troops. Some Japanese bunkers proved too thick for tank cannon and even naval gunfire to penetrate and had to be taken out by close assault using hand-placed demolitions and flamethrowers. The inner defenses dominating Peleliu proved almost inaccessible to vehicles, even when dozer tanks tried to cut makeshift roads. The tanks and armored amphibians tried mightily to assist the infantry, but the rocky center spine of the island defied their best efforts and the infantry took terrible losses. Mechanized flame weapons helped in some cases. The Navy Bureau of Ordnance had developed a Mark I flamethrower with a 100-yard range for possible use in landing craft, sending several of them to Hawaii in 1944 for testing. Six arrived in the 1st Marine Division base at Guadalcanal in time for the Peleliu operation and the marines mounted them in LVT4s. With a 200-gallon tank, they could fire for 71 seconds and proved useful, despite the vulnerabilities of the vehicle. The 1st Tank Battalion also operated the army's E4-5 flamethrower kits for the medium tank. This weapon replaced the bow machine gun with a flame weapon, but it suffered from the same weaknesses as the earlier field expedients using the infantry flamethrower, lack of range, sufficient fuel, and reduced tank armament. The first six of these kits had worked effectively on Guam, with the 3d Tank Battalion. The Corps made them a standard issue for the tank battalion (24 units in each) by the end of the year. The E5 flame gun had a 60-yard range, using thickened fuel (rarely available) carried in the E-4 24-gallon fuel tank, located in the right sponson of the tank.[33]

Tanks still lacked an integral tank-infantry communications means and the 1st Tank Battalion again resorted to the field expedient of mounting a standard field telephone on the rear of the tank using a spot-welded ammo can, with wires running to the turret. This assisted the already close bond developing within the 1st Marine Division between the tankers and infantrymen, whose risktaking to support one another became legendary. Infantry frequently hailed passing tanks en route to support another assigned unit. Usually, the tankers rendered assistance before proceeding on their assignment. Of the thirty-one officers of the tank battalion, eight were killed and only eight escaped being wounded. No tank fell to the persistent enemy close assaults, thanks to the attentive and close work of the infantry. Although all but one Sherman was knocked out of action by one or another cause, only nine became total losses, and sixteen to twenty vehicles remained in action on a daily basis. Even after the 1st Marine Division had been relieved on Peleliu, LVT detachments of 1st Amtrac and 3d Armored Amphibian Battalions remained on the island in support of the 81st Infantry Division, which worked on reducing the Japanese rock stronghold until 27 November, when resistance finally ceased.[34]

The aptly named Operation Stalemate revealed a new feature of the Japanese defensive doctrine, a defense in depth, using the natural fortifications of rock formations in which the garrison tunneled and fortified its positions in defilade from the dominant American naval gunfire. When the initial enemy counterattack failed, the Japanese commander wisely withheld further such efforts in order to exact the maximum delay and attrition on the attacking Americans by resisting from the strong and mutually supporting positions held in the rocky interior. In this battle, the enemy even reinforced his position from other island garrisons in the Palaus at night, using landing craft in almost suicidal runs to shore up the doomed defenses and buy more time. Prisoners remained very scarce, and resistance, in fact, continued after the island was declared "secure." The Japanese defenses faced in 1945 by the six divisions fielded by the Marine Corps in the III and V Amphibious Corps would prove just as daunting.

The Iwo Jima assault, the largest undertaken by a Marine Corps–only landing force, brought home the improved Japanese army antilanding doctrine to the troops of the 3d, 4th, and 5th Marine Divisions. The strongly armed and extremely well-fortified garrison would not waste its forces in an all-out counterattack of the landing beaches. Instead, the Japanese sought to draw the U.S. forces ashore into artillery concentrations and the lethal crossfire of antitank and infantry weapons hidden in a web of bunkers, caves, and trenches, almost all guarded by minefields of a greater effectiveness than yet seen in the Pacific war. More of the lethal 47mm antitank guns appeared in this battle, but the enemy light and medium tanks all became dug-in strongpoints in the defensive system at Iwo.

The 68 new LVT(A)4s of the 2d Armored Amphibian Battalion churned through the rolling seas and plunging surf on 19 February 1945, leading the 181 LVT2s and 222 LVT4s of the 3d, 5th, 10th and 11th Amphibian Tractor Battalions. These tractors all launched from LST mother ships and landed the assault elements of the 4th and 5th Marine Divisions side by side on the narrow neck of land separating the dominant Mount Suribachi from the airfields and lesser hill clusters on the larger northern end of the island. Losses on the approach to the beach remained very small, but like all the rest of the forces landed, the cumulative losses proved considerable, about one-third of the vehicles being lost in the month-long battle. Only twenty-eight men died in the amtrac battalions, however, demonstrating the difference between landing from deep water directly onto a beach and crossing the reefs such as at Tarawa and Peleliu. The armored amphibians again attempted to accompany the troops inland but wallowed in the loose volcanic sand. The low-velocity 75mm gun also proved less satisfactory in dealing with enemy emplacements. The tanks, as usual, provided the impetus for the attack, but at Iwo Jima they had to land from new LSM ships, each carrying six tanks, unloading directly on the steep beaches under the fire of any surviving Japanese antiboat gun. Most of the landing-ship skippers lacked experience and commanded green crews. Mines and shifting sands would make the offload of the desperately needed M4A3 mediums very difficult. The 5th Tank Battalion had a tank company loaded in LCM landing craft and managed to get the first vehicles ashore about 25 minutes after the leading LVT(A)4 had touched down. But four of these tanks threw track in the sand and another suffered an engine failure. On the 4th Division beaches, the tanks began to land another half hour later, losing three tanks to mines at beach exits.

Once ashore, the tanks of both battalions moved with the infantry to take out pillboxes and support the attack. Each battalion had with it four of the newly designed Sherman flame tanks. The Army Chemical Warfare Service (CWS) headquarters for the Pacific theater (POA) in Hawaii had worked with Marine Corps and navy experts to develop a flame weapon for the M4A3 medium tank in late 1944. A flame tube replaced the main gun in the turret, which also carried a 290-gallon fuel tank. The weapon used carbon dioxide at 300–350 pounds per square inch to project thickened fuel to a range of 60–80 yards. The flame equipment limited the traverse of the turret to 120 degrees to either side. But all this remained a marked improvement over the navy's Type 1 flame gun, which could only fit in an LVT. The army used depot facilities in Hawaii to construct fifty-four of these tanks, called the POA-CWS-H1 tankmounted flamethrower for a special battalion, the 713th Tank Battalion, to use with the 10th Army in the Okinawa campaign in support of army and Marine Corps operations. Marine commanders obtained the eight used on Iwo from these stocks, and the tankers of the 4th and 5th Tank Battalions put them into continuous use, supplying the crews. The battalion executive officer of the 713th accompanied the tanks to observe their use on Iwo and won the admiration of the Marine Corps tankers for his cool nerve under fire. The Chemical Corps then improved the flame tank by retaining the tank cannon (with only forty or twenty rounds of 75mm or 105mm ammunition) and making the flame tube a coaxial mounting. Flame-fuel capacity rose to 300 gallons, permitting a full two minutes of continuous fire. The FMF ordered seventy-two of these tanks, called the POA-CWS-H5, to be ready for the invasion of Japan, receiving seventy by the end of the war.[35]

Infantry casualties mounted, especially because nothing could counter the Japanese artillery and mortar fire originating from the northern redoubt of the Japanese garrison. The 5th Tank Battalion companies assisted in the taking of Mount Suribachi, while the 4th Tank Battalion overran the nearest of the three airfields on the island. The V Corps began to land the 3d Marine Division on D+2 and Maj. Holly H. Evans's 3d Tank Battalion entered combat. This reinforcement came none too soon, for the 4th Tank Battalion reported only twenty-eight tanks in action and the 5th Tank Battalion another thirty-four at the end of D+3. As the troops neared the second of the airfields, the V Corps approved Lieutenant Colonel Collins's plan for the massing of all three tank battalions to overrun this prize. Attacking on D+5, the plan failed as the tanks drove over the largest concentration of mines encountered to date, including many aerial torpedoes and sea mines turned into antitank mines. These oversize explosive devices shattered entire M4A3 tanks, sending their crews flying in the air, and a few of these tankers even managed to live through the experience. The tanks paused most of the morning for the mine-clearing efforts, then pushed on to the near edge of the field to support the infantry advance by fire. The airfield did not fall until D+7, after the infantry and tanks had picked their way across in face of intense fire from all arms. The intense fire of Japanese antitank guns, the worst seen at this point in the

Pacific war, threatened to undo the Marine Corps tank-infantry tactics. Still ahead lay the Motomaya Plateau and the main line of resistance of the Japanese army on Iwo.[36]

The tank-infantry force generated by three complete marine divisions on line, supported by all of V Amphibious Corps's artillery, hammered away at the Japanese positions. Ammunition consumption limited the time tanks could serve on the front lines. Frequent trips back to beach ammo dumps caused breaks in the tactical momentum that a unit might be able to develop. Commanders tried all types of tactical measures possible to effect a breakthrough and bring the carnage to an end. Marines attempted night attacks, day attacks, and even a floating end-around by the 2d Armored Amphibian Battalion, seaward of the 27th Marines to substitute for the tanks not able to come forward. The twenty LVT(A)4s knocked out some cave positions, but choppy water so affected their shooting that they had to return to the friendly shore. Slowly and deliberately, the advancing troops pushed the broken but still spirited Japanese into three small pockets. Armored bulldozers and tank dozers cut roads for the gun and flame tanks to approach and destroy the Japanese positions. Reducing these last positions lasted until 26 March, and small actions continued even after the V Corps had left the island. The 9th Marines's afteraction report concluded the obvious: "the most effective supporting weapon in this action was the tank."[37]

As the exhausted troops of V Corps returned to Hawaii and other bases, the 1st and 6th Marine Divisions geared up for the invasion of Okinawa, Operation Iceberg, where they would fight under General Geiger's III Amphibious Corps in the 10th Army. This largest of all operations in which the FMF participated in World War II saw the oldest and newest marine divisions committed to action. Counting army units, a thousand LVTs went into action as two marine and two army divisions landed near the Yontan and Kadena air bases on the island's waist and then swung north and south, respectively, to clear the enemy away. Landing in the first waves on 1 April 1945, the 1st and 3d Armored Amphibian and the 1st, 4th, 8th and 9th Amphibian Tractor Battalions drew little fire and lost no vehicles. The Borg-Warner LVT3 finally saw action in this landing, equipping the 1st and 4th Amtracs. The tanks landed from LCM and LSMs, except for one company each in the 1st and 6th Tank Battalions which used the novel T6 pontoon device to swim tanks into the beach, using their tracks as propulsion. Sometimes they struggled to get over the reefs, but they did in fact function as designed, and the tank crews detonated explosive charges to shed the pontoons and went into action, albeit a bit low on fuel. The LVT(A)4 furnished some direct support for the assault troops, but plenty of tanks arrived soon enough. The pioneering Lieutenant Colonel Metzger had already modified the training and mission of the armored amphibians to an artillery reinforcement role, and they went into action as self-propelled artillery once the artillery battalions had landed to coordinate fires. They also performed some excellent amphibious end-around movements as the campaign progressed.[38]

This "last battle" of the Great Pacific War would see the final development of Marine Corps armored fighting-vehicle doctrine, equipment, and tactics. It seems appropriate to note the presence of several of the key pioneers who had determined the ways and means for the employment of these weapons by the Marine Corps. Maj. Gen. Pedro del Valle, commanding the 1st Marine Division, had provided schemes in 1940 for the first division-size units studied by the headquarters staff, thus providing for the tank and amphibian tractor battalions. The 6th Marine Division commander, General Shepherd, had argued forcefully before the MCEB of 1938–39 that the Corps adopt heavier tanks from army procurement programs. His assistant on that board had been Lieutenant Colonel Denig, the second officer assigned to the old 1st Tank Company and the second officer assigned to the Marmon-Herrington plant as the Marine Corps representative. Denig had taken the first tank company on wartime deployment, B Company, 2d Tank Battalion, to Samoa, and all of his platoon leaders had risen to command. Two of them fought alongside Denig in the Okinawa operation, as Lieutenant Colonel Stuart led 1st Tank Battalion and Lieutenant Colonel Metzger the 1st Armored Amphibian Battalion.

Alone of the Marine Corps tank battalions, the 1st Tank Battalion still operated its trusty old M4A2 diesel tanks. The very determined Lieutenant Colonel Stuart had convinced General del Valle to fight up the chain of command and resist the substitution of the gasoline-powered M4A3 ordered by the headquarters. The standing argument over gasoline versus diesel would not be resolved at Okinawa, however, as losses in each of the two Marine Corps and eight army tank battalions related more to the hitting power of the Japanese guns than the resistance of the M4 tanks. The marines at first ran wild to the north of the landing site. The 6th Marine Division, in particular, pushed reconnaissance troops riding on tanks up the roads toward Nago and the Motobu peninsula with abandon. The tanks and armored amphibians substituted often for the artillery, which fell behind on the extensive but primitive roads of the island. The

1st Marine Division cleared the central part of the island and was first called into the 10th Army lines in the south, where the Japanese commander had prepared the now doctrinal last-stand redoubt. The army divisions had been roughly handled in their initial assaults on the "Shuri Line" of advanced defensive positions prepared by the Japanese. In a single morning on 19 April, the 27th Infantry Division lost twenty-two of thirty tanks, four of them the valuable flamethrower tanks of the 713th Tank Battalion. Many had fallen victim to the Japanese close-assault tactics of their infantry. But a single 47mm gun killed four army Shermans with sixteen shots as they moved down a road in column. The enemy also showed vigor in counterattacks, and the 3d Armored Amphibian Battalion, occupying defensive positions on the east coast, smashed a Japanese amphibious end-around counterattack on 4 May. Both Marine Corps and army tankers had much work cut out for themselves in this battle.[39]

The III Amphibious Corps entered the decisive southern battles on 6 May, with the 1st Marine Division assaulting the Shuri Heights and the 6th taking on Sugar Loaf. Thus began a virtual repetition of the attrition battle for Iwo, except on a larger scale. Both Stuart and Denig had convinced their division commanders to abandon the old doctrine of attaching tank companies to infantry regiments for the bulk of the campaign. Instead, the tank battalion commanders responded to the division orders and the regiments' needs by detailing tank companies or platoons to them as required by the tactical situation and the status of the tank units. Thus, the tanks remained at all times under the tank unit commanders, who furnished "direct support" to the infantry each day, but continued to enjoy the better maintenance and logistic support of their parent battalions. Near the end of the battle, when the 8th Marines reinforced the 1st Marine Division, Stuart attached Capt. Ed Bale's A Company, 2d Tank Battalion, although it continued to furnish support to that regiment. Thus the tank battalion moved slightly closer in this battle to becoming a true combat unit, instead of a mere source of tank companies for the infantry regiments.[40]

Except for one major counteroffensive against the 10th Army on 25–26 May, the Japanese commanders husbanded their forces for maximum resistance, counterattacking only locally to throw out initial advances of the infantrymen. At Okinawa the Japanese even withdrew from their main line of resistance at the end of May, before it became completely untenable. The army and Marine Corps forces thus would have to attack a second line of resistance, defended by Japanese forces who were rested after their successful withdrawal under fire.

That withdrawal had uncovered the Oroku Peninsula, where the Japanese navy portion of the island garrison characteristically decided to stay and fight on its own base rather than joining the army in the south. Here the 6th Marine Division made an amphibious end-around, moving a regiment shore-to-shore in amtracs, preceded by the armored amphibians. The amtracs proved scarce for the operation, having been run continuously for supply missions with little to no maintenance. The combined battalions mustered only seventy-two ailing tractors for the operation, including twenty-nine vehicles and crews from an army battalion. With armored amphibians in the lead, this mixed LVT force landed the 4th and 29th Marines by repeated shuttling, with twenty-four tanks following in LCMs. The naval garrison resisted the 6th Division's attack for ten days before the tank-infantry teams wiped it out.[41]

In the attrition war for successive ridgelines fought by the soldiers and marines until 23 June, the tanks and flamethrower tanks pressed their weight wherever feasible or wherever roads could be hacked using bulldozers and tank dozers. Artillery and air support could seldom find or neutralize the Japanese positions for any amount of time. When the tanks could approach the enemy lines, they operated ahead of the infantry, but close enough to receive protective fire from squads assigned to cover each vehicle. This measure stymied the Japanese close assault squads from using their lethal mines and satchel charges. Other tanks "overwatched" from the heights, looking for the telltale smoke of an antitank gun firing on the advancing vehicles. Many times, the tankers thought that they had encountered a new Japanese "super" antitank gun, but it seems likely that they were simply finding the excellent Japanese 47mm gun in greater numbers, very ably sited and served by its gunners. The Japanese gunners used the more open terrain of Okinawa to create fire-traps where several guns could fire upon advancing armored vehicles, which received priority fire. The attacking forces also found a few naval guns in inland bunkers and these certainly menaced the tanks with their larger and more powerful projectiles. One Sherman of the 6th Tank Battalion on the Oroku Peninsula ran up against a Japanese eight-inch naval gun, which destroyed the tank with two mighty hits.[42]

In the 1st Tank Battalion, the standard tank-infantry attacks against the Japanese positions became known as "processing." Lieutenant Colonel Stuart explained that this most successful employment tactic

against enemy fortress defensive areas, has consisted of the point *destruction* of emplacements by tanks, covered by [infantry] fire teams prior to a general advance. Tanks range out to positions up to 800 yards beyond our front lines, destroying positions on forward *and reverse* slopes within that distance, chiefly by point 75mm gun fire (appropriate shell and fuze settings) at cave entrances, apertures, OP's and likely locations of same. In addition, tanks *destroy* in a similar fashion enemy direct fire positions on forward slopes for an additional 1500 yards to the front beyond the farthest point of tank advance. Repeated relays of tanks are necessary. This "processing" then permits the infantry to advance lines under cover of neutralization fires of all types some 500 yards forward with relatively light losses and hold the ground. The procedure is then repeated in a zone extended further to the front. Japanese close assault tank hunters in spider holes, etc., employing both thrown satchel charges and strapped-on suicide demolition charges (both covered by enemy smoke) have been repeatedly encountered and necessitated positive infantry coverage—most effectively provided by our superb infantry as evidenced by the fact that not a single tank while in action (not abandoned) has been stopped or destroyed by tank hunters during the Palau and Okinawa operations, in spite of enumerable and varied attempts.[43]

Near the end of the campaign, as the 1st Marine Division approached Kunishi Ridge, the tankers' "processing" activity ran up against one of the larger caliber guns in a concealed firing position, losing several tanks. Lieutenant Colonel Stuart sent his intelligence officer aloft on one of the light planes now plentiful on the island to swoop down into the valley at the precise time that a "bait" platoon of tanks descended the slope, covered by the remaining tanks of a company. The officer spotted the gun's position and talked the fire of the overwatch tanks onto it for the final kill. The 4th Tank Battalion had used such direct air reconnaissance to speed its drive southward on Tinian through the cane fields, and here on Okinawa the possibility of direct air observation support for tanks again appeared.[44]

On the Kunishi Ridge, marines made their most amazing and innovative use of tanks. Two infantry companies of the 7th Marines had silently moved up a portion of the ridgeline under cover of darkness on the morning of 12 June. The Japanese response pinned the companies and inflicted casualties, while blocking any reinforcement by tanks and infantry during the day. In absolute frustration the tankers turned to battle-taxi duty, strapping on loads of urgently needed supplies and carrying six riflemen crammed inside each vehicle (leaving behind the bow gunner) and driving up the fire-swept slopes to the trapped companies.

Three tanks made three runs each to deposit fifty-four replacements and bring out casualties, using the belly escape hatch to load and unload personnel at the top of the ridge. The next night the remainder of two battalions made it to the ridge, but the enemy remained underground and directed incoming mortar and artillery fire into the position. Stuart's tank battalion continued its daily efforts to sustain this ridge enclave and a similar foothold of the 1st Marines at a cost of twenty-two vehicles knocked out or damaged. During a week, the tanks lifted some 550 troops forward with 90 tons of ammunition, medical supplies, rations, water, and wire. They returned over 600 men to the rear in the same effort.[45]

When the mopping up began on Okinawa on 23 June, the American forces had already paid the highest price for any campaign yet conducted in the Pacific war. Yet the doctrine, tactics, techniques, and equipment of amphibious war and island fighting had proven most effective. Tank-infantry tactics continued to serve as the only recommended method of fighting the Japanese fortified zone, especially when reinforced by the highly successful Sherman flamethrower tanks. General Shepherd wrote in his afteraction report that "if any one supporting arm can be singled out as having contributed more than any others during the progress of the campaign, the tank would certainly be selected."[46]

Preparing the End Game
Most of the III Amphibious Corps redeployed to Guam to prepare for the invasion of Japan. Operations Olympic and Coronet, planned for November 1945 and March 1946, would have landed invasion armies on the Japanese home islands of Kyushu and Honshu, respectively. The Olympic plan called for landing V Amphibious Corps with the 2d, 3d and 5th Marine Divisions on the southwest coast of Kyushu to seize the major city of Sendai and link with army forces across the island to hold the southern third of the island, avoiding a fight for the rugged northern half. The III Amphibious Corps would join the U.S. 10th and 11th Armies for the final Coronet landing on the Kanto Plain and the prosecution of the war until a Japanese surrender came.

As part of its preparation for these massive operations, the FMF Pacific headquarters hosted a tank summit conference on Oahu to assess the experience to date of the Pacific war and to consider changes necessary for the invasions yet to come. Dubbed the Conference on Tank Matters, the meeting marked a watershed for the use of the armored fighting vehicle in the Marine Corps. Since the early days of the MCEB meetings at Quantico, the fighting vehicles had evolved in unforeseen ways and the troops and leaders had devised tactics and techniques for using them largely ad hoc, with the minimal assistance of the headquarters staff that authorized the weapons and organizations that the FMF would use. For the first time since the war's beginning, Marine Corps leaders formally took stock of the armored fighting vehicle and its potential tactical value and employment in the conditions of warfare in 1945.

The Tank Matters conference convened on 25 April, while the Battle for Okinawa still raged, and brought together representatives of most of the tank battalions and other staff and ordnance officers to discuss a wide variety of themes. The meeting produced a new FMF Pacific standing operating procedure (SOP) document for "Tank-Infantry Coordination," which they intended to be the Marine Corps doctrine supplementing the army's Field Manual 17-36. A new tank battalion organization took form, moving maintenance largely to the battalion headquarters and increasing the strength of each of the three tank companies to seventeen tanks, with three platoons of five tanks each. A thirteen-tank flame-tank company rounded out the proposed battalion. The tankers urged the procurement of the new army heavy tank, as the T26 was then classified, in view of the losses already credited to the Japanese 47mm antitank gun and infantry close assaults with shaped charge demolitions. They considered the 90mm cannon essential for cracking the fortifications of the present and future campaigns. Until such equipment reached the troops, the M4-series tanks needed to be armored according to a uniform scheme among all the battalions, with the add-on plating removable for crossing poor terrain. The Chemical Warfare Service demonstrated the new H-5 version of its flamethrower Sherman, which won universal praise since it retained the tank cannon and featured improvements in the flame system, although it also lacked a 360-degree traverse for the converted turret. The rest of the conference agenda covered myriad topics ranging from communications equipment and frequency assignment to landing-craft procedures.[47]

In the end, the Marine Corps accepted none of the recommendations of the conference. The flame-tank procurement needed no additional impetus and the replacement tanks being shipped to the battalions for the Japan landings would be, as noted above, the 105mm gun M4A3 medium. The new tank battalion organization approved by the commandant in May simply added three flame tanks to the existing medium-tank company. The new FMF SOP did standardize tactics for Marine Corps tank units, but few variations probably existed among the divisions in 1945. It called for the centralized control of tanks by the parent battalion once the amphibious assault had brought all the tanks ashore with the supported infantry regiments. But that control simply represented a dispatching methodology, where tank units would be assigned to infantry regiments day by day, according to tactical requirements signaled by the division staff. The SOP cautioned all concerned that

> limited command facilities, maintenance and service equipment and inadequate personnel practically precludes the possibility of Marine Corps tank battalions engaging in armored attacks as such. Lack of facilities for moving large infantry units to close support of an armored attack further precludes this possibility, except in missions far in advance of supporting infantry.[48]

Thus, the FMF doctrine limited the tank battalion to an infantry-support unit, much akin to the amtrac, artillery, and engineers that typically operated only in support of larger organizations.

But the field reports from the corps and divisions indicated increasing disgruntlement with the tank situation imposed by higher headquarters. Maj. Gen. Harry Schmidt, commanding the V Corps, warned that "the number of special-purpose tanks has been inadequate. The recently developed flame thrower as a primary weapon in the tank proved indispensable in the Iwo Jima operation. . . . Furthermore the tank dozer also proved indispensable for opening routes so that flame thrower and assault tanks could get into firing positions." He recommended including fifteen dozer and twelve flame tanks in each tank battalion of seventy-four total tanks. In a separate letter Schmidt attacked the 105mm gun tank as providing "neither an advantage of armor nor muzzle velocity and parallels the mission of the M7B1 [self-propelled 105mm howitzer] and LVTA's now available to divisions." He noted the unanimous desire of his corps representatives at the Tank Matters conference for the M26 tank mounting the 90mm gun. He called for the provisioning of the tank battalions with the M26 and, failing that, the issue of the newer M4A3 with the 76mm gun or the older 75mm version.[49]

Unmoved by these arguments, the commandant attempted to quell the dispute.

> Tanks mounting high-velocity weapons as primary armament as requested in reference [requesting the M26] are not available. . . . It is believed that if a requirement for a heavier tank such as the M26 is fore-

seen for a particular operation, that representation could be made to the theater or other appropriate commander for the attachment of supporting Army units equipped with the desired weapons.[50]

This message hardly mollified the field commanders, and the arrival on Okinawa of the first army M26s after the fighting was over there probably exacerbated the intensity of the debate. The FMFPAC commander attempted to find a middle ground when he advised his corps commanders that, although the commandant's message precluded any procurement of new tanks with 90mm and 76mm high-velocity guns, there would be enough older Shermans to distribute for the coming operations. Enough M4A2 and M4A3 tanks with 75mm cannon remained in San Francisco shipping lots to equip the V Corps for its next operation. The total of those tanks already in Pacific theater depots would further rehabilitate the 1st and 6th Tank Battalions. However, any other resupply or refurbishment activities would necessarily consist of 105mm gun tanks, of which 600 would pass through San Francisco shipping lots by the first day of 1946. He also promised that the first lot of sixty-eight of these tanks, which lacked power traverse and gyrostabilizers, would be rolled back for use as flamethrower tanks and engineer vehicles, and that all tanks provided for combat purposes would have these features.[51]

Gradually the rebellion subsided. The commander of the 3d Marine Division told the FMFPAC commander that the 105mm gun tank would be acceptable as a replacement for the M4A2 tanks he had, provided they came with power turrets, gyrostabilizers, and the new suspension systems of the late-production Shermans. His tank battalion commander, Lt. Col. Rowland L. Hall, requested that the tanks come with modifications: welding thirty-two track blocks to the turret and a one-inch steel bar surrounding the hull-side sponson and rear to support sandbags. "It is felt that the vulnerability of the present medium tanks to projectiles and explosive charges makes these modifications very necessary." Conversely, the commander of the 1st Marine Division continued to complain and "recommended that the entire field of Marine Corps tank matters be reviewed. This review should be conducted with the end in view of formulating policies which will radically strengthen the tank arm of infantry combat commands." In a manner reflecting the hand of Lieutenant Colonel Stuart, his letter to the commandant decried the new battalion organization as weakening the tank battalion and called for a battalion of four tank and one flame-tank companies as the minimum necessary for assault landings.[52]

Happily for all concerned, the U.S. forces never executed the planned assault landings on the home islands of Japan. Marine Corps divisions headed for occupation duty in Japan and China or home for demobilization. There would be no test of which version of the M4 medium tank functioned best in battle in 1945–46, and the new LVT3s and LVT(A)5s never had to challenge the best defenses of the Japanese home islands. Assessment of the huge changes wrought by the Pacific war upon the Marine Corps remained largely incomplete.

Troops of the 2d Marines train with a King armored car in Haiti in the mid-1920s. These first armored vehicles in the Marine Corps served to support the infantry after the disbanding of the Armored Car Squadron in 1920.

With the demise of the King cars, the M1917 tanks of the Renault pattern alone remained available for duty with the Marine Brigade in China. Note the marine at the gate providing ground guiding to the driver as the tank is unloaded from a barge at Tientsin, 1927.

Marines might have preferred an amphibious tank to support their landing forces, but the early technology, such as the Christie "tank" (really a tracked 75mm gun) landing administratively at Culebra Island in 1924, showed almost no promise. *(U.S. Naval Institute)*

Capt. Nathan E. Landon, commissioned from marine gunner rank in 1917, took the first Marine Corps armored fighting vehicle unit overseas, leading the Light Tank Platoon in its service at Tientsin, 1927–28.

After sporadic experiments, the Marine Corps thought that this would provide the necessary support to the fledgling Fleet Marine Corps: the Marmon-Herrington CTL-3, a five-ton "light fighting tank," landing from a standard navy thirty-eight-foot tank lighter in September 1939. *(U.S. Naval Institute)*

The first USMC tanks in action, though, would be army-type light tanks, such as this M2A4 (one of only thirty-six acquired) of A Company, 2d Tank Battalion, landing for duty with the 1st Provisional Marine Brigade organized around the 6th Marines to garrison Iceland in July 1941.

Most of the Marmon-Herringtons would end up in Samoa for (thankfully) peaceful duty with the defense forces there. This exceptional photo shows the tank park of the 1st Separate Tank Company at Tutuila: the rare turreted Marmon-Herrington CTM-3TBD tanks (five made) can be seen, behind the CTL-6 in the foreground. The tank to the left is an M3 army-type light tank.

After the early experiences in the Solomons, the Marine Corps ordered the improved M5A1 light tank into service with all tank battalions. The 1st Marine Division, still in Australia, drew its new tanks from army depots, however. Here an M5A1 of 1st Tank Battalion trains at Balcombe.

The tank destroyers of the regimental antitank platoons and division antitank companies engaged the first enemy tanks on Guadalcanal and provided assault gun services throughout the war. They can be regarded more as mobile artillery than armored fighting vehicles. However, the intense fighting of the Pacific war drew all such weapons into the close-in fight against the Japanese. These are M3 75mm GMC halftracks of the 1st Marine Division, July 1943.

The improved LVT2, the "Water Buffalo," would lead the light tanks ashore in the 1943 and early 1944 amphibious assaults. Redesigned by FMC Company from the original Roebling "Alligator," these amphibious tractors would be pressed into service as assault vehicles against the defenses of Japanese island garrisons.

The results of such assault missions proved all too deadly for the tractor crews and the assault troops. Despite its makeshift armor plating, this LVT2 of the 2d Amphibious Tractor Battalion came to grief on the reef at Tarawa, November 1943. Note the turret visible to the rear of a sunken M4A2 of C Company, 1st Corps Tank Battalion. *(U.S. Naval Institute)*

Part of the solution correcting the carnage experienced at Tarawa came with the introduction of the armored amphibian. Ungainly and thinly armored, the LVT(A)1 would provide light tank firepower at the water's edge to assist in suppressing enemy defenses until the tanks could land and spearhead the inland drive of the landing force.

Another lesson of Tarawa, the inadequacy of the light tank in island combat, led to the wholesale refitting of Marine Corps tank battalions with the M4A2 medium tank in 1944. Working in close support with infantry squads, the medium tank overcame all enemy weapons, and could be brought into action in rugged terrain with the support of bulldozers or tank-dozers. Here, tank C-22, named "Comer," of C Company, 2d Tank Battalion, leads troops through the cane fields of Tinian.

In more open terrain, the tanks would lead the way across the zone swept by enemy fire, the infantry covering by fire from the rear and rushing into the Japanese positions once entered by the tanks. Here, M4A1 tanks of A Company, 1st Tank Battalion, head into the jungle at New Britain, January 1944.

The tank-mounted flamethrower worked best on the M4-series tank, after several experiments with light tanks and LVTs had proven too limited. Here, the CWS-POA-H1 flame tank reduces enemy positions on Okinawa.

Arthur J. Stuart, here a colonel, was perhaps the ultimate thinker and *eminence gris* of the USMC armored fighting vehicle officers. His cogent ideas set the post-war USMC armor policy goals, which took decades for later generations to accomplish. His concepts for the advanced amphibious assault have been regenerated in today's future-force planning. Somehow, it all started with little M3 light tanks on "duty beyond the seas" with B Company, 2d Tank Battalion, in Samoa 1941.

A candid picture of two of the architects of the World War II armored vehicle force of the Marine Corps. On Okinawa the commanding general of the 6th Marine Division, Maj. Gen. Lemuel Shepherd (*left*), takes a driving lesson in an LVT(A)4 with Lt. Col. Louis Metzger, commanding officer of the 1st Armored Amphibian Battalion. Shepherd had steered the Corps toward procurement of army tanks in 1939, and Metzger formed and led the first LVT(A) unit through a full twenty-five months of the war, writing most of the armored amphibian doctrine in the process. (*Courtesy of Louis Metzger*)

The postwar Marine Corps continued to hone its skills by practicing assaults on this fortified beach assault course developed at Quantico, Virginia. Note the LVT3C and LVT(A)5 teamwork depicted. *(U.S. Naval Institute)*

Initially the postwar Marine Corps soldiered on with its now-vintage equipment. Here M4A3 (105mm) tanks and LVT4s of the 2d Marine Division parade for the commandant of the Marine Corps on 23 April 1948.

The bitter fighting of the Korean War was made more bearable by the dispatch of the Corps's slim inventory of M26 medium tanks, carefully husbanded in depot storage in the late 1940s for just such an occasion. With its heavy armor and 90mm cannon, the tank dominated any battlefield it could enter. Although roadbound over much of the campaign, it provided a measure of security for Marine Corps operations throughout the war.

With the coming of the Korean "emergency," the depot at Camp Barstow went into a crash program to refit tanks and amtracs for the new conflict. Here the tank section of the depot refurbishes M4A3 flame tanks after their lengthy storage from 1945, fitting all with the 105mm gun alongside the coaxial flame tube. In the rear are M26 tanks being readied for issue, notably less faded by desert storage conditions.

In the decade following the Korean War, the Corps began to embrace "lightness" in its order of battle. An unintended complement to that policy was the Ontos M50 antitank vehicle. Designed as a replacement for medium tanks in the regimental antitank companies, this self-propelled 106mm recoilless rifle carriage seemed just the thing to retain in a marine division devoid of tanks, amtracs, and heavy artillery after 1958.

In tandem with the post-Korea tank production came a new family of amtracs, the largest of all being the new armored amphibian, the LVTH6, mounting a stabilized 105mm howitzer on the hull of the LVTP5 amtrac. Amtrac pioneers like Louis Metzger and Victor Croizat warned against its ungainly size, but the performance of the vehicle, fitted with the standard tank engine and transmission, proved impressive and its carrying capacity in both troops and cargo remained unmatched.

Ironically, the sole heavy tank of the U.S. postwar tank program entered service at the same time as the diminutive "Ontos." The M103 series tank (M103A2 pictured), was perhaps the "ugly duckling" of the army tank program and accordingly received no name, in contrast to all other U.S. tanks. Only the Marine Corps introduced it in active service, loaning seventy-two of them to the army when the latter experienced a brief change of heart. Its enormous firepower and singular size and weight made it a favorite of its crews, despite the chiding in the tank park of the medium-tank crewmen.

The use of the LVTP5 as a personnel carrier ashore for rather large numbers of troops left the latter rather uncomfortable with their surroundings. Unable to see or employ weapons, the troops sat or stood on a floor lined with fuel cells filled with gasoline. Thus, most opted to ride the vehicle topside, with sandbags providing protection and weapons support. Here, LVTP5s of B Company, 1st Amphibious Tractor Battalion, carry troops of 2d Battalion, 4th Marines, near Dong Ha on 12 March 1968.

In contrast, the final medium tank of the post-Korea production effort, the M48, proved well suited to the Vietnam War, and continued its service well into the 1970s. Here an M48A3 occupies a hide position while supporting 2d Battalion, 4th Marines on 9 February 1968.

The last Marine Corps armored fighting vehicle procured before the beginning of the Vietnam War was the long-awaited engineer vehicle, the LVTE1. Fitted with a mine plow and rocket-propelled line charges, the engineer vehicle represented a key technical development for the amphibious landing against defended and fortified beaches.

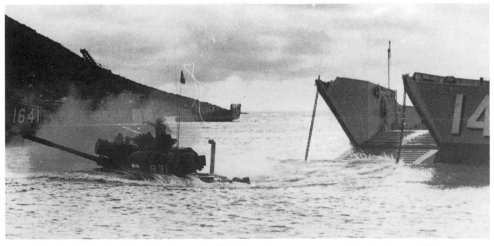

More simple fording gear permitted the tanks to remain in the forefront of the amphibious assault. The M48A3, pictured above, draws intake air through the turret hatches and requires only a thin exhaust stack to ford a depth of eight feet. A bilge pump and inflatable rubber grommet sealing the turret ring complete the ensemble. The tank is driving ashore from a navy landing craft at Capo Teulada, Sardinia, December 1970. *(Author's collection)*

The next family of amtracs to reach production proved highly successful. The LVT7 series saw a reduced size and a key use of water-jet propulsion to improve speed and handling in the water, as well as modern automotive components to boost land speed. The prototype LVTPX12, pictured here, sported a 20mm cannon that failed technical tests. The line charge apparatus would have been fitted to an engineer variant that fell on the chopping block of the budget.

The LVTP7 gave potential for employment of infantry in a mechanized tactical setting. However, the Corps remained resistant to adopting the doctrine and procedures that might have made it possible. Nevertheless, its handiness in mounting infantry, if only for amphibious landings, could not be denied. Here troops of the 31st MAU land on Iwo Jima, 5 May 1982.

The Persian Gulf conflict saw the last use of the M60-series tank by U.S. forces, as the Corps had only lately decided to convert to the newer M-1A1-series tank. This M60A1 sports the track-width mine plow and tows a rocket-propelled line charge in a trailer for overcoming hasty minefields during mobile operations. Mine-clearing equipment was among the last of the reforms demanded by Lieutenant Colonel Stewart's 1949 USMC Armor Policy Board to finally reach fruition.

Visions of "lightness" still dogged Marine Corps planners, however. In the mid-1970s, hopes ran high for the development of an eighteen-ton Mobile Protected Weapons System, which would furnish firepower to the marine division without the ensuing penalties of weight, bulk, and logistical burden. The AAI light tank, with its 75mm ARES high-velocity automatic cannon, was a late development of the concept, which failed in the face of improved main battle tank performance.

The interim mobile protected weapons system, the light armored vehicle (LAV) then became a weapon in its own right, spawning unit types and nascent concepts of a small, mobile, operational maneuver unit for the marine division. Here, LAV-25 vehicles depart an air-cushion landing craft on a beach in Thailand, May 1990.

The nature of the world threat and advancing armored vehicle technology in the end forced a strangely reluctant Marine Corps leadership to finally acquire the M1-series main battle tank in 1990. Almost too late for service in the Persian Gulf conflict, only six companies of these could be fielded. Here an M1A1 debarks a modern air-cushion landing craft (LCAC), a marked contrast with the Marmon-Herrington light tank exiting the navy landing craft in photo 5. *(U.S. Navy)*

For the near future, the running mate of the M1A1 will be the penultimate version of the now-venerable AAV-7 family, the AAV-7A1(RAM/RS). With improved power pack and suspension, it can handle the weight of increased armor appliqué kits and a larger weapons station, and still keep pace with the tank. For the twenty-one troops carried inside the vehicle, however, no set of doctrine or procedures prescribes how they might function as mounted infantry. The doctrinal match to the technological development still lags in the Marine Corps.

Much is expected from the medium-risk and high-technology advanced amphibious assault vehicle. With its high-speed skimming profile in water, it will carry its eighteen troops ashore from over-the-horizon shipping and act as a modern armored personnel carrier with laminate armor and NBC overpressure protection, and fight with its 30mm automatic cannon against a wide range of targets. The Marine Corps assembled fully engineered prototypes in 1999 and the vehicle will enter full production in 2008. Although touted for its role in the amphibious triad of AAAV-tilt-rotor aircraft–air cushion landing craft, the vehicle could just as easily prove the missing link for a fully developed doctrine and organization for mounted operations.

Chapter 6

Taking Stock, 1945–1950

> We Marines are inexperienced in antitank warfare. Unless we
> devote our attention to learn that which we haven't had the
> opportunity to learn by experience, it may cost us dearly the
> moment we engage a non-Japanese enemy. Some time
> between the final shot on Okinawa and the next D-Day of the
> future, we must learn how to stop hostile tanks.
>
> —Lt. Col. Arthur J. Stuart (1947)

> The American experience in World War II resulted in discarding
> the concept that the tank was an offensive weapon not
> intended for defensive combat against other tanks. The inabil-
> ity to find a feasible way to deploy tank destroyers led to their
> phasing out. From that point forward, it has been the U.S. Army
> mindset that the best and primary antitank weapon is another
> tank. This resulted in a "heavying" and upgunning of the
> American tank fleet.
>
> —Kris P. Thompson (1998)

Major Trends

Marines proudly recite their lore of ingenious preparation for the Pacific
war. Starting with the "prophecies" of Pete Ellis, the doctrinal evolution and early experimentation with landing operations of the 1920s
and 1930s led to the dedicated innovations leading into the first combat operations, after which lessons learned promptly became new doctrinal guidelines. Most of the events lend support to that legend only in
the most generalized manner. Numerous dead ends and frustrations led
to an astonishing range of directions pursued by the Corps leadership
and staff. The amazing transformation of the armored fighting vehicle
in the Marine Corps—from a mere novelty item to the weapon credited by General Shepherd as "having contributed more than any others" to the final campaign of the war—reflects well that phenomenon.

Shepherd himself had participated in the early quest for a "Marine
tank" that would provide the essential support to the infantry of the
landing force by knocking out defending machine guns at the beach,

and then assist the inland advance of the troops in manner not unlike that practiced in the last year of World War I. That Marine tank would weigh considerably less than those planned and produced for the U.S. Army, or any other army of the world, simply because the Marine Corps planned to fight island battles with little in the way of sustained combat operations after the landing operations had succeeded. In common with most military thinking of the late 1930s, the Marine Corps expected to use the antitank gun to deal with any tanks wielded by the enemy in such a brief campaign.

But World War II began as a European war, at least in the eyes of many Americans, and the early developments of that war impressed Marine Corps planners. Anticipating some employment against European opponents, the Corps ordered scout cars, motorcycles, and tank destroyers for a possible war of mobility. The army-type light tank had to be procured to find sufficient numbers to fill the tank battalions now considered necessary. Marines also bought large numbers of trucks and prime movers, which later languished on the docks, along with most of the scout cars, when the first units sailed into combat on board what few ships could be scraped up for the first "shoestring" operation.

The amphibian tractor, such a workhorse for the Pacific war, appeared first in the Marine Corps inventory as a cargo carrier. Marines pressed it into duty as an armored personnel carrier almost immediately, further developing it as an amphibious tank and later as floating, self-propelled artillery. The amtrac men of the division service troops passed into the ranks of assault troops all too quickly. They learned instinctively to add armor plating, how to fight their vehicles, and how to read the terrain and maneuver them through obstacles and avoid deadly antitank fire.

Curiously, the first offensive combat action of the Marine Corps, at Guadalcanal, followed closely the model landing envisioned in the deliberations of the Marine Corps Equipment Board in 1939. The light tanks fought a few machine guns opposing the landing, followed the troops inland, and served in counterattacks as necessary. The amphibian tractors brought cargo ashore and the 37mm antitank gun and the halftrack-mounted French 75s eliminated any tanks the enemy threw against them. Even the Bougainville landing of 1943, conducted at the end of the Solomons campaign, largely reaffirmed that doctrinal concept.

But the rest of the Pacific war waged by the Marine Corps exceeded the imagination of Ellis or any other thinker between the world wars. No one could have grasped the nature of "storm landings" against the meticulously fortified islands of the Japanese strategic defense perimeter, occupied by a fiercely determined enemy, capable of resisting beyond all perceived limits of human endurance. The ferocity of the great Pacific war almost defied the available military technology.

Just as the amphibian tractor changed in its Marine Corps role and mission, the tank, by late 1943, was fighting other tanks, antitank guns, and fixed fortifications. No longer used as independent units as at Guadalcanal, tank companies and platoons fought in close coordination with the infantry to blind, burn, and blast, "processing" the enemy-held territory yard by yard. By the war's end, demands for even larger and more powerful tanks came from tankers and senior commanders alike, including General Shepherd, who as a lieutenant colonel had urged the MCEB to abandon any notion of a peculiar light marine tank.

Ironically, the Japanese army and naval infantry followed the very lines of armored fighting-vehicle doctrine and development initially favored by the Corps in the 1930s: small, handy tanks for infantry support and trusting to the ubiquitous 37mm antitank gun for countering any enemy armor. U.S. Marines and soldiers had little difficulty in killing these smaller tanks with a variety of ground and mobile weapons in the war. By contrast, one can just imagine how well the CTL-6 light and CTM-3TBD improved model Marmon-Herringtons might have fared in the jungles of New Georgia and New Britain or at Tarawa, had the European war not stampeded the Corps to field army-type tanks.

The Postwar Marine Corps

The Japanese surrender announcement found most of the U.S. Marine Corps, then some 458,000 strong, deployed in the western Pacific with the III and V Amphibious Corps, the six divisions and four aircraft wings of Fleet Marine Force, Pacific (FMFPAC). Apart from demobilization concerns, their duties consisted of disarming Japanese forces and occupying parts of Japan and China. Postwar planning centered on a ready force of two divisions and two aircraft wings, plus corps troops, balanced between the East and West Coast bases, for duty primarily with the Atlantic and Pacific Fleets. Marines quickly terminated their occupation duties in Japan, but the deployments in China dragged on into early 1947. Nevertheless, by the end of 1946 barely 15,000 marines remained on the rolls of FMFPAC and an even smaller number in the fledgling FMFLANT.[1]

The Pacific war saw the refinement of amphibious doctrine and the expansion of the FMF far beyond the scope imagined by the planners and dreamers of the between-wars period. The amphibious tractor became the staple of the amphibious assault, spearheaded by its howitzer-armed and better-armored cousin, the armored amphibian. By mid-1945, three armored amphibian battalions and nine amphibian tractor battalions stood ready for the final assaults on Japan. The demobilization would leave only a skeletal battalion with one amtrac company and an LVT(A) platoon in each division, but the 10th, 11th and 12th Amtrac Battalions, each with an armored amphibian company included, would form on paper with the Marine Corps Reserve.

Some 18,621 amtracs had been produced during the war, but efforts to recover them from the western Pacific proved limited. Most were obsolete or worn out, and would be left for disposal in Marianas or Hawaiian staging bases. About 300 LVTs were shipped from Guam to the depot at Barstow, California. Several hundred more used navy opportune shipping from Oahu. Most recovered vehicles were of the latest LVT3 and LVT(A)5 types and the Barstow depot would retain about 1,500 amtracs by 1948, unfortunately in varied states of condition. Recovering the LVTs and a mountain of spares in Guam had required the temporary reactivation of the 1st Amtrac Battalion, under command of the redoubtable Lt. Col. Henry Lawrence, from May 1946 through June 1947. The last shipment from Guam to Barstow, ordered by headquarters in February 1949, liquidated an allotment of fifteen LVT(A)4 and seventy-four LVT3 vehicles apparently retained for a possible FMF presence in the western Pacific, fiscally impossible by then.[2]

Even the "local disposal" option of junking amtracs and tanks gave headaches to the headquarters staff. For example, the Corps sold two lots of unserviceable LVTs, 177 and 128 in number, to the Maui Boat and Yacht Club for the purpose of building a breakwater. Upon the failure to get the approval of authorities to dump them in the sea, the club attempted to resell them and then sold what little remained aboard them as salvage parts: seats, compasses, winches, radios, armor plate, and a few engines. Most of these last were old aircraft-type radial engines but a few twin Cadillacs came with the lots. The club paid one dollar per vehicle and realized about $14,000 gross sales from the salvage. The resulting investigation recommended tightened handling of the contracts.[3]

Tank units in the Marine Corps had endured rapid changes during the war in equipment and tactical employment. The light tank generally failed in the infantry support role so often demanded of it, and the light tank battalions and mixed battalions eventually gave way to medium battalions, six of which stood ready in their parent marine divisions for the final battles in 1945. The tank-infantry tactics evolving from the island battles of the Pacific stressed close support of squads of riflemen by individual tanks, and vice versa, the latter operating in platoons of four tanks each. By war's end, the flame-tank platoon of three vehicles had moved from the battalion structure to each medium tank company, reflecting its essential part in the tactical array. The medium tanks had proven unstoppable to all but the most desperate Japanese countermeasures and were widely credited within the Japanese army with unhinging the Japanese defensive doctrines. Although tied to the infantry support role, the tankers in the Corps still relished their independence to employ mobility and mass on the few possible occasions of the campaign: Roi-Namur, Guam, Tinian, and the planned but abortive airfield attack with three battalions on Iwo Jima.[4]

Unlike the development and production of the amtracs, performed for the Marine Corps by the Navy Bureau of Ships, the procurement of tanks by the Corps came to depend exclusively upon the army. Army production schedules and logistics support policies forced Marine Corps tank equipment decisions as early as 1944. The cherished twin-diesel M4A2 Shermans had to be replaced by gasoline-engine M4A3s rapidly, before the production line changed to the undesirable 76mm guns, simply to remain within army logistic support and design configuration policies. At war's end the marine tank fleet had to reequip with the M4A3 (105mm), as the army contracts shifted to production of the T-26 Pershing, keeping only the 105mm Sherman line open. Curiously, the advent of the M-24 caused the Corps to investigate once again the light tank, and ten were procured in 1945 for testing with a fording kit at Camp Pendleton for amphibious operations. They would remain in storage well after the Korean War.[5]

The recovery of tanks scattered throughout the western Pacific fared little better than that of the LVTs. An uneven flow of M4A2, M4A3, and self-propelled artillery M7B1 vehicles passed through Camp Pendleton. The M4A3 (105mm) remained standard issue for the postwar battalions, but the 2d Tank Battalion on the East Coast would have to make do with the M4A3 (75mm) drawn from local stores, as transportation funding shortfalls for the 105mm gun vehicles available in the West would delay transfer until 1947. More urgent was the requirement to ship tanks to North China, where the 1st and 6th Marine Divisions needed their tank battalions to better handle the incipient combat situation there. The platoons of 1st Tank Battalion fought some minor skirmishes with M4A3 tanks against Chinese forces well into 1946.[6]

The 75mm armed Sherman flame tanks of the CWS-POA-H1 and H5 designs were placed in storage, twenty-seven of them reconditioned for postwar requirements. By 1947 the Corps retained only two battalions of tanks, each of two companies, equipped with seventeen M4A3 (105mm) tanks and six flame tanks. The Marine Corps Reserve would form the 10th and 11th Tank Battalions.[7]

Training for the armored vehicles of the Corps crawled to a standstill after the war. The tank and LVT crewmen and mechanics courses were concentrated in a Tracked Vehicle School Battalion (later Company) at Camp Pendleton. In 1947 the school discontinued all courses except for LVT maintenance. Officer and NCO refresher courses conducted after war's end already had fallen aside. Many of the school personnel filled in deficiencies at the nearby 1st Amtrac Battalion, which then boasted only three officers and fifty-six men trained in the LVT. The postwar budget cuts had left little encouragement for the Corps at large, and the tracked vehicle units clearly bore their share of the impact.[8]

New equipment still concerned the Corps leadership, however, despite the clear lack of troops and operations funds. In a pattern to be duplicated almost every twenty-five years, the Corps obtained more modern tanks and LVTs and planned future organizations in midst of severe budget limitations. The LVT3 fleet, designed in 1943 and first used at Okinawa, clearly required design improvements. Following the swamping of several vehicles in Camp Pendleton exercises, a redesign was requested by the commandant in March 1948. The Bureau of Ships added 860 pounds of side armor, cargo covers, escape hatches, and a .30-caliber machine gun cupola, and extended the bow to improve buoyancy, resulting in the LVT3C. Continental's Prototype 2 won the design award, with minor modifications, and the commandant confirmed navy funds for the eventual rebuilding of 1,200 vehicles. A dedicated command vehicle, mounting a suite of five radios with an independent generator, first appeared with this LVT series. The Long Beach Naval Shipyard began work on the project, but after the first 50 LVT3Cs came off the line, the navy closed the shipyard and shifted the work to the San Francisco Naval Shipyard for the rest of the project, over the commandant's protest, starting in July of 1950. This interruption proved most untimely for the Korean War outbreak, as in so many other matters.[9]

The tank modernization proceeded from the twin pillars of dependency on army initiatives and the unchallenged Marine Corps recognition that the tank held as crucial a role on the battlefield of the future as it had in defeating the Japanese garrisons in the Pacific. In March 1946 the director of Marine Corps Schools warned the commandant of the prevailing views.

> In general, the tanks with which the Marine Divisions ended the war are now definitely obsolete. The tank for the future must be capable of withstanding greater punishment, be more mobile, and have improved hitting power. The present tanks are too slow and too vulnerable to antitank weapons.[10]

Actually, the commandant had already ordered the purchase of ninety-one M26 Pershing tanks in late 1945 under the FY 1948 budget. The same commandant earlier had withheld this tank from his Pacific war commanders planning the invasion of Japan. The 46-ton M26 medium (originally classified as a heavy) tank, mounting the excellent 90mm gun, was slow in reaching the FMF because of frequent budget reductions, which was partially rectified by supplementary appropriations and congressionally forced transfers from excess army stocks. Tankers liked its four to four and a half inches of frontal armor, but the reworked Sherman engine left this tank seriously underpowered. Thanks to the wartime acquisition of the 90mm antiaircraft gun as standard, the Corps had plenty of ammunition on hand for this tank, except for the M304 high-velocity armor-piercing (HVAP) round. The M26 tank entered service at this point as a mixed blessing, however. While introducing the excellent torsion-bar suspension, its fording gear required much local welding and reworking to function, and the transmissions and controlled differential steering units gave pause to marine tankers accustomed to their handy and robust Shermans. In the words of one veteran tanker,

> The M26 was a bastard! The engine was the same Ford 500 HP that was in the M4A3E8, it was under powered and the steering was done the same as the M4's, pull the levers with "brute" strength, good way to build the arms and upper body. There were NO dual controls and it was driven from the left side. There was no PIVOT and it took at least 60' to turn in. The engine was water cooled and had fan belts that would flex when shifting up or down. Yes shifting; the transmission was like fluid drive and a lever had to be moved very slowly so as not to jerk the transmission causing the flexing to dump the fan belts and the engine would overheat in seconds. Once your driver learned to shift up and down without loosing belts he would drive all day every day. We had live track with steel to the ground, good in dirt or mud, but hit cement in a turn and it was sliding to the flank

that made the heart jump, no fear of turning it over but running over the locals standing along side the road. On one long road march that went into the late night one of "A" company [1st Tank Battalion, Korea] tanks went sliding around a corner and took out a building and squashed one young kid, I helped pull the kid free but he was dead. Live track is more flexible in that it has a pin with rubber bushings that are very hard to remove. No end connector to pound on. When hitting a land mine the road wheels were blown away and more than likely the track would not be badly hurt. Fighting on a railroad track we backed off and pulled forward taking a 20' length of track with us for a very short way and it ripped the [M26] track but not enough to keep us from operating.[11]

In 1948 the commandant authorized the M26 to be placed in service in the two tank battalions as a special training allowance. The five tanks in each battalion could be used therefore for training purposes limited to special exercises, experiments, and demonstrations. Crew training on these vehicles permitted the planned use of the M26 in wartime emergency without wearing them out and expending parts with normal peacetime use. It was not to be used in amphibious operations, landing exercises, or maneuvers except by CMC authorization. The new commandant, Gen. Clifton B. Cates, rescinded this stricture only in late 1949, after the staff was satisfied that the battalions had sufficient experience with the tank. The 2d Tank Battalion received an extra platoon, with an eye to European contingencies requiring a heavier tank. The whole question of fielding a heavy tank already bothered many officers on the headquarters staff. Nor did the M26 make sense to some officers as a medium tank. In the spring of 1949 the commandant rejected the M-46, a conversion of the M26 featuring a superior engine, as not economical and an insufficient improvement. The staff considered a retrofit of the M-4s with the higher velocity 76mm gun. Internal memos expressed doubts about the M26 by the Corps's leadership in wake of an army offer of additional M26s in late 1949. The staff noted that

> CMC desires [that the] Heavy Tank requirement be broached in connection with [the] FY51 budget and [that the] M26 cannot be classified as "substitute heavy tank" at present.
>
> It is understood that [the] Marine Corps is only tentatively committed to the procurement of these additional tanks. It is requested that procurement not be finalized pending final determination of desirability of expenditure of funds for this equipment.

As soon as the T42 and T43 are in production, and if they prove superior to the M26, we should undertake to re-equip the Marine Corps with these tanks.[12]

Still, the commander of the 2d Tank Battalion, Lieutenant Colonel Denig, had asked in late 1948 that he be allowed to swap more of his authorized M4A3 for M26 tanks to facilitate the rotation of the better tanks on the now-standard Mediterranean battalion landing team deployments. With only two line companies in each tank battalion, the five M26 per company permitted little slack in operations.

At the end of 1949 the 102 M26 tanks in possession of the Corps mostly lay in the hands of depot personnel:

Camp Lejeune 37 (most in local depot storage)
Quantico 5
Barstow 55
Camp Pendleton 5[13]

In addition, the operating conditions for Marine Corps tankers seldom matched those of their army counterparts. Not only did tanks doctrinally remain shackled to infantry support missions, but the efforts of facilities engineers (and, later, environmentalists) posed problems. In October of 1948 the California Department of Public Works forbade the transport of either M26 or M4A3 (105mm) tanks on tank transporters between Camp Pendleton and San Diego. The last and most-feared quartermaster of the Marine Corps, Maj. Gen. W.P.T. Hill, ordered that tracked vehicles keep off of base roads, even in the training areas.

It is the policy of the Marine Corps not to operate tanks on paved roads, road shoulders or drainage structures. Where necessary to follow the direction of a road, parallel tank trains shall be used and where necessary to cross paved roads, concrete tank crossings shall be constructed.[14]

Marine Corps doctrine for the amtrac and the tank continued to reflect the experience of the Pacific war. The Amphibious Operations series of manuals were published during 1945–48 by the Marine Corps Schools as compendiums of that experience and guidelines for future operations. Most were focused on specific functions or units, including the *Employment of Tanks (Phib-18)* and *The LVT and LVT(A) (Phib-23)*. Each of these prescribed training, embarkation, ship-to-shore movement, and employment following the landing. The tanks were to support the infantry ashore, anchor the antimechanized defense, and provide specialized vehicles such as tank dozers and flame tanks to reduce field fortifications. A single page devoted to mechanized attack permitted the free use of tanks when terrain and enemy situation permitted. The amtracs executed typical wave movements against an enemy beach, with armored amphibians leading and providing last-minute suppressive fires. After landing the assault waves, the amtracs reverted to ship-to-shore resupply tasks and the armored amphibians furnished direct fire support as assault guns until the tanks landed, thereafter reverting to reinforcing artillery batteries for the remainder of the battle. These publications were converted with little change into the Landing Force Manual series of the 1950s and the Fleet Marine Force Manuals of the 1960s through the late 1970s (LFM 17 and FMFM 9-2 for *Amphibian Vehicles,* LFM 14 and FMFM 9-1 for *Tank Employment,* although the army FM-17 series was commended for tanks in land warfare). Not until 1981 would Marine Corps doctrinal publications outline task organizations for armored operations on a par with the army combined arms concepts of armored infantry and armor companies with appropriate attachments and supporting arms.

The doctrine for the armored amphibian reflected the seminal influence of Lt. Col. Louis Metzger. His final standing battalion order for operations for the 1st Armored Amphibian Battalion specified that these vehicles would first cover the ship-to-shore movement of the assault troops and advance no more than 100 yards inland. As assault guns, they would then move another 1,000 yards in support of the infantry, but no farther, since the high-silhouette, mechanical, and armor weaknesses rendered them too vulnerable. The final mission would have the platoons fire artillery missions for the infantry forward observers until the artillery had landed, whence the entire battalion would report for operations to the senior artillery commander. These precepts, repeated in the doctrinal publications noted above, endured the entire life of this vehicle type, until they were finally discarded in the 1970s. Doctrine seldom emerges from a single individual effort, but the officers of the 1942 B Company, 2d Tank Battalion proved very exceptional.[15]

Major General Shepherd reported to the commandant on the 2d Marine Division's amphibious landing exercise at Culebra Island in 1947. After watching the 8th Marines land, followed by A Company, 2d Tank Battalion an hour and a half later, he stated, "the time tanks should be brought ashore has always been subject to differences of opinion. I personally believe they should be landed as soon after the assault waves as possible, in order to provide direct support to the infantry during the most critical part of the landing." He also noted that the tank battalion still used M4A3 (75mm) tanks.[16]

Observing similar 2d Division exercises at Camp Lejeune in early 1950, amphibious expert Col. E. R. Smock wrote that tank units only had tank dozers for use in overcoming barriers. The need for more countermine and counterbarrier equipment could not be overstated. However, the use of tanks as independent units earned no praise from him. "I am becoming increasingly concerned by the growing tendency of tank officers to seek means of breaking away from and discrediting the battle-tested and proved tank-infantry team and the employment of tanks in providing direct fires in support of infantry units." He also faulted the infantry for letting LVT commanders direct their vehicles across inland waterway crossings, describing them as roaming along looking for landing sites instead of allowing the infantry commanders to direct the vehicle movement and disembarkation on the other side.[17]

The tank in the postwar Marine Corps came to represent the premier antitank weapon. Although the Corps at first copied the army's tank destroyer concept in the early days of World War II, the M3 GMC represented the sole procurement and it served mostly as an assault gun although it was issued to the antitank company of the infantry regiment and the special weapons battalion of the wartime division. Hopelessly obsolete in 1944, it had been replaced by the M7B1 self-propelled 105mm howitzer. The Corps had formed one antitank battalion during World War II, the 2d Antitank Battalion, but it never saw active service. In the postwar infantry regiment, the antitank company formed with two platoons. Of these two platoons, only the antitank gun platoon was manned in peacetime, its incredibly obsolete 37mm guns giving way at last to 75mm recoilless rifles. The tank platoon of five medium tanks remained on paper as a wartime organization. This structure remained in the division through 1957. Only during the Korean War did the regimental tank platoons enter service. Some leaders voiced opinions leaning toward retaining the tank destroyer doctrine. Major General Schmidt noted that some of his commanders favored the 57mm recoilless rifle as the replacement for the ancient 37mm guns. But he considered the 57mm to be primarily a bunker-buster for the infantry and only secondarily an antitank weapon. He advocated the 57mm gun or 75mm recoilless rifle as the AT gun of the future, so that the jeep could continue as the prime mover. But the future AT company would also require a 90mm or 76mm gun tank-destroyer platoon plus two towed-gun platoons.[18]

Assessing Future Prospects

Concerns over the medium and heavy tanks and the antitank weapons of the future necessarily reflected the war planning of the period. Although the Corps continued to form the naval infantry of the U.S. Navy, its wartime expansion and service with the field armies and corps of the U.S. Army left no doubt in the minds of its leadership that the service would fight in any continental conflict involving the United States and the Soviet Union. Postwar war plans emerged slowly as the tensions in Europe coalesced. In 1947 planning focused on the first twelve to eighteen months of a general war with the USSR. The outnumbered allied forces would have to defend strategic redoubts like the Iberian Peninsula, Sicily, the Middle East, and Japan, while occupying Iceland, Greenland, and the Azores. An eventual air and amphibious offensive, based upon the Suez-Cairo region, would attack the USSR in the event that the atomic air offensive failed and a long-term war ensued. By 1948 details of this concept included sending a marine division and an army infantry division to Sicily. The first strategic offensive would launch eight British and twelve American divisions into the Persian Gulf, aimed at recovering the oilfields. Further work increased the number of U.S. divisions to eighteen. These offensive moves included specific and implied Marine Corps tasks which undoubtedly placed them into direct conflict with the first-line units of the Red Army.[19]

By the end of 1949, a new series of war plans deployed Marine Corps units to Iceland, the Azores, and North Africa, building a divisional amphibious force in the Casablanca enclave within the first year. The eventual amphibious assault to retake Europe would require forty-two U.S. divisions landing in both the Mediterranean and northwest Europe. This plan remained in effect through 1951 and the continued planning of the following decades only reiterated the European alignment of Marine Corps mobilization and deployment.[20]

This European orientation for future wars proved demanding enough for the Marine Corps, but posed particularly bad news for its tank arm. Instead of the occasional charge by scattered tankettes of the Japanese army, Marine Corps tankers would have to face the seasoned mechanized breakthrough doctrine of the Red Army and defeat its medium tanks and assault guns, backed up by the much-feared JS-3 heavy tank, with its alarming eight inches of well-sloped frontal armor and 122mm cannon.

One of the first alarms sounded came in the work of Lieutenant Colonel Stuart. We recall his protests to General Vandegrift's decisions in the wake of the Tank Matters conference of 1945, when his commanding general's letter "recommended that the entire field of Marine Corps tank matters be reviewed. This review should be conducted with the end in view of formulating policies which will radically strengthen the tank arm of infantry combat commands."

After the war "Jeb" (the inevitable nickname) Stuart served on several future studies boards and taught at Quantico before reporting to the Plans and Policies Division as a staff officer as the "duty tank and amtrac officer," serving there until 1952. He wrote an especially thoughtful series of articles for the *Marine Corps Gazette* in 1947–50 which demonstrated not only a growing intellect but also an unusual prescience in amphibious theory. His serious conviction that the Corps had to make better use of modern tanks and consider the tank strength of its enemies, especially the USSR, led him to reassess the amphibious operation. His instincts told him that the amphibious operation needed to become more mechanized and its focus needed to shift from beach landings to inland maneuver. His amphibious concepts anticipated the institutional thinking of the Corps by almost fifty years.

Stuart's "We Must Learn to Stop Tanks" (October 1947) recalls his assessment of the Battle for Peleliu and how the battle against Japanese tankettes could have gone very badly against modern armor.

> We Marines are inexperienced in antitank warfare. Unless we devote our attention to learn that which we haven't had the opportunity to learn by experience, it may cost us dearly the moment we engage a non-Japanese enemy. Some time between the final shot on Okinawa and the next D-Day of the future, we must learn how to stop hostile tanks.
>
> This serious deficiency in our combat experience and fighting knowledge has come about naturally enough. Our erstwhile Pacific enemy injected many new weapons and tactics into the fight; but tanks worthy of the name and armored tactics were not among them.
>
> . . . We face a military world strong in armor. If the other fellow has that with which he can hurt us badly, then, it has always been the Marine way to learn his game and beat him at it. The other fellow has tanks and we have to learn how to stop them.
>
> We have got to study the thing we must learn to stop, the strong coordinated tank attack. It is an attack inherently characterized by

suddenness, surprise and great power. Tanks can be concentrated relatively quickly for the tank attack or the counterattack. They will be concentrated at the point of the enemy's selection. The attack will come on a relatively narrow front and its decisive phases will be of relatively short duration. It will often be preceded by artillery and aerial bombardment. The hostile tanks will be followed by infantry, and assisted by infantry weapons . . . direct support artillery and aviation. Tanks themselves will concentrate their tremendous firepower on our forces at the point of contact. . . .

In active antitank defense, each arm must develop streamlined time saving techniques specifically designed to be most effective against the hostile tank attack . . . to achieve near-automatic performance.

Such antitank weapons as infantry possess . . . have severe limitations. Although they are tank killers on the proving ground, they have three weaknesses: they are manned by exposed personnel; they are direct fire and so can be observed and their fire returned; and finally, in the normal infantry defense there aren't enough of them at any one place and they have such limited battlefield mobility that they can seldom be moved to oppose a tank attack after its commencement.

Our tanks must be flexibly employed in strength, for here again, a little is not enough. We must devise a doctrine for control of our tanks in antitank defense at division, corps, or at the very highest workable level, in order that we can counter-concentrate sufficient strength to meet and destroy the hostile tank concentration.

In all the history of antitank warfare the error most consistently and frequently recurrent is failure to bridge the gap between the proving ground or theoretical weapons capability and their actual capabilities *in the face of and under the conditions of hostile tank attack.* . . . The antitank functioning of the several arms must be shockproof. It must have staying power. . . . The problem is to prevent a breakdown in the antitank functioning of the several arms during the very period that it is so vital that they function. . . . We must eliminate the frequent and almost fatal miscalculation of the past between the theoretical and the practical. The necessity of keeping this important factor ever in mind in antitank warfare can not be over-emphasized.

We must achieve the coordination of the antitank roles of all arms. Thus the antitank roles of tanks, infantry, aviation, artillery and the passive antitank functions of engineers must be carefully coordinated into one integrated defensive system.

We saw the enemy fall helpless before the guns and flame of our tanks. We know the tank is inherently designed to strike without being struck. It is a weapon which very definitely requires a defense against it, with the cost of failure annihilation. Against the Japanese we had a virtual monopoly of these powerful weapons. That is no longer the case.

The study of antitank defense led inextricably to the amphibious assault itself, and here Stuart saw a weak system at work. In his "Strengthen the Beach Assault" (August 1948) he stated:

Our amphibious doctrine in World War II, so successful and so superior to that of World War I, had this one great weakness. It employed infantry, supported only by armored amphibians, to assault the hostile beach. The armored amphibian was designed to fight waterborne, and it was altogether invaluable in its primary role of leading assault infantry ashore and destroying or neutralizing hostile beachline weapons commanding the boat lanes. However, once infantry had disembarked and moved across the sands of the beaches, the assault amphibians' designed role was over and it ceased to have any major significance as a supporting arm. Once the assault infantryman of the last war had crossed the foreshore, he *stood essentially alone* for a very definite period of an hour or more until effective fire support was built up ashore. Infantry, realizing its limited offensive power while still unsupported, avoided initiation of other than the most urgent assault action and generally but sought to hold on and cover the landing of tanks, naval gunfire and air support agencies, and artillery. The general concept was thus to wait until the landing of support before undertaking serious assault action beyond the beachline. . . .

Thus the success of our beach assaults must properly be attributed more to *the efficacy of these extraordinary measures to insure the enemy's local weakness* by intense preparatory bombardment and effective isolation of the landing area—*rather than to the power of our own initial assault.* However, the margin of success in many cases was dangerously slender, and the price was often exceedingly high.

In the beach assault, as always in warfare, it is *fundamentally dangerous* to depend upon hostile weakness.

Even if hostile reactions not encountered in the Pacific could be ruled out, it would still remain highly desirable that we utilize the time now available to us to develop a combined arms beach assault commencing at H-hour. The forward movement of the assault would then *never* stop but would continue inland *rapidly* to seize key terrain and observation commanding the landing area. Exposure to observed indirect fires would be shortened, at the same time rapidly gaining dispersal room ashore for following landing waves. The combined arms assault is the surest way of preventing the assault becoming bogged in a narrow strip along the beaches for hours and days, without adequate dispersion and more or less at the mercy of hostile fires—which cost us dearly on occasion during the recent war. The combined arms attack is *the best insurance that early hostile counterattacks can be beaten off* of whatever type.

. . . The proper timing of the landing of tanks is simply resolved— *they must be landed in strength with the assault.* Therefore, to strengthen our beach assault, we must not only have more tanks, but we must land them in *their normal assault formation* where they are most effective—with or slightly preceding assaulting infantry, not an hour or more later!

There are really no insurmountable difficulties preventing the landing of tanks in the first assault waves. . . . Less than a fraction of one per cent of the hundreds of Marine tanks landed during the Pacific War were lost through destruction of tank landing craft. Covered by pre-H-hour bombardments, there seems to be really no reason why suitably designed tank landing craft cannot land in the first or any assault wave.

Thus, we can, and must substitute the tank-infantry assault for the infantry assault in amphibious operations. This is the most urgent, and perhaps the easiest, step in achieving a combined arms beach assault.

. . . *Everything must be tried, and the solution somehow found, so that artillery, like all arms in the amphibious assault, can participate in and support the beach assault.* If conventional artillery cannot in this sense be made amphibious, then we must *develop a new type of artillery!*

The question of providing infantry with armored carriers should be *carefully studied as a means of protection against the VT fuze.* Such carriers should probably be of the smaller improved LVT type with all-around splinter-proof armor. While it is hardly conceivable that infantry can fight solely from carriers, *it can, and may have to, fight in and out of such carriers.*

In conclusion, *the* simple truth that the strength of the *whole is greater than any of its parts dictates replacement of the infantry beach assault by the combined arms beach assault.* This is indisputable, and the only valid question is practicability of realization.

By 1949 Stuart had decided upon what today's doctrine writers call the "seamless maneuver from ship to objective," which he had called the previous year a "combined arms assault . . . [which] would then never stop but would continue inland rapidly." He developed that concept in a two-part article, "Mechanization of the Amphibious Attack" (July and August 1949). We can read here a progenitor of the modern amphibious theory, less the undreamed-of vertical assault possibilities that only later made practical sense with modern helicopters.

Apart from conventional and atomic aerial bombardment . . . World War II produced three major innovations in warfare—the mechanized attack, the amphibious attack, and the airborne attack. . . . It is not at all surprising that the next step, integration, was not achieved. World War II was too short to produce in anything resembling integral form either the amphibious-airborne attack, the airborne-mechanized attack, or the amphibious-mechanized attack. Nevertheless, such integration is logical and is clearly indicated for the future. There are indeed great possibilities in the cross-breeding of these three types.

Both geography and current military trends abroad indicate that defense against amphibious attack will be mobile rather than a fixed infantry beach-line defense. The military world has seen the consistent defeat of the fixed infantry waterline defense, and has had ample opportunity to note its ineffectiveness in stopping the amphibious attack. Yet, if any future enemy had not learned that lesson, simple geography would largely preclude its use in theaters involving coasts hundreds or thousands of miles long. Linear coastal defense would require prohibitive dispersion and dissipation of strength. The mobile defense built around armor, artillery, and aviation is logical from every consideration. *It is so logical that it must be anticipated and its impact on the amphibious attack carefully evaluated now.*

The amphibious attack of the past is geared too slow to cope with the geographic time and space factors of future amphibious theaters. It is poorly adapted to cope with the most probable type of enemy defense. The issue of battle is always decided, in the absolute sense, by the determinants of fire power and its control, or, in short—*by fire*. If an enemy can effect a more rapid build-up of firepower at the landing area, the amphibious attack *will inevitably be defeated* and be thrown back into the sea. Just as certainly, if at any time during or after a landing the enemy can bring to bear equal (or even inferior) forces of greater mobility—the landing force faces the same fate through defeat in detail.

Something, then, must be done about the amphibious attack. It cannot remain frozen in its World War II form, despite brilliant success under World War II conditions. If it is to cope with a mobile defense, its tempo must be stepped up so that objectives can be seized prior to the build-up of the enemy's forces even though they be highly mobile. Final beachhead lines, key terrain features—all will have to be seized much more rapidly than hitherto. This cannot be done by infantry attacks; foot infantry simply cannot move rapidly enough. But it can be done by mechanized attack.

To pursue this concept further, the enemy's problems of defense in land warfare would immediately be multiplied. In the past the enemy could establish a continuous defensive zone in depth, echelon reserves and otherwise concentrate his forces to advantage along a linear front. However, it would be manifestly impossible for him to achieve any such coordinated defensive strength also along his entire coastline. Thus the threat of sudden mechanized (or even infantry) attack in flank or rear from "beachheads which weren't there the day before" would pose for the enemy an extremely difficult problem.

So if the success of the future mechanized land offensive depends so largely upon gaining the hostile rear as it has in the past, exploitation of amphibious mobility as described could not but result in great new advantage. As offensive armor thus increased its mobility, defense against it would proportionately become more difficult. The lightning amphibious seizure of beachheads by mechanized landing forces is thus a major potential corollary of the mechanized land offensive.

All general characteristics of amphibious and mechanized combat support and favor the realization of the amphibious-mechanized attack. The beach assault always has been, and always must be, launched against defenses weak at the time of assault—weak either as a result of surprise effect or through reduction by pre-landing bombardment. In land warfare the mechanized attack has been most successful against weak defenses. The essential conditions for successful mechanized action in respect to immediate hostile capabilities thus already exist in the amphibious attack. Denial of the air to the enemy is already a requisite of the amphibious attack. It is highly favorable, if not essential, to successful mechanized action. The amphibious assault depends on overwhelming power for success, as does the mechanized assault. Very strong air and naval gunfire support is available to the amphibious landing force; vehicle-borne forward observers and limited modification of control techniques are all that is needed to adapt this support to the increased tactical mobility of a mechanized landing force. Thus, the major over-all conditions essential to success exist with remarkable similarity in the mechanized and amphibious forms of attack.

The fully mechanized landing attack is an entirely practical development within the general framework of amphibious and mechanized tactics and employing standard materiel—although some modification of techniques and certain improvement of materiel is desirable.

Just as the landing force successfully adapted infantry tactics to amphibious warfare the mechanized amphibious attack can be developed most logically through the adaptation of proven mechanized doctrine.

The zone of intelligence coverage must be deepened inland and primary intelligence effort focused on the following:

1. *The hostile antitank defense (and mobile reserves)—including location, nature, and strength and*
2. *Terrain considerations—particularly trafficability, vehicular cover, and vehicular concealment.*

A continuous landing beach is not necessary and the location of inland objectives and the nature and trafficability of beach and terrain inland may dictate several separate landings. However, landings should be in general proximity to each other to provide mutual support; also, so that success and breakthrough inland anywhere will at once outflank and render untenable hostile positions which might be holding up the attack in other landing areas.

The ship-to-shore movement would be greatly accelerated as a result of mechanized passage of the beach and mechanized assault inland. If a ten-knot speed on water and land was achieved, good vehicular dispersion could be obtained by a one-minute interval (300-odd yards distance) between waves. Even with slower speeds and greater interval a powerful force could be landed in the first hour, a far greater force than during the entire first day of past landings. With this sharp speed-up of the attack two alternatives become possible. The assault waves could continue inland beyond initial beach objectives, pushing out reconnaissance and varying formation in accordance with previous plans and the unfolding situation to seize inland (final) objectives, leaving for following waves the task of screening and defense of the landing area. Or, initial assault groups could establish the landing area screen by fanning out inland to seize dominating and protective terrain, with following task forces making the main thrust inland. In either case, both the establishment of the landing area screen and attack inland would be executed almost simultaneously, and the choice of method and sequence would hinge largely on local conditions. If the initial assault group established the landing area screen, tank units and other heavy elements not required for its maintenance could be shifted to task forces driving inland. If later waves established the screen they could be specially composed as required.

. . . Only sufficient strength should be deployed in the assault to insure the positive and rapid overrunning of beach defenses and directly opposing hostile positions without risk of failure or delay. The remainder of the landing force should be landed as balanced tactical units prepared for instant action . . . disposed as required to execute planned missions inland, and they would follow or pass through, reinforce or be reinforced by assault groups as planned to accomplish the drive inland.

. . . However, regroupment should be minimum and insofar as possible, preplanned.

The mechanized amphibious attack is entirely feasible logistically. Shipping of required types exists today in sufficient quantity to land powerful mechanized landing forces. Shipping of *more efficient* types could be constructed on a war basis in much greater quantity. Supply requirements would be heavy *but could be met.* A future beachhead of 25 mile depth probably could be seized without refueling assault vehicles, being well within the fighting radius of modern combat vehicles. With surprise and speed drastically reducing the enemy's capability of reaction, it is likely that most assault units could seize final objectives without rearmament. However, at least sufficient fuel and ammunition for a single complete servicing and rearmament of all equipment should be embarked, mobile-loaded, and landed immediately after follow-up troops to provide supplies as required *to complete the seizure of the beachhead* and for prompt servicing of combat vehicles to ready them for beachhead defense.

. . . Certain materiel improvements are clearly needed. Improved tank flotation devices are desirable to give greater water-borne tank speed and maneuverability. A completely new armored amphibious carrier of greater speed on water, vastly improved performance on land, and with all-around splinter-proof armor—to replace the amphibian tractor and most if not all wheeled vehicles of combat units—is next in importance.

Although the mechanized landing force is entirely within our capability of attainment, we must avoid three principal pitfalls. First, total mechanization is essential, for any dismounted element slows the entire force, any unarmored element exposed to destruction of neutralization jeopardizes the balance and effectiveness of the whole force. Second, there is the *danger of compromise or hedging;* a weak, faltering mechanized attack can only result in certain and costly failure. Finally, although mechanized tactics and techniques of combat are clearly defined, they are *complex in detail* and require the comprehensive training of all ranks and all arms to achieve the coordinated, near automatic teamwork at troops level. To give good troops good equipment will not be enough; mastery of vehicular combat including precision fire and maneuver—long established requisites of successful mechanized action—can be achieved only *through thorough and detailed individual and unit training* with full equipment in conjunction with all other partners of the armored team.

The advent of the Korean War cut short any more developments of these themes by Lieutenant Colonel Stuart, who immediately had to deal with the 1950 tank crisis as well as the amtrac modernization and replacement and the problems of antitank weapons development. However, his thoughts on "The Beach Minefield" had already been accepted for the October 1950 issue of the *Gazette*. In it, he studied another of the perennial difficulties facing modern amphibious operations, calling for the development of mechanized mine-clearance systems.

> It is clear that the landing force must ever be capable of overcoming all types of beach obstacles and that the beach minefield can never be allowed to become insurmountable. Fortunately, the landing force of today can breach the beach minefield. Yet it is equally true that the current landing force methods and means for overcoming beach minefields are seriously lacking in speed, precision and economy—and are far below the general level of landing force proficiency in the amphibious assault. When it is considered that beach minefields will become more, rather than less, difficult to defeat in the future—the problem of the beach minefield must be recognized as one of the more serious threats to future amphibious success.
>
> The best known of the mechanical mine-clearing devices are the mine-exploder tanks. These tanks push a flail, roller or other device to detonate mines. . . . All of the mechanical means of mine clearance are at present characterized by short life even under average conditions. But beach minefields are usually shallow: and, by accepting losses, these devices can be employed to successfully penetrate beach minefields, as they were at Normandy [in the British Sector]. They are definitely superior to manual clearance for landing force assault use because of their *greater speed and ability to function under heavy fires.*
>
> Nevertheless, the landing force mine clearance plan of today should utilize the explosive line charge, placed by the method most suited to local conditions and available means—as the primary means of clearance. But the current major limitation of the line charge—the limited length practical to place with present methods (even though additional charges can be consecutively placed in approximate extension)—renders the line charge still unsuitable as the sole means of clearance because of the probability of uncleared gaps due to the lack of precision of present placement techniques. So until means of laying line longer continuous charges are developed to completely penetrate beach minefields, and as long as gaps in clearance are probable—line charges must be supplemented by other means. This supplementary role is best executed by the mine clearing tank, and the landing force clearance plan should provide a section or more of these vehicles for each lane to be cleared.

Not content with publishing his notions, Stuart used his position on the headquarters staff, starting in 1948, to engineer the complete reassessment of all armored fighting vehicle concepts and programs. No longer content with merely reviewing the "entire field of Marine Corps tank matters," as he had advocated earlier, he now sought the detailed development of the amphibious mechanized attack he had proposed in the *Gazette,* along with the preparation to face the combat arms of the Red Army, as the war plans now required.

There was no shortage of apparent motives. In January 1949 the commandant canceled any further deployments of the M26 by the 2d Tank Battalion to the Mediterranean with the routine floating battalions, citing excessive consumption of scarce spare parts. Inexplicably, the message also contained his statement that he believed that the M4A3 (105mm) tank was adequate for missions in that area. Stuart wrote a staff comment that the commandant's message could be interpreted as a precedent that he considered the M4A3 (105mm) a satisfactory tank for expeditionary duty. "[I]t is considered most doubtful that the 105mm howitzer tank can in fact satisfactorily execute tank combat missions except as a minor supporting weapon for and in conjunction with other tanks."[21]

Stuart secured his Plans and Policy director's approval of an armor policy board around the same time, and Maj. Gen. O. P. Smith signed the convening order on 22 March 1949. The seven-officer board, headed by Col. William F. Coleman, the G-3, gathered five trustworthy tanker lieutenant colonels and a captain recorder. With himself, Stuart added Metzger, McCoy, and Harvey Walseth (who had commanded A Company at Guadalcanal) from the headquarters staffs and managed to snare Denig temporarily from 2d Marine Division. They met day to day from 4 to 14 April to cover a broad agenda of topics. As their charter, they undertook

1. To examine and evaluate the Marine Corps doctrine on amphibious warfare and base defense in connection with the Marine Corps mission, for the purpose of recommending a Marine Corps armor and associated equipment policy consistent with this doctrine.
2. Based upon the foregoing to make recommendations relative to present and long range modification, development, procurement and distribution of armor and its associated equipment within the Marine Corps.[22]

The Armor Policy Board reported a rather dismal situation for the moment. It found the Marine Corps tank and amtrac inventory holding mostly obsolescent materiel (see Table 6.1). While the inventory matched the total numbers of tanks required for equipping a peacetime

Marine Corps of two divisions, schools, and reserve battalions, the wartime requirement of four divisions, three force battalions, and two training commands could not be met in either type nor numbers.

The amphibian tractor inventory looked comparatively favorable. These figures assured the board that not only peacetime equipment, but also wartime requirements totaling 1,062 LVT3 and 299 LVT(A) vehicles for four amtrac and three armored amphibian battalions and schools, could be met with the existing inventory, with the exception of the desired 299 armored amphibians.

The development horizons appeared technically favorable to the board, with the army tank program having new model light, medium, and heavy tanks completely designed, with critical components such as engines, transmissions, guns, and fire-control equipment successfully developed. "Therefore, new tanks of radically improved performance can now be developed within the limits of existing developed components." The LVT program also expected similar results from new component development, to include a 105mm howitzer carrier and improved armored personnel carrier characteristics.

Therefore, the board confidently recommended a significant set of goals as the long-range Marine Corps policy for armored fighting vehicles.

Table 6.1. Marine Corps Tank and Amphibian Tractor Inventory, 1949

Vehicle Type	Serviceable	Unserviceable
M26	99	3
M4A3 (105mm) (manual traverse)	33	7
M4A3 (105mm) (power traverse)	170	9
M4A3 (75mm)	16	133
M4A3 (105mm) with flamethrower	7	27
M4A3 (75mm) with flamethrower	4	1
TOTAL	335	180
LVT3	1578	
LVT4	72	245[a]
LVT(A)4	14	
LVT(A)5	118	71[b]

Source: Armor Policy Board Report, part II, pp. 3-4, 5-6.
[a] A total of 245 LVT3s and LVT4s were categorized as unserviceable.
[b] A total of 71 LVT(A)4s and LVT(A)5s were categorized as unserviceable.

1. The tank force would consist of all heavy tanks in the wartime-only force tank battalions and all mediums in the divisional tank battalions. The divisional tank battalion would include a flame-tank platoon in wartime, but in peacetime this platoon would have the heavy tank in order to provide training and familiarization of cadre for the force battalions. No light tanks would be required.
2. The continued need for flotation devices came from the need to land tanks as early as possible, preferably in the scheduled assault waves of the amphibious landing.
3. The armored amphibian would remain necessary and the LVT(A)5 remained the standard until a better vehicle became available.
4. Armored personnel carriers to make the assault landing completely mobile dictated the continuation of the LVT modernization program.
5. The flame tank remained essential, with an integral turret weapon. However, the M3-4-3 kits for mounting flamethrowers in the bow machine gun position would be discarded. The army concept of a trailer-mounted flame weapon, to be towed into action by a tank, was rejected as impractical.
6. Reconnaissance vehicles were considered but armored cars ruled out. The Marine Corps reconnaissance units needed a light armored truck, but would use the jeep as an interim vehicle.
7. An armored engineer vehicle would use an angled blade to remove mines under fire, project line charges, place other explosives, transport bridging kits, and operate a mechanical/electronic mine detection and clearance device. The tank dozer kit remained a standard requirement.
8. Mine detection and clearance equipment for both the tank and the armored engineer vehicle required development.
9. Self-propelled artillery for the landing force would come in the form of the LVT(A) or a self-propelled artillery weapon with flotation equipment, in order to make artillery amphibious and mobile in keeping with the all-mobile assault force concept.
10. A mobile antiaircraft weapon, also amphibious, became a stated requirement.
11. Finally, an armored observation and communication vehicle for fire support required development. Fielding would be two per tank battalion in peacetime, four in time of war. These would provide mobile spot teams for air, artillery, and naval gunfire support.

Modified M4s would suffice for the mission, to be replaced by the standard medium tank conversion.

The board studied the tank battalion and concluded that tank units would perform missions:

- as elements of the assault to provide close support in the attack and defense with machine gun and cannon fire
- as the spearhead of a mechanized landing force to land and move quickly to the support of a helicopter of other airlanded force
- as the principal element of a mobile antiboat, antiairborne, or antimechanized attack
- to support other tanks, that is, providing heavy tanks in support of medium tanks
- to provide direct fires on the beach and the adjacent area when employed in the leading wave of the ship-to-shore phase of the landing operation
- to destroy fortifications with direct fire
- to provide reconnaissance forces with sufficient firepower to permit aggressive search for information, counter-reconnaissance, and security missions[23]

Most of these missions would be performed by the medium tank of the division's tank battalion and the tank platoon of the regimental antitank company. The board advocated the heavy tank as an essential destroyer of heavy armored vehicles such as the Russian JS-3, which remained beyond the capability of any medium tank known or under development. Such a vehicle would also act in support of the medium tanks and assist in the destruction of heavy fortifications. They did not desire a light or reconnaissance tank, although they speculated that long-range overland operations with the army might require such a vehicle.

The board provided numerous details of the vehicle characteristics, supporting equipment, and components that would be necessary for the optimum tank force. For example, it specified that the landing craft developed to carry these tanks should permit firing of the main gun while afloat. Night driving and gunnery aids, communications sets fully compatible with other air, ground, and naval gunfire arms, electronic recognition devices for identifying tanks for friendly aircraft, special crew clothing and helmets, and automatic position-locating and navigation equipment all would require development.

Finally, although the board considered the acquisition of Army T42 and T43 medium and heavy tanks as the only possible solutions to the required capabilities, it did not consider them the last word in development. They particularly desired a medium tank with greater firepower and armor protection to provide the infantry support role specified for the divisional tank battalions.[24]

In considering the LVT portion of Marine Corps armor policy, the board revealed a concept of future amphibious landings which consisted of assault forces made entirely mobile, riding amphibious vehicles in order to overcome all hydrographic and terrain obstacles and advancing inland, "thus eliminating the necessity for disembarking on or near the beaches." The members found the current amphibious vehicles to be inadequate, and called for the development of a true armored assault personnel carrier that would not only serve the infantry requirements but also transport the ammunition and other cargo to support the tank and self-propelled artillery units in the assault force. The LVT(A) remained necessary for supporting the beach assault, but the board expected it to be replaced eventually by more capable self-propelled artillery. Curiously, the members found no need for specialized command vehicles, which they rejected along with amphibious flamethrower vehicles and fully submersible amphibious vehicles as unworthy projects for the future.

General Smith praised the Armor Policy Board Report and recommended its approval, except for the portion covering heavy tanks, which he feared would draw attention to the Marine Corps playing the role of a second land army. He advocated following the development of the heavy tank without committing the Corps to heavy tank units. But General Cates approved the report without exception on 27 April.[25]

Now, almost 25 years after General Russell had first ordered tanks for the FMF, the Marine Corps had a rational basis for its acquisition, fielding, and operation of armored fighting vehicles. The Armor Policy Board report of 1949 reflected much experience of the Pacific war, but also took into account the nature of a new threat, technological improvements, and a futuristic concept for amphibious operations that lay more years in the future than the time spent since the early Caribbean landings. When the MCEB met in 1950 to forecast the future requirements of all its components, the Armor Policy Board Report was adopted in its entirety, with the exception of flotation devices for tanks, which the board thought would be corrected by large landing craft designs then being drafted. This represented the personal triumph of Lieutenant Colonel Stuart in his quest for a comprehensive review of Marine Corps tank and armored issues, together with an airing of his concepts for mechanizing the amphibious operation. This last element would prove daunting, however, for many other officers. The president of the MCEB sought to assure his fellow generals that he had not intended to characterize the amphibious operation as a mechanized one. He just thought that the future amphibious vehicle should be able to go further inland before debarking troops and serve as land transport.[26]

Amazingly, the study stood as the single example of comprehensive armor guidance in the Marine Corps through the 1980s, either a significant feat for a few visionaries of 1949 or testimony of Corps reticence over the ensuing generation. No similar study or guidance ever again emerged from the Corps leadership. However visionary in its outlook, the board perhaps placed too much faith in the emerging technology and in the ability of the American military-industry cooperative to produce quality armored fighting vehicles on time and with the expected capabilities. Only the light tanks of the 1940–50s development and production programs emerged without the technical engineering and production quality-control problems that dogged the U.S. tank-automotive industry through the 1980s. The heavy and medium tanks and the new families of amphibian tractors all experienced teething problems and production delays. A complete failure to develop mine-clearing equipment may be blamed largely upon the army materiel system, but it received too little attention in the Marine Corps as well. The amphibious artillery, armored engineer, and supporting arms observation vehicles similarly never emerged and the jeep remained the sole mounted reconnaissance vehicle through the 1970s. The LVT remained inadequate as an armored personnel carrier well into the 1900s and the board failed to foresee the requirement for sophisticated command and communications vehicles for battalions and regiments engaged in mounted operations.[27]

The force structure created to reflect the policy consisted of a divisional tank battalion of four medium tank companies of seventeen tanks each, together with the existing regimental tank platoons. The force (corps echelon) tank battalions would be formed with three companies, each of seventeen heavy tanks. The commandant's guidance for FY 1951 stated that the peacetime divisional battalions would field thirty-five medium and five heavy tanks, with two force heavy tank companies of seventeen tanks each, but the force companies soon fell out under succeeding revisions. Amtrac unit strength remained unchanged in peacetime and two tank and three amtrac battalions remained in the Marine Corps Reserve.

The medium tank would be the T42 design (later superseded by the T48 series), under development by the army since 1946.[28]

These measures altered nothing in the immediate future or the readiness of the Marine Corps for its next battlefield. On 22 May 1950 the Inspector-Instructor of the 10th Tank Battalion, Marine Corps Reserve, reported that he had on hand only four M4A3 tanks and one recovery vehicle, all in poor condition. One month later, North Korean forces attacked the Republic of Korea.[29]

Chapter 7

Arming for Pax Americana, 1950–1965

> Positive information exists that spaced and laminated armor
> were features of current Soviet tank development and possible
> modifications of present tanks. [The 90mm lacks power and
> range] whereas the current requirement . . . could be met by
> the planned hyper velocity 120mm gun, the main armament
> of the T43 heavy tank.
>
> —Lt. Col. Arthur J. Stuart (1950)

> As the helicopter capability increases, the need for surface land-
> ing craft and land vehicles will decrease.
>
> —Gen. Randolph M. Pate (1956)

Korea and Expansion (1950–1955)

Marine Corps forces mobilized and improvised in 1950 from a weak
peacetime posture to fight the most varied five-month campaign in
Corps history. The 1st Marine Brigade took the few ready units to the
defense of the Pusan Perimeter. Then a 1st Marine Division, hastily
amalgamated from the rest of the active forces and initial Marine Corps
Reserve mobilization, landed at Inchon and, reinforced by its third
infantry regiment, cleared most of Seoul. The division then shifted by
sea to the east coast of Korea, landed administratively, and pushed
north toward the Yalu River only to collide with the Chinese counteroffensive and withdraw ignominiously to the port of Hungnam and
reassemble near Pusan. At the end of 1950, the Korean War would then
change character and become, first, a slugfest to establish equilibrium
on the former demarcation line between the two Koreas, and then a
wearying war of attrition to hold the line for an eventual peace.

The 1st Provisional Marine Brigade formed hurriedly in July 1950
for immediate embarkation. The Barstow depot provided M26 tanks to
replace the M4A3s of Company A, 1st Tank Battalion and new LVT3s
for the 1st Amtrac Company. The battalion commander, Lt. Col. Harry
T. Milne, carefully selected the officers and men for this important mission. His company commander, Capt. Gearl M. English, was a typical
veteran tanker with considerable World War II experience. "GM" or

"Max" English had crewed an M2A4 in 1941 on Iceland with A Company, 2d Tank Battalion, returning to the United States to be a driving instructor in Rip Collins's Tank School at Jacques' Farm. His supervisor, Capt. Bob Neiman, saw English as his best instructor and pleaded with Collins to transfer English, with a field commission, with him for duty with the company he was forming in 4th Tank Battalion. So Max went to war as a platoon leader with C Company, 4th Tank Battalion, earning a Silver Star on Iwo Jima. Now he would face a new enemy with untested vehicles, but veteran tank commanders.

The tank company had only one day on the range with two tanks to familiarize crewmen with the M26: each gunner and loader team fired two rounds of 90mm ammunition. Many of the crewmen, however, remained down on the docks in San Diego, unpacking and removing preservatives from the twenty-two M26s they would take to Korea. The five extra tanks probably had been ordered for the wartime tank platoon of the infantry regiment deploying with the brigade, the 5th Marines. English considered them his "spare" vehicles, however, and manned them with his headquarters personnel, led by the company tank leader, as the senior tank NCO was called. No one from 5th Marines intervened or complained. The shift in equipment to the M26 seemed obvious given the terror already generated by the T34s of the North Korean People's Army (NKPA). With the 5th Marines understrength (two rifle companies per battalion), the performance of the tank company would provide key assurance against disaster.[1]

Not to say that the opening moves proved auspicious, however. The tank and amtrac companies sailed aboard two navy amphibious dock ships, one of which accidentally flooded its well to a depth of five feet. Fourteen tanks and 300 rounds of scarce 90mm ammunition were damaged. Upon return to port the tanks were repaired and the ship sortied again.

Arriving at Pusan on 2 August 1950, the tanks saw action beginning on the tenth, eight years after the first Marine Corps tank actions had been fought on Guadalcanal and Tulagi. Captain English achieved the first complete gunnery practice for his company with their new tanks by zeroing the 90mm guns on hillside targets from the flatcars carrying the tanks out of the port area. The regiment commander, Lt. Col. Raymond Murray, kept English in his "hip pocket" so that the tank platoons could be assigned to any battalion in need of support. But bad luck stayed for a while with one platoon. During the 5th Marines' attack on Paedun-ni and Kusong, 1st Platoon tanks crossed a river. One tank crashed through the bridge and the second threw track crossing the stream, stalling a long column of vehicles. The surviving section continued to support the rifle companies of the vanguard. Two days later, five tanks accompanied the 1st Battalion, 5th Marines (1/5) on an 11-mile road march toward Sachon. The NKPA attempted an ambuscade, but the tanks, roadbound but mobile forts, provided dominant fire support to neutralize and break the attackers.[2]

This seasoning came none too soon, for the brigade was rushed into the 1st Battle of Naktong when the NKPA 4th Division occupied a bridgehead with six battalions and at least four T34 tanks. The marines of 1/5 and 2/5 jumped off in the counterattack on 17 August, each accompanied by a tank platoon. At 2000 1/5 detected the approach of three T34s. The tanks came into the prepared positions of 1/5 and a volley of 3.5-inch bazooka and 75mm recoilless rifle rounds. The first tank was crippled, receiving the coup de grâce from an M26; two M26s combined on the second enemy tank, and all weapons killed the last T34. The first tank-tank encounter for the Marine Corps since 1944 had gone perfectly well. Ironically, the Marine Corps tank credited with killing the first T34 tank was the 3d Platoon's A34, commanded by T.Sgt. Cecil Fullerton. The M26 platoons worked with the infantry to clear the ridges and eject the NKPA from the brigade's zone of the Naktong Pocket. In early September the sequence virtually repeated itself in the 2d Battle of Naktong. 2d Platoon, Company A tankers, despite losing their platoon leader earlier in the day to a machine-gun burst, caught three T34s napping and killed them outright, going on to scatter accompanying infantry. Later a fourth tank was killed in a thicket and a fifth captured, abandoned by its crew.[3]

The brigade commander, Brig. Gen. Edward A. Craig, wrote on the 17 August engagement with the T34s to the chief of staff of the Army, as requested by the local army commander. His detailed report makes it clear that the NKPA tank troops would be no match for properly trained and equipped U.S troops.[4]

Three enemy T-34/85mm tanks attacked our positions at 172005 August. Enemy tanks were moving northwest along road toward our position. . . . The enemy tanks fired approximately four rounds of HE ammunition at our troops without results. The enemy came under fire of our tanks, 75mm recoilless rifles and 3.5" rocket launchers almost simultaneously. Three M-26 tanks moved 900 yards southwest down the road and positioned themselves overlooking a curve in the road. Two of our tanks were abreast and opened fire at a range of 100 yards as the first two enemy tanks came around the curve in the road.

The first M-26 fired two rounds of APC [armor-piercing, capped; a conventional solid shot round] ammunition at each of the enemy tanks, a total of six rounds. All rounds fired at the hull penetrated the enemy armor.

The second M-26 fired one round of APC at the first enemy tank, one round of HVAP [high-velocity armor-piercing] and two APC at the second tank and four rounds of HE ammunition at the third enemy tank. Our second tank fired the HE ammunition through a penetration made previously by APC ammunition through the machine gun bow mount, front slope plate of the third enemy tank.

All enemy tanks were penetrated by APC ammunition when fired at the hulls. . . . All the enemy tanks were burning at 2015, and although two rounds were fired by the enemy at our tanks, all were misses.

During the tank attack 75mm recoilless rifles and 3.5" rocket launchers successfully damaged the enemy's tanks. The first enemy tank was hit by four rounds of recoilless rifle fire and halted; the right track of the second enemy tanks was hit and blown off by 3.5" rocket fire at a range of 75 yards and set on fire. As a result the second enemy tank ran into a ditch. The recoilless rifles fired four rounds of ammunition at the first tank; one round each at the second and third enemy tanks all at ranges of 100 yards. Rocket 3.5" hit all enemy tanks.

Although hit by 75mm recoilless rifles and 3.5" rockets the enemy tanks continued firing and only one was completely immobilized. One enemy crewman attempted escape from enemy tank No. 2; and three crewmen from No. 3; all were killed by small arms fire.

No Marine aircraft participated in the attack on the enemy tanks since the Tactical Air Coordinator (airborne) called planes off to prevent endangering our troops.

Lieutenant Colonel Stuart laconically remarked on the copy of Craig's letter that he routed throughout headquarters:

Apparently 75 recoilless & 3.5 bazookas took hostile tanks under fire first, followed by our own tanks.

It is significant that hostile tanks were "hit by 6 rds of 75 recoilless & all hit by 3.5" *without* stopping fire from any hostile tanks (para 7). The efficiency of HEAT type "penetration" has often been questioned & this tends to prove that such penetrations *cannot* be counted upon to *positively put a tank out of action*. This *not* meant to infer that HEAT AT weapons are of no value or should be eliminated.

In all these fights, the M26s remained practically roadbound, but untouchable to the 45mm antitank guns attached to the NKPA infantry. A few tank commanders were wounded by small arms as they exposed themselves searching for targets. The single setback came on 5 September when two T34s and an armored personnel carrier (APC) accompanied a company of NKPA infantry against 1/5's lines. With radios inoperable, the 1st Platoon rushed to the action and the two lead M26s traversed their turrets in the wrong direction. The T34s knocked out both, but the marine tankers successfully bailed out. The infantry killed the enemy vehicles in a hail of 3.5-inch rockets, but too late. Of the eight hulks now occupying that stretch of road, two were M26s.[5]

While the Naktong fighting peaked, the rest of the 1st Marine Division (less the reinforced 7th Marines Regiment, still assembling in California) straggled into Japanese ports and prepared for the amphibious landing aimed at the key port of Inchon, on the coast west of Seoul. Only 3,450 troops had remained at Camp Pendleton with the division cadre after the sailing of the 1st Marine Brigade. First to arrive as replacements were companies of the Organized Marine Corps Reserve: the 13th Infantry Company from Los Angeles, the 12th Amtrac Company (San Diego) and the 3d Engineer Company (Phoenix). As the regulars were shaken out of barracks, bases, and the 2d Marine Division, and more reservists reported in, an order from the secretary of Navy to keep troops under 18 years of age out of the fighting resulted in the deliberate crippling of the 1st Armored Amphibian Battalion, by receiving 500 of the division's minors. The bulk of the combat-ready marines with tracked vehicle or weapons experience went to the 1st Tank Battalion, but many men without driving or gunnery experience had to be assigned as crewmen. Flame-tank crews trained briefly on the vehicles at the Barstow depot as they were being issued. B Company stood up on 21 July. The next eighteen M26s arrived on 5 August, as did A Company, 2d Tank Battalion, immediately redesignated as C Company, 1st Tank Battalion. The battalion began to embark for Japan on 16 August, but D Company would not form and catch up until late in September.[6]

The Inchon landing operation of 15 September 1950 remains shrouded in the legend and lore of the Marine Corps. The truly legendary part should be the degree of improvisation resorted to by the navy and Marine Corps planners, who could conveniently draw upon all the recent experience of the Pacific war against an opponent hardly reminiscent of that conflict. Thanks to the earlier disabling of the 1st Armored Amphibian Battalion, the army's A Company, 56th Amphibian Tractor Battalion had to be used for the LVT(A)5 spearhead. These eighteen armored amphibians would lead 164 LVT3 (including 50 rebuilt LVT3Cs) and 85 DUKW vehicles ashore from LSTs to land the 1st

Marines southeast of the Inchon limits. The 5th Marines, swinging around from Pusan and the now-disbanded 1st Brigade, would land from landing craft directly in the port.

The key to success lay in the precursor assault on Wolmi-do, an island guarding Inchon harbor, to which it was connected by a causeway. Landing craft brought in a battalion of infantry, supported by a detachment of the experienced A Company, 1st Tank Battalion: six M26, one flame and two dozer Shermans, and a retriever. These quickly blasted and burned the NKPA troops from their caves and entrenchments as the infantry quickly overran the island. The causeway proved free of obstructions and the tanks linked with the rest of the landing force already passing through the town.

The main landings took place with little resistance. The LVT waves of thirty vehicles each became disorganized after the first three touched down. Most LVTs stayed on the beach or bogged down trying to push inland. A floating supply dump of twenty-four LVTs had to delay until the next day as ten amtracs bogged on the mud flats. The tanks landed over the next day through the port and joined the two infantry regiments as they pushed east on the road to Seoul. Five miles ahead marine pilots spotted six T34s moving without infantry support toward the town. Eight Corsairs hit them with rockets and napalm, killing two but *claiming* all six. That afternoon, the regiments settled in on their beachhead perimeter. The deadly 3d Platoon of A Company, 1st Tank Battalion spotted three intact T34s at the site of the morning's air strike and killed them with twenty rounds fired by two M26s. Two hulks remained from the air strike, but T34 number six was never seen.[7]

The advance continued and the 5th Marines halted the night of 16–17 September on the approaches to Ascom City. That morning, yet another incredibly inept NKPA detachment of six T34s, this time with about 200 infantry, blundered into the marine position. This event provided vengeance for the 1st Platoon of A Company, 1st Tank Battalion, which had lost two tanks on the Naktong position to the T34s. The M26s fired forty-five rounds of AP as the marines of two adjacent battalions added bazooka and recoilless rifle fire. All of the NKPA were wiped out in the brief firefight, and tanks claimed five of the six tank kills. Certainly their hits had proved most destructive, but all weapons hit all the tanks, save the first one taken out by an outpost bazookaman. The combat had barely concluded when Gen. Douglas MacArthur, Adm. Arthur Struble, and a dozen other generals drove up with X Corps staff officers and a gaggle of reporters. The made-to-order publicity scene lay before them, as the marines surveyed their handiwork. The Kimpo airfield fell to the tank-infantry teams that day and the Han River presented the last obstacle on the advance to Seoul.[8]

Crossing the Han presented another opportunity for the Marine Corps's amphibious art to be practiced. Early in the morning of 20 September the 5th Marines attempted the crossing, on the heels of a reconnaissance party that had used rubber rafts. The ubiquitous army armored amphibians and 1st Amtrac Battalion LVT3Cs were in direct support. Tanks and artillery would cross later on bridge ferries. The result was a fracas, as four LVTs stuck in the mud and the rest returned to the near shore. Greatly embarrassed, the marines reorganized and crossed in daylight, the second battalion of infantry remaining mounted into the hill objectives, stopping only when swamps and light bridges barred further movement. The army LVT(A)5 company led the 2d Battalion, Korean Marine Corps Regiment (2/KMC) mounted in DUKWs in trace of the 5th Marines.

The 1st and 5th Marines closed on Seoul to the south and east on foot through rugged hills and growing NKPA resistance. The amtrac battalion ferried the 1st Marines, the army 32d Infantry, and the ROK 17th Infantry on 24–25 September across the Han, setting the stage for the clearing of the capital city.[9]

The marine infantry narrowly avoided a setback as a platoon of T34 tanks cruised leisurely around the industrial park at Yongdung-po the night of 21–22 September. A rifle company, under the command of Capt. Robert A. Barrow, a future commandant, remained dug into a berm, curiously immune from the fire of the 85mm guns. Volleys of 3.5-inch rockets finally convinced the tanks to withdraw and the company continued its mission.[10]

The clearing of Seoul was spearheaded by the 1st Marines, with B Company, 1st Tank Battalion in support. Many prisoners were netted by the tank-infantry teams. Several tanks were disabled by mines but recovered as the advance continued. A flame tank was lost to a surprise infantry close assault, and tank-infantry coordination improved with that example. Two SU-76 self-propelled guns fell to marine tank cannon in the city center, and fighting ended on 27 September. The 1st Marine Division claimed a total of thirty-eight enemy tanks destroyed during the Inchon-Seoul operation, but aircraft probably accounted for a dozen of these. The commander of 1st Tank Battalion, Lieutenant Colonel Milne, had operated with mostly untrained and inexperienced crews, "yet tanks have been able to operate efficiently and aggressively."

He counted one flame, one dozer, and five M26 tanks lost to enemy action, but claimed that approximately thirteen tanks and fifty-six anti-tank or antiaircraft guns had been destroyed by his men.[11]

During the next month, the 1st Marine Division moved to the east coast and joined the UN Command drive toward the Yalu River and total victory. This part of the Marine Corps campaign then concluded in the massive riposte by the Chinese army (PLA) and the concomitant breakout of the division and neighboring army units from the Chosin Reservoir sector. The 1st Amtrac Battalion and the HQ, 1st Tank Battalion remained in Wonsan and Hungnam rear areas. The 1st Tank Battalion would fight with the division using its four medium-tank companies as well as the newly activated tank platoons of the regimental antitank companies, attached for administrative and maintenance support.[12]

In brief, the division was strung out in late November along a narrow, unimproved 45-mile road from the port of Hungnam to the front lines at Yudam-ni, where the 5th Marines prepared to continue the attack northwest through the 7th Marines. The division headquarters occupied the middle point at Hagaru-ri, with its auxiliary airstrip. The 1st Marines chafed further south at Koto-ri. Army troops and their M4A3 (76mm) tanks operated to the northeast, using the same main service road. That no tank terrain existed was noted by author Eric Hammel, who described the arrival of a single tank from a platoon of D Company, 1st Tank Battalion at Yudam-ni, the evening of 27 November as an "arduous ascent to the [Taktong] pass, teetering on the brink of bottomless chasms, scraping against rock outcroppings, squeezing by the abandoned [Army] Sherman tank."[13]

The PLA offensive struck the forward regiments of the 1st Marine Division and 7th Infantry Division on the night of 28 November. The marines held their positions against heavy attacks, but the army 31st Tank Battalion failed in its relief of the army vanguard east of the Chosin Reservoir. An attempt by the 1st Marines to push forward a reinforcement to Hagaru-ri ended in a similar disaster, despite the use of eleven tanks of B Company. The center of the long column, isolated from the tanks at either end, was devastated and routed by the PLA forces. On 2 December the general pullout began, starting with the 5th and 7th Marines and army stragglers in the north. Tank D23 led the way, engine conking out, batteries expiring, and tracks skidding into ditches, but somehow remaining in action and destroying roadblocks all the way to Hagaru-ri. Infantry battalions cleared the flanking hillsides and tank-infantry teams cleared the roadway as the regiments moved into Hagaru-ri, by then under siege from all sides. On 10 December the 1st Division moved toward Koto-ri and the 1st Marines. Bringing up the rear this time were the forty-six tanks of B and D Companies, 1st Tank Battalion, the battalion HQ dozer tank platoon, the 31st Medium Tank Battalion, and the tank platoons of the three infantry regiments. They remained at the end because of the doubtful condition of the vital bridge at the Changjiu Power Plant No. 1. In the end, all but the last eight M26s made the crossing. A breakdown came at a tense moment when refugees and PLA troops pressed from the rear and men began to abandon their trapped vehicles. The bridge was blown and the column continued to fight its way to the port. One of the isolated tanks, B22, would fight all night, after which the crew escaped, only to be captured two days later. Lieutenant Colonel Milne reported a total of fourteen tanks and ten trucks lost in the Chosin breakout, but surprisingly few casualties in the tank battalion (four missing, four wounded and thirty-one nonbattle casualties).[14]

The marines evacuated Hungnam and reassembled at Masan, in the old Pusan Perimeter, for rest and equipping. For the tankers the rest and maintenance would be put to good use. The shortage of twelve M26s and seven M4A3 dozer tanks would be made up from new shipments from the United States, and the support of the army 328th Ordnance Battalion proved exemplary. The division performed counterguerrilla missions in the Pohang area, with the tank battalion assigned to a 15-by 15-mile quadrant south of Pohang, but no actions resulted. The tank companies then split up to support the three USMC and one KMC regiments in Operation Ripper, the first of a long series of short-legged counteroffensives designed to return the UN forces to the original demarcation line before the war. The advance continued in the summer into the Punchbowl zone and the lines remained static into 1952. The tank-infantry work produced no novelties and the routine support of tank platoons for infantry battalions and tank companies for regiments was hardly altered. Even the PLA spring offensives brought little change to tank tactics. The 90mm cannon dominated the battlefield wherever it could be brought to bear. Bunkers provided the bulk of targets, and some tank-infantry raids occurred in the fall defensive period. Attempts to dragoon the tankers into reinforcing the artillery with indirect fire were eventually thwarted by the prospect of wearing out the 90mm gun tubes with no replacements on hand. The tank battalion, filled out to almost 1,000 marines in number, operated and maintained its tanks and those of the regimental antitank companies. Mines proved to be the greatest problem for tanks, but few became total losses. Ammunition expenditures averaged over 3,000 rounds per month for the main gun (over thirty per tank, considering the ninety-seven authorized in the division, not counting the nine flame tanks). During July–November, the tank units received the M46 tank as replacements for their venerable M26s, a great improvement in mobility, but too late for the more mobile phases of the war.[15]

In March of 1952 the 1st Marine Division made its last shift on the front, taking responsibility for the west coast and the frontage past the Panmunjon Peace Corridor to the left boundary of the Commonwealth Division. The division thus recovered close proximity to its amtrac and armored amphibian battalions. The latter had remained since 1950 on the Kimpo Peninsula attached to the I Corps Kimpo Provisional Regiment (KPR). The Amtrac Battalion spent the post-Masan period in the Ascom City zone and the Kimpo Peninsula, with B Company detached to Pohang to offload supplies for Marine Aircraft Group 33 there. D Company stood up at Camp Pendleton in late 1950, but remained there for the war's duration.

The long and tortuous front occupied in 1952 remained vexing to the 1st Marine Division leadership. The KPR remained much the same under 1st Marine Division control. The 1st Amtrac Battalion was placed into the line to the east of the KPR and west of the KMC regiment. The three USMC infantry regiments rotated in and out of the line for the rest of the front. The 1st Tank Battalion remained in division reserve, with two companies in support of front-line regiments and the other two companies in reserve assembly areas. The amtrackers responded to their infantry duties with aplomb, reviving the tradition of Guadalcanal and reinforcing a doctrine of readiness to serve as an infantry battalion as a secondary mission. Some thirty positions on a 14,000-yard frontage were manned by three LVT platoons and the divisional reconnaissance company. Weapons included 106 heavy and light machine guns, four 60mm and six 81mm mortars, and fourteen 3.5-inch bazookas. Company A, 1st Amtrac Battalion provided waterborne patrols of the river and estuary.

The static positions created no other missions for Marine Corps armored fighting vehicles. The 105mm guns of the flame platoon and 90mm guns of D Company, 1st Tank Battalion were pressed into artillery reinforcement in April 1952. A KMC tank company was trained in the use of their new M4A3 (76mm) tanks and attached to the tank battalion. Tank raids, now including the much-feared flame tanks, broke the monotony of occasional sniping and bunker shoots on the main line rotation of the tank companies. A number of M39 APCs were received from the army and operated by the tankers. They primarily served as part of a rescue element kept ready during Panmunjon talks, but they also formed an "armored utility vehicle" platoon for general use in the battalion, including rearming the tanks on the front lines. Other improvisations occurred, such as the borrowing of an M4A3 (76mm) platoon and some 90mm AA guns by the 1st Armored Amphibian Battalion on receipt, and manning them with battalion headquarters personnel in support of the KPR. The regimental antitank companies also acquired 90mm antitank guns for use in the front lines.[16]

As truce talks proceeded, the UN troops grew to mourn the earlier monotony, as several fierce fights broke out in the late summer and fall of 1952 over the outpost line, mostly at night. Thanks to the new 18-inch (incandescent) searchlights mounted on the M46 tank, the tankers could provide firepower to support many of the outposts, but not all could be saved by fire alone. Infantry casualties caused the division to send replacements from the amtrac battalion and place thirty-five LVTs out of service in Ascom City.

During March–June 1953 the division rotated out of line and into corps reserve. The tank and artillery units remained in place, however, and supported the Turkish Brigade and the 25th Infantry Division in more outpost fights. When the division returned to the front in June, a platoon of M46s was used to reinforce a key outpost, named Boulder City. It held against a fierce PLA attack on 24–25 July. Marines now considered the "Army method" of occupying firing positions full-time to be better than the earlier notion of occupying firing positions only after the action had begun. Overall, the defense of the outpost positions during 24–27 July had involved over thirty tanks, which fired approximately 1,300 shells and 55,000 bullets. Ironically, the armistice took effect on 27 July, after one of the most costly months of fighting endured by the division.[17]

The fighting over, the 1st Marine Division would remain in Korea until its 1955 redeployment to Camp Pendleton. A new main line of resistance and fallback positions demanded the construction of some 200 tank slots. The 1st Tank Battalion turned over its M46s and M39s to the army's 6th Tank Battalion on 17 March (armistice terms froze equipment in Korea for a specified period) and embarked at Inchon for Pendleton and a new issue of M48A1 tanks. The 1st Amtrac Battalion would remain in Japan and Okinawa and serve with the 3d Marine Division.

The impact of the Korean War upon armor policy in the Marine Corps can be minimized. The Corps leadership had already determined a modernization policy for tanks and amtracs in the face of discouraging budget reductions, and this had paid off handsomely in the war from a materiel standpoint. The M26, regarded with some suspicion and purchased with evident caution, had provided a necessary overmatch against the NKPA armor. The policy of keeping the bulk of the M26s in war reserve, ready for issue in the case of contingencies, had proven sound. Since the PLA used no armor and had no artillery to speak of before the final static phase of the war, the Marine Corps tank policy saw no further testing. The LVT3C had performed well in the hands of necessarily inexperienced personnel, and no continuing amphibious campaign had ensued to demonstrate Corps proficiency in the art. Tactics had remained those of the Pacific war, in keeping with the character of the Corps itself.[18]

Innovations were few, more in line with mere equipment upgrades, such as improved vehicles, tank searchlights, and command vehicles. An innovation quickly forgotten was the "porcupine tank," which featured extra radios and antenna to direct air and artillery support from a tank. Both M46 and Sherman models were developed in depot and in the field, yet no command or fire-support control tanks emerged in the aftermath of the war.[19]

Operations in Korea also witnessed the introduction of the helicopter as a source of tactical mobility for the infantry formations. It seemed to offer the infantry complete freedom from the tyranny of terrain restrictions. This factor would prove of far more importance to Corps armored fighting vehicle policy and doctrine than did any accomplishment or omission of the tank and amtrac troops themselves. The impact of Marine Corps fascination with the helicopter, however, would take a decade to unfold.

The Korean War and the mobilization of national resources it spawned allowed the Marine Corps to achieve many of its program objectives otherwise unattainable in the 1940s. An entirely new family of amtracs would be designed and produced, and the tank program would be fleshed out to the approximate levels that the 1949 Armor Policy Study had recommended. The sudden outbreak of hostilities found inventories and industrial capacity severely lacking. Mobilization of men and materiel proved sluggish and brought home many lessons in war planning and preparedness in general for U.S. forces. Both the army and Marine Corps staffs spoke openly of the "tank crisis" of 1950, reflecting the immediate needs of both U.S. forces in Korea and the rest of the forces required to face the Red Army in war plans, as well as the feared continuation of Communist bloc aggression elsewhere in the world.

Not only did the Corps bring the 1st and 2d Marine Divisions up to strength in the year after the war's outbreak but it also formed the wartime organizations already provided for in the FMF structure. These latter included the 7th and 8th Tank Battalions, the reinforcing "force battalions" provided for in postwar planning and endorsed by the Armor Policy Board. The battalions formed on 30 September 1950 and their command rolls recalled the glory days of the Pacific war. Maj. Leo B. Case formed the 7th Tank Battalion at Camp Pendleton, to be followed by Lt. Col. Holly Evans until Alexander B. Swecensky relinquished command of the 1st Tank Battalion, USMCR, at San Diego to take command. Case, who had led the charge of M2A4s at the Tenaru River in 1942, received promotion to lieutenant colonel in 1951 and served as its last commander. On the East Coast, Charles W. McCoy commanded the 8th Tank Battalion for most of its service.[20]

Finding men for these battalions proved easier for the harried headquarters staff than finding the machines. Nobody knew how "big" the Korean War might become, and the 7th Tank Battalion seemed destined for shipment overseas, following the departure of the 1st Marine Division. However, the Corps lacked heavy tanks for the force battalions and had too few M26 mediums remaining after outfitting the rest of the 1st Tank Battalion for war. Accordingly, the commandant ordered the 7th Tank Battalion equipped with M4A3 (105mm) tanks as training vehicles and gained assurances from the army that it would provide M46s prior to deployment. Even graver circumstances faced the 8th Tank Battalion, which received by the same orders a shipment of the last serviceable M4A3s, thirteen with the 75mm gun. General Cates ordered the tank inventory scoured for repairable vehicles and cautioned all commanders to conserve tanks and spares. Had these tank battalions deployed to Korea with last-minute issue of M46s, their experiences would have repeated those of the 1st Tank Battalion in July and August. In November Cates advised:

> By copies of this letter, Force Commanders are informed that the Commandant of the Marine Corps realizes that the foregoing special tank materiel arrangements, necessitated by the current national shortage of modern tanks, are not entirely satisfactory even on an interim basis, and every effort is being made to expedite procurement of modern tanks in adequate quantities.[21]

The files of headquarters reveal just how difficult the early days of the Korean War must have been. On 18 June the G4 summarized the current materiel situation for the Plans and Programs director. The army's crash program to field the new light tank, T41, would make it available in January 1951. The tank plants would convert those M26 mediums remaining in the United States to M46s and commence production of a hybrid T42 medium in April. The heavy tank, T43, would debut in August of 1951. Spares for the M4 through M46 became crash programs. But Marine Corps tanks remained scarce (see Table 7.1).

The report judged the M4 tank as totally inferior to the T34, not capable of surviving combat against enemy tanks with its 105mm low-velocity gun. Therefore it remained totally unsatisfactory for employment in the situation they faced. The wartime tank battalion needed four tank companies, and the antitank companies of the regiments required their tank platoons. Adding a force tank battalion of 53 tanks (heavy when available) would raise the required tanks to 147 per division committed to combat.[22]

As the 1st Marine Division prepared to embark for the Far East, the Corps ordered its first eighty M46s, essentially M26 tanks fitted with the Continental 12-cylinder engine coupled to a modern cross-drive transmission. Further purchases of the M46 gave way in October 1951 to the army's new production M47 series, the M46 hull married to the turret of the newly developed T42. M47s would equip the new 3d Tank Battalion, deploying to Japan in 1953 with its parent division, as well as the rebuilt 2d Tank Battalion. The M47s also outfitted the training pools of the two reserve battalions (now designated 1st and 2d Tank Battalion, USMCR). All tank-school training converted to the M47 in October 1952, despite the retention of the M46 in the 1st Marine Division for the rest of its service in Korea.[23]

The M47 introduced an improved 90mm cannon and the first rangefinder coupled to a mechanical ballistic computer to the Corps but

Table 7.1. Marine Corps Tank Inventory (June 1950)

Type	Issued to troops	Serviceable	Unserviceable
M26	28	74[a]	—
M4A3 (105mm)	41	149	26
M4A3 (75mm)	23 (USMCR)	28	157
M24 light tank	—	9	—

[a]16 more being acquired.

otherwise had little effect, for the M48 series replaced it in short order. The 3d Tank Battalion kept it the longest (1959), owing to its isolation in the western Pacific, where that battalion began its tradition of withering at the extreme marches of the limited Marine Corps logistic support system.[24]

The M48-series medium tank, derived from the T42 through T48 prototype series, began to enter Marine Corps service in 1954. It would remain in service the longest period of any tank in the Corps. Rushed to production as part of the Korean War rearmament program, it suffered an inordinate amount of teething problems and production delays, exceeded only by its heavy tank stable mate. Marine Corps medium companies of both divisional and force battalions operated it in the now-standard seventeen-tank company, one of these vehicles receiving the dozer kit (reduced from the three extra tanks ordered per company for the Korean War in 1957). Outfitting the active and reserve battalions would not be completed until 1959.[25]

Although superficially similar in performance to the preceding M47 medium-tank model, the M48 offered improved armor thickness (4.33-inch hull front and 7-inch turret front) and shaping, better fire control by moving the rangefinder to the commander's vice gunner's position, larger ammunition capacity, and a cupola for the commander's machine gun. The bow gunner or assistant driver now disappeared, reducing the required crew to four. The driver occupied a center hull position with better vision and simplified controls. However, the weight now reached 52 tons fully loaded and the range fell to a disappointing 70 miles. The improved 90mm gun installed in both M47 and M48 tanks fired a 44-pound AP shot at 3000 feet per second (fps) and a 32-pound HEAT projective at 4000 fps. This performance permitted the deletion of HVAP ammunition from use, as it caused very high bore wear in service.[26]

The initial order of M48s in 1952 also reflected twenty-eight of the eventual seventy-four flame-tank variants, the M67 (formerly T66), which substituted a flame projector for the main gun, using a mock 90mm tube to conceal its special nature. The fully rotating turret fired 365 gallons of flame fuel in 70 seconds to a distance of 150 yards. With the provision of M48 dozer kits and flame tanks, the Sherman tank would disappear from the Corps battalions in 1959.[27]

The flame-tank development remains a singular case of Marine Corps tank procurement of a separate weapon within the army materiel system. In November 1949 the commandant advised the army that he considered the army's plans to develop a trailer-type flame-tank weapon unsatisfactory. He requested development of an integral main armament flamethrower based upon the T42 medium tank. Staff conferences with the Army Chemical Center had informally agreed that the "package turret" could be developed, but with Marine Corps funding, since no land warfare requirement currently existed. The commandant asked for a cost and prototype-construction time estimate. The army's response indicated that a T4 turret could be developed, slightly short of the specifications of the Armor Policy Board Report, for $100,000 in two and a half years. Such funding would have to await wartime measures, and when the Corps came up with it the army then undertook the project.[28]

Wartime also brought a reassessment of the light tank in the Corps. The Armor Policy Board had rejected its acquisition but stated that the Corps should display continued interest in it. The G2 staff thought that a light tank was required for reconnaissance missions. Jeb Stuart's response from the P&P Division declared that the light-tank requirement for reconnaissance stemmed from plans to deploy parts of the FMF to desert operations, for which army units could be borrowed. The Korean War had revealed the unlikely need for this type of unit, so Stuart recommended study of a reconnaissance capability at the division level, equipping light-tank platoons of three sections of two tanks each in the division reconnaissance companies.[29]

The unique acquisition of the heavy tank in the postwar Marine Corps suffered a tortuous sequence of decisions and events. The last of the T41–43 family of light, medium, and heavy tanks developed from 1946 by the army, the sole postwar heavy tank to reach production owed much of its existence to the Marine Corps. The USMC Armor Policy Board of 1949 and the Marine Corps Equipment Board of 1950 had recommended that all force (corps level) tank battalions be heavy. This concept was reversed by the Basic Organization Structure Board of 1952, which held that the Corps had no need for a heavy tank, but that it would still accept the T43 in production. The commandant, now General Shepherd, decided that the heavy tanks would go first to the 8th Tank Battalion, but that the force battalions would initially receive the M48, pending the receipt of an acceptable heavy tank.[30]

The T43 design represented the pinnacle of U.S. tank engineering of the late 1940s, with its cast elliptical hull and turret, Continental AV-1790 engine and cross-drive transmission, and torsion bar suspension. A rangefinder and mechanical computer directed a 120mm main gun in a novel electrohydraulic turret, among other features. In 1950, it existed only as a full-scale mockup. The outbreak of war brought a rush order

in December 1950, which led to a complete production run of 300 vehicles, considered sufficient for army and Marine Corps requirements.

The production T43E1 or M103 heavy tank featured the following
characteristics:

Weight:	64 tons loaded, 61.5 light
Crew:	5 (two loaders)
Radius of action:	80–100 miles on 280 gallons of gasoline
Speed:	23 mph
Armor:	Hull—front, 5 inches at 60 degrees; side 2 inches at 40 degrees. Turret—front, 10–5 inches; side, 5–3 inches at 0–40 degrees.
Armament:	120mm T123E1 with 34 rounds (later 38); .50-caliber M2 with 1,000 rounds; .30-caliber M37 with 5,250 rounds.
Suspension:	torsion bar, seven road wheels, six return rollers each side.

The 120mm gun proved exceptionally powerful, firing a 51-pound solid
shot at a muzzle velocity of 3500 fps or a 31-pound HEAT round at 3750
fps with 48,000 psi chamber pressure. Penetration performance against
30-degree sloped armor compared very favorably to the current 90mm
(T119) gun:

120mm AP	221mm at 1,000 yd./196mm at 2,000 yd.
90mm AP	119mm at 500 yd./117mm at 1,000 yd.
90mm HVAP	221mm at 500 yd./199mm at 1,000 yd.

Also available for the 120mm gun were HE, white phosphorous (WP),
and training (TP) projectiles. The recoil of this impressive tank cannon, in spite of the considerable weight of the vehicle, caused the gunner to lose sight of the target upon firing, as the sight picture jumped
completely over the target image. This effect required the gunner both
to reacquire the target and to sense the tracer or impact of the round
as the sights and tank rocked back down, to determine any corrections
to aim, if necessary. In an effort to reduce this condition, the army and
Chrysler Corporation design team tested a suspension locking device,
which prevented the suspension roadwheel arms from moving during the firing, hence reducing this rocking of the tank. The Marine
Corps officer at the Aberdeen Proving Ground refused to fire the modified tank with a crew. Upon remote firing with the suspension lock

installed, the gun came out of its trunnions and slammed into the rear of the turret, demolishing the radios and rangefinder. No further changes came from the designers and the M103 gunners learned to cope with the problem.[31]

From the outset, the M103 heavy tank served to offset the uncertainty that the heaviest Russian tanks could be destroyed on the battlefield. Studies based its "level of effectiveness" compared to the medium tank on the probability of a first-round hit that would ensure immobility of a Soviet JS-3 tank:[32]

Tank	1,000 yards	2,000 yards
M48A1	.61	.23
M103A1	.69	.38

The army proved hesitant to complete the development and fielding of this immense and complicated tank, and the project manager had to fight a rear-guard battle against elements in the Army Staff to keep the program alive. The staff had advanced the notion that planned 90mm HEAT munitions would prove effective against the heaviest Russian armor. Lieutenant Colonel Stuart assisted the harried program manager's office with Marine Corps support in the heavy tank program. He advanced a Department of the Navy position decrying the 90mm HEAT ammunition as unproven, lower in velocity, and with accuracy expected to fall off after 1,000 yards range:

> Positive information exists that spaced and laminated armor were features of current Soviet tank development and possible modifications of present tanks. [The 90mm lacks power and range] whereas the current requirement is for 75% probability of a first round hit at 2500 yards which could be met by the planned hyper velocity 120mm gun, the main armament of the T43 heavy tank.[33]

As might have been expected from the rush to production, the T43E1 failed its initial trials at Fort Knox, mostly for erratic gun controls and poor ballistic performance of the projectiles. A modification program (of over 100 discrepancies) resulted in the standardization of the T43E1 as the 120mm gun combat tank, M103, in 1956. Throughout all these perturbations, the Marine Corps maintained its interest in the tank and applied its program funds to the appropriate modifications as well as storage costs pending the reworking of the 218 tanks it took from the project.[34]

The Marine Corps alone would participate in the M103A1 upgrade of turret controls, sights, rangefinder, and ballistic computer. Even so, the delicate combination of vacuum-tube amplifiers to the servo systems controlling the hydraulic turret drives made for a temperamental gun-pointing system for the remainder of the tank's service. These new heavies finally reached the troops during 1958–59. Had the army assigned the tank a higher priority in its materiel system, the deliveries might have happened sooner. Ironically, the M103A1 proved so impressive that the army took seventy-two of them on temporary loan from the Corps to outfit its sole heavy-tank battalion in Europe during 1959–62. The heavy tank proved fairly popular with the troops, who above all respected the powerful armament it carried. Many challenges to the crewmen, such as the job of the second loader to hand-ram both the projectile and the propellant cartridge into the chamber in a single movement within the confines of a narrow turret, were taken on with a sense of pride. It shared all the teething problems of the M48 series, exacerbated by its unique turret and problems resulting from the extended storage period of the tanks while awaiting successive modification programs.[35]

The amphibian tractor program benefited equally as the tank program did from the exigencies of the Korean War. But at first the LVT modernization program had little to offer. The first fifty LVT3C modernization vehicles from the Long Beach Naval Shipyard went to the 1st Amtrac Battalion as it mounted out for Korea, but the remaining vehicles for the battalion had to be the LVT3s out of depot storage, and not all of these in the desired condition. The San Francisco Naval Shipyard managed to convert 66 more LVT3C vehicles and deliver all but 10 to the Corps by the end of September, too late for the Inchon landing. The navy set continuing production goals of 25 vehicles per week but initial rates hovered around 10 per week. The commandant informed the navy that he needed a total of 1,194 LVT3C and 199 LVT(A)5 amtracs in order to field two amtrac battalions at war strength (four companies each) and two armored amphibian battalions at reduced strength (two companies each). After modernizing the 700 LVT3Cs provided for in the FY51 budget, a shortage of 264 LVT3Cs and 99 LVT(A)5s would yet remain. Desert depot storage contained some 400 old LVT3s, but these required a complete overhaul, and considerable refurbishing. Only 28 LVT(A)5 remained in storage. He concluded that new production of these vehicles now became necessary. But producing a 1943 design hardly made sense.[36]

Development of the new amphibian tractor became a high priority. Not only was a new design possible, but a complete family of carrier and specialized support vehicles came into service through the efforts of the Navy Bureau of Ships (BuShips) and Marine Corps collaboration. The LVT Continuing Board, functioning since 1943, came under control of the Marine Corps membership in the 1950s, beginning with the switch of the senior member assignment from BuShips to the president of the Marine Corps Equipment Board.

In December 1950 BuShips contracted the Borg-Warner (Ingersoll Division) Corporation to design a family of amtracs, drawing upon engineering developments that had continued since 1946. The LVTP-5 personnel carrier variant would be accompanied by similar developments of an armored amphibian (LVTH-6), command (LVTC-5), air defense (LVTAA-1), recovery (LVTR-1), and combat engineer/breaching (LVTE-1) vehicles. The navy also contracted a competing design from the FMC Corporation, based upon the Army M59 APC, and development proceeded on this series as the LVTP-6. But the Borg-Warner LVTP-5 proved superior in seaway and surf handling and entered full production in 1952. A total of 1,112 P-5s and 210 H-6s were built by 1957. Although the AA version failed surf testing, some 58 command vehicles were modified, 65 R-1s built, and 55 E-1s modified. As with the Army T43- and T48-series tanks, the rush to production of the new LVT resulted in numerous defects requiring extensive modification by the factory, provided in the end by the FMC Riverside plant. The resulting delays permitted extended troop tests of the initial vehicles, compounding the requests for changes to the design and modification kits. Headquarters ordered the rebuilding of 500 LVT3Cs in April 1953 to cover the gap until the P-5 family finally entered full service in 1956.[37]

For all its mechanical woes, the LVTP-5 family provided a superior mechanized amphibious assault capability to the Marine Corps. With the same engine and cross-drive transmission of the M48 tank series, the P-5 could carry its troops and cargo at speeds of 5.6 knots in water and 30 mph on land. One P-5 test rig, fitted with remote controls, crossed surf 13.5 feet in height (80% plunging) in Monterey Bay in 1957. Only 15-foot waves caused it to strike bottom at a 43-degree impact angle. Production models remained restricted to nine feet of surf, however, because of air-intake limitations. Armor protection resisted small arms and artillery fragments, but not heavy machine gun AP rounds. A cupola-mounted .30-caliber machine gun provided close-in protection. Its cavernous covered troop compartment and large bow ramp permitted carrying a large troop complement (rated at thirty-six men, but not achieved with infantrymen carrying typical field equipment loads) or five tons of cargo, including a jeep or a partly disassembled 105mm howitzer. Although designed mainly for waterborne operations, its improved torsilastic suspension provided a better ride ashore for occupants than the earlier generation LVT. However, despite initial enthusiasm for its potential as an APC, extended land use of the new LVT, twice as heavy as its predecessor, only increased the difficulties of maintenance. Engine or transmission replacement remained a day-long task, and the crew of three usually had its hands full keeping this large vehicle operational.[38]

The specialized vehicles proved highly innovative. The H-6 armored amphibian featured a fully stabilized (the LVT[A]5 had only vertical stabilizing) armored turret with a 105mm howitzer and stowage for 151 rounds, reduced usually to 100 rounds while waterborne. A .30-caliber coax and .50-caliber antiaircraft mount machine gun completed the weapons suite. The E-1 carried an angled blade-type mine excavator, capable of clearing a 12-foot lane to a depth of 16 inches. Two palletized line charges could be fired from water or land for explosive lane clearance. The communications vehicle contained a large suite of radios of various types for use by an infantry battalion or regiment commander and his principal staff.[39]

The final and perhaps most unusual armored program conceived by the Marine Corps in wake of the Korean War came in the development of a highly mobile, light antitank vehicle for the division. The regimental tank platoons were not manned in peacetime, and the tank required specialized supply and maintenance support barely adequate in Marine Corps tank battalions, let alone the infantry units. Moreover, the weight and size of the medium tank had rendered it roadbound for too much of the Korean War campaign. Although the army had abolished the tank destroyer as a concept and equipment after World War II, and the Marine Corps's mimicking with the M3 GMC had ended in 1944, the Marine Corps development of the M50 Ontos ("Thing") must be considered as a reversion to that doctrine.

In 1951 the Corps and the Allis-Chalmers Corporation began the development of a light vehicle that would employ the new and more powerful 106mm recoilless rifle, using highly mobile "shoot and scoot" tactics to reinforce the division's infantry, which would use the same rifle on a fixed mount at the battalion level. The result was a fully tracked, three-man vehicle, weighing in at nine tons, capable of firing its six rifles in sequence, pairs, or together in a single devastating volley, using simple telescopic sights and .50-caliber spotting rifles. A

145-hp gasoline engine drove it on band track at 30 mph. Carrying eigh-teen rounds of ammunition, the Ontos would equip the new divisional antitank battalions with forty-five vehicles each. Manned by the infantry, the antitank battalions supplanted the antitank companies of the infantry regiments, entering service in 1958. Production of the M50 commenced in September 1956. The installation of a Chrysler 361B engine developing 180 hp and new track during 1963–64 produced the M50A1, which had sufficient automotive improvements to enable it to reach designed speeds.[40]

Operation of the Ontos was simplicity itself, with the steering, sight-ing, and spotting designed to minimize the training demands usually associated with armored fighting vehicles. At first the design included no intercom for the crew. The "night fighting" capability installed in the M50A1 consisted of a quadrant and azimuth indicator to permit range-card firing. The spotting rifle tracers burned out at 1,500 yards, hence extended range firing was by burst-on-target technique. After fir-ing the six rifles, the loader had to reload each rifle from outside the vehicle, at a halt, from the external ammunition stowage, under the rear of the vehicle. The limited traverse (40 degrees to each side, elevation -10/+20 degrees), light armor, and telltale backblast of the rifles forced the Ontos crews to train to fight from the ambuscade. The five-vehicle platoons typically were attached to individual infantry battalions for deployments and the fifteen-vehicle company usually operated in direct support of the regiment, although the division commander could in the-ory wield the battalion as an antitank reserve.[41]

Reorganization and "Lightness" (1955–1965)

The provision of antitank battalions to the marine division at least had the favorable effect of relieving the tankers from the close-in antitank support of the infantry as a task, freeing them for more conventional armored missions. However, a greater doctrinal change in the Corps would moot the issue. The helicopter had matured sufficiently as a technological development, such that Marine Corps planners looked to it to solve most of the traditional mobility concerns of the Fleet Marine Force. Study groups at Quantico since the late 1940s had forecast great potential for the helicopter in the landing force and by the mid-1950s were ready to assume that new models would lift artillery and prime movers ashore. Neither the performance nor the numbers of helicopters sufficient for the all-helo "vertical assault" would ever materialize, but the conceptual seeds were sown. The commandant, Gen. Randolph M.

Pate, instructed the 1956 FMF Organization and Composition Board, later known in the lore as the Hogaboom Board:

> The helicopter will become the primary means of achieving tactical surprise and flexibility. However, surface landing craft and land vehicles will continue to be the primary means of mobility at the objective until sufficient helicopters of improved capability . . . are available to permit the landing, tactical maneuver and logistic support of all assault elements of a Marine Division. As the helicopter capability increases, the need for surface landing craft and land vehicles will decrease.[42]

The board responded by recommending the reduction of the division in size and weight of equipment, to at least gain full air transportability (i.e., in cargo aircraft), and enhancing the division's potential to employ vertical assault. Pate ordered the reorganization to the M-series tables in 1957, placing all tracked vehicles (except the Ontos), the heavy artillery, and much of the transportation and engineering equipment of the old World War II–pattern Marine Division into the Force Troops, replacing some of the remaining artillery howitzers with heavy mortars, and realigning personnel in the infantry regiments. The divisions conducted early field trials of the reorganization. The addition of a fourth rifle company and a complete (footmobile) reconnaissance battalion scored well with the critics, but artillery remained weak in counterbattery potential and the antitank firepower improved only for "the initial encounter."[43]

> . . . the mortality rate of the Ontos is still an unknown and highly critical factor.
> The armored shock power of the division is negligible.

The new division organization remained in force well into the 1980s, modified only by the eventual return of conventional artillery, amtrac, and tank units to the division in the 1970s as a response to a renewed orientation to the Russian-pattern ground threat. Regardless of how the helicopter developed or failed in the aftermath of the Hogaboom Board, its direct effect upon Marine Corps armored fighting vehicle concepts was to reduce their importance both tactically and in the budget program. The search for "lightness," which had influenced the initial tank program in the Marine Corps, emerged with new fervor.

The three amphibian tractor battalions switched to the Force Troops and continued to perform their missions relatively unchanged. After all, they had often performed their World War II missions from the corps support troops. For the tank battalions, however, the reorganization cancelled some of the provisions of the 1949 Armor Policy Board. The divisional and force battalions had differing missions, organizations, and equipment. While the 3d Marine Division, deployed in the western Pacific in Japan and later Okinawa, retained its share of the new force units as integral to a reinforced division concept, the tank battalions on the East and West Coast all became, in theory, force tank battalions, of which only one had remained active after the Korean War, the 8th Tank Battalion, slated to receive the M103 heavy tank upon its long-awaited debut. Yet the medium tank served as the desired infantry support tank, and the force tank battalion existed to give heavy firepower support as needed to the divisional tank battalion.

Ultimately, the Corps adopted the compromise solution of changing the 1st and 2d Tank Battalions to mixed battalions, with two medium- and one heavy-tank companies. The 3d Tank Battalion remained on the original peacetime divisional battalion organization, with three medium companies. The 8th Tank Battalion cased its colors on 12 May 1958 (the 7th had disbanded on 8 September 1952), later to return in the reserve establishment. The wartime organizational charts reflected a fourth (medium) company in the battalions and a separate heavy tank company in the Force Troops, and the reserve tank strength grew accordingly.[44]

Doubts continued well into the 1960s, however, and numerous studies recommended changes to the division organization to return the tanks and amtracs to divisional control. The criticism of the M50 Ontos increased with an unusually poor provisioning of spares upon introduction and the quartermasters admitted a total lack of parts in the FMF. Moreover, the effectiveness of the 106mm recoilless rifle as a tank killer looked inferior to the new generation of antitank guided missiles now entering service. Even the Marine Corps Reserve saw inadequacies, as only two Ontos per company were provided as training vehicles.[45]

The Marine Corps Reserve reorganized its armored vehicle units at the end of the Korean War. This establishment reduced the three reserve amtrac battalions, each with an armored amphibian company, to the 1st and 2d Amphibian Tractor Battalions, USMCR, both located on the East Coast, and the 1st and 2d Armored Amphibian Companies, USMCR, remained at Gulfport, Louisiana, and Treasure Island, California. The 1st and 2d Tank Battalions, USMCR, remained at San Diego and Mattydale (near Syracuse), New York, with a varying number of companies. With the organization of the 4th Marine Division USMCR within the reserve establishment in 1963, the requirements changed and only one battalion each of tank, amtrac, and antitank (later including 4th LAI Battalion;

see below) units became necessary. However, the reserves included additional tank, antitank, and amtrac companies as necessary to fill out wartime organizations of the regular FMF. In 1967 the 8th Tank Battalion reactivated in the reserve as a force heavy tank battalion.[46]

The few operations conducted in the decade following the Korean war varied in the extreme, and produced only minor lessons, mostly in readiness issues, for the Corps. The Lebanon Crisis of 1958 saw successive battalion landing teams (BLT) of the Sixth Fleet landing at Beirut to stabilize a tottering national government and threatening international tensions. BLT 2/2 and 3/6 landed 15–16 July under the command of Brig. Gen. Sidney Wade, commanding the 2d Provisional Marine Force. After securing the airport, Wade led an armored column of tanks, LVTs, and Ontos into the city to take control of the port area and bridges over the Beirut River, as well as to guard the U.S. embassy and residence complex. The Lebanese army cooperated with Wade and no fighting occurred. This proved fortunate for the tank platoon of 2/2, for it had two tanks and all of its tank ammunition on board an LSD on route to Malta for repairs, and these tankers landed without main gun ammunition. After 1/8 landed as reinforcement, the 2d Force counted on an array of fifteen M48 tanks, ten Ontos, and thirty-one LVTP5s for armored vehicle support. Until 27 July and the arrival of an army medium tank battalion from Germany, these vehicles alone performed the security and armored patrols, each one using typically two to three tanks, three LVTs, and a rifle platoon in a show of force. The withdrawal of these FMF units began on 14 August.[47]

The coming of the Cuban Missile Crisis in 1962 saw a large mobilization of active and reserve Marine Corps forces. For a brief interval, the Marine Corps contemplated active operations against the Russian army long anticipated in its planning. Apart from the strategic weapons exchange and general war consequences, which both sides threatened, the immediate prospect of an invasion of Cuba to neutralize the missile and air bases would have brought Marine Corps forces in contact with some of the 20,000 troops of the Red Army, including four tank battalions equipped with T-54 medium tanks as well as SU-100 tank destroyers and unspecified numbers of the primitive "Snapper" antitank missile. The deteriorating relations with Cuba had already caused the 2d Marine Division to furnish a garrison detachment to the U.S. Naval Base at Guantanamo, beginning in 1961. The initial tank platoon deployment there eventually led to a rotating assignment for a heavy tank platoon and flame-tank section, with an Ontos platoon added for good measure.

Eventually, this garrison became a permanent defense force, with an organic tank platoon and Ontos platoon, a curious throwback to the World War II defense battalion.[48]

These operations demonstrated to the Corps the continuing requirement for armored fighting vehicles, and the tank program received additional scrutiny in the 1960s in spite of the doctrine of "lightness" imposed by the 1958 reorganization. Although the Marine Corps would give the new M60 "main battle tank" (a term adopted to describe an amalgam of medium- and heavy-tank characteristics) a troop test in 1961, the G4 asserted the evident satisfaction with the M48/M103 combination. The staff rated the M103 capable of killing the JS-3 and its replacement, the T-10 Russian heavy tank, with both AP and HEAT ammunition. The M48 garnered high marks as an infantry-support tank and could kill all Soviet armor except the JS-3/T-10 with AP and could kill the heavies with HEAT rounds. Acquiring the M60, its ammunition, and spares would cost the Corps $243 million. The staff advocated waiting for the next-generation tank, for which the army had developed a 152mm combination gun and guided-missile launcher. In April of that year, however, the staff received news that the army would not undertake its Future Main Battle Tank program, leaving no replacement for the M60 series in the near term. The G3 advised the commandant, Gen. David M. Shoup, that he must consider a modernization of the current vehicle fleet or acquisition after all of the M60. The army's M551 Sheridan program still continued, however, and bore watching as a replacement for the Ontos, using a similar 152mm gun/launcher.[49]

Difficulties with tank ammunition complicated the decision process at the same time. The HEAT ammunition for both the 90mm and 120mm tank cannon had fuzing problems that made safe handling of the rounds in the confines of a turret problematic, and the Corps notified the army in March 1961 that it still refused to accept delivery of the 119,000 rounds already bought and another 56,000 previously ordered until the problems had been solved. Such difficulties dogged the HEAT ammunition almost all of its service life, including reliability problems of ammunition stored over long periods in magazines. Needless to say, the doubts over ammunition required for the defeat of the heavy Russian tanks weighed heavily on the future of the tank fleet.[50]

Shoup made his decision in June to modernize the existing tanks and forego the purchase of the M60 series. A G-4 staff study, called the "Interim and Mid-range Tank Plan," demonstrated good rationale for upgrading the M48 and M103 from both cost and performance criteria.

Essentially the tanks would be brought up to M60 automotive standards by providing them with identical diesel-engine installations. The coincidence-type rangefinder would reduce the training burden of the original stereoscopic instruments, and the program also upgraded turret controls. Finally, a collective gas particulate system would provide state-of-the-art protection against nuclear, biological, and chemical (NBC) weapons, using hoses to connect crewmen gas masks to a central unit. Assuming that the HEAT ammunition entered service, the older tanks would remain just as potent as the newer M60 with its British-designed 105mm gun, and the armor protection remained the same or better (in the case of the M103). If the army's 152mm gun/launcher proved superior to current guns, then the Corps would consider later rearming the tank fleet with that weapon.[51]

The modernization of the tank fleet prolonged the remaining effects of the 1949 Armor Policy Board decisions on the organization and operation of tank units. The 421 medium M48A1 tanks would enter the M48A3 overhaul program in December 1962 at the rate of 25 per month, and the Anniston and Red River Army Depots also upgraded the 73 M67A1 to M67A2 at five per month. The 160 M103 heavies (of 218 on hand) cycled through their rebuild beginning in August 1963 at the rate of 25 per month. The Corps refitted its Ontos to the M50A1 model at the same time as the M103 upgrades.[52]

The Corps did pursue a series of new developments in hybrid high-speed amphibious landing vehicles, employing various concepts such as planing hulls and hydrofoils, combined with wheels or tracks. These did not progress to the stage of fighting vehicles, but rather projected a high-speed cargo carrier, replacing the DUKW, which would "transit non-mobile loaded cargo directly from ship to inland beach dumps without the laborious landing craft–crane–truck transfer operation presently required at the shoreline." Corps amtrackers fervently hoped for a new series of LVTs emerging from such testing, but none of the designs attempted during the 1960s proved successful, although much engineering knowledge was obtained in hull forms and water-jet propulsion systems.[53]

Just as doctrine remained static for "land vehicles" in the Corps, training also became stultified. Although some forty students used army schools at Fort Knox in FY55, by FY58 the number had declined to twenty-three. The Marine Corps Schools Catalog of 1958 omitted mention of the Fort Knox basic course for new officers and set the advanced-course goal at zero attendance for captains. Six officers were slated for the abbreviated fifteen-week course for company-grade officers. More and more, the training of officers and crews became relegated to on-the-job training. In response to a request to extend officer training in the basic tank/amtrac course at the Camp Pendleton tracked vehicle school from four to six weeks, the headquarters training staff disapproved. While recognizing that the proposal would produce a better-trained officer, the staff asserted that the purpose of the course was to orient the officer to his anticipated duties in order to continue his military education on the job. "The temptation to use these and other courses to qualify officers in an MOS [military occupational specialty] cannot be followed, however, without undue loss of service in the operating forces and increase in students and overhead in the training base." The situation slowly improved from that 1957 nadir, and the Pendleton school trained officers, NCOs, and mechanics in increasing numbers. The officer course reached nine weeks in length by the end of the 1960s.[54]

The training levels in the FMF, never particularly high after the Second World War, probably declined during the period that the tank and amtrac battalions remained in the Force Troops, separated from the infantry units that they doctrinally supported, except for formally scheduled exercises. Amtrac crews practiced day and night water operations and ship orientation, while tank crews performed rudimentary vehicle maneuver and gunnery drills into the 1980s, using facilities dating from the Korean War. The 3d Tank Battalion on Okinawa kept its tanks on administrative deadline during much of 1961–62, too short of spares to perform any training. The delivery of a tank turret trainer from the Naval Training Devices Center in 1961 to the 2d Tank Battalion for test and evaluation perhaps summarized the situation. A response to a 1952 project, the center built the device on an M47 turret, thus rendering it completely unsuited for M48 and M103 crews. The headquarters staff promptly terminated the project![55]

The three active amtrac and three antitank battalions remained unchanged from the mid-1950s through the Vietnam War. The last force tank battalion disappeared in 1958, and the heavy tanks made up the third companies in the 1st and 2d Tank Battalions. The USMCR battalions were designated 4th and 8th on the West and East Coast, respectively, with the 8th and C Company, 4th Tank Battalion retaining the rest of the heavy tanks. A force tank company requirement remained on paper, with the same "destroyer tank" mission of 1949, to be activated from the reserves when necessary. The tank battalions thus fielded 53 medium or heavy tanks, nine flame tanks, and four M-51 heavy tank retrievers, the latter never dieselized. The amtrac battalions had 190 LVTP-5s, 10 command, 6 retriever, and 8 engineer variants. The sole remaining armored amphibian company went to depot storage with 18 H-6, 2 P-5, and an R-1 on paper strength. The antitank battalion continued unchanged with its 45 Ontos vehicles.[56]

The mature tank and amtrac force emerging from the Pacific war suffered from postwar reductions and changed priorities as did the rest of the FMF. The Corps leadership, however, remained sensitive to the need to upgrade armored materiel and used what little funds remained to partially improve the equipment. The 1949 Armor Policy Board forecast a broad range of advancements and the coming of the Korean War made most of these financially achievable. The actions of A Company, 1st Tank Battalion in the Pusan Perimeter and later at Inchon, proved that the Korean War tankers retained their mettle of the 1941–45 war. The amtrac battalion proved adequate, with its obsolescent machines, in performing their primary mission at the Inchon landing and the Han Rivor croooing, but oaw littlo uoo latcr in thcoc miooiono. After the Korean War concluded, however, the flow of new model equipment lasted until 1959 for tanks and 1963 for amtracs.

Unfortunately, the American tank and automotive industry fell short of the technical promise endorsed by the Armor Policy Board. The troubled development experienced by the tank and amtrac programs of the 1950s and the frequent defects or substandard performance of the machines hardly matched the goals of Lieutenant Colonel Stuart and his team. When combined with the wholehearted rush toward "lightness" and the false hopes of the helicopter conducted by the Corps under General Pate, the armored units began to languish in Force Troops organizations that constituted unit pools rather than fighting organizations. In the divisions of the FMF, the Ontos-equipped antitank battalions represented a gamble that armored vehicles could be minimized on future battlefields. A low tempo of operations and training with somewhat upgraded 1950-vintage designs characterized the armored units of the Corps on the eve of its next conflict.

Thus, as the Corps edged toward its seven-year campaign in Vietnam, its armored fighting vehicle situation perhaps approached its nadir.

Chapter 8

From Jungle to Desert, 1965–1991

> Get a ROC [required operational capability] out on XM1 as soon as possible. . . . [T]he Marine Corps has paid lip service to Combined Arms Training too long and must take major efforts in Combined Arms Training.
> —Gen. Lewis Wilson (1975)

Vietnam War Interlude (1965–1970)

Increases in military spending under the Kennedy administration improved readiness in the Marine Corps across the board: manpower, training, and materiel in particular. One demonstration of the renewed verve in Marine Corps operations was the execution of the two largest postwar amphibious exercises at almost the same time in the Atlantic and Pacific. Operation Steel Pike (October–November 1964) saw the II Marine Expeditionary Force (MEF—a combined division–aircraft wing team) embark over 21,000 troops for a landing near Huelva, Spain. Not only did the three full infantry regiments land (eight USMC and one Spanish naval infantry battalions), but also the MEF commander put ashore forty-five tanks, thirty-five Ontos, and fifty LVTs. A mere three months later, Operation Silver Lance (February–March 1965) saw III MEF land 15,000 troops, including thirty-six tanks and twenty-four LVTs at Camp Pendleton. In these landings the new navy landing craft of the LCU and LCM-8 type took part, their sides and ramps specially constructed to permit tanks to fire in the forward arc while afloat, one of the last elements of the 1949–50 armor and equipment policy board concepts to be accomplished. Although the exercises allowed little in the way of operations ashore, many of the tanks broke down. The dieselized tanks had not reached the units in sufficient numbers, however, and this was the last use of the older M48 and M103 "A1" versions with gasoline engines.[1]

As war clouds loomed in the western Pacific, a reprise of the Lebanon landings occurred in the Dominican Republic, and once again the Marine Corps BLTs had to land and assist in restoring order to a troubled capital city. On 28 April 1965 helicopter-borne troops of BLT 3/6 began to land in Santo Domingo. On the following day, the platoons of tanks, LVTs, and Ontos landed and an armored column joined the rest of the BLT in the city. The troops of the BLT advanced against the rebel zone in small units, sometimes subdivided down to a rifle platoon with two LVTs and a tank. Small arms fire hit around the troops, but both sides agreed to a ceasefire the same day. Reinforcements from Camp Lejeune brought the remainder of a full company each of tanks, LVTs, and Ontos with the 4th Marine Expeditionary Brigade (MEB, a combined regiment-aircraft group team), landing on 8 May. But no fighting remained of any sort and the additional armored vehicles added much to traffic congestion in the capital. Marines withdrew by 5 June, leaving army troops to complete the presence mission.[2]

Nothing could prepare the Corps fully for its longest war and the greatest challenge to its institutional fiber, the Vietnam War. There would be fewer shocks than in the Korean War, but once again the Corps would undertake tremendous expansion while continuing to operate in strength in other parts of the globe. The Corps's strength peaked in 1969 at over 314,000 (from over 190,000), with over 80,000 on duty with III MEF in Vietnam. Another division, the 5th, would activate, with its constituent tank, amtrac, and antitank battalions. In all the Corps sent two and one-third divisions into combat in Vietnam, fighting a combination campaign of pacification within the northern provinces of the Republic of Vietnam, and a more conventional border conflict against the Army of the People's Republic of Vietnam (NVA).[3]

Tank, Ontos, and amtrac companies landed with the 9th MEB at DaNang to begin the formal campaign in March–July 1965. Overall command remained with Maj. Gen. "Rip" Collins, the commanding general of III MEF until his normal relief in June, to this day the highest tactical post ever held by a Marine Corps tanker. Within a year the tank, amtrac, and antitank battalions of the 1st and 3d Marine Divisions had arrived. The 5th Marine Division's armored vehicle battalions activated in July 1966, but equipment and personnel shortages would plague these units. Each battalion furnished a company to deploy with the 27th Marines to Vietnam in the summer of 1967. Except for the M103 heavy tank, all the equipment procured in the preceding decade would receive a rigorous trial by fire. (See Table 8.1.) Unlike the North Koreans, the enemy infantry in Vietnam held capable antitank weapons in the form of rocket propelled grenades (RPG) and recoilless rifles. Full of fight and operating in infantry-favorable terrain, the NVA and their local Viet Cong (VC) henchmen proved their mettle on more than one occasion against marine tracked vehicles and their crews.[4]

The armored fighting vehicle units strove to contribute to the Vietnam campaign. The newly added xenon tank searchlight offered an improved night-fighting capability with its 75-million-candlepower output and infrared capability that projected 25-million-candlepower "black" light out to a kilometer for engagement with new main gun infrared sighting devices or the new suite of infantry weapons scopes. During the dry weather period in Vietnam (March–September) officers like Lt. Col. Walter Moore, a tanker since 1944 now commanding the 1st Antitank Battalion, urged the infantry regiment and division commanders to make greater use of the vehicles and their firepower to provide direct fire support to the infantry and to conduct motorized reconnaissance. Moore chafed at the use of Ontos for protecting command posts, artillery positions, and bridges (the saying went, "two on the ridge, three on the bridge," for such tank and Ontos platoon missions), and ventured so far as to quote from a draft Vietnamese army field manual.[5]

> In counterinsurgency the primary tradeoff is between security forces for fixed installations and forces available for offensive employment. The greater firepower of armored vehicles tempts some to use them for the defense of especially important installations. This is a gross waste of every characteristic of armor except firepower and must be steadfastly resisted. *All* of the Armor and as much as possible of the regular infantry must be free for offensive use. So freed, they will be able to contribute directly to the security of many installations in the role of reaction forces while still carrying the war to the enemy.

The tactics of tank-infantry close support and armored column procedures remained, as in the previous conflicts. Most tank and antitank companies operated in direct support of designated infantry regiments, furnishing platoons to infantry battalions as required. A few company sweeps occurred with tanks and LVTP-5s, the latter seeing considerable use out of their primary element in the role of APCs. The Ontos proved extremely vulnerable to the principal threat of mines and spent most of the war in static positions, guarding bridges and other vital points. It also displayed a nasty tendency for accidental firing of its recoilless rifles. Tanks made road sweeps, operated in tank-infantry operations with companies in direct support of infantry regiments, defended during the monsoon season, and fired the much-despised indirect fire missions to reinforce the artillery. In the absence of enemy armor, the Marine Corps tanks dominated any battlefield that they could enter, and the 90mm's superb mix of ammunition ideally suited it for the missions.

Collateral missions mounted, for example, when the 1st Marine Division tasked 1st Tank Battalion in 1967 with operating the Southern Sector Defense Command at DaNang.

The personnel drain in 1969 caused the battalion commander to cadre one tank company in order to field two full companies in support of the three USMC regiments and the 2d Brigade of the Korean Marine Corps. Meanwhile, the marines of the neighboring 1st and 3d Amtrac Battalions, when not operating vehicles, served as temporary dismounted infantrymen patrolling the "Rocket Belt" cordon around the DaNang Airport or occupying the estuary of the Cua Viet River. The 1st Amtrac essentially became a full-time infantry battalion, reprising its role from the Korean War, while 3d Tracks pulled more of the troop resupply, convoy, perimeter, and landing-zone security type of duty.[6]

The LVTP-5, with its belly fuel cells full of gasoline, proved vulnerable to mines, so its use as an APC became strictly limited. Frequently, the infantry would ride on the roof, with crew-served weapons up to 106mm sandbagged and secured to the vehicles. In the Marble Mountain sector, minings of LVTs averaged 2.7 per month. One LVTP-5 suffered the ignominious fate of being sunk in a river in 1967 by RPG-2 hits. The armored amphibian returned to war, with the activation of 1st Armored Amphibian Company in June 1966. One platoon had preceded it in 1965 and the LVTH-6s would work as assault guns and reinforcing artillery until their final, definitive decommissioning in 1970.[7]

In all some 300 LVTs were lost or damaged beyond unit repair capability during the Vietnam War, reflecting a high rate of use. Most of the sixty-two landings by Corps units of III MEF and the Seventh Fleet used the LVTP-5s, but only a few, such as Operation Starlite, attained any scale. Mines inflicted most losses. Tank and Ontos losses proved fewer and are not reliably recorded, many having been returned to action by support or depot repair. Logistic support proved inadequate, coming as no surprise to units long frustrated with the peacetime procurement of spares. The tanks fared best because of the army's use of the M48A3 in the war and the support available from its supply system and tank depots on Okinawa and Japan. The 1st and 3d Antitank Battalions decommissioned in Vietnam in December 1967, their surviving A companies being attached to the constituent tank battalions.[8]

Almost right away in 1965, the Corps attempted to put its amphibious specialty to work against the VC guerrilla bands operating in the I Corps military region assigned to Marine Corps forces in Vietnam. Operation Starlite, conducted 17–24 August, saw two rifle companies of the 2d Battalion, 7th Marines landing by LVT on the eighteenth, with two platoons of tanks, a flame-tank section, and two Ontos platoons also landed by LCM. These units proceeded inland to link with a helicopter-borne battalion, and the tanks and infantry routed the VC on first contact. The battalion commander then called for a noon resupply via five LVTs, and assigned the three unsupported flame tanks as escorts. The column got lost and ran into what became a common ambush situation during the war, and the flame tanks rather helplessly sprayed the area with machine-gun fire. A single M67A2 returned to the command post and the battalion executive officer led an impromptu relief with a single M48A3 tank, the flame tank and accompanying Ontos and infantry. The tank received a disabling recoilless rifle shot right away and a general melee ensued against the dug-in VC. The engagement resulted in twenty-two casualties (five dead) and the group had to remain overnight guarding the disabled vehicles. Only two tanks remained to support the general advance. Although the regiment commander praised the armored vehicles as preventing further casualties, the evidence remained of poor tactical handling of the armored vehicles. The similar Operation Piranha saw limited success in September and featured the first employment of the LVTE-1 to clear beach mines.[9]

By 1967, the 1st and 3d Marine Divisions occupied the north and south sections of the I Corps region and conducted separate operations for the most part, to guard the DaNang airbase complex and block infiltration of the NVA across the border, respectively. The 3d Division found the most contact with the NVA and small-scale tank employment gave little edge to the battles. Typical was the combat by 3d Battalion, 4th Marines on 27 February in which a heavy firefight, developed by L Company, quickly was dominated by the supporting tank platoon. But later a tank threw a track and "the tanks now proved to be a handicap. Company G would not leave [and] . . . was ordered to establish a night position and evacuate wounded." The next day the NVA hit from three sides at 0630 with mortars, small arms, and RPG fire. RPGs hit two tanks, one catching fire, but both continued to support the infantry company with turret .50-caliber machine guns. By the end of the action at 0900 the troops had repulsed the enemy three times. Another small unit action occurred on 28 July when the 2d Battalion, 9th Marines made a spoiling attack into the demilitarized zone (DMZ) with an attached tank platoon, three Ontos, three LVTE-1 amtracs, and engineer support. The force had to use the same road into and out of the DMZ, however, and the enemy took advantage of that knowledge and typical skill with the terrain. Moving into prepared positions covering the route, they stopped the column with a command-detonated bomb in the road and opened a withering fire. Running this gauntlet cost 23 dead and 251 Marine Corps wounded for a return of only 32 killed NVA and an undetermined number of enemy wounded.[10]

At the mouth of the Cua Viet River, the 1st Amphibian Tractor Battalion had an easier time of it, virtually running its own war to control Coastal Enclave C-4, with an attached rifle company, artillery support, and a platoon of the 1st Armored Amphibian Company. On 10 December the attached infantry spotted a reinforced platoon of NVA and pursued. The battalion commander, Lt. Col. Edward R. Toner, called in two provisional rifle platoons from his B Company, accompanied by two LVTH-6s as assault guns. The following day, these moved in on the NVA. The H-6s fired at 50–150 meters and the other four H-6s provided indirect fire support. The NVA counterattacked but died in battle, leaving fifty-four dead and uncovering a supply dump and mortar position. The cost to friendlies was only twenty wounded.[11]

The "defining year" for the Marine Corps in Vietnam—1968—saw several extremes of employment of fighting vehicles by the FMF, perhaps indicating some of the quandaries existing. Marines still found difficulties with small detachments, as shown by a 24 January NVA ambush of four trucks in the 3d Marine Division zone. The reaction force, consisting of only one M48A3, one M67A2, and two M42 self-propelled 40mm vehicles (army) and led by the commander of Company B, 3d Tank Battalion, ran into the usual ambush prepared for the usual relief force. Capt. Daniel W. Kent died in action when a recoilless rifle round hit his tank. The enemy broke and ran when helicopter gunships responded.[12]

The Battle for Hue began on 30 January when eight battalions of NVA infantry infiltrated the city and the NVA 2d Division threatened to reinforce. The responding Marine Corps forces included tank platoons from both 1st and 3d Tank Battalions, and Ontos of A Company, 1st Antitank Battalion. Here, with the enemy in known and observable positions, the armored vehicles gave key support to the embattled infantry and undoubtedly provided the measure of superiority. The key Marine Corps infantry battalion commanders fighting there differed in their opinions but valued the support equally. Lt. Col. Ernest Cheatham, commanding 2/5, liked the Ontos for its speed and agility and thought that the tanks drew too much fire. Lt. Col. Robert Thompson of 1/5 preferred the tanks for their armament and staying power. Both tanks and Ontos received frequent hits by RPG and recoilless rifle rounds. Several tanks went through up to five crews and remained in action. Three of the Ontos stayed knocked out of action when hit. Most commanders rated the 90mm fire best, provided that the tankers had and used concrete piercing fuzes on their HE rounds. Otherwise, the 106mm projectiles of the Ontos worked better in knocking down buildings and walls to facilitate the infantry advance. Both Thompson and Cheatham had to hold up their advance at times for lack of 90mm and 106mm ammunition, illustrating the essential role of their armored fighting vehicles.[13]

The single tank platoon and two Ontos platoons assigned to the 26th Marines during the 77-day siege of Khe Sahn provided arguably less decisive support to that embattled outpost than had occurred at Hue. The vehicles remained in "hide" positions during the day and emerged to occupy fighting positions during the night. Tankers fired most of their ammunition, however, as indirect fire missions, since their cannon outranged the artillery available to combat outpost. When NVA light tanks made their long-anticipated appearance in I Corps, attacking the combined special forces camp at nearby Lang Vei with twelve PT-76s, there was no possibility of getting the marine Corps tanks or Ontos into action. The regiment commander had planned only an infantry reaction force to move overland through jungle, instead of facing the predictable road ambush on the way to the camp. In the end nothing was done beyond requesting air support for the beleaguered special forces and their native troops.[14]

In fact, one discerns almost a singular lack of Marine Corps interest in employing armored fighting vehicles in any significant numbers during the Vietnam campaign. The only effort seemingly made by the Marine Corps in Vietnam to form a large mechanized team came with Task Force Robbie in the 3d Marine Division. Ostensibly named for the assistant division commander, this unit consisted of a tank company of the 3d Tank Battalion, augmented with a pair of army M42 "duster" 40mm vehicles, two army truck companies carrying some quadruple .50-caliber mounts and one or more rifle companies. Tank officers planned the routes, fire support, and operations, which focused on the rapid reinforcement of any position threatened in the division area. This concept of a mobile division reserve had merit, but the force usually saw action in a piecemeal manner. Certainly nothing approaching army mounted operations occurred in the two Marine Corps divisions, despite fairly large numbers of vehicles and a notably absent enemy armor threat. Ironically, the army made some use of excess Ontos acquired from the Marine Corps in Vietnam. Formed in Company D, 16th Armor, for use with the 173d Airborne Brigade, the former Marine Corps vehicles gave good support to the troops when flown into action by the flying crane heavy-lift helicopters supporting the brigade.[15]

Marine Corps forces began to redeploy out of Vietnam in 1969, a gradual withdrawal only completed two years later. The tank and amtrac battalions rotated early, since fighting had ebbed considerably in the III MAF zone. By mid-1970, all had relocated to their former garrison bases. After the Corps processed large numbers of discharges and disbanded the 5th Marine Division units and the remaining 2d Antitank Battalion, the remaining tracked vehicle units picked up a new direction for training and operations, as the Corps began to prepare for Europe and NATO commitments as its main raison d'être. Although the Corps could anticipate little in the way of additional funding in the 1970s, the need to prepare for conflict involving large mechanized forces blew new life into the tank and amtrac units.[16]

Redeployment and Reorganization (1970–1980)

The fluid and often confused nature of Vietnam War engagements left little legacy for the Corps. Interservice rivalries, especially over the control of air power, and lesser-scale spats over the command of large ground formations left many senior Marine Corps commanders wary of the future

Table 8.1. USMC Armored Fighting Vehicle Inventory, 1967

Vehicle	Authorized	Possessed	Distribution
M48A3	457	409	195[a] (189)[b]
M103A2	160	160	34 (33)
M67A2	75	73	36 (34)
M51 VTR	73	101	42 (39)
LVTP-5	820	1085	447 (441)
LVTC-5	82	85	42 (41)
LVTR-1	67	78	28 (28)
LVTE-1	40	47	28 (28)
LVTH-6	340	329	18 (18)
M50A1	281	352	170 (159)

Source: Equipment distribution and condition report in Dept. of Navy Installations and Logistics letter, 16 Oct. 1967, RG127/71A4525/8.
Note: 265 LVTP-5s, 5 LVTC-5s, 14 LVTR-1s, 237 LVTH-6s, and 81 M50A1s were in storage.
[a] Actual units.
[b] Ready.

American way of war. Marines felt reassured that their emphasis on small-unit tactics and leadership had proved rewarding. There remained less certainty, however, in heavy weapons and weapons systems, and how much they had contributed to success or failure in the long and agonizing campaign, with its seemingly indifferent outcome.

On the other hand, the traditional Cold War enemy remained in place and the Corps clearly returned to post–World War II concepts of mobilization and reinforcement of the European theater. With that renewed emphasis, one could anticipate a reassessment of the firepower and mobility resident in the Fleet Marine Force, and the modernization of armored fighting vehicles not deemed crucial to operations in Southeast Asia. Studies and wargames conducted at Quantico during 1967–68 already pointed to possible changes in equipment and organization. The war games evaluated various mixes of armored vehicles and antitank weapons in both conventional and mixed battalions in action against Red Army units of T62 and T54 medium tanks and the PT76 light reconnaissance tank, with the usual array of accompanying mechanized infantry equipment. The Marine Corps tank and amtrac units used M60-series, MBT70, and M48-series tanks, the M551 light reconnaissance vehicle and a proposed LVTHX-5 armored amphibian for comparative purposes. The infantry units employed 106mm recoilless rifles, TOW and dragon antitank missiles, and light antiarmor weapons (LAAW) in these "tests."

The Quantico studies and war games concluded that the current inventory of tanks and antitank weapons no longer sufficed for the threat at any level of warfare. Lt. Gen. Lewis J. Fields, commanding the Development and Education Center at Quantico, endorsed the reports, recommending the disbanding of the antitank battalions and the procurement of the M551 light reconnaissance vehicle, with its powerful 152mm-gun launcher, as a light armored combat vehicle (LACV), and the rearming of the M48 tanks with the 105mm gun of the M60 tank, pending the development of the army's MBT70 (Main Battle Tank 1970, the successor to the earlier Future Main Battle Tank program of 1961). The recommended tank battalion consisted of thirty-six tanks and twenty-four LACV, four flame tanks, and four retrievers. Fields warned that the MBT70 program merited caution on the part of the Corps, and he steadfastly resisted the creation of a Force Mechanized Group (an armored vehicle regiment) introduced in the studies:

> For example, the war games do not provide a rationale to completely support the conclusion . . . that "a Force Mechanized Group consisting

of the combined tank-LACV battalion, the amphibian tractor battalion and the armored amphibian battalion would provide more effective tank, antitank and mechanized support." There is considerable reservation on [the statement] ". . . that the Force Mechanized Group original concept should be applied to current and follow-on MC mechanized assets."[17]

The first new amtrac in the Corps armored vehicle acquisitions after Vietnam eventually proved to be a thoroughbred. CMC had hoped to field it in FY67 and contracted in June 1962 for six LVTPX-11 prototypes to be delivered by the end of 1963. With such a development schedule, a proposed refit of the LVTP-5 fleet with the tank diesel engine and transmission seemed unnecessary. The headquarters staff took direct charge of the development program, charging the Landing Force Development Activity (later the Developmental Center) as the program manager.[18]

The project received design proposals from FMC, Borg-Warner, Pacific Car and Foundry, and the Chrysler Corporation. These ranged from 14 to 20 tons weight, employing a Cummins V-8 diesel engine (with a gas turbine option planned) of 315 hp to achieve speeds of 40 mph on land and 6–7 mph on water. A modern suspension system featured ten to twelve large road wheels, supported by either conventional steel torsion bars or rubber torsion devices. The vehicles carried twenty-six to twenty-nine troops or four tons cargo, with the troops positioned in impossibly cramped seating as specified for the thirty-six men in the old P-5. The rather boxy vehicle shapes (average 21 x 10 x 9 feet) still relied on tracks for water propulsion and carried the usual cupola-mounted machine gun. Only the Pacific Car and Foundry candidate differed markedly from the pack of candidates, relocating the engine to the front to permit a rear ramp mounting and a bow trim vane to improve stability at sea.

The contract went to Borg-Warner, specifying improvements such as a Lycoming gas turbine, electric drive, band track, and improved armor. Unfortunately, the program would be canceled in mid-1963, as the design proved unfeasible because of propulsion limitations and the unfortunate beam-length ratio. Smarting from these setbacks, the Corps sought a redesigned tracked vehicle in collaboration with the FMC Corporation.[19]

Between 1967 and 1968, the Corps took delivery of fourteen prototypes of the LVTPX-12, a 19-ton carrier for twenty-five troops, using a torsion bar suspension and 400 hp Detroit Diesel linked to water jets to drive it 40 mph on land and 8 mph in water. Testing through 1969 revealed it to be highly superior in all measures to the LVTP-5 family except in internal volume. It particularly distinguished itself in surf, crossing through plunging surf in excess of 10 feet in height, fully loaded. Although a 20mm/7.62mm machine-gun combination in an electrical power turret armed the prototypes, the first production version delivered for testing in October 1971 would feature the .50-caliber M85 machine gun. The Hispano-Suiza M139 20mm had caused problems and project officers feared the heavier weapon would cause its employment as an assault gun.[20]

The new LVTP-7 began to reach the FMF in 1972, but only additional recovery and command variants would be produced, no engineer or armored amphibians, owing to budget limitations. The original armament, despite the deletion of the 20mm gun, never proved successful. As early as 1973 the field complaints came in. The commander of the 2d Amtrac Battalion reported the weapons station required a high level of training to operate and maintain. Trips to the gunnery range had produced disappointing results: nine weapons firing almost 5,000 rounds with twenty-three stoppages and four others firing 5,700 rounds with twelve stoppages, using average crews. He predicted better results from more experienced crews when corrections to the gun, mount, and ammunition feed chutes occurred, but the system never proved popular with the troops.[21]

The same year that the P-7 reached the FMF, the Corps retired the M103 and M67 tanks and established the four-company all-medium tank battalion as standard. Hopes ran high that the XM803 tank could be purchased and a state-of-the-art tank replace the aging M48. But the failure of this last vestige of the Army MBT70 program threw the Corps into a quandary. The M48, even if upgunned, could not be expected to fare well in the NATO theater. The army would not continue standard logistic support for this tank in the future. Once more the standard production army tank had to be acquired, and the M60A1 replaced the M48s in 1974. The addition of the 105mm gun and its modern discarding-sabot ammunition (APDS and APDSFS) gave the tank battalions a better anti-tank weapon, but other characteristics remained much the same as the M48 tank, with a slight increase in fully loaded (combat) weight. However, new improvements followed in 1977 with a changeover to the newest production M60A1: passive night sights, main gun stabilization, and a "reliability improved" engine.[22]

Much work remained to be done, however, for Marine Corps units and leaders lacked experience in the conduct of mechanized operations. The tank battalion and assault amphibian battalions returned to the division organization from force troops in 1976, marking the end of the "light" period brought on by the Hogaboom Board. Even with an improved amtrac, redesignated an assault amphibious vehicle (AAV) in 1985, and the current main battle tank, modern notions of combined arms would be slow to grow in the FMF. Marines did poorly in NATO Exercise Strafer Zügel, in which a Marine Amphibious Unit (MAU) participated in an exercise in northern Germany. Restricted from using helicopters in the accustomed way, the marine reinforced battalion with its platoon of M48A3s and LVTP-7s was hopelessly outmatched by fast-moving *panzertruppen.*[23]

Early trial mechanized exercises with the 2d Tank Battalion and 2d Marine Regiment had begun in 1972, using M48A3 tanks and trucks as surrogate amtracs, repeated twice in 1975 with M60A1 tanks and the LVTP-7s at Fort Stewart, Georgia. In 1976 the FMF transferred a reinforced platoon of LVTP-7s to the desert training base at Twenty-nine Palms, California, where 3d Tank Battalion had returned from its former base in Okinawa, and the "Palm Tree" series of mounted fire-support exercises began in earnest. Thus when Marine Corps units returned to the fall NATO exercises in 1976, it was with a new impetus, built around a complete 4th Marine Amphibious Brigade (MAB), including a half tank battalion (two tank companies) with M60A1 tanks and a half battalion of LVTP-7s, mounted by troops now more familiar with basic mechanized tactics. Success in that year's Exercise NATO Bonded Item 76 carried over into an even better NATO Bold Guard 78, where the 4th MAB brought 53 tanks and over 100 LVTP-7s, with fire support provided by a self-propelled artillery battalion combined with the full panoply of marine aviation: helos, attack planes, and missiles. By mid-1979 tankers at Camp Lejeune could even maneuver freely across and along the base roadways, at last overturning the restrictions imposed in the late 1940s by the quartermaster of the Marine Corps.

The Corps introduced the TOW and Dragon antitank missiles into the FMF in 1975. However, the twenty-four-launcher TOW platoons were concentrated (three each) in a large antitank company added to the tank battalion for improved maintenance support. This measure reprised the divisional scout company of 1941, also attached to the tank battalion. But in this case, the jeep (M151 at this stage) served as the missile launcher's mobility, so the maintenance of almost 130 more of these small vehicles became part of the battalion logistic load. Yet the jeep hardly qualified as a combat vehicle, and the TOW sections, of eight launchers each, usually supported individual infantry battalions. These were part of the growing pains that Marine Corps tacticians would experience as the combined arms skills grew haltingly in the FMF.

Much of the Corps leadership viewed any change in doctrine to mechanized operations on the European continent with considerable trepidation. The Corps retained its historic paranoia over appearing superfluous as a second land army. Many generals wished to abandon what appeared to be the "heavy" armored concept of operations and return with new enthusiasm to the amphibious specialty of World War II, an indispensable capability for the United States, viewed from within the Corps as a traditional sea power. But even the new assault amphibious vehicle had only improved its water speed by a few knots. An amphibious landing force for the 1980s would have to do better, especially to gain notice of the NATO strategists.

Accordingly, the Corps issued its requirement in August 1974 for a new LVA (landing vehicle, assault), to be produced by the mid-1980s, later extended to 1990. Compared to the automotive evolution represented in the LVTP-7 series, the LVA called for revolutionary progress through a high- to medium-risk development of a planing hull with retracting suspension, powered through the water at 25 mph by new stratified-charge rotary engines of great compactness but high power. The USMC Amphibian Vehicle Test Branch evaluated industry proposals in 1975, recommending against surface effect and hydrofoil designs, based upon the complexity, transition problems from high to low speed, surf zone, and riverine hazards. Estimating that technical feasibility could be achieved by 1988, they urged the continuation with the 1500-hp rotary engine as key, with a gas-turbine alternate design. Two developmental contracts were issued for an air cushion and a planing hull design solution. Some 932 LVA (77 with command and control modules) were planned to replace 855 LVTP-7 and 77 LVTC-7 models, with 54 retrievers to be replaced in kind. The concept of operation was for the LVA to land an infantry regiment from 25 miles offshore through Sea State 2, across eight-foot surf, and then continue to attack ashore at 40 mph as an APC using a 25mm automatic cannon in a stabilized turret. Tanks and other support would make the same landing in trace, using air-cushion landing craft already under development by the navy to replace conventional landing craft.

In 1979, however, cost estimates had shot up so that the Corps could not proceed, given the unresolved technical risks. The LVA program was canceled and an immediate requirement emerged for an improved

AAV, called LVX, which would improve upon the land-fighting characteristics of the AAV-7 (formerly LVTP-7) to approximately the same as the army's M2 Bradley, while retaining the same performance of the AAV-7 in water. The LVX would act as a true infantry fighting vehicle, with provision for the thirteen or, in alternate design, twenty-one infantrymen to fight from within the vehicle.[24]

Alas, the complexities of merging the two types of vehicles resulted in cost estimates no better than the LVA. Thus in 1985 the Corps reversed itself again and embarked on an AAV7A1 program to extend the life of the AAV7 through the end of the century. New engines, weapons stations, and suspensions, as well as a series of other components, including applique armor, would keep the AAV7 in service and tactically viable.[25]

At the center of the controversy remained the questions of doctrine and organization. The tank, assault amphibian, and infantry battalions lacked any common means of operating under a modern combined arms concept. Infantry manuals dated from 1970 and the new tank and AAV manuals written through 1976 merely reflected the new vehicle characteristics, with no new approach. The army had embarked on a new FM 100-5 series, ultimately leading to their air-land battle concept. Yet the dissimilarities of army and USMC maneuver battalions prevented any simple copying. In the end USMC units would have to task organize the three distinct FMF units to mount infantry for extended periods in AAVs, and mix these with tank units into combined arms task forces, either tank or infantry-heavy. Yet the AAV leaders insisted on maneuvering the vehicles, leaving the infantry mere riders, as if embarked in landing craft or helicopters. The tankers wanted the infantry to come out of their mental foxholes and directly embrace the goals of combined arms, relegating the amtrackers to simple custodians of the equipment.

In the mid-1970s military journalists and defense analysts joined with Congress to charge the Marine Corps with remaining too wedded to World War II amphibious operations, thus making them unsuited for the demands of NATO operations. In the sparse budget years following the Vietnam War, being found so irrelevant appalled the Corps leadership as certain institutional death. The Senate requested a comprehensive six-month study by the Marine Corps on its mission, force structure, manpower, and quality in May 1975. The manpower and efficiency report alone would take that much time, and in June the commandant, Gen. Louis Wilson, ordered his director of operations, Maj.

Gen. Fred C. Haynes, to undertake a separate one-year study of Marine Corps force structure.[26]

General Wilson's guidance for the Haynes Board imposed few restraints. No weapon or organization remained sacred, save the recently reorganized combat service support echelon in the FMF, which Haynes could study but not offer organizational changes. Wilson considered the A-4 and AV-8 aircraft valuable, but remained noncommittal on fighters and wanted reconnaissance aircraft held as a low priority. He wanted heavy artillery to be eight-inch caliber and directed a reduction in trucks and specified the strength of the infantry battalions. On tanks, Wilson ordered the acquisitions chief to show a Marine Corps requirement for the army's new XM1 main battle tank, the successor to the dead MBT70 program. He specified the return of the 3d Tank Battalion to the United States, leaving only four platoons in the western Pacific. Wilson, who had won the medal of honor on Guam in 1944, fumed that "the Marine Corps has paid lip service to Combined Arms Training too long and must make major efforts in Combined Arms Training."[27]

The Haynes Board reported out on 17 March 1976 and suggested the creation of permanent "mobile assault regiments," one on each coast, in which the infantry, tank, and assault amphibian (formerly amtrac) battalions would live and work together to create the combined arms force deemed necessary for operations in NATO. More and heavier artillery, additional antiaircraft missile batteries, and activation of the fourth company in the assault amphibian battalions (to increase the tactical mobility of the infantry) rounded out the core changes Haynes urged. He also advocated improved combined arms training and a review of Marine Corps tactics for the mid- to high-intensity conflict. Above all, he later asserted, the board sought to drive the institutional thinking of the Corps toward what it saw as likely future conflict, especially in the oil-resource regions of the Middle East.

The mobile assault regiment concept General Haynes proposed combined two infantry battalions, two tank battalions, one assault amphibian battalion, and a self-propelled artillery battalion. The tank battalions grew from three to four in Haynes's study, but they were smaller, using the same total number of tanks in the current inventory.[28]

But few of the senior officers could bear to see such a decisive alteration of FMF organization, given the doubts and fears associated with army-like organizations in the Corps. The opposition grew, rallying around the formidable figure of Gen. Samuel Jaskilka, the assistant commandant. One year later, the official policy statement held that the capabilities of the mobile assault regiment (MAR) existed already in the various units of the FMF:[29]

> Initial indications are that these capabilities can be effectively main-tained within the existing structure through training emphasis, and can be provided to satisfy operational requirements by task organizing. This approach would have the advantage of training the full flexibility of the current structure, while ensuring the operational capability envisioned by the Haynes Board recommendation [for the mobile assault regiment].
>
> Other than funding to support the additional training emphasis described . . . [above] no funds have been allocated toward forming a MAR and no new equipment requirements have thus far been identified.

The Haynes Board remained stillborn, the heavy assault regiments never formed and proved sorely lacking in the 1990–91 Persian Gulf conflict. Major General Haynes retired a few years later, in the same grade.

Attempts at Combined Arms (1980–1990)

Tentative doctrine for fighting with combined arms using the existing FMF organizations emerged from Quantico in the form of Education Center Publication (ECP) 9-3 (1978) and later Operational Handbook (OH) 9-3B (1980). These introduced the concept of "Marine Combined Arms Task Forces," organized at the battalion level, controlling "mobile assault companies." The resulting procedures effectively translated con-ventional mechanized doctrine and made it applicable to Marine Corps line units. Here, at last, the way stood clear for effective tactical growth for Marine Corps combined arms and later a spirit of maneuver warfare using Marine Corps infantry units, mounted in AAVs, moving in con-cert with tank units, with a full array of artillery, naval gunfire, and air support. The combined arms exercise program at Twenty-nine Palms continued to refine these concepts, just as the army worked at Fort Irwin and its National Training Center to convert the doctrine to experience.

However, doctrinal cohesion was never obtained in the Corps, despite lessons learned and repeated at Twenty-nine Palms, Camp Pendleton, Camp Lejeune, and during excursions to army bases for training. The principal factors preventing a true mechanized doctrine centered on the uneasiness of the leadership with mechanization, doubts about the strategic lift costs of so much heavy equipment, and apparent nostalgia for an almost mythical state of "lightness," which would leave the infantrymen supreme, devoid of technological burdens. After all, tanks and AAVs had not proven decisive in the Vietnam War, where the current leadership had earned their professional reputations. Had not the commandant, Gen. Robert Barrow, as a company commander approaching Seoul, shrugged off the NKPA T34s with a few volleys of 3.5-inch rockets? Somehow, there had to be a way for marines to be different and not simply be imitating the NATO armies.

Enter the light armor. Lighter armored fighting vehicles, in the 16- to 18-ton range, could be carried in slings under the newest heavy-lift helicopter, the triple-engine CH-53E, entering service in the late 1970s. If such vehicles could be made effective against Warsaw Pact armor, then the Corps could return to its long-cherished notions of vertical envelopment and discard the heavy mechanized regiments advocated by the noisy but few armor advocates in the Corps. The Developmental Center at Quantico proposed, in a 1973 study, that a mobile protected weapons system (MPWS) be designed, a "light weight, highly mobile and agile, helicopter-transportable weapons system capable of supporting the infantry against armor, materiel and personnel targets, an assault gun in the force beachhead and for subsequent operations ashore." Several Department of Defense agencies began to support such a project, and the Marine Corps received approval to lead a joint project, with the army as junior partner, called the Advanced Combat Vehicle Technology (ACVT) Program. The army, ever reluctant to see programs threatening main battle tank research and mindful of growing criticism in political and defense circles over the tank programs, past and future, nevertheless participated out of a need for an air-dropable combat vehicle for the airborne and airmobile forces.[30]

The ACVT Program centered upon two research vehicles and a field exercise. The 45-ton high-mobility and -agility vehicle (HIMAG) chassis evaluated a 1,500-hp gas turbine, and the high-survivability test vehicle, light (HSTV-L), used a 650-hp gas turbine on a 20.5-ton chassis. Both vehicles would carry minimum armor protection against small arms, trusting to "agility" to evade killing shots on a smoke-filled and confused battlefield. That tactical concept was evaluated in 1980 by the Corps and army at Fort Hunter Liggett in an instrumented test named the Advanced Anti-Armored Vehicle Evaluation (ARMVAL). A new hypervelocity automatic-loading 75mm cannon would be featured as the primary weapon envisioned in these and other projects. The Corps published its formal requirement for the MPWS in 1978, seeking a 16-ton vehicle with great agility (0–20 mph in 8 sec. acceleration) and emphasizing its antitank capability. A family of vehicles akin to the AAV system gained favor at the Development Center as well. A fully developed and engineered vehicle would enter service in 1988 (initially 1985), but if a hybrid vehicle could be converted from existing light-tank or armored-car designs, then a 1986 service date could be attained. Forty years after the arrival of the first Marmon-Herrington "light fighting tanks" at Quantico, the Marine Corps found itself again proposing a unique lightweight design to perform tank functions on the battlefield.[31]

Clearly, the MPWS could not be produced in the near future, yet the Corps accepted more commitments with major NATO and theater commands that faced mechanized potential opponents in Europe, the Far East, the Middle East, and Southwest Asia. The Corps would align troops to the three brigade (3d, 6th, and 7th MEB) sets of equipment to be stored on board maritime prepositioning ships (MPS) and ready for operations by the mid-1980s. The brigades had to meet Defense Department guidance calling for the equivalent of an army mechanized brigade on the ground, together with the other components of a marine air-ground task force. All the active tank and assault amphibian battalions would be required to man and equip these brigade sets. Thus, one element of Corps war planning continued to move toward the heavy-assault regiment requirement, at the same time that the light force advocates searched for weapons to make their program effective under the same conditions of operation.

Congressional testimony by key Marine Corps generals in 1980 confirmed that the Corps needed a near-term version of the MPWS in the form of a light armored vehicle (LAV) to keep the bulk of the infantry viable in the modern maneuver warfare envisioned in the war plans. Thus, Congress came to the Corps's rescue with funds, beginning in 1981, for the purchase of LAVs available "off the shelf" in the world armaments industry. After a rushed series of tests, the Corps selected the General Motors–Canada LAV candidate, an eight-wheeler based upon the Mowag "Pirate" design, as the basis for a family of vehicles. The LAV-25 began to reach units in 1983. The 15-ton vehicle with a three-man crew mounted a 25mm automatic cannon and two 7.62mm machine guns in a stabilized turret. Protected against small-arms fire, it had great maneuverability and good cross-country performance with a maximum speed of at least 50 mph and could ford streams using rear propeller drive. Most important, it could be airlifted in C130 and larger aircraft and the new air-cushion landing craft could carry five of them in the place of a single tank.

The USMC LAV battalion started out as almost a landlubber clone of the amtrac battalion, with a 25mm-gun infantry carrier as a base vehicle, and variants for command, recovery, mortar, supply, antiaircraft, and assault gun (the last planned and designed but not bought) missions. Organic infantrymen would be added only as an afterthought in the late 1980s, as the battalion moved in typology from a mobility/firepower (LAV) unit to a motorized infantry (light armored infantry—LAI) and finally a mobile reconnaissance battalion (light armored reconnaissance—LAR), all in the first ten years of existence. It seems clear that the Marine Corps generals advocating the LAV battalion sought a miniature operational maneuver group that would give a theoretical rapid-maneuver option to a marine division still capable of mounting only one infantry regiment in AAVs, shuttling one regiment via helicopters and retaining the third regiment as footmobile. Ironically, the near-term solution to light armor became the final solution, for the technical promise of the MPWS faded in face of main battle tank armor technology, the false hope that agility equaled protection, and the limited availability of heavy-lift helicopters.[32]

The LAV series vehicles gradually began to appear in the field as the Marine Corps began to experience a number of "small wars" challenges both overseas and nearer to home. The combat debut (in U.S. hands) of the LVTP-7 and the M60A1 tank came with the curious Grenada intervention of 1983. Two companies of BLT 2/8 landed by helicopter on 25 October near Pearls Airport, but a second effort to secure the governor's residence on the other side of the island at St. George's brought a landing of another company in AAVs with the tank platoon and antitank section at Grand Mal Bay. The armored vehicles marched down the coast to St. George's that night, to relieve a team of Special Forces that had secured the governor's residence. The government troops fled at the sound of tracked vehicles in the night, and only sporadic shooting occurred. Accompanying infantry knocked out a government APC with a LAAW, but no serious challenges developed. That proved fortunate, for once again, amazingly, the tanks had landed without main gun ammunition, crowning the tenser moments of this operation with a bit of comic opera.[33]

The same BLT 2/8 that participated in the seizure of Grenada continued on its original mission as a relief unit in Lebanon, where the Marine Corps mission there had just turned into a combat situation. The first three rotations of MEU (Marine Expeditionary Unit, a BLT—aircraft squadron team) had landed at Beirut Airport under benign, administrative conditions, not even landing artillery and tanks until the second rotation. The third relief unit used its AAVs to render aid to civilians caught in a severe snowstorm in the Lebanese mountains. But the fourth rotation in Beirut, the 24th MEU, had begun taking part in the conflict, first with artillery support for the government troops, and then firing five rounds from a tank at a recoilless rifle aiming at one of the rifle company positions on 4 September 1983. On 16 October the commander moved the tanks to a more visible position, hoping to discourage other attempts to harass the Marine Corps's lines. Quite unexpectedly, the next strike came early on 23 October in the form of a suicide attack with a large truck bomb, which flattened the 24th MEU headquarters building in the resulting explosion.

Into this fray came the 26th MEU and BLT 2/8, fresh from its combat initiation in Granada. Fighting broke out on several occasions in December, and this time all arms came into use, with a vengeance; the tanks and antitank missiles scoring several hits on rebel centers of resistance. But the American withdrawal from Lebanon came all too quickly, and with a bitter taste of disaster.[34]

The next overseas expedition brought the new LAV units into play, an ideal constabulary role for these vehicles and troops. As tensions grew between the U.S. forces in the Panama Canal Zone and the local government, the theater commander, Gen. Frederick Woerner, requested these unique vehicles as reinforcements for his garrison forces. Companies of the 2d LAI Battalion began to rotate into the zone every three to four months, beginning in May 1989. When General Woerner decided to begin the action on 20 December, D Company, 2d LAI had its place in the sun. Using fourteen LAV-25s manned with ten scout teams drawn from a force security company, the LAI platoons overran government troops posts, broke roadblocks, protected the U.S. embassy, and supported other units with fire. The vehicles and troops performed well against very light resistance.[35]

Having procured the upgraded AAV7A1 and new LAV vehicles in the 1980s, the main battle tank now became a concern to Corps planners as the armor threat represented by the T-72- and T-80-series tanks had demanded a new generation of tanks from the NATO powers, including the M1 (former XM1) Abrams tank on the part of the U.S. Army. Five different commandants had a hand in the long and painful decision process by which the Corps finally decided to acquire the M1. Retaining the obsolete M60A1 or going to the industry's super-M60 option would have run against the army logistics support priorities, all converting to the M1 program. As an interim measure, the Corps took over the management of an active add-on armor kit in 1988, abandoned by the army, which offered substantial improvements to the frontal 70-degree arc of the tank. Continued use of the M60A1 into the 1990s by the Marine Corps, however, would have risked shortages quite soon in gun tubes, engines, and fire-control components. The M1 appeared and disappeared from Corps budget forecasts starting in 1981, when it was first fielded in the army. Finally a decision memorandum of February 1985 by the commandant, Gen. Paul X. Kelley, would stick, fixing an objective of 490 M1A1 (120mm gun) tanks to replace the 716 M60s then in the Corps fleet of three active and two reserve battalions, three afloat MPS sets, and planned war reserve stocks. Changing to a four-tank platoon permitted some reductions, but mostly the depot and prepositioning requirements would be shaved to set the lesser requirement.[36]

The officer most closely connected with the procurement of the M1 tank repeated the essential 1948–50 role of Lt. Col. Arthur Stuart in determining Marine Corps armor policy in many ways. A passionate advocate of tanks and armored doctrine for the Marine Corps, Lt. Col. Martin R. Steele secured the telling 1985 decision from the commandant, after several years' effort which included his being scolded and thrown out of two commandants' offices on several occasions. Emerging from service in Vietnam with 1st Tank Battalion as a corporal, Steele earned a commission and commanded tank platoons and companies and an amtrac company before being ordered to Detroit in 1977 as the Marine Corps liaison officer to the Army Tank and Automotive Command (TACOM). With characteristic toughness and professional courage, Steele corrected Marine Corps problems with M60A1 tank engines and solved universal flaws in the M60A1 fire-control system, drawing on the knowledge of civilian experts at TACOM and then overcoming heavy bureaucratic inertia to field the corrections. Ordered to headquarters as a lieutenant colonel, he occupied the same post from which "Jeb" Stuart had engineered the Armor Policy Board and had overseen the orders for the medium and heavy tanks of the 1950s. Steele had no success in prompting new armor policy deliberations, but he was able to "sell" the M1 tank program after years of effort. He then went on to command the 1st LAV Battalion, bringing his considerable knowledge to bear in wringing out flaws in its design and logistic provisioning. Like Stuart, he commanded the 1st Tank Battalion but, in contrast, later saw his career soar until retiring as a lieutenant general in 1999.[37]

Original planning for the M1A1 fielding called for training all battalions on the initial sixteen tanks at Twenty-nine Palms during 1991, and completing the active force issue in 1992. The Persian Gulf campaign would alter that schedule, however.

Gulf War Shootout (1990–1991)

In wake of the Iraqi seizure of Kuwait in August 1990, the president of the United States ordered the U.S. Central Command to reinforce and defend Saudi Arabia and the other Persian Gulf states, in concert with a growing coalition determined to resist and ultimately expel the Iraqi forces. Among the first U.S. forces to arrive in Saudi Arabia for this purpose was the 7th MEB, which deployed to the key port and petroleum center of Al Jubayl, with its aviation based further south on the Gulf of Bahrain. Offloading heavy equipment, including 53 M60A1 tanks, 28 LAVs, and about 100 AAV7A1, from its dedicated Maritime Prepositioning Squadron 1, the brigade reported ready for operations on 25 August, a mere ten days after arrival in theater and weeks ahead of any U.S. Army armored force.

The brigade stood alone only for a few days before the follow-on elements of the I MEF began to arrive. Eventually growing to a force of over 90,000 marines and navy personnel, the Marine Forces, Central Command, included two reinforced divisions, an enlarged aircraft wing containing the majority of the USMC aircraft inventory, and the bulk of two force service support groups. Over 20,000 marines and navy personnel of the 4th and 5th MEBs remained afloat while the I MEF moved into the Kuwaiti-Saudi frontier.

Both the M60- and M1-series tanks saw their first American combat employment against enemy armor with the Corps, the latter tank hurriedly issued to 2d Tank Battalion and two companies of the 4th Tank Battalion as they arrived in theater. The M60A1s also received "Blazer" active armor applique kits, a Corps-wide modification delayed for the vehicles stored on board the MPS.

Turning to the mission and threat at hand, marines prepared to fight what was widely perceived as a combat-seasoned mechanized army, eighth largest in the world. The ground units dug themselves in north of the Jubayl area and rehearsed antitank tactics, while marine airmen scoured the skies, patrolling over land, and covering the fleet units then in the Persian Gulf. The tank, light armored infantry, and assault amphibious battalions came into their own as the 1st and later the 2d Marine Divisions girded themselves for classic desert warfare. Unfortunately, no new progress in doctrine and training had occurred in the previous ten years, and the tank battalions had to "hold school" for the infantry regiments and their attachments on an ad hoc basis. In the end, each division and regiment developed its own procedure for joining AAV, infantry, engineer, tank, and antitank units into combined arms teams.

All the active and most of the Reserve armored vehicle battalions in the U.S. bases were sent to the force, with companies of tanks and AAVs attached to each of the two floating brigades. These provided sufficient resources for each division to field two mounted regiments. In addition, the 1st "Tiger" Brigade, 2d Armored Division reported to the I MEF for operations, eventually serving with the 2d Marine Division. At sea, the growing amphibious forces maintained a vigilant stance, practicing when feasible under the difficult hydrography and limiting geography of the Persian Gulf.[38]

After the allied coalition had reached sufficient strength to assure the defense of the Gulf states, the strategic posture changed to preparing an offensive to liberate Kuwait. Now marines began to grapple with the problems of overcoming an impressive system of field fortifications built by the Iraqi defenders facing the coalition. Marine commanders responded to these problems with an intensive period of training and the fielding of specialized engineering equipment, designed to break the successive obstacles of mines, wire, ditches, and berms that they faced. For most marines, this would be the most thorough training effort they experienced in their entire careers, as smaller and then larger unit battle drills were learned and rehearsed. The service support units struggled with long supply lines and harsh desert conditions to not only maintain the forces already present and arriving, but also to amass and store the sixty days of supplies determined by the commanders as their combat requirement. In the end an entire logistic support base for the ground combat element was excavated in the desert a short distance from the Kuwaiti border, almost under the noses of the enemy. Aviation units worked hard to provide their sorties under the stiff maintenance and operational considerations, knowing that they would likely open the combat phase of the campaign long before any marine placed his boot on Kuwaiti soil.

On 24 February 1991 the 1st and 2d Marine Divisions attacked into Kuwait, opening the coalition offensive by forcing their way through the Iraqi barriers and brushing aside the frontline resistance. Mounted in a variety of tanks, assault amphibious vehicles, trucks, and light armored vehicles, the attacking regiments destroyed or captured whole battalions of Iraqi troops and swept through the burning oilfields toward the capital of Kuwait City. Artillery barrages and repeated strikes by fighter-bombers and attack helicopters supported the advance of the regiments, halting only at night in order to prevent accidental combat among the allied and Marine Corps units.

A few counterattacks were beaten off with hardly any casualties. The two marine divisions and the army armored brigade pressed onward to the outskirts of the capital, cutting it off while the Iraqi forces attempted to withdraw. After 100 hours of combat, these forces dominated southern Kuwait and the capital was mopped up by the Arab coalition forces.

In what marines still refer to as "the drive-by shooting," the ad hoc mounted regiments overran airfields and Iraqi battle positions without serious resistance, after passing through the uncovered and poorly maintained minefields. The only armored vehicle casualties in the assault came with the mine clearance teams, which lost a few dozer tanks and amtracs, which were disabled while proofing the minefield lanes. The 1st and 3d Tank Battalions, with their M60A1s, claimed 116 Iraqi tanks and 32 APCs destroyed in their movement with the 1st Marine Division, mostly at ranges under 1,000 meters because of poor visibility on the battlefield. The 2d Marine Division held the M1A1-equipped 2d Tank Battalion in reserve, while the two M1A1 companies attached from the Marine Corps Reserve 4th Tank Battalion attached to the 8th Marine Regiment and the 8th Tank Battalion attached with its M60A1s to the 6th Marines of the 2d Marine Division. In the only large firefight in this zone, B Company, 4th Tank Battalion killed or assisted in the destruction of 59 tanks (including 30 T72s) and 35 APCs. The tanks fought at ranges of 1,100–2,600 meters. No Marine Corps tank received a single hit from any antitank weapon in the 100-hour "war." The 580 AAV7A1-series vehicles performed equally well in mounting the bulk of four regiments, engineer teams, and waiting on board ships for the amphibious assaults that never took place.[39]

Among the many emergency measures taken by the Corps to prepare for the campaign, the provision of adequate mine-clearing devices and systems responded to the last of the original 1949 Marine Armor Policy Board requirements. The mine roller and plow kits for both tanks performed well, and the line charge trainers and AAV7A1 launcher kits permitted the engineer teams to operate with great success against the large Iraqi barriers.

The performance of the LAV units in the Gulf War reflected the confused circumstances of their procurement and the doctrinal hybrid under which they operated. Finally organized with a few "scout" riflemen in the LAV-25 squads, the redesignated light armored infantry (LAI) battalions deployed to Saudi Arabia and generally operated in the style of U.S. Army armored cavalry squadrons in screening and minor reconnaissance missions. Deployed on a weak outpost line before the ground offensive began, two of the companies engaged Iraqi battalions on the frontier during the Iraqi spoiling attack on 29–30 January 1991 known as the Battle of Khafji. They scored impressive hits with their TOW missiles and held the old medium tanks and APCs in check with a large volume of 25mm fire. Yet friendly fire from TOW missiles and aircraft claimed two of their own vehicles. Moreover, the MEF and divisions held no maneuver reserve in the vicinity of the outpost line to support the LAI battalions in the event they had to fall back.

During the offensive the LAI maneuvered in feints and flank guard, never serving the mobile assault regiments as "eyes." The groping of the MEF units forward became so disoriented that the forward command posts of the MEF, 1st Marine Division, and 1st Marine Regiment were each in turn menaced by intruding Iraqi tanks, most of which simply surrendered.[40]

But the enemy in this war either did not fight or lacked the skills necessary to inflict damage when it did. One LAI company commander summarized,

> Well, I think in a lot of ways we were lucky. . . . The Iraqis were real poor gunners; their tank gunnery skills just stunk. We could hit them at 3000 meters with our main gun (25mm) sabot. And they'd shoot at us with tanks at 3000 meters and they couldn't hit us with tank fire, which is inherently more accurate. Bigger round, more stable than these (25mm) sabot rounds— they couldn't hit us. There's a lot of reports—Charlie Company had some— pretty close encounters with tanks, and they just couldn't hit people.[41]

Assessing the armored fighting vehicle performance after the Gulf conflict, the headquarters staff expressed satisfaction with all the vehicles and units. The improvements now needed included thermal night sights (only fitted then in the M1A1 tank and the antitank LAV-AT), electronic position-locating equipment, improved radios, and an identification system equivalent to the aviation "identify friend-foe" equipment. Assessment teams deployed from the Quantico commands collected many comments and critiques on equipment, training, tactics, and procedures from the units in Kuwait, but converting them into "lessons learned" would require dedicated efforts in the aftermath of the campaign.

Chapter 9

Paradigms for the Future

Any conceptual future enhancement of the Maritime Pre-positioning Force would envision an expansion to accommo-date the forward positioning afloat of Naval Construction Battalion engineering equipment, a fleet hospital, an expe-ditionary airfield, and Joint Task Force capable command and control equipment and would not hinge upon increased armor.
—Gen. Carl E. Mundy Jr. (1994)

The AAAV will be the Marine Corps' primary means of accom-plishing surface power projection and forcible entry against any level of defended littoral. It . . . will be the principal means of armor protected water and land mobility and direct fire support to Marine infantry during combat operations to include an NBC environment.
—Brig. Gen. James Feigley (1998)

Gulf War Aftermath (1991–1995)

The Gulf War propelled the FMF into the heavy mechanized fighting that its leaders had sought to downplay as a priority since 1958. After some initial hesitations on the meaning of that war and the Marine Corps experiences in it, the leadership reduced its heavy component and begin to theorize once again on the merits of lightness in the force, seeking technical improvements to the infantry and aviation compo-nents to reduce requirements for fighting vehicles.

A force structure board, headed by Maj. Gen. Charles C. Krulak, ini-tially sought in 1993 to rectify the weaknesses of the Gulf War with a series of improvements capped by a resurrection in effect of the mobile assault regiments of the Haynes Board. In this case, the Krulak Board designed a more modern and capable "combined arms regiment" (CAR) by motorizing its two infantry battalions with organic LAVs. The study called for converting four such infantry battalions for duty in two CARs, which also included the two surviving active tank battalions of the reduced postwar FMF. For amphibious assaults, the Corps continued to count upon developing a high-speed amtrac designated the advanced amphibious assault vehicle (AAAV).

But within six months the Corps abandoned many of the important parts of this ground-force structure overhaul. The two combined arms regiments became too costly in face of the AAAV program's priority. The squeamishness in the Corps leadership toward mechanizing ground units too much had reappeared all too soon in the aftermath of the Gulf War. Infantry units remained foot-mobile but capable of riding helicopters and AAVs to the battlefield, thus not ready for mounted combat without a dedicated training period. The three LAI battalions converted to light armored reconnaissance (LAR) battalions and two tank and two assault amphibian battalions remained in place. Artillery lost a proposed mobile artillery rocket system, replaced with a support agreement with the army to provide such units. As partial compensation for the death of the combined arms regiment, a countermobility platoon augmented the assault amphibian battalion to carry engineers and line charges. Also the authorized strength of the assault amphibian battalions of the active and reserve forces grew to four companies each. The infantry battalions finally received the TOW missiles from the old tank battalion TOW company and the regimental TOW platoons. The Dragon antitank launchers gave way to a smaller number of the more effective Javelin systems.

The antitank weapons developed to face the future generation of tanks developed for the Russian army finally began to reach the troops. The TOW IIB heavy antitank missile with an improved top attack type warhead went into production in 1992. The Javelin (former AAWS-M) medium missile began production in 1996 to replace the Dragon. For close-in work, the Corps's Predator had a highly successful demonstration and validity test and entered engineering and manufacturing development in 1994. A replacement for the AT-4 unguided rocket in the rifle companies, the Predator system fires a 19-pound, fire-and-forget, top-attack missile effective to 600 meters with development potentially extended to a kilometer.

The Marine Corps tank program creaked along toward reaching the requirement originally funded in FY91–93, but bankrupted in bureaucratic shuffling. With only 221 of the 490 M1A1 vehicles originally specified, shortages existed in the Reserve, depot, and MPS stocks in 1993. Congress acted in the FY94 and FY95 authorizations to transfer 50 and 132 tanks, respectively, from the army to the Corps. The original money for the 490 M1A1s came to the Corps in the form of funding "fenced" by Congress in FY90–93 to keep the plants running. The commandant, Gen. Alfred M. Gray, acted against staff advice to terminate the Corps's buy at the halfway point and attempted to use the funding for other programs, with the result that both tanks and funds were lost. The next commandant in line, Gen. Carl Mundy, briefed Congress that he held no concerns for the apparent shortfall in tanks, citing the experience of the army armored brigade assigned to the I MEF in Saudi Arabia as a preferred alternative to spending more funds on Marine Corps tanks. After much hesitation, he accepted the additional army tanks, bringing the Corps essentially to its planned objective in 1995.[1]

The programmed replacement for the AAV7A1 recalled the LVA concept of the mid-1980s, but benefited greatly from advances made since then in engineering and technology. The AAAV project sought to develop an advanced technology hybrid skimmer vehicle carrying eighteen troops across State 3 seas at 20+ knots and performing as a state-of-the-art armored fighting vehicle upon reaching the shore. Costs remained very high, especially after the Corps kept the requirement for these vehicles on its maritime prepositioning ships and brought the overall requirement to over 1,000 (instead of about 600) such vehicles. But the budget in the late 1990s now permitted a $7.6-billion program to go forward, despite the era of defense austerity. With AAAV development extended and quantity production delayed until 2007, however, a newly refurbished AAV7A1, incorporating Bradley fighting vehicle automotive upgrades, became necessary as the Corps's personnel carrier for the next decade.[2]

Almost half a century after the 1949 Armor Policy Board recommendations, the Marine Corps enjoyed at last a well-equipped tank battalion with superior tanks, fully supported by organic scout, antitank, and tank-launched bridge units and capable of coordinating all forms of fire support. The assault amphibian battalion employed amtracs (but no armored amphibians) fully capable of mounting infantry with mobility equivalent to the tank and under adequate armor protection. Both these battalions operated special mine-clearance systems. The Corps outfitted a lavishly equipped battalion for the armored reconnaissance capability, originally dismissed by the planners of 1949. Even the mechanized form of amphibious attack pondered in the late 1940s by Arthur J. Stuart became attractive to programmers working on the future amphibious requirement.[3]

Training for the armored vehicle units improved immensely with the incorporation of new training and readiness standards for crews and units. Adapted from aviation qualification methods long available, the armored fighting vehicle battalions received dedicated allocations of ammunition, modern training ranges and maneuver areas and a system of "combat readiness percentages" by which commanders at all levels could assess the day to day readiness of units.[4]

The Corps's infatuation with lightness continued to place obstacles, though, in the proper operation of armored forces in the FMF (after 1992, the preferred term became Marine Corps Forces). Policy changes had forecast the reductions in the numbers of battalions, including tank battalions, in the FMF prior to the Persian Gulf conflict. However, the lessons learned in the Gulf upon converting infantry regiments into ad hoc mechanized units, wrought with such sweat and fears, had little impact later in the Corps. No doctrinal solutions have surfaced yet treating the problems of using the different units for combined arms operations. Instead the Corps embraced the trendy doctrine of "military operations other than war" (MOOTW), which seemed made to order for a slimmer, lighter Marine Corps, ever more anxious to gain a prominent niche for the postwar budget stakes. Leaders began to talk of employing smaller units that would use "leveraged technologies" to seek out and destroy enemy forces, primarily with precision weapons delivered by ground and naval launchers and aircraft.[5]

Incredibly, the Marine Corps seemingly took no further interest in the enduring power of armored fighting vehicles to accomplish combat missions at great savings in casualties. Tank platoons at one point or another fell out of the peacetime deployments of MEUs to the Mediterranean, Middle, and Far East. But events once again reinforced the obvious factors. During the Corps's moderately successful involvement in Somalia (1992–93), the troop contingent originally destined for use (a reduced division) fell away to only a few battalions of infantry and light armored vehicles. However, when the time came to disarm the major rebel camps around Mogadishu, some containing M47 and T55 tanks, the rush was on to locate and stand up the few tanks that had been unloaded in desultory fashion on the piers. A tanker cadre composed of a captain, a staff NCO, and four crewmen, fleshed out by some selected nontanker personnel, manned four M1A1 tanks, with a fifth vehicle kept ready as a spare. The first operation put these vehicles into action armed with only 200 rounds of .50-caliber and 400 of 7.62mm machine-gun ammunition. The 120mm tank ammunition had been reloaded to the MPS ships and some 13 days elapsed before two pallets of main gun ammunition arrived by air! On 10 January 1993 a "sort of" tank versus tank combat occurred as the scratch platoon battled six M47s using coax and .50-caliber fire. Amazingly, the rebels bailed out of their obsolete but lethal tanks, sensing that ranging machine guns had their mark and deadly 120mm rounds soon would follow. In the end, the tanks operated for two and one-half months, averaging 2,500 miles, and proving themselves highly useful in a light-force, MOOTW deployment.[6]

The light armored vehicles of the LAR battalions, by contrast, continue to find favorable employment in the myriad of constabulary duties undertaken by Marine Corps forces in peacetime. The latest excursion to the Balkans, in wake of the NATO prosecution against Serbia in 1999, saw a reduced LAR company operating with Lt. Col. Bruce Gandy's 3d Battalion, 8th Marines in mobile security and armored reconnaissance missions in the province of Kosovo. Operating day and night, the LAV-25 patrols resembled the type of security actions long performed by similar units of the British and French armies in their overseas constabulary roles of yesteryear. However, the LAR units remain wedded to army cavalry doctrines and generally view motorized infantry work as an anomaly.[7]

Thus, the continuing use by the Marine Corps of its modern armored fighting vehicles and organizations remains shrouded in doubts. Doctrinal gaps and institutional habits pose potential obstacles for any effective employment.

Program Continuations (1995–2000)

With the complete acquisition of the M1A1 tank, the Marine Corps returned to a tank policy of battlefield superiority more like that of the decades following the Great Pacific War, with the advantage that this time the U.S. tank-automotive industry was producing one of the finest main battle tanks in the world. The M1A1 carries the 120mm gun, but this time an advanced smoothbore cannon, firing discarding sabot ammunition at a muzzle velocity twice that of the 120mm gun of the M103 and with fixed caseless ammunition stored in a blastproof magazine. Three machine guns augment the stabilized main gun, which has a laser rangefinder coupled to thermal day-night sights and a digital computer enabling the gunner or tank commander to fire on the move at a moving target over 3,000 meters distant at a high probability of a first-round hit. The armor protection, developed from years of allied research on spaced armor and laminates, makes the tank invulnerable to all shaped charge weapons and most tank cannon in the frontal arc and sides. Although the weight has climbed over 68 tons, the 1,500-hp gas-turbine engine gives the tank a high speed and great cross-country mobility on a highly flexible suspension system, with thermal viewers enabling the driver to maneuver in all conditions of visibility.

The M1A1 tank will remain in service with the Marine Corps through 2020. The continuing program of modifications and upgrades ensures the adequacy of the tank compared to all other main battle tanks in the world. The cost of spares and ammunition will continue to vex some of the leadership still pining for a lighter force. But the M1A1 will remain the absolute insurance of battlefield superiority just as the M26 procurement of 1947–49 ensured success in Korea.[8]

The follow-on to the M1A1 main battle tank may come from a conceptual program started in 1998 to produce an "expeditionary family of fighting vehicles" that would reprise the old MPWS concept but use advanced technology modules to permit armor and weapons packages to be added or removed from a basic vehicle. The concept includes such exotic components as directed energy weapons, composite materials and alloys, sensor data fusion suites, vehicle integrated defense systems, and propulsion not based upon petroleum fuels. The vehicles would link with all kinds of battlefield surveillance systems and itself form part of an imaginative command and control system that would instantly share information and targeting data among all units employed.[9]

Already leaning toward the exotic, the AAAV has demonstrated high-speed performance in water with a planing hull and great land mobility with a pneumatic suspension system, using separate test vehicles for each mode of travel. General Dynamics Corporation, the producer of the M1A1, won the AAAV contract and began delivering full engineering prototypes for testing in 1999. The production schedule calls for delivering 1,013 production vehicles during 2006–12. This 32-ton vehicle only marginally resembles its LVT ancestors, and appears more as a state-of-the-art infantry fighting vehicle of the sort used by the most well-equipped land armies, but adapted for operations at sea. Using a 12-cylinder diesel generating 2,775 hp at sea and 850 hp on land, the AAAV will carry eighteen troops skimming at 25 knots over water and rolling across land at 45 mph. The suspension retracts under hull extensions, so that 23-inch-diameter water-jet pumps can propel the hull onto a planing attitude in the water, in order to travel at high speeds. Armed with a 30mm or larger automatic cannon in a stabilized turret, the vehicle will keep pace with the battle tanks and protect its occupants against 14.5mm gunfire and provide collective NBC protection to its occupants.[10]

In contrast to the technological advances featured in the tank and AAAV programs at the end of the century, the light armored vehicle program will continue with a modest service life extension program beginning in 1999. The LAV vehicles will receive general component upgrades and new improvements to fire controls, but otherwise will remain similar in performance to the first production vehicles. That is a far cry from its original billing as an interim vehicle for the late 1970s project for an MPWS for land or helicopter-borne operations. But the vehicles remain very handy and relatively simple to operate and maintain. The next projected replacement would be a variant of the expeditionary family of fighting vehicles noted above, but that would require the LAV-25 to serve almost 40 years, and that seems most doubtful.[11] (See Table 9.1.)

These armored fighting vehicles will serve the Marine Corps after 2000 in battalions unchanged since the middle 1990s. The Marine Corps Forces will continue to emphasize small-unit operations, but remain capable of organizing large land formations or amphibious landing forces based upon the marine division and the MEF. Amphibious doctrine taking advantage of the new tilt-rotor aircraft replacing helicopters, the air-cushion landing craft, and the AAAV will emphasize landing combat units from ships 25 miles or more offshore. The air and surface landings from these ships will project combined arms forces deep inland to route the enemy by maneuver and fire superiority.[12]

Conclusions: Historical Trends in USMC Armor Policy

The armored fighting vehicle entered Marine Corps service as a novelty, an experimental weapon requiring evaluation, like so many others of the late machine age. The armored car attracted attention first. Its simplicity and tactical value seemed attractive and Marines wanted it for constabulary duty in Haiti and China. The vehicle designs proved inadequate and unreliable, however, and the experimental light tank platoon deployed to China in 1928 instead of armored cars. These light tanks earlier had served to evaluate the ability of Navy ships and landing boats to place some kind of fighting vehicle ashore to counter the beach defenses facing the typical amphibious landing conceived in the 1920s. The obvious requirement focused on eliminating machine-gun positions threatening the infantry exposed on a beach. Marines preferred an amphibious tank to overcome these defenses, but no designs seemed worthwhile, and so the light tank, transported in a lighter to the beach, would have to suffice.

This amphibious requirement caused the commandant, General Russell, to include "light fighting tanks" in his list of components needed for the formation of the Fleet Marine Force, dedicated to the

Table 9.1. USMC Armored Fighting Vehicle Inventory, 1985-2012

A. Main Battle Tanks

Year	M60A1	M1A1 (CT)	M1A1[a]
1985	716	0	0
1986	716	0	0
1987	716	0	0
1988	716	0	0
1989	716	0	0
1990	714	0	0
1991	711	0	0
1992	667	221	0
1993	280	221	0
1994	143	221	50
1995	8	221	50
1996	—	221	182
1997	—	221	182
1998	—	221	182
1999	—	221	182

[a]Army transfers, including 48 "Common"; rest from seventh year of production, without heavy armor. The original M60A1 requirement was 759, and 490 for M1A1.

B. Amphibious Assault Vehicles

Year	Troop Vehicles	Command Carrier	Recovery Vehicles
1999–ca. 2010[a]	1151 AAV7A1	106 AAV7CA1	64 AAV7RA1
	599 (RAM)	46 (RAM)	35 (RAM)
2005	12 AAAV[b]		
2006	39		
2007	101		
2008	301		
2009	501		
2010	701		
2011	901		
2012	1013		

[a]377 more AAV7A1 (non-RAM upgrades) to be retained in MPS storage.
[b]Plus 14 prototypes.

C. Light Armored Vehicles, 1999

Type	Quantity
LAV-25	409
LAV-AT	95
LAV-L	94
LAV-C2	50
LAV-M	50
LAV-R	45
LAV-AD	17 (all in 4th LAR)
MEWSS	12 (all in Radio Battalion)
Total:	772 LAV chassis (plus a few loaned to Army, ANG, etc.)

Sources: M1A1 Tank System Modernization Plan (July 1997), 8 MCSC TkSect; PM-AAV7 to author, 21 June 1999; 1997 program brief, AAAV Technology Center, Woodbridge Va., 9; Colebaugh interview.

amphibious assault and defense of forward naval bases. The Corps's unique pursuit of a tankette of minimal size and capability in the 1930s stemmed from the limited view of beach defenses and the restricted capacity that ships and craft of the period displayed. In effect, the Marine Corps only needed enough of a tank to land and knock out the opposing machine guns, and then accompany the infantry inland to support a short-term operation. One discerns the beginnings of "lightness" as a Marine Corps dogma: the concept that Marine Corps forces, unlike the U.S. Army, fight in a "light" configuration using special methods and tactics thus requiring distinct equipment types.

Ensuing developments in the formation of armored vehicle units in the Marine Corps came more by accident than design. The Marine Corps Equipment Board noticed the amphibian tractor at a time that none of the Navy's landing craft prototypes demonstrated great promise, and it demonstrated certain utility as a cargo carrier. The provision of armor plating, its employment as a personnel carrier, and the development of a type of amphibious tank from its design all proceeded from this rather inauspicious beginning. The light fighting tank, or "Marine Tank," experienced delays and mechanical problems through the end of the decade, largely because of the size limitations imposed by the Marine Corps, but also because of the limited experience of the truck manufacturer that won the initial contract. The opening campaigns of the European war in 1939, meanwhile, demonstrated to all observers that the tank would play a greater role in combat than had been forecast. Moreover,

U.S. war planning following the fall of France offered the possibility of early conflict against the Axis or Vichy French forces by the new brigades and planned divisions of the Marine Corps. The "Marine Tank" could not be readied in time for such operations in sufficient numbers. The early opposition of the commandant and other senior officers to procurement of the U.S. Army's light tanks fell aside, and the Marine Corps now placed increasingly urgent orders for U.S. Army light tanks, scout cars, and tank destroyers in ever growing numbers.

The new tanks and amtracs filled out the tank and amphibian tractor battalions of the 1st and 2d Marine Divisions, and the scout cars and halftrack tank destroyers went to other division organizations, except that the divisional "scout company" tended to group with the tank battalion for better maintenance, under most organizational schemes.

As the officers and men struggled to unpack and learn the operation and maintenance of a number of new weapons and machines, the focus of Marine Corps operations then veered away from European conditions of warfare and focused again on the Pacific. The scout cars and tank destroyer battalions fell by the wayside as the divisions loaded the slender number of transports and cargo ships available for the South Pacific and the first American offensives against the Pacific outposts of the Japanese empire.

At Guadalcanal, the primitive doctrine of landing against and occupying an enemy base worked, presenting few challenges to the system. The few tanks going into action, independently of any support, worked well enough and their presence in reserve virtually guaranteed the holding of the all-important airfield. The cargo amtracs performed equally well, until lack of parts and maintenance effectively neutralized them and the troops took up rifles as infantrymen. So far, so good.

But the brutal fight for Tarawa caused a major turning point in armored vehicle use by the Marine Corps, as in practically every other aspect of the amphibious landing art. The fortifications and fighting spirit of an alert and well-handled island garrison proved almost too much for a marine division to handle, despite seeming superiority in all types of weapons. The larger medium tank now became essential, along with a flamethrower tank, and the Marine Corps pressed the amtrac into service as an armored personnel carrier, at least as far as the water's edge. The armored amphibian, already under development, now became an essential component of the assault formation. As a result of the upgrading of armored fighting vehicles in both doctrinal mission and equipment quality, the infantry would never again face extinction at the high-water mark. Improvements also came in the aircraft and naval gunfire support of the Navy, but the armored and troop-carrier amtracs brought the troops safely ashore and the medium tanks escorted them inland, eliminating all enemy weapons that could be approached. A doctrine of integrated infantry-vehicle close-support tactics developed empirically in each marine division, despite the handicaps of radio communications of the day, and the FMF later enshrined these procedures in printed manuals.

Achieving such a level of capability did not come easily. The original architects of the tank program could not have foreseen the carnage of Tarawa. But Major Withers had provided essential criteria for mechanical reliability of the Marine Tank, and Lieutenant de Zayas brought much energy to the early troop tests and practical demonstrations. Lieutenant Colonel Shepherd, aided by Captain Denig, influenced the move to army tank procurement, and, finally, Lieutenant Colonel Blanchard may have performed real miracles in guiding the chaotic process of start-stop procurement and standardization in the early war years of largely unproven equipment, much of which had to be changed as models and requirements evolved. These pioneers, together with the ingenious Donald Roebling, inventor of the amtrac and armored amphibian, paved the way toward the development of a mature system of fighting vehicles that the Marine Corps achieved during the Great Pacific War. The wartime improvements depended upon improvisations from the battalion commanders like Metzger, Lawrence, Stuart, and Denig, as well as numerous company commanders, all operating independently until the FMF collated experiences of the various divisions into a force SOP. In the Armor Policy Board of 1949, five veteran tanker lieutenant colonels extended this system into formal institutional planning, with accompanying technological upgrades that appeared attainable.

The Corps became accustomed to and then dependent upon army materiel policy early in the history of tanks. The willingness of the army to continue logistic support and maintenance management of a particular model tank frequently determined Marine Corps decisions on tank procurement. The exception to this rule lay in the persistence of the flamethrower tank in USMC service, which caused the Sherman to be retained very late in the 1950s. Resources frequently curtailed the desires of the leadership for a first-rate tank fleet, but limited purchases permitted the fielding of a technically superior tank in Korea in the M26, replaced in following years by full allocations of the M46, M47, and M48 in quick succession. But then the conversion of the Corps leadership to a new dogma of "lightness" left most Marines content with a smaller tank force based upon the M48-M103 series, which served into the 1970s. The M48 served well in support of the infantry in Vietnam, and many tankers cherished their combat experience in these vehicles. As a result, the tankers themselves, unlike the amtrackers, remained curiously wedded to their Vietnam-vintage hardware. Many would complain later of the M60 and M1 purchases, stating, "We never should have given up the 48s."[13]

The old tankers thus presented some of the same obstacles as did the infantry officers in attempting to modernize armored fighting vehicle doctrine and admit more modern concepts of combined arms. The infantry officers, generally dominating the Corps leadership, could not face the implications of large-scale mobile operations in which tanks and mounted infantry would play key roles. The tankers, for their part, insisted that the tank battalion already was capable of combined arms operations as a maneuver battalion, even in an infantry regiment or marine division devoid of mechanized doctrine. The tankers maneuvered, sometimes with their Ontos brethren, into the early 1970s in California and on the East Coast without combined arms attachments. No armored vehicle battalion yet included functional sections for fire-support coordination or command and control, nor did they practice the integration of infantry, engineers, artillery, or attack helicopters as required for combined arms operations.

The politics of armored fighting vehicle modernization and acquisition reflected these points and more. After 1958 the infantry leadership could not agree upon the need for any heavy combat vehicles, let alone of what vintage. General agreement occurred over the need for a modern LVT, but its use beyond the high-water mark of the beach remained problematical. The problem of tank and amtrac modernization usually cited was fiscal. The purchase of a tank or amtrac often required 75 percent of the available funds for ground equipment acquisition for several years. Therefore, at any budget decision point, a tank or amtrac buy supplanted a dozen or so desired programs of interest to the leadership. On top of that, the evident personalization of such budget decisions, such as General Barrow's refusal to even consider a tank buy in his commandancy, or the equivocations of Generals Gray and Mundy, could only exacerbate the established trends.

By the time of the Gulf War, all these forces could be detected. Over a hundred major decisions were made by the commandant and his headquarters staff in the fall of 1990 as the I MEF prepared to fight a mobile campaign in the desert. Ironically, the most difficult and tortuous decision centered on whether to accelerate the M1A1 acquisition process and equip the USMC tank battalions then moving or preparing to deploy to the Gulf. The army posed no objections to loaning the vehicles, as the advantages of the M1A1 were understood widely. But Marine Corps generals feared that the tankers were simply advancing their agendas with scare tactics highlighting the evident weaknesses of the M60 series. Many thought that the current equipment was good enough, or that the TOW missile would defeat the Iraqi armor. In the end, only one and one-half of the four and one-half deployed tank battalions received the M1A1, although all could have been converted. In the late 1990s many officers continued to believe that the antitank missile would kill all the tanks, hence removing any need for tanks in the Corps. USMC doctrine never provided for the tank as the basis of offensive power, as leaders learned and acknowledged frequently in the Great Pacific War, but instead continued to treat it as a key antiarmor weapon system.

Completing the M1 buy in the mid-1990s ultimately required that the commandant eat his words to Congress on the sufficiency of the tank fleet. The army initially opposed completing the targeted buy of M1A1 tanks in the Corps, believing that furnishing the Tiger Brigade to I MEF in the Gulf conflict was the agreed model for the future. Gen. Carl Mundy twice wavered, fearing to offend the army chief of staff and a cohort of army planners who feared Marine Corps encroachment in ground warfare. Finally, the Corps pointed to the unpaid debt accruing from the free transfer of the USMC M48 fleet to the army for its M48A5 program. Although 159 M60s had been given the Corps for its MPS stocks in the 1980s, the army's eventual payoff came in excess M1A1s to fill out the Corps requirements. Thus, the Marine Corps, as in 1948, gained a modern tank force at the behest of congressional pressure to share excess army tanks. The commandant's nervousness to the end exemplified the personalization of such decisions, as the Corps completed acquisition of the M1 some 15 years after it became the army standard.[14]

Training and doctrinal processes continued to lag in the Marine Corps in the use of armored fighting vehicles. After the Korean War, Marine Corps combat arms officers earned their spurs on peacetime deployments. A noticeable problem of "BLT-itus" originated in the formation of battalion landing teams to perform nearly all deployments. In the BLT, the tank, amtrac, Ontos, artillery, and engineer officer attachment commanders

provided technical and tactical expertise, leaving the infantry officer free
to "take the hill." No growth in the tactical skills associated with various arms could occur under that system. The successor method bode no
better. Specialization showed as the chief characteristic of the MEU
deployments. Typically the tactical focus lay in a MEU "playbook" of battle drills. Each rifle company specialized in either a raid, helicopter-
borne, or mechanized type of operation. Hence any exposure to armored
or mounted operations for the majority of infantry officers came on an
incidental basis. The Corps accelerated supporting arms training at its
Twenty-nine Palms, California, desert training base with tank and amtrac
attachments for infantry battalions and even tested mobile combined
arms regiments on long-distance maneuvering on a few occasions. But
neither organizational nor doctrinal changes ensued. The Quantico commands printed new doctrinal manuals for the employment of tank, AAV,
and LAR units in the late 1990s; however, to date no interest has been
taken in publishing new doctrine on the combinations of these units with
infantry, engineers, and artillery for the conduct of mounted operations.
War planning continues to emphasize the force list generated for the MPS
equipment sets, the equivalent of a combined arms regiment, but exer-
cising such a unit proves too costly. A return to a situation akin to the
Gulf War will rely on the operations procedures resident in separate
units, requiring more ad hoc organizations and tactics in the absence of
mounted doctrine.

The continuing Marine Corps tendency to use armored vehicles in
small numbers, another version of "lightness" in practice, probably had
its origin in the Korean War. When the commandant decided not to send
the 7th Tank Battalion as reinforcement, the single battalion of tanks,
admittedly swollen with regimental tank platoons and sections of dozer
tanks, generally operated platoons assigned to infantry battalions and
companies in support of regiments, although up to thirty tanks at a time
engaged in the outpost battles in the last weeks before the armistice. The
1st Tank Battalion prepared itself on paper to counter any Chinese
armored attack with massed companies. But such an enemy move would
have proven suicidal against prepared UN positions and air supremacy.
The tankers of the Second World War had instinctively moved beyond
this pennypacket assignment of tanks, employing entire companies
together to support a regiment's main attack, or massing three tank battalions for the abortive attack on Airfield no. 2 at Iwo Jima.

But the long-term association of tank platoons with infantry battalions as a normal assignment, reinforced by peacetime deployments of

BLT and MEU-type units, caused an institutional rejection of mass as a principle of armored fighting vehicle employment. In Vietnam ambushes of single and paired tanks, or even a platoon of five, could be attempted by the enemy forces with some chance of success, whereas coping with an entire company of tanks (or Ontos) with riflemen in close support, might have proven prohibitively costly. Although no tactical assessment has ever emerged from that conflict, many of the tactics continued to the present day. Fighting vehicle unit commanders who plead for mass use may frequently find themselves either ostracized as egoists or simply ignored by the senior infantry commanders. The clear exception here in recent years appeared in the increasing use of the LAV units, remaining much in vogue as acceptably "light." Commanders have used the LAV-25-series armored cars in larger numbers, although the failure to develop a doctrine for mounted operations for ground forces of the Corps has left these units in a doctrinal vacuum, generally free to embrace U.S. Army cavalry doctrine, however relevant it might be to the Marine Corps Forces.

The Corps leadership perhaps lost its sense of need for modern armor. The commandant retiring in 1999, Gen. Charles C. Krulak, stated that he "would eliminate the tank fleet found in the Marine Corps today if I could." The World War II and Korean War generation of leaders knew how much the tanks and amtracs had saved in casualties and how they had facilitated the offensive use of infantry against all types of objectives. After the Vietnam War, however, the senior commanders viewed the tanks and amtracs more as an expensive burden required for the amphibious assault. Large-scale operations had not occurred as a routine in Vietnam, and the use of armored vehicles to reinforce the offensive use of infantry and reduce casualties generally was not appreciated. Instead, memories of disabled or mired tracked vehicles holding up operations remained current. [15]

Despite the increased emphasis by Marine Corps forces in major war plans after the Vietnam War, little doctrinal thought was given to the increased value of armor in the large-scale operations envisioned. Equipment upgrades for tank, amtrac, and antitank units, and the introduction of the LAV as a surrogate mobile weapons system, seemed sufficient for the Corps leadership. This factor may have stemmed from the limited tactical experience of the Marine Corps in large-scale operations. Unlike their army counterparts, few generals in the Marine Corps commanded major units for any significant period of time. Many of them, even some commandants, had never commanded combat units larger than battalions. Larger ground units seldom deploy to the field, even for training. In addition, almost half the decisionmakers of the Marine Corps were the aviation generals, with neither experience nor use for expensive land fighting systems and generally favoring the "lightness" creed that devolves more emphasis upon aviation support. Thus, the continued maintenance of a modern tank fleet did not see much favor in the post-1970 Marine Corps. Corps doctrine did not develop the means of fielding real combined arms units, nor were the tank and amtrac battalions especially fitted for the demands of modern armored warfare until the 1990s. Hope for dominant antitank munitions for infantry and aviation consistently retarded the decision to field modern fighting vehicles and units. The Gulf War found the Corps at a point when most of these problems had been determined and corrective measures undertaken, but early combat against a determined opponent in that campaign would have exposed serious weaknesses.

The Marine Corps has evolved as a military institution for over two centuries, but we can see its most significant developments and acquired characteristics by observing patterns of the last sixty years, or two or three generations. Some key trends identifiable in the story of the Corps and the armored fighting vehicle seem to indicate the following:

> A closed system of institutional goals and values, with doubtful feedback and analysis loops, seldom extending to foreign practices; exogenous variables, such as army procurement practices, and a cult of personality.

Today, the Marine Corps maintains a precarious balance in its armored fighting vehicle inventory, with modern units fielding capable weapons. The lessons of the Gulf War reside mainly in the archives and with the collective but fading memories of the armored units themselves. Just as in 1945 one cannot speak of "armor" in the Marine Corps, just tank, amtrac, and now armored reconnaissance units, which may or may not be used in modern combined arms or limited military operations with imagination and verve. We can expect to see a continuing search by the Marine Corps for the "light fighting tank" or even a tankless fighting vehicle force. The doctrinal weakness for operating mechanized forces may continue, as well as the emphasis on the smallest of units, especially with the reluctance to attempt costly mechanized and amphibious operations or exercises of any appreciable scale. However small, the virtues of a technically and tactically superior fighting vehicle force remain a marked Marine Corps tradition. It only remains for its leaders to take the fullest advantage.

Appendix 1

Armored Fighting Vehicles in Marine Corps Service

TANKS

M1917 Six-Ton (acquired 1923)

Crew: Two

Weight: 13,400 pounds

Armor: 0.6 inch (15mm) maximum, hull and turret

Armament: 37mm M1916 gun or .30-caliber machine gun

Engine: Buda HU, 4-cylinder, 42 hp

Speed: 5.5 mph

Range: 30 miles

Misc.: Three acquired on loan from the Army for amphibious exercises in the Caribbean, growing eventually to eight such machines in the light tank platoon, Marine Corps Expeditionary Force formed at Quantico. Five deployed to China with the platoon in 1927–28. Discarded in 1935.

Marmon-Herrington CTL-3 (1936)

Crew: Two

Weight: 9,500 pounds (10,900 pounds for CTL-3A)

Armor: 0.25-inch

Armament: Three .30-caliber machine guns

Engine: Lincoln V-12 110 hp; Hercules 6-cylinder 124 hp in CTL-3A

Speed: 33 mph

Range: 125 miles

Misc.: Turretless tank; prototype fitted with one .50- and two .30-caliber machine guns; band track. Five built; five more CTL-3A delivered in 1939 with 10.5-inch track and reinforced suspension. The CTL-3s were rebuilt in 1941 as CTL-3M. Equipped 1st Tank Company, FMF, later the tank platoons of 1st and 2d Scout Companies. All discarded in 1943.

M2A4 Light Tank (1940)

Crew: Four

Weight: 23,500 pounds

Armor: 1-inch maximum hull and turret

Armament: One 37mm M5 and one .30-caliber machine gun in turret; one .30-caliber AA (antiaircraft gun) on turret; three .30-caliber machine guns in hull.

Engine: Continental W-670 radial, 262 hp

Speed: 36 mph

Range: 70 miles

Misc.: Thirty-six acquired from U.S. Army in 1940 as it became apparent that Marmon-Herrington designs could not be delivered in time. Equipped 3d and 4th Tank Companies, FMF, which became A Companies, 1st and 2d Tank Battalions in 1941. First eighteen saw action at Guadalcanal with A Company, 1st Tank Battalion, the only combat employment of the M2A4. Discarded in 1943.

Marmon-Herrington CTL-6 (1941)

Crew: Two

Weight: 12,500 pounds designed, 14,775 pounds actual

Armor: 0.4375–0.5-inch (0.25-inch engine louvers)

Armament: Three .30-caliber machine guns

Engine: Hercules WXCL-3, 6-cylinder, 124 hp

Speed: 33 mph

Range: 125 miles

Misc.: Turretless tank; improved version of CTL-3, with track and suspension components similar to M2A4. Only twenty built, discarded in 1943 on Samoa.

Marmon-Herrington CTM-3TBD (1941)

Crew: Three

Weight: 18,500 pounds designed, 20,800 pounds actual

Armor: 0.4375–0.5-inch (0.25-inch engine louvers)

Armament: Two .50-caliber in turret; three .30-caliber machine guns in front hull.

Engine: Hercules DXRB diesel, 123 hp

Speed: 30 mph

Range: 125 miles

Misc.: Turreted version of CTL-series tank, with track and suspension components similar to M2A4. Only five built; discarded in 1943 on Samoa.

M3 Series Light Tank (1941)

Crew: Four

Weight: 25,600 pounds (26,000 for the M3A1)

Armor: Hull: 1.5-inch front, 1.0-inch side. Gunshield: 2.0-inch (first production had only 1.5). Turret: 1.5-inch front, 1.25-inch side.

Armament: One 37mm M6 and one .30-caliber machine gun in turret; one .30-caliber AA on turret; three .30-caliber machine guns in hull (one in M3A1).

Engine: Continental W-670 radial, 262 hp; some fitted with Guiberson T-1020 9-cylinder radial diesel, 245 hp

Speed: 36 mph

Range: 70 miles (90 miles diesel)

Misc.: Standard tank in USMC tank battalions through end of 1943. Used for flamethrower tank, 1943–44, as well. M3 introduces vertical gyrostabilizer for gun mount. M3A1 and later U.S. World War II tanks fitted with power turret.

M5A1 Light Tank (1943)

Crew: Four

Weight: 30,800

Armor: Hull: 1.75-inch lower front, 1.0-inch side. Gunshield: 2.0-inch. Turret: 1.5-inch front, 1.25-inch side.

Armament: One 37mm M6 and one .30-caliber machine gun in turret; one .30-caliber AA on turret; one .30-caliber machine gun in hull.

Engine: Twin Cadillac V-8, 296 hp

Speed: 36 mph

Range: 100 miles

Misc.: Issued to USMC tank battalions beginning in late 1943 (summer 1943 for 1st Tank Battalion from Army stocks). In action in Cape Gloucester and Roi-Namur battles, a few remain at Saipan. Discarded late 1944.

M4A2 Medium Tank (1943)

Crew: Five

Weight: 66,000 pounds

Armor: Hull: 2–4.25-inch lower front, 2.5-inch upper front, 1.5-inch side. Gunshield: 3.5-inch. Turret: 3.0-inch front, 2.0-inch side.

Armament: One 75mm M3 and one .30-caliber machine gun in turret; one .50-caliber AA on turret; one .30-caliber machine gun in hull.

Engine: Twin GM diesels, 12-cylinder, 410 hp

Speed: 25 mph

Range: 150 miles

Misc.: Issued to 1st Corps Medium Tank Battalion in 1943, partial issue to all USMC tank battalions beginning in late 1943 (M4A1 with gas engine in summer 1943 for 1st Tank Battalion from Army stocks). All USMC tank units converted during 1944. Sole U.S. user of diesel M4 tanks.

M4A3 Medium Tank (1944)

Crew: Five

Weight: 66,400 pounds

Armor: Hull: 2–4.25-inch lower front, 2.5-inch upper front, 1.5-inch side. Gunshield: 3.6-inch. Turret: 3.0-inch front, 2.0-inch side.

Armament: One 75mm M3 and one .30-caliber machine gun in turret; one .50-caliber AA on turret; one .30-caliber machine gun in hull; 2-inch mortar M3 (smoke) in turret.

Engine: Ford GAA V-8, 500 hp

Speed: 26 mph

Range: 130 miles

Misc.: Issued to USMC tank battalions beginning in late 1944. All USMC tank units converted during 1945; 1st Tank Battalion was the last. Postwar model is M4A3 with 105mm howitzer M4. Bulldozer and flamethrower variants continued in USMC service until 1959.

M26 Medium Tank (1948)

Crew: Five

Weight: 84,000 pounds

Armor: Hull: 3-inch lower front, 4-inch upper front, 2–3-inch side. Gunshield: 4.5-inch. Turret: 4.0-inch front, 3.0-inch side.

Armament: One 90mm M3 and one .30-caliber machine gun in turret; one .50-caliber AA on turret; one .30-caliber machine gun hull.

Engine: Ford GAF V-8, 500 hp

Speed: 25 mph

Range: 100 miles

Misc.: 5–10 vehicles issued to 1st and 2d Tank Battalions in 1948. Complete issue to 1st Tank Battalion in 1950. Introduced torsion bar suspension. No further use of gun-mount stabilizers in USMC tanks until 1976. Discarded in 1951.

M46 Medium Tank (1951)

Crew: Five

Weight: 92,800 pounds

Armor: Hull: 3-inch lower front, 4-inch upper front, 2–3-inch side. Gunshield: 4.5-inch. Turret: 4.0-inch front, 3.0-inch side.

Armament: One 90mm M3A1 and one .30-caliber machine gun in turret; one .50-caliber AA on turret; one .30-caliber machine gun hull.

Engine: Continental AV-1790-5A, V-12, 810 hp

Speed: 30 mph

Range: 80 miles

Misc.: Rework of M26 tank with new power pack, introducing V-12 engine series and cross-drive transmissions. Used only by 1st Tank Battalion, Korea.

M47 Medium Tank (1952)

Crew: Five

Weight: 92,900 pounds

Armor: Hull: 3–3.5-inch lower front, 4-inch upper front, 2–3-inch side. Gunshield: 4.5-inch. Turret: 4.0-inch front, 2.5-inch side.

Armament: One 90mm M36 and one .30-caliber machine gun in turret; one .50-caliber AA on turret; one .30-caliber machine gun hull.

Engine: Continental AV-1790-5B, 810 hp

Speed: 30 mph

Range: 80 miles

Misc.: Another interim Korean War production vehicle, remaining in service until 1959 (3d Tank Battalion). Introduced rangefinder. Last tank with bow machine gun.

M48A1 Medium Tank (1955)

Crew: Four

Weight: 97,000 pounds

Armor: Hull: 2.4–4-inch lower front, 4.33-inch upper front, 2–3-inch side. Gunshield: 4.5-inch. Turret: 7.0-inch front, 3.0-inch side.

Armament: One 90mm M41 and one .30-caliber machine gun in turret; one .50-caliber AA in turret cupola.

Engine: Continental AV-1790-5B to -7C, 810 hp

Speed: 28 mph

Range: 70 miles

Misc.: Final version of postwar medium-tank design effort. Introduced cast hull. M67 was the flamethrower tank variant, using mock 90mm gun as flame tube.

M103A1 Heavy Tank (1959)

Crew: Five

Weight: 121,000 pounds

Armor: Hull: 4.5-inch lower front, 5-inch upper front, 1.75–2-inch side. Gunshield: 4–10-inch. Turret: 5.0-inch front, 2.75–5.38-inch side.

Armament: One 120mm M58 and one .30-caliber machine gun in turret; one .50-caliber AA on turret.

Engine: Continental AV-1790-5C, 810 hp

Speed: 21 mph

Range: 80 miles

Misc.: Final version of postwar heavy-tank design effort, ordered into production in 1950, but engineering and quality controls delayed introduction. Two loaders for separated 120mm ammunition. USMC M103s were only operational U.S. heavies; seventy-two were loaned to Army.

M48A3 Medium Tank (1963)

Crew: Four

Weight: 101,000 pounds

Armor: Hull: 2.4–4-inch lower front, 4.33-inch upper front, 2–3-inch side. Gunshield: 4.5-inch. Turret: 7.0-inch front, 3.0-inch side.

Armament: One 90mm M41 and one .30-caliber machine gun in turret; one .50-caliber AA in turret cupola.

Engine: Continental AVDS-1790-2A, 750 hp

Speed: 30 mph

Range: 300 miles

Misc.: Conversion to turbocharged diesel engine, coincidence rangefinder, NBC particulate unit. First combat use of M48A3 was by USMC in 1965. Extended service of M48 fleet to 1974. M67A2 served until 1972.

M103A2 Heavy Tank (1964)

Crew: Five

Weight: 123,000 pounds

Armor: Hull: 4.5-inch lower front, 5-inch upper front, 1.75–2-inch side. Gunshield: 4–10-inch. Turret: 5.0-inch front, 2.75–5.38-inch side.

Armament: One 120mm M58 and one .30-caliber machine gun in turret; one .50-caliber AA on turret.

Engine: Continental AVDS-1790-2A to 7C, 750 hp

Speed: 23 mph

Range: 300 miles

Misc.: Conversion to turbocharged diesel engine, coincidence rangefinder, NBC particulate unit. Extended service of M103 fleet until 1972.

M60A1 Main Battle Tank (1974)

Crew: Four

Weight: 97,000 pounds

Armor: Hull: 3.35–5.63-inch lower front, 4.29-inch upper front, 1.4–2.9-inch side. Gunshield: 5-inch. Turret: 10-inch front, 5.5-inch side.

Armament: One 105mm M68 and one 7.62mm machine gun in turret; one .50-caliber AA in turret cupola.

Engine: Continental AVDS-1790-2A, 750 hp

Speed: 30 mph

Range: 300 miles

Misc.: Initial issue replaced in 1977 with late-production M60A1 with improved engine, passive gunner and driver viewing devices, and two-axis gun stabilization. First combat of M60 series tank in U.S. service by USMC at Grenada, Lebanon, and Gulf War. Last USMC service in 1994.

M1A1 Main Battle Tank (1990)

Crew: Four

Weight: 135,000 pounds and growing

Armor: Composite, laminated, and spaced armor; some vehicles use depleted-uranium reinforcing layer in turret front.

Armament: One 120mm M256 and one 7.62mm machine gun in turret; one .50-caliber AA and one 7.62mm machine gun on turret.

Engine: AGT-1500 gas turbine, 1500 hp

Speed: 41.5 mph (25 mph in reverse)

Range: 275 miles

Misc.: Two-axis stabilized gun, thermal sights and vision devices, digital computer, laser rangefinder, combustible cartridge case ammunition. NBC overpressure protection and numerous other advances. Issued first to 2d and 4th Tank Battalions for Gulf War, remainder in 1991–93. Will serve through 2020.

ARMORED CARS

King Armored Car (1917)

Crew: Three

Weight: 5,500 pounds

Armor: 0.25-inch

Armament: M1908 Benet-Mercie one-pounder automatic cannon (37mm); later .30-caliber Lewis machine gun.

Engine: V-8, 70 hp

Speed: 45 mph

Misc.: Assembled by the Armor Motor Car Company, Detroit, on King touring car chassis. Equipped the 1st Armored Car Squadron, 1st Marine Regiment, Philadelphia Barracks, 1917–21; later service in Haiti with the 2d Marines until 1927. Discarded in 1934.

White Model 15-B Armored Car (1927)
Crew: Three
Weight: 6,500 pounds
Armor: 0.25-inch
Armament: M1917 Browning .30-caliber machine gun
Engine: V-8, 70 hp
Speed: 40 mph
Misc.: Single vehicle procured (Chassis no. 740, originally no. 624, changed by QMMC, letter, 12 May 1931), likely to have been followed by more as replacements for King cars, but became fiscally impossible by end of decade.

M3A1 Scout Car (1942)
Crew: Three
Weight: 10,000 pounds
Armor: 0.25–0.5-inch
Armament: One .50-, two .30-caliber machine guns
Engine: Hercules 6-cylinder, 110 hp
Speed: 55 mph
Range: 250 miles
Misc.: 4 x 4 drive, issued to scout companies, and other units briefly in 1942.

LAV Series (1983)
Crew: Three (seats additional four to six troops)
Weight: 24,418 pounds
Armor: 0.5-inch aluminum (appliqué kit effective vs. 14.5mm AP at 300m)
Armament: One 25mm M242 cannon and one 7.62mm in turret, one 7.62mm machine gun on turret.
Engine: Detroit Diesel 6V53T V6, 275 hp
Speed: 60 mph land, 6.5 mph water
Range: 430 miles
Misc.: 8 x 8 wheel drive, based upon Swiss Mowag design built under license by GM-Canada. Fully stabilized gun. Variants include 81mm mortar, TOW antitank missile, command, logistics, recovery, and air defense vehicles. An assault-gun variant was canceled in 1991. With the addition of thermal sights, it will serve well into the next century.

TANK DESTROYERS
M3 Gun Motor Carriage (1942)
Crew: Five
Weight: 17,620 pounds
Armor: 0.25–0.5-inch
Armament: One 75mm M1897 gun
Engine: White 160AX, 128 hp
Speed: 45 mph
Range: 200 miles
Misc.: Issued two per infantry regiment, twelve per divisional special weapons battalion until early 1945. The 2d Antitank Battalion formed with three batteries of twelve each, but disbanded in 1943 without entering operations.

M50 Ontos (1958)
Crew: Three
Weight: 16,200 pounds
Armor: 0.5-inch
Armament: Six 106mm M40A1C recoilless rifles, four .50-caliber spotting rifles, one .30-caliber AA machine gun.
Engine: GM 302 V-6, 145 hp
Speed: 30 mph (governed)
Range: 150 miles
Misc.: M50A1 rebuild in 1963–64 fitted the Chrysler 361B engine developing 180 hp and new track. Last vehicles were withdrawn from service in 1980.

AMPHIBIOUS FIGHTING VEHICLES
LVT1 (1941)
Crew: Two to three (18 troops)
Weight: 17,300 pounds
Armor: None as built; 0.25-0.50-inch pin-on added for combat.
Armament: One .50-, two .30-caliber machine guns
Engine: Hercules 6-cylinder, 150 hp
Speed: 12 mph land, 6 mph water
Range: 120 miles land, 50 miles water
Misc.: Original Donald Roebling design. Roller-in-groove track system required overhaul every 100 hours.

LVT2 (1943)
Crew: Two to three (20 troops)
Weight: 24,250 pounds
Armor: Pin-on 0.25–0.5-inch
Armament: One .50-, two .30-caliber machine guns
Engine: Continental W-670-9A 7-cylinder radial, 262 hp
Speed: 20 mph land, 7.5 mph water
Range: 150 miles land, 100 miles water
Misc.: FMC redesign of original Roebling tractor.

LVT(A)1 (1943)
Crew: Six
Weight: 29,050 pounds
Armor: Hull: 0.5-inch front, 0.25-inch sides maximum. Turret: 2.0-inch front, 0.5-inch side.
Armament: One 37mm M6, one .30-caliber machine gun in turret; two .30-caliber machine guns in mounts behind turret.
Engine: Continental W-670-9A 7-cylinder radial, 262 hp
Speed: 25 mph land, 7 mph water
Range: 125 miles land, 75 miles water
Misc.: Adaptation of M3A1 light tank turret to LVT4 hull. In service through 1945.

LVT4 (1944)
Crew: Two to three (30 troops)
Weight: 27,400 pounds
Armor: Pin-on 0.25–0.5 inch
Armament: One .50-, two .30-caliber machine guns
Engine: Continental W-670-9A 7-cylinder radial, 262 hp
Speed: 20 mph land, 7.5 mph water
Range: 150 miles land, 75 miles water
Misc.: LVT2 redesign with rear ramp.

LVT(A)4 (1944)
Crew: Six
Weight: 39,460 pounds
Armor: Hull: 0.5-inch front, 0.25-inch sides maximum. Turret: 1.5-inch front, 1.0-inch side.
Armament: One 75mm howitzer M3 in turret; two .30-caliber machine guns on turret sides, one .30-caliber machine gun hull.
Engine: Continental W-670-A 7-cylinder radial, 262 hp

Speed: 25 mph land, 7 mph water

Range: 125 miles land, 75 miles water

Misc.: Adaptation of M8 GMC turret to LVT4 hull. The LVT(A)5 in 1945 added hydraulic power and vertical stabilizer to the turret and remained in service through 1955.

LVT3 (1945)

Crew: Three

Weight: 30,000 pounds armored

Armor: 0.5-inch cab, 0.25-inch pin-on armor

Armament: One .50-, two .30-caliber machine guns

Engine: Twin Cadillac V-8, 296 hp

Speed: 17 mph land, 6 mph water

Range: 150 miles land, 50 miles water

Misc.: Designed with rear ramp. LVT3C conversion beginning 1949 added roof to troop compartment and reduced armament to a cupola mounted .30-caliber machine gun.

LVTP5 (1956)

Crew: Three (34 troops, 25 optimal)

Weight: 64,200 pounds (82,750 pounds LVTE-1)

Armor: 0.6-inch

Armament: One .30-caliber machine gun in cupola

Engine: LV-1790-1 liquid-cooled V-12, 810 hp

Speed: 30 mph land, 6.8 mph water (LVTE-1 24.9/6.2 mph)

Range: 190 miles land, 57 miles water

Misc.: Additional variants included armored amphibian (LVTH-6), command (LVTC-5), air defense (LVTAA-1), recovery (LVTR-1), and combat engineer/breaching (LVTE-1) vehicles. The AA vehicle failed surf testing however.

LVTH-6 (1957)

Crew: Six

Weight: 74,210 pounds

Armor: Hull: 0.5-inch maximum. Turret: 1-inch front, 0.75-inch side.

Armament: One 105mm M49 howitzer, one .30-caliber machine gun in turret, one .50-caliber AA machine gun on turret.

Engine: AV-1790 liquid-cooled V-12, 810 hp

Speed: 30 mph land, 6.8 mph water

Range: 190 miles land, 57 miles water

Misc.: The last of the armored amphibians, fitted with gyrostabilizer.

LVTP-7 Series (1972)
Crew: Three (25 troops maximum)
Weight: 38,370 pounds
Armor: 1.2–1.8-inch aluminum
Armament: One .50-caliber in electric-hydraulic turret
Engine: Detroit Diesel 8V53T two-stroke turbocharged V8, 400 hp
Speed: 8.4 mph water, 45 mph land
Range: 480 miles land, 59 miles land
Misc.: Redesignated AAV-7. Introduced torsion-bar suspension.

AAV-7A1 (1999)
Crew: Three (21 troops maximum)
Weight: 48,060 unloaded AAV7A1 RAM/RS
Armor: 1.2–1.8-inch aluminum (appliqué kit effective vs. 14.5mm AP
    at 300m)
Armament: One M2 .50-caliber and one Mk19 40mm machine gun.
Engine: Cummins VTA-525, 4-cylinder V-8, turbocharged diesel, 525 hp
Speed: 45 mph land, 8.2 mph water
Range: 200 miles land, 57 miles water
Misc.: Originally LVTP-7. AAV-7A1 redesign of 1977 added new Continental
    4-stroke VT400 diesel (400 gross hp), passive night driving viewer, upgun
    weapons station with 40mm/.50-caliber combination, smoke launchers,
    appliqué armor, fire-suppression system, electric turret. Continuing
    RAM/RS upgrades, using Army M2 Bradley Fighting Vehicle engine and
    suspension systems will carry the AAV7A1 well into the next century.

AAAV Project (2006)
Crew: Three (18 troops)
Weight: 62,880 pounds
Armor: Protected against 14.5mm AP at 300 meters
Armament: One 30mm Bushmaster II cannon, one 7.62mm machine
    gun in turret.
Engine: MTU MT883 V-12 turbocharged, 850 hp land, 2575 hp water
Speed: 45 mph land, 25 knots water
Range: 300 miles land, 65 nautical miles water
Misc.: Preproduction engineering prototypes delivered in 1999. Armament
    fully stabilized with thermal sights, digital fire control. Fitted with NBC
    overpressure FLIR sensors, hydropneumatic suspension, and other
    advanced systems.

Note: All weights are empty unless otherwise indicated (manufacturing differ-
    ences cause as much as 4 percent variation). Armor figures are maximums.

Appendix 2

Armored Fighting Vehicle Units in Marine Corps Service

1917–1941

1st Armored Car Squadron (1917–21)

Light Tank Platoon, Marine Corps Expeditionary Force (1923–28)

1st Tank Company, 1st Marine Brigade (1937–41), *redesignated*
1st Scout Company, 1st Marine Division

3d Tank Company, 1st Marine Brigade (1940–41), *redesignated*
A Company, 1st Tank Battalion

4th Tank Company, 2d Marine Brigade (1940–41), *redesignated*
A Company, 2d Tank Battalion

1st–2d Tank Battalions (1941)

1941–1945

1st Scout Company, 1st Marine Division (1941–43)[a]

2d Scout Company, 2d Marine Division (1941–43)[a]

1st–6th Tank Battalions (1941–45)

1st–5th, 8th–11th Amphibian Tractor Battalions (1942–45)

2d Antitank Battalion (1942–43)

1st Corps Medium Tank Battalion (1943–44)

1st–3d Armored Amphibian Battalions (1943–45)

6th Amphibious Tractor Battalion (1944)

1st Separate Tank Company (1942–43), *redesignated* C Company,
3d Tank Battalion

2d Separate Tank Company (1942–44), *redesignated* B Company,
6th Tank Battalion

1946–1949

1st–2d Tank Battalions

1st–2d Amphibian Tractor Companies

1st–2d Armored Amphibian Platoons

10th–11th Tank Battalions, USMCR

10th–12th Amphibian Tractor Battalions, USMCR

1st–2d Armored Amphibian Companies, USMCR

1950–1958

1st–2d Tank Battalions

7th Tank Battalion (1950–52)

8th Tank Battalion (1950–58)

3d Tank Battalion (1952–58)

1st–2d Amphibian Tractor Battalions

3d Amphibian Tractor Battalion (1952–58)

1st–2d Armored Amphibian Battalions, *redesignated* 1st–2d Armored
  Amphibian Companies (1956)

1st–3d Antitank Battalions (1957–58)

10th–11th Tank Battalions, USMCR, *redesignated* 1st–2d Tank Battalion,
  USMCR (1953)

10th–12th Amphibian Tractor Battalions, USMCR, *redesignated* 1st–2d
  Amphibian Tractor Battalions, USMCR (1953)

1st–2d Armored Amphibian Companies, USMCR

1959–1972

1st–3d Tank Battalions

1st–3d Amphibian Tractor Battalions

1st–2d Armored Amphibian Companies

1st–3d Antitank Battalions (1959–67; 2d, 1970)

1st Armored Amphibian Company (USMCR, 1959–66; FMF, 1966–70)

5th Tank Battalion (1966–69)

5th Amphibian Tractor Battalion (1966–69)

5th Antitank Battalion (1966–69)

1st–2d Tank Battalions, USMCR (1959–62)

4th Tank Battalion, USMCR (1962–72)

8th Tank Battalion, USMCR (1967–72)

1st–2d Amphibian Tractor Battalions, USMCR (1959–62)

4th Amphibian Tractor Battalion, USMCR (1962–72)

2d Armored Amphibian Company, USMCR (1959–70)

4th Antitank Battalion, USMCR (1962–72)

1973–2000

1st–2d Tank Battalions

3d Tank Battalion (1973–92)

2d–3d Amphibian Tractor Battalions (1973–76)

2d–3d Assault Amphibian Battalions (1976–2000)

1st Amphibian Tractor Battalion (1973–76)

1st Tracked Vehicle Battalion (1976–88)
1st Armored Assault Battalion (1988–92)
1st Combat Support Group (1992–94)
1st Combat Assault Battalion (1994–2000)
1st–3d LAV (1984–88), *redesignated* LAI (1988), *redesignated*
   LAR (1993) Battalions
4th Tank Battalion, USMCR
8th Tank Battalion, USMCR
4th Amphibian Tractor Battalion, redesignated Assault Amphibian
   Battalion, USMCR (1976)
4th LAV, *redesignated* LAI (1988), *redesignated* LAR (1993) Battalion,
   USMCR (1987–2000)

[a]The divisional scout companies became dismounted units in 1943.

Notes

Chapter 1. Ideas and Experiments

1. Allan R. Millett, *Semper Fidelis: The History of the United States Marine Corps* (New York: Macmillan, 1980), remains the essential study.

2. Quartermaster of the Marine Corps (QMMC) to Major General Commandant (hereafter CMC, or commandant of the Marine Corps), 28 July 1916 and 28 Oct. 1916, and A. B. Drum to Commanding Officer (CO), Marine Barracks, Philadelphia, 15 Aug. 1916, Record Group 127, Entry 140A, Box 163 (hereafter RG127/E140A/163), National Archives, Washington D.C.; SecNav, letter, 31 Oct. 1916 (file 776:3173), RG80/E19/2435, and RG127/E18/163, General Records of the Department of the Navy.

3. CMC, memo to QMMC, 2 Jan. 1918, RG127/E140A/163; various QMMC letters of 1927–38 referring to the King cars are in File 273-2, Vehicle, Armored Car, NARA/RG127/E140A/126. B. T. White, *Tanks and Other Armored Fighting Vehicles, 1900 to 1918* (New York: Shepperton, Allan, 1970), 162; note in *Leatherneck* (Jan. 1927): 14; clipping file, Reference Section, History and Museums Division, Marine Corps Historical Center, Washington D.C. (hereafter RefSect).

4. Maj. Andrew B. Drum to CMC, 25 Nov. 1919, RG127/E140A/163.

5. Philadelphia Depot QM to QMMC, 12 Oct. 1933, and survey of Cadillac [King] armored car, M.C. no. 728, RG127/E140A/126.

6. CINCAF, message to Navy Dept., 19 March 1938, "desire shipment from west coast or 14th Naval District of 3 light armored cars equipped with .30 caliber machine guns of the same type as used by the Army. These are urgently needed by the 4th Marines for use in patrolling their sector and cannot be obtained in the Philippines." HQMC, message to CINCAF, 21 March 1938, RG127/E140A/126. The USMC Air-Ground Museum at Quantico exhibits a surviving King car. The Corps probably considered procuring more White armored cars, but fiscal pressures probably made this impossible, and the problems in China proved fleeting. The White model 15-B truck purchased 8 Dec. 1927 had a 121.5-inch wheelbase and quarter-inch armor, and was fitted with one M1917 Browning .30-caliber machine gun; CMC, letter to CO, 4th Mar, Shanghai, 21 Feb. 1933, RG127/E140A/File 273-2.

7. Advance Base Operations in Micronesia OpPlan 712H (declassified 1961), HAF 165, USMC Research Center Archives, Quantico, Va. Contrary to Millett, *Semper Fidelis,* 326n, however, it makes no mention of light tanks as required either in offense or defense.

8. Tank instruction formed part of the curriculum of the first field officers' course conducted postwar at Quantico: "Marine Corps Schools," *Marine Corps Gazette*

(Dec. 1920): 410, cited in Arthur E. Burns III, "The Origin and Development of U.S. Marine Corps Tank Units: 1923–1945," student paper, Marine Corps Command and Staff College, Quantico, Va., 1977, 2.

9. RG80/E19/559/File 11112-1800HW. The wheels moved slowly: First Lieutenants Grover C. Darnall and James W. Flett first completed this course in September 1926.

10. On Christie and his amphibious tank see Kenneth J. Clifford, *Progress and Purpose: A Developmental History of the United States Marine Corps, 1900–1970* (Washington, D.C.: HQMC, 1973), 34, or the exhaustive treatment by George Hofmann in *From Camp Colt to Desert Storm: A History of U.S. Armored Forces,* ed. George F. Hofmann and Donn A. Starry (Lexington: University of Kentucky Press, 1999). Burns, "Origin and Development of U.S. Marine Corps Tank Units," 4–6. Letters, Cdr Scouting Fleet, 26 Dec. 1923, to CNO requesting, and CNO to Cdr Scouting Fleet, 28 Dec. 1923, approving request to take on board a marine tank for purposes of experiments in connection with the winter maneuvers, RG80/E19/814/File 20392(1394).

11. RG80/E13/773, File War Dept., Aug. 1923–Apr. 1925; note that these tanks followed the two other M1917 tanks transferred to the USMC on verbal agreement for the Fleet Exercise of 1923–24. Eight vehicles were declared for disposal by another SecNav to SecWar letter of 12 Sept. 1935. Curtis D. Wilbur was the SecNav in 1925.

12. QMMC to Lieutenant Colonel Noa, Marine Barracks, Quantico, Va., 26 Jan. 1927, and HQMC, memo, 2 April 1927, RG127/E140A/126; Millett, *Semper Fidelis,* 222–28.

13. HQ 3d Brigade (Bde), Brigade Training (Bde Trng) Order #2, 7 Sept. 1927, RG127/A1(245), Records relating to marine activities in China, 1927–38, Box 5.

14. Final report of Brig. Gen. Smedley D. Butler (July–Dec. 1928), 14 Jan. 1929, in ibid.

15. 3d Brigade Operations (Bde Ops) B2, report of 30 Sept. (#8), in ibid.; SecNav, letter to SecWar, 12 Sept. 1935, reports eight M1917 on hand at Quantico: serial numbers 18282, 18124, 18235, 18254, 18367, 18428, 20717, and 20797. All were considered unserviceable, and the letter requested authority to dispose of them. Subsequent letters transferred them to the navy for disposal: RG127/E18/270.

16. Millett, *Semper Fidelis,* 329.

17. Ibid., 336; Clifford, *Progress and Purpose,* 43–46.

18. On landing craft trials and tribulations, see Clifford, *Progress and Purpose,* 48–54.

19. Quoted in ibid., 54.

20. CMC to Cdr Special Service Squadron, USN, 19 June 1934, RG127/E18/76.

21. Withers file, RefSect; Army C/S, letter to CNO, 18 July 1935, and AsstCMC, message to USS *Chicago,* 25 July 1935, RG127/E18/57.

22. CMC, letter to QMMC, 29 Nov. 1935, RG127/E140A/128.

Chapter 2. Early Rearmament

1. *Small Wars Manual, 1940* (Washington, D.C., 1940), sec. 2-44, pp. 50–51.

2. CMC to QMMC, 29 Nov. 1935, RG127/E140A/128.

3. AsstCMC, memo, 3 Dec. 1935, RG127/E140A/128.

4. Correspondence between HQMC and the Marmon-Herrington Company, 1937, RG127/E18/164; tank data from Fred Crismon, *U.S. Military Tracked Vehicles* (Osceola, Wis.: Motorbooks International, 1992), 65–66.

5. Chairman, Marine Corps Equipment Board (MCEB), to Major Withers, 23 March 1936, RG127/E140A/128.

6. Navy Dept. (BuSup) to Marmon-Herrington Co. Inc., 5 June 1936; Aberdeen Proving Ground (APG) to CMC, 22 Sept. 1936, reported passing quarter-inch armor plates for Marmon-Herrington (M-H) light tank. Test was 100 yds .30 AP and 50 yds .30 ball; both achieved partial penetration only. RG127/E140A/128.

7. QM, Quantico, letter to QMMC, 26 Feb. 1937, and QM, Quantico, letter to CG, FMF, 20 Feb. 1937, reporting acceptance of CTL, factory numbers 1329–33 (Marine Corps numbers were T-1 through T-5) for use by 1st Tk Co, 1st Marine Bde, FMF, upon its formation. "Tanks in test run have demonstrated ability to: 1. Run a hundred and twenty-five miles without addition of gas, oil or water. 2. Make a complete three hundred and sixty degree turn in either direction within a circle of eighteen feet in diameter by turning on one locked track. 3. Bridge a trench fifty inches wide. 4. Negotiate a forty-eight inch vertical drop without turning over. 5. Negotiate a twenty-two inch vertical rise." CMC to CG, Marine Barracks, Quantico, 10 March 1937, directs installation of one USN radio receiver, type RU, in one of the CTL. Photos of the period show only one tank per CTL-3 platoon fitted with a radio. RG127/E140A/128.

8. FLEX4 reports, NARA, Washington Regional Records Center, Suitland, Md., accession number 64A-4552 (hereafter RG127/64A-4552), cited in Burns, "Origin and Development of U.S. Marine Corps Tank Units," 24–27.

9. CMC, letter to BuOrd, 18 Sept. 1937, requesting contracting M-H for five more CTL at a $14,680 bid, but the contract itself is dated 14 Sept. 1937, Director, Ops/Trng, memo to CMC, 21 Sept. 1937, RG127/E140A/128.

10. CMC, letter to BuOrd, 1 Oct. 1937, reporting crack in center bottom plate of CTL-3, requesting purchase of new one; CMC, letter to CG, 1stBde, 27 Nov. 1937; A. W. Herrington, President, M-H Co., letter to BuSup, 27 Sept. 1937; BuOrd, letter to M-H, 26 May, approved change; RG127/E140A/128.

11. MCEB notes, 9 Dec. 1937, RG127/E18/76.

12. CMC to Chief, BuSup, 14 Sept. 1938, RG127/E18/164.

13. Director, Ops/Trng, memo to CMC, 8 Nov. 1938, notes M-H letter to CMC, 7 Nov., stating test tank ready on 15 Nov.; CMC, letter to BuSup, 25 Nov. 1938; M-H, letter to HQMC, 7 Dec. 1938, presenting contracts for final signatures; BuSup, letter to M-H, 23 Dec. 1938, accepts. RG127/E18/129.

14. The vehicles had factory numbers 1434–38. M-H plant inspector to CMC, 25 July 1939, RG127/E18/129.

15. President, MCEB, to CMC, 19 Sept. 1938, RG127/E18/164.
16. Gen. Lemuel C. Shepherd Jr., transcript of oral history interviews, 1966–67, Marine Corps Historical Center, Washington D.C., 1967, 38–40.
17. CMC to President, MCEB, 19 Oct. 1938, RG127/E18/164.
18. Chief of Ord to CMC, 26 April 1938, and minutes of MCEB meeting, 31 May 1938, RG127/E18/76.
19. CMC to BuOrd, 29 June 1936, budget estimate for FY38; CMC to BuOrd, 15 May 1937. "The present procurement plans call for two tank companies with eighteen light tanks each."
20. QMMC, letters, 23 Jan., 10 April, and 16 July 1931, 8 July 1936, 21 June 1937, 23 Sept. 1938; MCEB memo, 17 April 1939; CO, 1/10, letter to QMMC, 10 Feb. 1933, reports on Chevrolet cross-country car USMC #703 tested over three-month period: it needed better ground clearance of at least six inches and dual or better traction tires; RG127/E140A/128; 1stBde Annex 3 to AdminOrd 10-39, 21 Dec. 1939, RG127/E140A/File 169-1. CMC to CG, FMF, 22 Sept. 1936, RG127/E18/270.
21. Clifford, *Progress and Purpose,* 52–53; Burns, "Origin and Development of U.S. Marine Corps Tank Units," 28–30; CO, 1st Tk Co, to CMC, 9 Dec. 1938, RG127/E18/164.
22. Shepherd to CMC, 31 May 1939, RG127/E140B/154.
23. P&P, memo to CMC, 20 July 1939, RG127/E18/1230.
24. QMMC file on FLEX6 notes general satisfaction with tanks, especially the second series of five with its improved track, RG127/E140A/File 169-1. Burns, "Origin and Development of U.S. Marine Corps Tank Units," 32; cf. Frank O. Hough, Verle E. Ludwig, and Henry I. Shaw Jr., *Pearl Harbor to Guadalcanal,* vol. 1 of *History of U.S. Marine Corps Operations in World War II* (Washington, D.C.: Historical Division, HQMC, 1958), 23–32, and Clifford, *Progress and Purpose,* 52–53, on lighters, although both erroneously note that the Corps had given up on the M-H tank by 1939.
25. CMC to President, MCEB, 23 Feb. 1940, RG127/E18/1229.
26. Minutes of MCEB meeting, 3 April 1940, RG127/E140B/154; for pithy comments on the MCEB members and these proceedings, see Gen. Merrill B. Twining, oral history transcript, 1967, Marine Corps Historical Center, Washington D.C., 1975, 70–71.
27. Director, P&P, to CMC, 8 April 1940, decision memo on number, type of tanks, RG127/E140B/154.

Chapter 3. Preparing for War

1. Hough, Ludwig, and Shaw, *Pearl Harbor to Guadalcanal,* 54; Millett, *Semper Fidelis,* 345.
2. Millett, *Semper Fidelis,* 347.
3. President, MCEB, to CMC, 13 April 1940; CMC to QMMC, 19 April 1940; CMC to Chief, BuOrd, 14 June 1940, RG127/E18/1229.
4. Director, P&P, memo to CMC, 24 June 1940; CMC to QMMC, 2 July 1940, orders five M2A4 tanks ($165,000) and 31 13.5-ton M3s ($1,023,000); Chief,

BuOrd, letter, 7 Aug. 1940, notes verbal orders of CMC, 31 July 1940, and modified above order to 36 M2A4 at $1,188,000. RG127/E140B/154.

5. President, MCEB, to CMC, 27 June 1940; SecNav to SecWar, 8 July 1940, refers to both 11.5- and 13.5-ton models of the M2A4, but the latter already had been designated M3. RG127/E18/1229.

6. Richard P. Hunnicutt, *Stuart: A History of the American Light Tank* (Novato, Calif.: Presidio, 1992), 119–20.

7. Burns, "Origin and Development of U.S. Marine Corps Tank Units," 33–36.

8. Nov. 1940 muster rolls, RefSect; Burns, "Origin and Development of U.S. Marine Corps Tank Units," 36, 41.

9. CG, 1stBde, to CMC, 23 Jan. 1941, RG127/E18/1229.

10. CMC to CNO for Chief, BuAero, 17 Oct. 1940, requesting aircraft radios; Base MTO, San Diego, to QMMC, 4 Nov. 1940, notes receipt of 18 M2A4, 31 Oct. 1940, issued to 2dBde, FMF. ser. nos. 487–549; CO, 4th Tk Co, 2dBde, to QMMC, 5 Dec. 1940, requested tools for eighteen tanks received, signed by J. S. Cook Jr. Fifth endorsement, 8 Jan. 1941, is CMC to QMMC noting "the organization of tank battalions having a headquarters and maintenance company is contemplated"; Cdr., Rock Island Arsenal, to Chief, BuOrd, 2 Oct. 1940, notes parts shipped with the 18 M2A4 shipped to Quantico and San Diego (18 in each set?): two engines, two transmissions, nine pair track assembly, gauges, eighteen filters, 290 piston rings, two and one-half pages of parts. RG127/E40B/154.

11. CMC to CG, Amphib Corps, Atlantic, 5 Dec. 1941, RG127/E140B/182; MTO, San Diego, to QMMC, 21 Dec. 1941, received five CTL-3 tanks; QMMC to Chief, BuOrd, 26 Feb. 1942; QMMC to Chief, BuOrd, 13 Aug. 1942, orders 141 M3A1 scout cars; QM, SplTrps, 2dMarDiv, to QMMC, 18 June 1942; QMMC to BuOrd, 20 July 1942; OrdSect, QMMC to QM, 2d Antitank Battalion (AT Bn), 11 Sept. 1942, RG127/E140B/226; BuAero, AirMailGram, 20 Feb. 1942, states 62 cars shipped from International Harvester Springfield to QM San Francisco, 24 of these earmarked for shipment overseas to Pearl Harbor (probably for defense battalions); QM, SplTrps, 2dMarDiv, to QMMC, 18 June 1942: 2dMarDiv has 19 scout cars, M3A1 on hand, USMC nos. SC-22 to -32, 50051–59, RG127/E140B/227; muster rolls, RefSect; Burns, "Origin and Development of U.S. Marine Corps Tank Units," 36, 41; Robert M. Neiman, interview with author.

12. CMC, decision memo, 15 Dec. 1942, orders replacement of the scout cars in the division scout company (now attached to the tank battalion) with one-quarter jeeps, and that an armored 6 x 6 scout vehicle (penned note says "T-24") be procured when developed by the army. Scout company to go to DivSpl troops; CMC to QMMC, 22 Dec. 1942: due to scout cars deleted from T/O of scout company, cancel orders for 40 M3A1 cars. RG127/E140B/226.

13. Director, P&P, memo to CMC, 26 Aug. 1942, AT Artillery; CMC to QMMC, 7 Sept. 1942; RG127/E18/1227; P&P, internal memo, 7 Jan. 1942, announcing army three-inch-gun motor carriage (tank destroyer). Penciled memos:

Director, P&P, to M-3 (Ops staff officer): "for consideration: a tank destroyer Bn in Div Spl Trps and a tank destroyer btry in each Def Bn." M3 to Director: "We already have on order 60 mounts for 75mm guns for the same purpose. Suggest we follow development with view to possible substitution for 75mm or added weapon later. Believe we should put M-H tanks in Defense Battalions when we get more scout cars and M-3 tanks for divisions." (Overwritten in red pencil, "M-3 OK [initials].") QMMC to Chief, BuOrd, 20 Jan. 1942, requests 30 75mm motor gun carriages with mounts without gun, 75mm, M1897, USMC to provide guns, RG127/E18/1228. On the M5 motor carriage, see Hunnicutt, *Stuart*, 295–96.

14. Sept. 1942 and Nov. 1943 muster rolls, RefSect.

15. Clifford, *Progress and Purpose*, 54–56; Alfred Dunlop Bailey, *Alligators, Buffaloes, and Bushmasters: The History of the Development of the LVT through World War II* (Washington, D.C.: History and Museum Division, HQMC, 1986), 34–41; cf. message 231850, Dec. 1942, in Bailey, *Alligators, Buffaloes, and Bushmasters*, 31–32.

16. Bailey, *Alligators, Buffaloes, and Bushmasters*, 40–41; CMC to CG, FMF, 16 Sept. 1940; QMMC to Chief, BuShips, 17 Sept. 1940, RG127/E140B/154. BuShips to BuSupAccts, 19 Sept. 1941: Contract 89992 covered 100 amtracs, serials C-4139–4238, plus 10 unnumbered. New contract 78806 for 200 amtracs, numbered C-2644–2843. All contracts made with D. Roebling, specifying manufacturer as FMC. RG127/E140B/157.

17. QMMC to CMC, 18 Sept. 1940; P&P, memo to CMC, 20 Sept. 1941, notes the following: 10 amtracs delivered to Dunedin, now in use for training. Four others are shipped to Norfolk, two more to Quantico on 20 Sept. Thereafter deliveries will be five per week until 1 Nov., and then ten per week. Uncorrected defects in design limit operations to 100 hours before major overhaul. Desire to restrict deliveries to divisions until service facilities at their bases become adequate. Forecast only eight machines to 2d Div on 8 Nov. of the first 140 machines. RG127/E140B/154; Bailey, *Alligators, Buffaloes, and Bushmasters*, 43.

18. QMMC, letter, 31 Dec. 1941, and CMC to CO, Amtrac det Dunedin, 3 Nov. 1941, RG127/E140B/157. Bailey, *Alligators, Buffaloes, and Bushmasters*, 41–42.

19. General Marshall's statement in Millett, *Semper Fidelis*, 351.

20. CMC to QMMC, 5 Feb. 1941, RG127/E140B/184.

21. Hunnicutt, *Stuart*, 127–53.

22. Ibid., 153; on tank engines see Constance M. Green, Harry C. Thomson, and Peter C. Roots, *The Ordnance Department: Planning Munitions for War* (Washington, D.C.: Chief of Military History, Department of the Army, 1955), 287–301.

23. CMC to QMMC, 21 March 1941, orders 39 M3 tanks at $1.365M; CMC to CG, 1st and 2d Div, 29 July 1941: schedule for activation of tank units; M-H plant Inspector (Lt. Col. Fred S. Robillard) to CMC, 12 May 1941, RG127/E140B/184; Crismon, *U.S. Military Tracked Vehicles*, 66–67. In this work, I have reflected

upon battalion organizations only at significant benchmark points and have not provided a comprehensive guide to peacetime and wartime organizations. The organizations apparently varied considerably in World War II, owing to local exceptions to the published tables of organizations, as well as the understandable tendency to retain excess vehicles and weapons.

24. Report of board of investigation, loss of tank T-8, 24 June 1941, RG127/E140B/184; Neiman interview.

25. QMMC to MTO, Camp Pendleton, 9 Oct. 1941, notes ten M3 light tanks received 22 Sept. 1941 for 2d Div tank company, USMC #60047-56. QM, 1stTkBn, 1stDiv, New River, N.C., to MTO, Phil, 28 Oct. 1941, reports receipt of ten M3 light tanks, USMC #60057-66, RG127/E140B/184; muster rolls, RefSect; Burns, "Origin and Development of U.S. Marine Corps Tank Units," 45–46. Only twelve of A Company's M2A4 tanks reached Iceland, as its 3d Platoon unloaded at Charleston with six tanks, probably to make room for attachments from the 1stMarDiv. The twelve M2A4 vehicles remained on Iceland when U.S. Army troops relieved the 6th Bde of this duty. Swackhammer interview.

26. CO, B Co, 2dTkBn, to QMMC, 12 Nov. 1941, and QMMC to Chief, BuOrd, 18 Nov. 1941, RG127/E140B/184; officers to Ft. Knox and Louisiana maneuvers, November muster rolls, RefSect; B Co test fire from Metzger int., letter to author, 8 July 1999.

27. CO, B Co., 2dTkBn, to CMC, 6 May 1942, RG127/E46A/7; see also the delightful tale by one of Denig's platoon leaders, Louis Metzger, "Duty Beyond the Seas," *Marine Corps Gazette* (Jan. 1982): 28–37.

28. Bio file, RefSect.

29. Hunnicutt, *Stuart,* 142–43.

30. RG127/E46/7.

31. OrdSect, memo to QMMC, 31 Aug. 1942, RG127/E140B/182.

32. QM file 273-16 (Jan.–Aug.) RG127/E140B/226; it remains unlikely the tank was ever rebuilt, reported as still a bare hull by QM, PhibCorpsPAC, to QMMC, 23 Sept. 1942, RG127/E140B/227.

33. QMMC to Chief, BuOrd, 28 Feb., 18 April, 8 July, and 13 Aug. 1942 (three letters same date), RG127/E140B/226.

34. Inspector, M-H plant, to QMMC, 16 Feb. 1942, and QMMC to M-H Inspector, 23 Feb. 1942, RG127/E140B/226; QM, 2dTkBn, to CMC, 20 April 1942, and Hercules Motors Corp. to CMC, 7 May 1942, RG127/E18/1227. It seems unlikely that the order to rebuild the five CTL-3As as CTL-3Ms was ever accomplished.

35. CO, 2d Sep Tk Co, to CO, 22d Marines, 8 June 1942, RG127/E18/1227.

36. CMC to CG, PhibCorpsPAC, 17 June 1942, RG127/E140B/226. Muster rolls show the 2d Separate Tank Company arriving on Samoa, 29 July 1942, RefSect. One version relates that the company arrived in Samoa with twelve M-Hs, and the rest M2A4s (presumably from the old 3d Platoon, A Company, never sent to Iceland), and one M3. They were later issued new M3A1 tanks with stabi-

lizers and power turrets, but British radios with USSR markings, intended for Lend-Lease; Doug Brown, interview with author, 8 Oct. 1998.

37. Muster rolls, RefSect. Captain Mattson committed suicide on 6 Dec. 1942, perhaps reflecting the personal toll of deployments and isolated posts. The remaining five CTL-3M tanks in the USMC probably stayed at Camp Elliott, with the 2d Scout Company, mustering with 2d Tank Battalion starting in Aug. 1942.

38. Muster rolls, RefSect; Brown interview; Fred Chapman, interview, 23 April 1999; Jacques Jost, "Marmon-Herrington AFVs in the Netherlands East Indies," *AFV News* 32, no. 1 (Jan.–April 1997): 7.

39. Numerous QMMC letters, Sept.–Oct. especially QMMC to Chief, BuOrd, 25 Sept. 1942, RG127/E140B/227; QMMC to QM (Signal) Depot San Diego, 7 Nov. 1942, notes total of 329 British army no. 19 radio sets for USMC M3 tanks; Brown interview; Millett, *Semper Fidelis,* 376, notes that the limitations of the San Francisco depot led to the establishment of the main USMC Depot at Barstow, California.

40. Muster rolls, RefSect; QMMC to QM, New River, 19 Nov. 1942, RG127/E140B/227.

41. 3dMarDiv to QMMC, message 231850, Dec. 1942, notes that the 100-hour check was not performed on their M3A1 tanks due to lack of tool sets. The tanks were now nearing 200 hours and tools were requested urgently.

Chapter 4. Going to War

1. Hough, Ludwig, and Shaw, *Pearl Harbor to Guadalcanal,* 254–68; Richard B. Frank, *Guadalcanal: The Definitive Account of the Landmark Battle* (New York: Random House, 1990), 77–79; casualties from muster rolls, RefSect.

2. Cates quote from Jeter A. Isely and Philip A. Crowl, *The U.S. Marines and Amphibious War* (Princeton: Princeton University Press, 1951), 121.

3. Victor Croizat, *Across the Reef: The Amphibious Tracked Vehicle at War* (London: Blandford Press, 1989), 55. Croizat, a pioneer amtrac officer, served at Guadalcanal and later commanded amtrac battalions supporting the 4th Marine Division.

4. Richard Tregasis, *Guadalcanal Diary* (New York: Random House, 1943), 142, cited in Frank, *Guadalcanal,* 155; Lt. Leo B. Case, the platoon commander of this first tactical success with Marine Corps tanks, later commanded the 7th Tank Battalion when organized in the Korean War expansion.

5. Hough, Ludwig, and Shaw, *Pearl Harbor to Guadalcanal,* 291, 308; casualties from muster rolls, RefSect.

6. Marine Corps operations in New Georgia are covered in Henry I. Shaw Jr. and Douglas T. Kane, *Isolation of Rabaul,* vol. 2 of *The History of U.S. Marine Corps Operations in World War II* (Washington, D.C.: Historical Division, HQMC, 1963), 54–163 passim.

7. Burns, "Origin and Development of U.S. Marine Corps Tank Units," 53.

8. Curiously, the Corps at first rejected the M5 series, perhaps still sensitive

due to the plethora of production variants they had experienced in the M3 light-tank series, until settling on a single M3A1 model, QMMC, letter to ChOrd, 26 Sept. 1942, RG127/E140B/227. On 15 Jan. 1943 a P&P Division memo noted the first M5 tanks (M5A1 was not yet allocated to the USMC) would arrive for training use in January, with 210 more in March. The M5 also had an escape hatch after the first 800 vehicles of the production run; only the enlarged radio installation in the turret bustle would distinguish the M5A1, RG127/E18/1227. Hunnicutt, *Stuart,* 172–87.

9. QMMC to Chief, Ord, 8 Oct. 1942, noting release of six M4A4 tanks to USMC. Requested shipment to the base at San Diego for the training center; 13 Nov. letter notes sixteen more M4A4. RG127/E140B/227. Muster rolls, RefSect.

10. Green, Thomson, and Roots, *The Ordnance Department,* 290–301; R. P. Hunnicutt, *Sherman: A History of the American Medium Tank* (Belmont, Calif.: Taurus Enterprises, 1978), 122–53 passim.

11. CO, TkSchl, to CMC, 26 Nov. 1942, preliminary report on medium tanks; CO, TkSchl, to CMC, 16 Dec. 1942; Collins, memo for Lt. Col. S. T. Clark, 18 Dec. 1942, RG127/E18/1228.

12. P&P memos, 28 and 30 Nov. 1942, and OrdSect, QMMC penciled memo, 13 Jan. 1943, RG127/E18/1228.

13. P&P memo, 3 Nov. 1943, notes Force Plan of 31 Aug. 1943 forecast 1944: one medium-tank battalion, six divisional tank battalions; RG127/E18/1225.

14. Memo for the Director, Personnel, 17 Jan. 1944; CMC, airgram to FMF, 23 April 1943, on urgent modification to M4A2s in hands of 1st Corps Tank Battalion and Tank School: All 168 mediums to be returned to the army, 100 in first flight, then 68 after 100 new tanks issued [N.B.: What was the modification? Probably a change to cylinder linings permitting higher power output]; RG127/E18/Box 1225.

15. Colonel Whitehead, Investigation report to CMC, 31 Dec. 1943, RG127/E18/1225.

16. H. L. McCormick (Army Ordnance), report given to Capt. Gordon Guiberson, Tank Automotive Center, Detroit, 3 Aug. 1943, RG127/E18/1225.

17. Report, 4 Nov. 1943, RG127/E18/1225.

18. P&P memo, 12 April 1943, RG127/E18/1226.

19. P&P, memo to CMC, 28 Oct. 1943, on radio installation in tanks.

20. Croizat, *Across the Reef,* 63; Bailey, *Alligators, Buffaloes, and Bushmasters,* 59–68.

21. Naval Material Inspector, FMC Co. to distribution list (including CMC), 23 March 1942; CMC to CG, Quantico, 20 May 1942; CMC to CG, FMF, San Diego Area, 12 Oct. 1942: RG127/E140B/184. BuShips to BuOrd, 29 Oct. 1942, requested an M5A1 tank turret gun, mount, and periscope for use in the FMC LVT(A) pilot model, but no further action seems to have occurred, RG127/E18/1228. Unit folders, RefSect.

22. Croizat, *Across the Reef,* 63; Bailey, *Alligators, Buffaloes, and Bushmasters,* 157–59, 225–26. A P&P report, 23 Aug. 1943, on the test of Borg-Warner's Model

B, the LVT-3 prototype, on 30 July–3 Aug. in the San Diego area notes it consistently outperformed the LVT2 accompanying test vehicle; RG127/E18/1226.
23. Croizat, *Across the Reef,* 63.
24. B Co., 1st Corps Medium Tank Battalion left 3dMarDiv control on 27 March
1944, departing Guadalcanal on 15 April, arriving Pearl Harbor 30 April;
muster rolls, RefSect; Philip Morell, interview, 29 Sept. 1999.
25. Shaw and Kane, *Isolation of Rabaul,* 349–86; Burns, "Origin and Development
of U.S. Marine Corps Tank Units," 63–65; Roland Hall, letter, *MCTA Newsletter,*
no. 299 (June 1999): 7. The army turned over the first 24 M4A1 medium tanks
arriving in the Southwest Pacific Area to A Company, 1st Tank Battalion, in
May 1943, the only use of this model by the USMC; Benis M. Frank and Henry
I. Shaw, *Victory and Occupation,* vol. 5 of *History of U.S. Marine Corps
Operations in World War II* (Washington, D.C.: Historical Division, HQMC,
1968), 703.
26. Arthur P. Alphin, "A Bigger Hammer," instructional ms., The Armor School,
Ft. Knox, n.d., 155–57; Shaw and Kane, *Isolation of Rabaul,* 392–93, 431.
27. Joseph H. Alexander, *Utmost Savagery: The Three Days of Tarawa*
(Annapolis, Md.: Naval Institute Press, 1995), 99–100.
28. Bailey, *Alligators, Buffaloes, and Bushmasters,* 83–86.
29. Citation for Navy Cross medal awarded to Lawrence; Lawrence file, RefSect.
30. Alexander, *Utmost Savagery,* 112–16; Croizat, *Across the Reef,* 96–97; Henry
I. Shaw, Bernard C. Nalty, and Edwin T. Turnbladh, *Central Pacific Drive,*
vol. 3 of *History of U.S. Marine Corps Operations in World War II*
(Washington, D.C.: Historical Division, HQMC, 1966), 108; Lawrence quote
from Victor Croizat, letter to author, 4 May 1999.
31. Alexander, *Utmost Savagery,* 121–205, 238; Alphin, "A Bigger Hammer,"
130–40; Shaw, Nalty, and Turnbladh, *Central Pacific Drive,* 53–109; Steve
Zaloga, *Armour of the Pacific War* (London: Osprey, 1983), 16–17. Shoup told
Bale years later that he regretted the wording of the "tanks no good" message;
he had asked only that the halftracks be landed as the tanks had become disabled, but the message became transformed by his assistants or the radio operator; Ed Bale to author, 7 June and 8 July 1999; Frank Stewart, interview, 27
July 1999.

Chapter 5. Armored Victory

Epigraph: Frank and Shaw, *Victory and Occupation,* 386.

1. CMC to CG, 1st Marine Amphib Corps, July 1943, T/O file, RefSect.
2. Muster rolls, RefSect; Neiman interview; Schmidt, son of the 4th Mar. Div. and
later V Amphib. Corps commander Maj. Gen. Harry Schmidt, was yet another
of Robert Denig's lieutenants of the old B Company, 2d Tank Battalion, to take
command. The first M4A2 company formed in a divisional tank battalion was
Ed Bale's company on Tarawa, which became A Company, 2d Tank Battalion,
the former A Company going to the 1st Corps Tank Battalion.

3. Croizat, *Across the Reef,* 67–68.
4. Shaw, Nalty, and Turnbladh, *Central Pacific Drive,* 143–52.
5. Ibid., 155–67; Neiman interview.
6. Shaw, Nalty, and Turnbladh, *Central Pacific Drive,* 167–75; Alphin, "A Bigger Hammer," 159–62.
7. Shaw, Nalty, and Turnbladh, *Central Pacific Drive,* 199–213. The 2d Separate Tank Company remained a poor cousin of the tank battalions, now receiving their M2A4s as hand-me-downs including Ed Bale's 13 recovered from Tarawa; Bale to author, 2 June 1999.
8. Croizat, *Across the Reef,* 243–44.
9. Hunnicutt, *Stuart,* 374; Neiman interview.
10. Neiman interview; C. B. Ash, letter to editor, *MCTA Newsletter* 7 (Jan. 1994): 9.
11. Croizat; *Across the Reef,* 118–19; Neiman interview; Shaw, Nalty, and Turnbladh, *Central Pacific Drive,* 267–71; CO, 4th Tank Battalion, complained that the hydrographic information proved very inaccurate. The use of LVTs to guide tanks across the reef was a failure; they lacked communications links, coordination, and planning, and frequently had too many missions at the same time; CO, 4thTkBn, undated handwritten questionnaire of CG Expeditionary Troops for Saipan, RG127/E46A/23.
12. Shaw, Nalty, and Turnbladh, *Central Pacific Drive,* 271–78; Zaloga, *Armour of the Pacific War,* 22.
13. CO, 23d Mar, to CG, V Corps, 18 July 1944, and CO 1/24 to CG, Northern Force and Landing Force, 17 July 1944, RG127/E46A/23. Box 23 also contains an undated enclosure: "Recap of LVTs (Cargo and Tank) used in Forager Operation to date," showing combined losses of the 733 amtracs of all types used at Saipan by the army and Marine Corps as a total of 184, of which total losses to fire and sinking were 79 LVT2 and -4, 31 LVTA1 and -A4.
14. Shaw, Nalty, and Turnbladh, *Central Pacific Drive,* 284–86; Zaloga, *Armour of the Pacific War,* 22.
15. Shaw, Nalty, and Turnbladh, *Central Pacific Drive,* 415.
16. Muster rolls, RefSect; A Company, 1st Corps Medium Tank Battalion, replaced the company in 3d Tank Battalion.
17. Croizat, *Across the Reef,* 124–26; Shaw, Nalty, and Turnbladh, *Central Pacific Drive,* 458–73.
18. Shaw, Nalty, and Turnbladh, *Central Pacific Drive,* 483, 499; Zaloga, *Armour of the Pacific War,* 23.
19. Shaw, Nalty, and Turnbladh, *Central Pacific Drive,* 508–12.
20. Ibid., 503–47.
21. Ibid., 552–64. On 26 July the battalion commander of 2/3, Lt. Col. Hector de Zayas, was killed by a sniper, ending the career and life of the second commander (1937–39) of the old 1st Tank Company.
22. CO, 4thTkBn, undated handwritten questionnaire of CG Expeditionary Troops for Saipan, RG127/E46A/23; Shaw, Nalty, and Turnbladh, *Central Pacific Drive,* 575.

23. Croizat, *Across the Reef,* 244.

24. P&P, memo to CMC, 2 March 1944, RG127/E18/2148.

25. CO, 4thTkBn, to CG, FMFPAC, 24 Sept. 1944, RG127/E46A/21.

26. P&P, decision memo, 16 Sept. 1944, RG127/E18/2148.

27. P&P memo, 16 Sept. 1944, and CMC, 31 Oct. 1944, RG127/E18/2148.

28. Muster rolls, RefSect; the last tank unit formed 10 Sept. 1944 in the U.S. was Tank Company, 29th Marines (later C Company, 6th Tank Battalion), commanded by the Jacques' Farm gunnery instructor, Capt. Hugh Corrigan. One of the platoon leaders, 2d Lt. Richard M. "Roughhouse" Taylor, would become a favorite of USMC tankers as a company commander in the Korean War and battalion commander in Vietnam.

29. Files of the tracked vehicle schools in RG127/E18/532, 533, and 497. The CG, San Diego area, in his message of 24 Nov. 1943, reported the maximum capacity of the tank operator's course to be 850 troops; Box 533.

30. Croizat, *Across the Reef,* 134–36; Burns, "Origin and Development of U.S. Marine Corps Tank Units," 80; Joseph H. Alexander, *Storm Landings* (Annapolis, Md.: Naval Institute Press, 1997), 112; George W. Garand and Truman R. Strobridge, *Western Pacific Operations,* vol. 4 of *History of U.S. Marine Corps Operations in World War II* (Washington, D.C.: Historical Division, HQMC, 1971), 91–105.

31. Garand and Strobridge, *Western Pacific Operations,* 109–25; Zaloga, *Armour of the Pacific War,* 24.

32. Garand and Strobridge, *Western Pacific Operations,* 125.

33. Hunnicutt, *Stuart,* 376, and *Sherman,* 403–4; Burns, "Origin and Development of U.S. Marine Corps Tank Units," 81, 141.

34. Burns, "Origin and Development of U.S. Marine Corps Tank Units," 83; Garand and Strobridge, *Western Pacific Operations,* 154–264, 274 passim.

35. CG, Army Forces, POA memo, 7 Dec. 1944, forwarded by CINCPAC to CG FMFPAC, suggesting FMF initiate request for flame tanks, RG127/E238D/3; Hunnicutt, *Sherman,* 406; Neiman interview.

36. Garand and Strobridge, *Western Pacific Operations,* 535–36, 563–65.

37. Ibid., 620, 708; Alphin, "A Bigger Hammer," 177, 183.

38. Croizat, *Across the Reef,* 164–71; Burns, "Origin and Development of U.S. Marine Corps Tank Units," 90–93; One T6-equipped tank apparently brushed with a destroyer, causing wags to claim the only instance of such a collision at sea; Bill Henahan, "Another First for the 1st!" *MCTA Newsletter,* no. 198 (Feb. 1998): 4.

39. Frank and Shaw, *Victory and Occupation,* 703; Burns, "Origin and Development of U.S. Marine Corps Tank Units," 92; Roy E. Appleman, James M. Burns, Russell A. Gugeler, and John Stevens, *Okinawa: The Last Battle* (Rutland, Vt.: Charles E. Tuttle, 1960), 204; Croizat, *Across the Reef,* 172. Joseph Alexander notes that the 10th army staff at first wanted the 1st Tank Battalion assigned to the southern front, but the 1st Marine Division commander would tolerate no such breakup of his team; *Storm Landings,* 162.

40. Ed Bale, letter to author, 26 May 1999.

41. Croizat, *Across the Reef,* 173–74; Appleman et al., *Okinawa,* 431–34.

42. Frank and Shaw, *Victory and Occupation,* 324.

43. CO, 1stTkBn, to G-3, 1stMarDiv, 25 May 1945, RG127/E46A/18.

44. Neiman interview.

45. Frank and Shaw, *Victory and Occupation,* 337–42; Walter Moore, "The Battle for Kunishi Ridge," *MCTA Newsletter* 3 (July 1992): 17–21.

46. Frank and Shaw, *Victory and Occupation,* 386.

47. R. K. Schmidt, memo for C/S, FMFPAC, 3 May 1945, Conference on Tank Matters, and CG, FMFPAC, 21 May 1945 report of conference, RG127/E46A/18.

48. Burns, "Origin and Development of U.S. Marine Corps Tank Units," 141; draft SOP, enclosed in CG, FMFPAC, 21 May 1945 report of conference, RG127/E46A/18.

49. CG, V Corps, to CG, FMFPAC, 19 April and 24 June 1945, RG127/E46A/18.

50. CMC, letter to CG, FMFPAC, 18 June 1945, RG127/E46A/18.

51. CG, FMFPAC, to CG III, V Corps, 13 July 1945, RG127/E46A/18. A cargo ship bearing an emergency army shipment of twelve M26s arrived at Naha port and put the first of these tanks ashore via LCTs on 30 July; Richard P. Hunnicutt, *Pershing: A History of the Medium Tank T20 Series* (Berkeley, Calif.: Feist Publications, 1971), 41–44.

52. 3dDiv, message to FMFPAC, 14 June 1945; CO, 3dTkBn, to CG, FMF, 5 July 1945; CG, 1stMarDiv, to CMC, 27 July 1945, RG127/E46A/18.

Chapter 6. Taking Stock

Epigraph: Kris P. Thompson, "Trends in Mounted Warfare," *Armor* (May–June 1998): 43–45, and (July–Aug. 1998): 55–58.

1. Millett, *Semper Fidelis,* 438–47.

2. James Ralph Davis, "From the Sea: The Tactical Development of Marine Corps Tracked Amphibian Vehicles," M.A. thesis, University of San Diego, 1995, 396–422. Davis cites Darslow inventory of 1 Sept. 1048: 1,273 LVT3, 50 LVT4, 14 LVT4(A), 80 LVT(A)5 "new," 11 LVT3, 22 LVT4, and 52 LVT4(A) "used"; Croizat, *Across the Reef,* 200; Subsequent experience would show that maintenance in storage of such materiel remained beyond the capabilities of the depot system in this period; CMC to QMMC, 16 Aug. 1950, National Archives—Suitland, Md., Headquarters Marine Corps Correspondence, Record Group 127, 63A-2000, Box 191 (hereafter RG127/63A-2000/191); CMC to CO, 5th Depot (Guam), 2 Feb. 1949, noted 66 of these last worn or unserviceable LVT3 were ordered disposed of locally; National Archives—Suitland, Md., Headquarters Marine Corps Correspondence (classified), Accession 0008113, Box 35 (hereafter RG127/8113/35).

3. CMC to CNO, 26 May 1950, RG127/8113/35.

4. Burns, "Origin and Development of U.S. Marine Corps Tank Units," 105–7. On Japanese army inability to cope with tank attacks, see Meirion Harries and Susie Harries, *Soldiers of the Sun* (New York: Random House, 1991), 353.

5. CMC memo, 18 April 1948, RG127/E18/2148.

6. Ord Sup Div, memo to P&P, 18 Oct. 46, and CG, FMFPAC, message, 9 Dec. 1945 (ordered fifty M4A3 to China for 1stMarDiv; seventeen were lost in typhoon), RG127/E18/2148.

7. CMC memo on flame tanks, 6 May 1946, and CMC to QMMC on postwar allowance, 11 June 47, RG127/E18/2148. The POA-CWS-H5 version, upgraded with the 105mm gun, would serve in Korea.

8. CMC to FMF, 16 Dec. 1948, continues policy of his 4 March 1947 decision cited in P&P memo, 17 April 1947, RG127/E18/497.

9. CMC to Chief, BuShips, 19 Oct. 1949; HQMC cover sheet, 8 May 1950, to SF Naval Shipyard report of progress for 11 March 1950–30 April 1950 (n.d.); RG127/8113/35; Davis, "From the Sea," 420, 463. The LVT(A)5 also received a turret cover and bow extension. Good sources on LVT evolution are Steve Zaloga, *U.S. Amphibious Assault Vehicles* (London: Osprey, 1987), and Robert J. Icks, *AFV Profile 16: Landing Vehicles Tracked* (Windsor, England: Profile Publications, n.d.). A lucid essay by an LVT pioneer is Victor J. Croizat,"Fifty Years of Amphibian Tractors," *Marine Corps Gazette* (March 1986): 69–76, expanded later in his *Across the Reef.*

10. Director, MC Schools, to CMC, 22 March 1946, RG127/E18/487.

11. QMMC to CMC, 29 Sept. 1947, citing CMC memo of 12 Oct. 1945; CMC to QMMC, 23 Oct. 1947; Chief, BuOrd to Army Chief of Ord, 23 Oct. 47; RG127/E18/2148; Donald Gagnon to author, 8 June 1999.

12. CMC to C/S Army, 25 April 1949, subject medium tank, G3, memo to G4, 4 Nov. 1949, RG127/8113/40. G4 annotation on CG, 2d Div message 052220Z, July 1949; P&P, memo to Ord Supl Section, 27 Oct. 1949; RG127/18/2148.

13. P&P Division, memo to Ord Supl Section, 27 Oct. 1949, RG127/18/2148.

14. Calif. Dept. of Public Works, 1 Oct. 1948; QMMC to Director, MC Schools, 13 Sept. 1951, on approving request for tank platoon for Quantico Schools Battalion. RG127/63A-2000/191–93.

15. SOP for 1st Armored Amphib Bn, 22 Jan. 1946, RG127/E46A/2.

16. Shepherd to CMC, 20 March 1947, RG127/63A-2000/1118.

17. Smock to Director, P&P, 10 May 1950, RG127/63A-2000/1099.

18. CG, V Corps, to CG, FMFPAC, 4 Aug. 1945, RG127/E46A/18.

19. Steven T. Ross, *American War Plans, 1945–1950* (London: Frank Cass, 1996), 49, 67–70, 88–90.

20. Ibid., 114–17. Still later, the Marine Corps Objective Plan 1961 (MOP61), 22 Jan. 1958, makes assumptions that the 2d Marine Division and two-thirds of the 2d Marine Aircraft Wing would deploy to Europe one month after mobilization, the West Coast Division/Wing deploy the second month and the USMCR 4th Division/Wing the sixth month. One other Division/Wing would remain in the Pacific. This is not a war plan, but next best; RG127/60A2514/1.

21. CMC to CG, FMFLANT, 27 Jan. 1949, RG127/8113/40; G4 memo, 24 Jan. 1949, citing earlier message version; RG127/8113/38.

22. Armor Policy Board Report, 15 April 1949, RG127/8113/38.

23. Marine Corps University Archives, Marine Corps Equipment Board 1950 (hereafter MCEB50), 101.
24. MCEB50, 103–8.
25. Armor Policy Board Report, 15 April 1949, RG127/8113/38.
26. MCEB50, 109. Lieutenant General Metzger has assured me that the Armor Policy Board was indeed the brainchild of Jeb Stuart, who virtually ran its agenda and report from start to finish; Louis Metzger, interview with author, 19 March 1999. Senior member, MC Board, to Executive Director for Review of MCEB50, 14 Nov. 1950, RG127/8113/20.
27. The MCEB 1950 document similarly prescribed operational concepts and materiel acquisition goals for most arms of the Corps which remained firmly enshrined at least until the demands of the Vietnam War accelerated the emerging military technology for general-purpose forces. It should be treated as a seminal document in any study of Marine Corps doctrine and acquisition practices.
28. CMC memo, 23 June 1949, on FY51 tank requirements, citing Armor Policy Board Report; RG127/18/2148. CMC to QMMC, 14 April 1950, directed buy of max. qty. T42 for $2.45M, for war reserve; RG127/18/6853. Director, P&P, to chair Ind Plan Group, Army War Pl Branch, 31 Oct. 1949, showed modest acquisitions continuing for the current medium M26 and proposed heavy T43:

Type	Initial Issue	Replacements	Stock
M26	68/0	16/16	8/0
T43 or later	12/0	3/3	1/0

The same document stated the cumulative requirements for the first mobilization year as 1,000 M26 and 504 T43 tanks. RG127/8113/40.
29. RG127/E18/2148.

Chapter 7. Arming for Pax Americana

Epigraphs: P&P to OP-09M, 3 April 1950, Current Dev. of Army Tank Policy, RG127/08113/40; Davis, "From the Sea," 502.

1. Neiman interview; Gearl M. English, interview with author, 7 Oct. 1998; Donald Gagnon, interview with author, 18 March 1999. For the story of the 1st Marine Brigade, see Lynn Montross and Nicholas A. Canzona, *The Pusan Perimeter,* vol. 1 of *U.S. Marine Operations in Korea, 1950–1953* (Washington, D.C.: Marine Corps Historical Center, 1954).
2. English interview; Montross and Canzona, *Pusan Perimeter,* 50–51, 63, 129, 144.
3. Montross and Canzona, *Pusan Perimeter,* 175, 192–95.
4. CG, 1stBde, to C/S Army, 23 Aug. 1950, with attached photos and routing sheet, RG127/8113/33 and 40.
5. Montross and Canzona, *Pusan Perimeter,* 219–25; For an evaluation of the Russian 45mm AT gun vs. the M46, see Spl Report Type C, AT Co, 1st Marines: eleven hits at 1,400 yards, summarizing superficial damage; RG127/65A1099/70.

6. Lynn Montross and Nicholas A. Canzona, *The Inchon Seoul Operation,* vol. 2 of *U.S. Marine Operations in Korea, 1950–1953* (Washington, D.C.: Marine Corps Historical Center, 1955), 24, 76, 131. 1stTkBn War Diary for Aug. and Sept. 1950, RG127/65-A5099/81.

7. Montross and Canzona, *Inchon Seoul Operation,* 90–139.

8. Ibid., 147–56.

9. Ibid., 188–251.

10. Ibid., 229. This incident may well form the basis for Barrow's refusal as CMC to modernize the USMC tank fleet.

11. Ibid., 259–97. 1stTkBn War Diary for Sept. 1950, RG127/65-A5099/81.

12. 1stTkBn War Diary for Nov. and Dec. 1950.

13. Eric Hammel, *Chosin: Heroic Ordeal of the Korean War* (New York: Vanguard, 1981), 50.

14. Ibid., 273–80, 409–18. 1stTkBn War Diary for Dec. 1950.

15. Lynn Montross, Hubard D. Kuokka, and Norman W. Hicks, *The East-Central Front,* vol. 4 of *U.S. Marine Operations in Korea 1950–1953* (Washington, D.C.: Marine Corps Historical Center, 1962), 13–216, passim. The huge size of the tank battalion stems from the incorporation of the three antitank company tank platoons (five M26) of the infantry regiments, plus three M4A3 dozer tanks per tank company (seventeen M26) authorized in the war; 1stTkBn War Diary, Jan–Dec. 1951. Perhaps as a sign of improved morale, the commander reported twenty cases of gonorrhea at Masan the first week of January.

16. Pat Meid and James M. Yingling, *Operations in West Korea,* vol. 5 of *U.S. Marine Operations in Korea, 1950–1953* (Washington, D.C.: Marine Corps Historical Center, 1972), 17–98, passim. Cmd Diary, AT Co, 1stMarDiv, April 1953, NARS/Suitland/65-A5099/70. Cmd Diary, 1st Arm Amphib Bn, Dec. 1952, Box 72. Cmd Diary, 1st Amtrac Bn, Box 71.

17. Meid and Yingling, *Operations in West Korea,* 114–392, passim. 1stTkBn, April–July 1953.

18. G4ord (Lieutenant Colonel Stuart), memo to G4, 13 July 1950: Tanks: "The Marine Corps has intentionally conserved its limited stocks of M26 tanks for operational contingencies, providing only a platoon in headquarters company to enable peacetime tank battalions to become proficient in the use of the M26, should re-equipment for major operations be dictated (Armor Policy Board Report dated 15 April 1949). This policy proved most wise." RG127/8113/40.

19. 1stTkBn War Diary, June 1951, RG127/65A5099/81. Sup Dept, QMMC, letter to CMC, 27 March 1951, RG127/63A-2000/191. The Porcupine tank, albeit advanced in concept, exceeded the available technology: the power demand proved too much for vehicle batteries, and HF radios required grounded pole antennae, which were erected with wires, and struck for movement; Prentiss Baughman, interview with author, 8 Oct. 1998. The Camp Lejeune Depot reported to CMC, 11 Sept. 1951, on the slow progress

on building ten Porcupines, hence the program may have been abandoned; RG127/63A2000/191.

20. Muster rolls, 1950–58, RefSect.

21. G4 order for tools for 7thTkBn (M4A3, M46 tanks), 18 Sept. 1950; CMC to QMMC, 17 Nov. 1950; CMC to CG, FMFLANT, 26 Dec. 1950, notes cadres for 8th Tank Battalion still in 2d Division, hence allocates all M4 tanks to 2d Division; RG127/8113/40.

22. G4 to P&P, 18 June 1950; Fiscal to QMMC, 20 Dec. 1950, advised of T43 heavy tank production delayed delivery until 1952; Suppl. budget had $95M for 190 tanks, RG127/8113/40.

23. Ord Sect, memo to G4, 11 Aug. 1950; CMC decision on acquiring M47 by memo to QMMC, 2 Oct. 1951; issue to 2dTkBn, USMCR, QMMC, letter to Inspector and Instructor, Syracuse, 13 Nov. 1952; CG, Camp Pendleton, to CMC, 30 Dec. 1952, on M47 in schools; RG127/63A-2000/191.

24. Command diaries, 3dTkBn, Jan.–Dec. 1955, showing 35–55% deadline rates, RG127/65-A5099/94. QMMC, letter to G4, HQMC, 1 Dec. 1958, notes shipping of M48 to 3d Marine Division, with M47s to be disposed of "in best interests of government," RG127/63A-2000/191.

25. G4, memo to Ord Branch, 19 July 1952 on T48 deficiencies; CG, 2dMarDiv, letter to CMC, 28 Dec. 1954, on modifications to M48; QMMC, letters to CMC, 2 Dec. 1955 and 15 July 1955, notes CMC intention to equip 8th Tank Battalion with M48 until heavy tank ready; CMC, letter to CG, 2dMarDiv, 7 Jan. 1956, citing M48 dozer kit in production, Sept. 1956. Marine Corps M48s became M48A1 tanks through the normal depot overhaul cycle, commencing in 3d quarter FY57, CMC to Ch, Army Ord, 28 Nov. 1956, RG127/63A-2000/191–93.

26. R. P. Hunnicutt, *Patton: A History of the American Main Battle Tank* (Novato, Calif.: Presidio, 1984), 86, 434–36.

27. On the M67/T66, see CMC, letter to CG, Army Chem Corps, 18 June 1952, RG127/63A-2000/191; and Hunnicutt, *Patton*, 252, 444.

28. CMC to C/S Army, 17 Nov. 1949; Army Chem Ctr to Log Div, Army Staff, 29 Dec. 1949, RG127/8113/26. CMC to QMMC, 22 Aug. 1950, orders $100,000 transferred to the army for flame tank, pursuant to 23 March conference, RG127/8113/40. CMC to C/S Army, 22 Dec. 1950, urging design and production of flame turret for T42 tank, expediting viz. marine division requirement, RG127/8113/38.

29. Senior member, MC Board, to Executive Director for Review of MCEB1950, 14 Nov. 1950, RG127/8113/20. R&D, memo to P&P, 24 Nov. 1950, citing G2, 27 Sept. 1950, comment; P&P tank/amtrac/antimech officer (Stuart), memo to executive director, P&P, 8 Dec. 1950; RG127/8113/40. The M24 tanks acquired in 1945 for amphibious testing still languished in storage at Barstow, albeit reduced by one to nine; QMMC to P&P, 29 May 1950, request to return to army was denied on 9 June 1950 with instructions to keep on hand, RG127/E18/2148.

30. CMC, letter to Director, Education Center, 3 Dec. 1952; QMMC to CMC, 2 Dec. 1955, citing CMC decision of 15 July 1955; RG127/63A-2000/191.

31. Richard P. Hunnicutt, *Firepower: A History of the American Heavy Tank* (Novato, Calif.: Presidio, 1988), 219; Don Beal, interview with author, 29 Dec. 1997.

32. G3, Troop and Organization program, FY62–71, 14 Sept. 1961, RG127/64A3742/2.

33. P&P to OP-09M, 3 April 1950, Current Developments in Army Tank Policy, RG127/8113/40.

34. AC/S G4 to Material Requirements Branch, G4, 24 Jan. 1958, Heavy tank T43 status: notes for expected congressional hearings. Army system treats T43 as low priority. USMC has $120M investment thus far. Troop basis approved by C/S, 21 Jan. 1958: the division tank battalion will be two M48, one M103 company. Separate force heavy tank company in each FMF, activated for mobilization only (i.e., USMCR). Thus 51 peacetime in units plus 4 in schools = 55, plus mob stocks of 164 = 219 total; RG127/60A2514/2. HQMC files contain copies of 114 quality deficiency reports turned in April 1953 on the T43E1, RG127/63A2000/191.

35. Hunnicutt, *Firepower,* 113–28. The initial M103A1 tank issues went to the third companies of 1st and 2d Tank Battalion with later distribution to the reserve battalions. There was a plan to equip the 1st Tank Battalion entirely with M103A1 tanks, treating it as a force tank battalion for support of the 3d Tank Battalion overseas, and CMC ordered this implemented in December 1958. This never occurred, and the 1st Tank Battalion turned in forty M103A1 vehicles in 1961, apparently kept on its supply account but not issued to the troops. CMC to CG, FMFPAC, 12 Dec. 1958, RG127/60A2514/3; QMMC, letter to G4, 7 March 1961, RG127/67A6485/29. On the loan of 72 tanks, Army DC/S Logistics, letter to G4, HQMC, 15 Sept. 1959, RG127/66A4849/17. The long storage period produced serious deterioration of the engine oil coolers, which suffered high failure rates, but funds existed only to rectify under the later depot overhaul cycle, CMC, letter to CG, Barstow, 6 Feb. 1959, RG127/66A4849/17. See also QMMC, letter to CMC, 19 July 1958, announcing first shipments in Oct. 1958, Ord Section memo, 26 July 1956, with shipping instructions. For 104 M51 retrievers, CMC to C/S, army message 282002, March 1956, requesting modification of USMC heavy tanks as soon as possible, with no requirement for dozer kits; RG127/63A-2000/193. Thanks to MSgt. Dan Shepetis for explaining the inner workings of the M103 turret to this one-time user, letter to author, 17 July 1999.

36. CNO to CO, SFNS, 20 Sept. 1950; CO, SFNS, 29 Sept. 1950, reports progress; RG127/8113/3; P&P, memos to OP-09M, 10 and 15 Aug. 1950, MC FY 92 requirements for LVT and LVT(A); CMC to QMMC, 25 Aug. 1950, set the distribution priorities of the initial production: replace losses in 1st Amtrac Battalion, five to the Training and Replacement Regiment, one to test center, replace all remaining 1st Battalion vehicles, then 255 to East Coast depot; RG127/8113/35.

37. BuShips, memo for file, 18 July 1951, on LVTP5/H6 production; CMC to FMF commanders, 14 April 1953, on LVT3C rebuild; HQMC chief of staff to

G4, 3 Jan. 1953, on initial deliveries; advance logistic data for LVTE1, 31 July 1963, the last of the production; RG127/63A-2000/191. G4 to CMC, 9 Sept. 1963, Staff Study 4-63, Annex A, "A History of LVT Management 1940 to 1962," RG127/63A-7645/19. The archives of the Amphibious Vehicle Test Branch (AVTB), operating since 1948 at Camp Pendleton, contain the details of the engineering development and testing of all amtrac and related amphibians considered by the Corps since then. The pioneer amtrackers Metzger and Croizat urged the Corps staff *not* to build the LVTP5 design in 1950, because it offered too few technical advances since 1945 on too large a vehicle; Metzger interview.

38. See also Zaloga, *U.S. Amphibious Assault Vehicles.* After action report, B Co, 3d Amtrac Bn, 7 April 1955, on landing Army 38th RCT in exercise near San Simeon, using 56 LVT3C and four LVTP5 during Feb.–March 1955; RG127/65-A5099/Box 94. Surf test by LVTP5 no. 49, 7 Oct. 1957, AVTB Archives. The rival LVT6 program was canceled on 10 Oct. 1956 by CMC, the design retained as an easily mass-produced alternate LVT in general war. CMC reported to BuShips in letter, 28 Dec. 1956, that the Corps was "satisfied" with the integral armor of the P5 and H6, and had no interest in pin on armor kits, preferring welded kits in the event of future requirements; RG127/63A-2000/191.

39. Borg-Warner Corp., "Research, Investigation, and Experience in the Field of Amphibian Vehicles for the U.S. Marine Corps," Final Report (December 1957), copy in AVTB Archive.

40. William B. Allmon, "The Ontos," *Vietnam* (Aug. 1994): 12–16; E. L. Bale Jr., "Ontos," *Marine Corps Gazette* (Oct. 1957): 48–50. Regimental antitank companies disbanded 20 Dec. 1957; press releases and unit histories from Ontos file, RefSect; QMMC to G4, 15 June 1956, on Ontos production; QMMC to G4, 15 Oct. 1961, on M50A1; RG127/63A-2000/191. Advance logistic data on M50A1, 16 Oct. 1963, RG127/69A-7645/19. G4, memo to C/S, 7 Feb. 1961, provides procurement history of Ontos; QMMC, memo of 19 July 1956, request for maximum number of M50 for $22.514M earmarked in budget. Objective was 349 vehicles. CMC to QMMC, 20 Dec. 1954, directed procurement under FY56 funds and 296 were bought that year, RG127/64A3742/2.

41. LFB-16, *Employment of the Rifle, Multiple, 106mm, Self-propelled M50(T165E2)(Ontos),* 5 Nov. 1955, and LFB-23, *Employment of the Antitank Battalion,* 23 Dec. 1959, gave way in 1965 to the FMFM 9-3, *Anti-mechanized Operations.*

42. Davis, "From the Sea," 502. Millett, *Semper Fidelis,* 524–27.

43. 1stMarDiv, Final Report of Reorganization Test, 4 June 1957, NARS/Suitland/ 65A-5099/4770.

44. CMC to FMFPAC, 19 Nov. 1958, decision to reequip one company of each force battalion, 1st and 2d, with M103, RG127/60A2514/2. CMC to CG, Barstow depot, 11 April 1958, 3d Division will reequip with M48 tanks and M67 flame tanks (thus ending the M4A3 service in the USMC), RG127/60A2514/5. CMC to CG, FMFLANT, 13 Feb. 1958, to deactivate 8th Tank Battalion, 3d Co, 2dTkBn, to receive M103 when available. As late as

13 Feb. 1958 CMC considered sending a heavy tank company to the 3dTkBn: CMC, speedletter to CG, FMFPAC, RG127/60A2514/1.

45. FY63 Annual Program Objectives (8 March 1961) shows return of tank and amtrac battalions to division in FY63, RG127/64A3742/2. G3 to MC Planning & Program Committee, 13 June 1961: Recommend return of tank and amtrac units to division; increase of tank company to four platoons, parallel to four rifle companies; notes that old tank platoon, AT Company of regiment, was typically given to supporting tank company as its fourth platoon. All this is for mid-range plan period, impact on five-year procurement, RG127/64A3742/1. Combat Unit Evaluation, FMF Orgn Test Prog., 23 March 1961, proposes division tank battalion of four companies (one heavy) each 22 tanks (four platoons), with two guns, nine flame tanks in Battalion HQ, RG127/67A6485/9; QMMC to G4, 20 March 1958, also notes shortages for M51 and amtracs, RG127/60A2514/2; G4 to Director, USMCR, 15 Nov. 1961, on shortages of M50 in USMCR.

46. Muster rolls, RefSect; Director, USMCR, to CMC, 10 April 1963, has enclosed list of tank requirements and assets, RG127/67A6045/1.

47. Jack Shulimson, *Marines in Lebanon, 1958* (Washington, D.C.: History and Museums Division, 1966, 1983), 18–25, 27, 37, 40; Beal interview; The BLT in theory was a task-organized unit for amphibious operations, but in practice it became a standardized reinforced battalion with an attached artillery battery and platoons each of tank, amtrac, antitank, engineers, trucks, and reconnaissance and service troops.

48. SecDef Press Conference, 6 Feb. 1963, RG127/71A4525/8; G-3, memo, 13 June 1961, items for newsletter: notes FMF augmentation to Guantanamo naval base: one rifle company, tank platoon, artillery battery, two HRS helos, RG127/64A3742/1; Beal interview. The heavy tank assignment to Cuba, justified by the presence of Russian JS-2 heavy tanks, proved the sole overseas use of USMC M103 tanks.

49. G4, memo to C/S, 25 Jan. 1961: status of ordnance, and G-3, memo to CMC, 8 April 1961, on army weapons systems objectives, RG127/64A3742/1–2.

50. G-4, brief to CMC, 16 March 1961, on type classification of T153 (120mm) and T300 (90mm) ammo, RG127/64A3742/2.

51. G4, memo to Plans, 4 Aug. 1961, forwarding G4 staff study #2-61, and G3 to distr Troop&Org Program, FY62–71, 14 Sept. 1961, RG127/64A3742/2.

52. QMMC, letters to G4, 7 Aug. 1961 and 15 Nov. 1961, RG127/67A-6485/29. Advance Log Data for M103A2, 15 May 1964, RG127/70A-5214/20. The DON Installations and Logistics (I&L) to ASD (I&L), 16 Oct. 1967, equipment distribution and condition report shows only 160 M103A2 in inventory, RG127/71A4525/8.

53. CMC to various CG on tracked vehicle modernization, 17 May 1962, NARS/Suitland/68A-4244/18. CMC to CNO, 16 June 1965, on LCA vehicle, NARS/Suitland/70A-5214/20.

54. CMC, letter to C/S Army, 29 Oct. 1956; Formal Schools Training program, HQMC, 22 May 1958; CMC to CG, Camp Pendleton, 17 April 1957; RG127/63A-

2000/128. HQMC Schools report, 31 Dec. 1964, RG127/71A6199/3. Millett, *Semper Fidelis,* 534, notes overall decline in the training establishment from 23.5 to 17.5% of total personnel strength during 1957–61.

55. On 3d Tank Battalion, Robert C. McInteer, interview with author, 7 Oct. 1998, and Charles J. Barone, interview with author, 8 Oct. 1998. On turret trainer model 3-T-1, CMC to LFDevAct (Landing Force Development Activity), 8 Feb. 1961, RG127/67A6485/9.

56. Numbered battalions corresponded to parent divisions, except for the 1st Amtrac Battalion; stranded in the Far East after the Korean War, it remained thereafter attached to the 3d Marine Division. The 3d Amtrac Battalion supported the 1st Marine Division. One company each of the 1st Amtrac and 3d AT Battalion served in Hawaii with the 1st Marine Brigade.

Chapter 8. From Jungle to Desert

1. Steel Pike folder, RefSec; Barone interview.

2. Jack K. Ringler and Henry I. Shaw Jr., *U.S. Marine Corps Operations in the Dominican Republic, April-June 1965* (Washington, D.C.: Historical Division, HQMC, 1970), 18–20, 24–25; "The 2d Antitank Battalion in the Dominican Crisis," n.d., 2d AT file, RofSect.

3. Millett, *Semper Fidelis,* 559–60, 577.

4. Command Chronologies (CC), 5th Tank, Amtrac and AT Bns, Operational Archives, Marine Corps Historical Center. Unit history sketches and copies of the personnel diaries are held by the Reference Section. The heavy tank C Company, 1st Tank Battalion, was refitted with medium tanks and left its M103A2s in Camp Pendleton, for a new D Company, attached to 5th Tank Battalion. 5th Tank Battalion received its last required M48A3 in Feb. 1969, and was deactivated at the end of the same year. 5th Amtrac experienced a 50% admin. deadline rate (no crews) in mid-1968. But the 5th Antitank Battalion busied itself, firing 3,200 and 7,750 rounds of 106mm ammunition the last semester of 1968 and first of 1969.

5. 5th MarDiv, press release on xenon searchlight, 5thTkBn file, RefSect; CO, 1st AT Bn, to CO, 1st, 5th, 7th Mar, and CG, 1st MarDiv, 30 April 1966; 1st AT Bn file, RefSect; two on the ridge cited by Stephen L. Parrish, "A Light Tap with a Strong Arm: Doctrine and Employment of Marine Corps Armor from 1965 to 1975," *Armor* (Sept.–Oct. 1992): 18.

6. CC, 1stTkBn, Sept. and Dec. 1968, April and Dec. 1969; CC, 3dTkBn, Jan.–Feb. 1966, March–April 1966, Aug.–Sept. 1967, Jan. 1968; Davis, "From the Sea," 545–66. Highly critical of USMC tactics in Vietnam is Parrish, "Light Tap with a Strong Arm."

7. Davis, "From the Sea," 536ff.

8. Ibid., 568–69, 576. Allmon, "The Ontos," 16. Comparing 1962 and Oct. 1967 inventories shows twelve fewer M48, perhaps representing combat total losses to date. Many M48s in later service bore marks of previous shaped-charge penetrations, as did many of the LVTP family of vehicles.

9. Jack Shulimson and Charles M. Johnson, *U.S. Marines in Vietnam: The Landing and the Buildup, 1965* (Washington, D.C.: History and Museums Division, HQMC, 1978), 72–78; Croizat, *Across the Reef,* 222–23. Two men received Navy Cross medals for heroic actions at the LVT ambush site, hardly compensating for the tactical handling of the action; the commander of the infantry battalion also received the Navy Cross.

10. Gary L. Telfer, Lane Rogers, and V. Keith Fleming, *U.S. Marines in Vietnam: Fighting the North Vietnamese, 1967* (Washington, D.C.: History and Museums Division, HQMC, 1984), 11, 125–28; CC, 3dTkBn, July 1967.

11. Telfer, Rogers, and Fleming, *U.S. Marines in Vietnam,* 145–46; By early 1968, the amtrac battalion had support of three 4.2 mortars of 12thMarDiv and frequently had support by local engineers, Vietnamese army and militia, USMC tanks and recon, and army mechanized infantry; Jack Shulimson, Leonard A. Blasiol, Charles R. Smith, and David A. Dawson, *U.S. Marines in Vietnam: The Defining Year, 1968* (Washington, D.C.: History and Museums Division, HQMC, 1997), 38.

12. Shulimson et al., *The Defining Year,* 119.

13. Ibid., 186–216; CC, 1stTkBn, 3dTkBn, Feb. 1968; the four tanks of 3d Tank Battalion received 28 hits by recoilless rifle and RPG, one M48 becoming a total loss. A Co, 1stTkBn, reported 34 RPG and two mine hits, no losses; three Ontos became total losses.

14. Shulimson et al., *The Defining Year,* 255, 544; Parrish, "Light Tap with a Strong Arm," 20; CC, 3dTkBn, July 1967–Jan. 1968.

15. Shulimson et al., *The Defining Year,* 253, 544; Parrish, "Light Tap with a Strong Arm," 20; On army use of Ontos, Robert Swartz, interview with author, 26 April 1999, keyed by his letter in the April 1999 *Marine Corps Gazette.*

16. The Ontos stationed with the Guantanamo Bay garrison continued to operate until April 1980, by then with only one vehicle still operational and two used for parts; Jeffrey Wilkinson to author, 28 June 1999.

17. CG, MCDEC report, 31 Dec. 1968, on project 30-67-09: Report on FMF Capabilities for Antitank Warfare (Mid-Range Period), 4 vols. Study based on two wargames of MEF faced by large mech. forces; 33% of engagements were under 1,000m, hence Dragon was favored over TOW antitank missile; no discussion of missions, tactics; RG127/71A4525/6.

18. CMC, letter to BuShips, 29 Jan. 1962, NARS/Suitland/70A-5214/20. CMC, letter to BuShips and Director, USMC Landing Force Development Acty, 25 Nov. 1963, Director, Landing Force Development Activity, 22 July 1963; NARS/Suitland/69A-7645/19; misc. notes from AVTB Archives.

19. LVTPX-11 Project, RG127/68A4244/21–22.

20. Zaloga, *U.S. Amphibious Assault Vehicles,* 39–41; CG, Development and Education Center (MCDEC), to CMC, 25 March 1969, Service Test Final Report demonstrated the following results for maintenance reliability of the LVTPX-12, compared to the LVTP-5 (P7/P5): mean time between failures 7.1

hours/2.61; mean mileage between failures, 85.8/25.4; availability percentage, 54/34; maintenance hours per 110 miles, 6.16/20; 5th Amtrac Bn, report of troop test, 24 Oct. 1968; 1968 trials of the tank diesel installation in the P-5 (a possible backup to further development failures) produced definite overheating problems; LVTPX-12 files, AVTB Archives.

21. CO, 2d Amtrac Bn, 17 July 1973; work stopped on the 20mm mount in Sept. 1969; subsequent trials that month of the .50 mount revealed failures in the electric charger and feed chutes, 7,650 rounds fired with 28 stoppages, but FMC claimed that 17 of the stoppages cleared by recharging the weapon; PX-12 files, AVTB Archives.

22. CMC to various cdrs, 10 Nov. 1971, M67A2 flame tanks, RefSect.

23. CG, FMFLANT, to CG, 2dMarDiv, 251808, Aug. 1976, on attachment of 2d Amtrac Bn to 2dMarDiv, 2d Amtrac Bn file, RefSect; Brig. Gen. Harold Glasgow, the MAU commander in Germany, confirmed the outcome of Exercise *Strafer Zügel* in a briefing he gave officers of BLT 2/8 prior to their exercise at Twenty-nine Palms, Feb. 1979, attended by author and Dennis Beal; the author's tank company included veterans of these and other NATO exercises of the period.

The demise of the flame tank, long insisted upon by the Corps as a distinctive ordnance development item, deserved more than a terse statement of HQMC. Citing its poor reliability and maintainability, low usage rate in peacetime, and, most significantly, the cost of developing or converting such a weapon for the newer M60-series tank, the final letter of instruction determined it "an uneconomical investment." CMC, letter to various commanders, 10 Nov. 1971, M67A2 Flame Tanks, RefSect.

24. LVA and LVX general data from Zaloga, *U.S. Amphibious Assault Vehicles,* 41–43. LVA technical evaluation, AVTB, 20 Feb. 1975; LVA Operational Requirement, MCDEC, 21 Jan. 1975; AVTB archives.

25. New Cummins engines came after 1983, and an "upgunned weapons station," pairing a 40mm automatic grenade launcher with a .50-caliber machine gun, was fitted 1987–92. The P900 appliqué armor kit (189 bought) gave protection to front and side vs. 12.7mm fire and the follow-on AAK kit protected against the Russian 14.5mm at 300m distance. Production lines resumed 1983–86 for another 329 vehicles for the MPS storage (see below); Davis, "From the Sea," 616, 621–40. The penultimate rebuilt of the now-venerable AAV-7 series, now weighing 28–31 tons, will be the "RAM" upgrade entering service in 1999: Bradley engine and suspension, new transmission; AVTB brief to author, April 1997.

26. Senate Report 94-106 (19 March 1975); CMC to Major General Haynes, 19 June 1975, RG127/94-0085.

27. CMC guidance, including "get ROC [required operational capability] out on XM1 as soon as possible" contained in 19 Jan. 1975 letter and route sheet, signed by Maj. Gen. Keith Smith, RG127/94-0085.

28. Public Affairs Branch draft press release, memo for corresp., and Q&A list, 17 May 1976; Major General Haynes, news briefing transcript, 24 March

1976; Requirements, Program and Resources (RPR), memo to Public Affairs and Information (PAI), 5 May 1977; RG127/94-0085.

29. RPR, memo to PAI, 5 May 1977, signed by Maj. Gen. Edward J. Bronars, RG127/94-0085; Fred Haynes, interview with author, 29 June 1999.

30. David R. Stephanson and Maurice A. Roesch III, "The Selection of a Light Armored Vehicle for the Marine Corps," research paper, Industrial College of the Armed Forces, 1982, 9; Francis T. Klabough, "Mobile Protected Weapons System May Be a Substitute for Tanks," *Marine Corps Gazette* (March 1978): 31–34.

31. LAV Directorate, MCDEC, MPWS Final Test Report (1980), VI-1–6; The testing at Fort Hunter Liggett included all current antitank and armored weapons, and a surrogate MPWS design based upon M551 chassis with more powerful engines; ARMVAL After Action Report, 1981 (unclassified), Research Library, Marine Corps University.

32. Documents including the Solicitation of Award (14 April 1981), Purchase Description (Feb. 1982), and LAV Directorate Program Management Folder (1982) are grouped in folders in the stacks of the Research Center, Marine Corps University; Kenneth W. Estes, "LAV: Quo Vadis," *Marine Corps Gazette* (Dec. 1981): 18–19. Andrew Findlayson to author, 21 April 1997. Klabough interview.

33. Ronald H. Spector, *U.S. Marines in Grenada, 1983* (Washington, D.C.: History and Museums Division, HQMC, 1987), 16–21. The actual first combat use of the M60A1 and LVTP7 came with the Israeli Army (1973) and Argentine Naval Infantry (1982), respectively.

34. Benis M. Frank, *Marines in Lebanon, 1982–84* (Washington, D.C.: History and Museums Division, HQMC, 1987), 27, 81, 123–25.

35. Nicholas E. Reynolds, *Just Cause: Marine Operations in Panama, 1988–1990* (Washington, D.C.: History and Museums Division, HQMC, 1996), 15, 22–26.

36. Appliqué armor briefing, 19 May 1990; logistics concerns cited in an undated 1986 point paper from the HQMC logistics staff. The final requirement for the M1A1 later was pared to 443, 430, and then 420 tanks, by reducing war reserve and maintenance float numbers, but some staff officers still consider the 490 figure the valid acquisitions goal; CMC to Congressman Earl Hutto, 2 May 1994; M1A1 Tank System Modernization Plan, July 1997; these notes and papers from Hist. File, Tank Section, Ground Combat Weapons Branch, Marine Corps Systems Command, Quantico, Va. (hereafter TkSect); copies in author's files.

37. Steele bio file, RefSect; Martin R. Steele, interview with author, 1 May 1997.

38. The 1st Tracked Vehicle Bn, formerly 1st Assault Amphib Bn, remained on Okinawa, but its AAV and tank companies went to the campaign. The 4th Tank Battalion sent only two tank companies.

39. CC, 1st, 2d, and 3dTkBn, Feb. 1991.

40. Charles J. Quilter II, *With the I Marine Expeditionary Force in Desert Storm and Desert Shield* (Washington, D.C.: Marine Corps Historical Center, 1993). Norman Friedman, *Desert Victory: The War for Kuwait* (Annapolis, Md.:

Naval Institute Press, 1991); USMC Armored Vehicles, brief for SecDef, n.d., and M1A1 program briefing for SecDef, 13 June 1991, TkSect; Stan Owen, "Marine Corps M1A1 Tanks in Operation Desert Storm," *Amphibious Warfare Review* (Summer/Fall 1992): 50–54; CC, 1st and 2d LAI Bn, Jan.–Feb. 1991. The 1stMarDiv forward CP was saved by the intervention of seven LAVs under Capt. Eddie S. Ray, who counterattacked about fifty Iraqi vehicles, earning one of the two Navy Crosses presented in the war (the other went to an attack helo squadron commander), Desert Storm Awards, RefSect; Davis, "From the Sea," 648, notes seventy-two line charge kits sent to Saudi Arabia prior to the start of the offensive. In a way reminiscent of World War I, many AAVs were equipped with two fascines, each made up of fifty-five six-inch plastic pipes, for use in crossing trenches and ditches.

41. Capt. Dennis Green, commanding A Company, 2d LAI Battalion, in Robert E. Osborn, *Sand and Steel: Lessons Learned on U.S. Marine Corps Armor and Anti-Armor Operations from the Gulf War,* Marine Corps Lessons Learned Data Base Section (Quantico, Va.: Marine Corps Combat Development Command, [1992]), 32.

Chapter 9. Paradigms for the Future

Epigraphs: CMC to Congressman Earl Hutto, 2 May 1994, in author's files. James Feigley, Operational and Technical Concepts for the Advanced Amphibious Assault Vehicle briefing paper, in author's files.

1. Stephen K. Scroggs, "M1A1 Tank Transfer," in Congress and Military Policy Course 231 (Carlisle, Pa., 1998), 58–115; Steel interview; Dennis Beal, interview with author, 29 Dec. 1997. The last active operations of USMC M60A1 tanks ended in May 1994 when the tank platoon of the Guantanamo Bay, Cuba, garrison deactivated; Jeffrey Wilkinson to author, 28 June 1999.

2. PM-AAV to author, 21 June 1999. Not an AAV7A2, instead a RAM-RS (Reliability, Availability, Maintainability, and Rebuild to Standard) program. The fleet numbers 1,321 AAV7A1 on hand: 1,057 kept in service: 680 RAM-RS (599P/46C/35R), 377 unmodified (including MPS stocks).

3. The bridging vehicles were issued in 1987. Only 221 of the Marine Corps M1A1 tanks are late-production common tanks with the depleted-uranium armor; the tanks transferred from the army came from earlier production runs: 48 army common tanks and 134 earlier production plain (no depleted-uranium armor) tanks. The USMC tank inventory at the end of the century stands at 403, M1A1 Tank System Modernization Plan (July 1997), 8, TkSect; The final reorganization of active and reserve tank battalions is in CMC message 112003, May 1992, TkSect; Kenneth W. Estes, "A Well-Led Corps . . ." *The Almanac of Seapower* (1994); Estes, "A New Day May Be Dawning for the Nation's '911' Force," *The Almanac of Seapower* (1995); Estes, "Force of Choice," *Armed Forces Journal International* (Sept. 1995): 46–50; "Armor in the Amphibious Force," USNI *Proceedings* (April 1986); "What Is Heavy, What Is Light?" *Marine Corps Gazette* (July 1987): 30. Estes,

"Implications of STOM for Armored Forces," *Marine Corps Gazette* (March 1999): 53–57.

4. Marine Corps Order 3501.23, "Tank T&R Manual," 20 Sept. 1995.

5. Estes, "Force of Choice," 49.

6. Interview with Maj. Michael F. Campbell, formerly in charge of the 1stTkBn detachment, Task Force Mogadishu. "MOOTW" has been supplanted already by the term "small-scale conflict" (SSC), doubtlessly a more satisfying term.

7. J. A. Marliewicz and P. C. Laing, "LAR: Peace Enforcers," two-page manuscript, author's files; 3dBn, 8thMar, fact sheet, "LAR/TOW Integration in the OOTW Environment," author's files.

8. M1A1 Tank System Modernization Plan (July 1997), 8, TkSect. Tank ammunition has remained a weakness in the Marine Corps programming: there were no projectiles capable of killing the Russian T-72 in 1979 in USMC magazines for the 105mm M60A1, nor could the 120mm rounds bought in 1992 likely kill the next-generation T-80 (upgraded).

9. USMC Future Force, "MAGTF Expeditionary Family of Fighting Vehicles" briefing, 30 Oct. 1998, TkSect.

10. Rollout of the first fully equipped vehicle came on 23 June 1999, attended by author; technical data sheet, 22 Aug. 1997, and 1997 program brief, AAAV Technology Center, Woodbridge, Va. No family of vehicles emerges from the AAAV program. Only a command and communication suit, perhaps in palletized form, will provide a variant differing from the troop carrier, which also loses the ability to employ line charges for mine clearance.

11. Interview with Maj. Brian C. Colebaugh, USMC, LAV Program Mgr Office, 22 July 1999: the fire-control improvements include second-generation thermal sights, laser rangefinder, and improved gunners controls.

12. "Tentative Landing Operations Manual 2014," Marine Corps Combat Development Command, Quantico, Va., 1998; Estes, "Implications of STOM for Armored Forces," 53–57.

13. Interview with Lt. Gen. Martin R. Steele. Lieutenant General Steele, the highest-ranking Corps tanker in its history, reflected upon his twelve years' experience as a key staff officer in planning and executing the fielding plans for the M60A1 and M1 series tanks in the USMC.

14. Steele interview.

15. Krulak, statement cited in *Marine Corps Gazette* (July 1999): 23.

Bibliography

Documents

Archives. Amphibious Vehicle Test Branch. Marine Corps Base, Camp Pendleton, Calif.

Archives. Marine Corps Research Center, Marine Corps University, Quantico, Va.

Command Chronologies (CC), Operational Archives. Marine Corps Historical Center, Washington, D.C.

General Records of the Department of the Navy, Record Group 80. National Archives and Records Administration. Washington, D.C., and Suitland, Md.

Headquarters Marine Corps Correspondence, Record Group 127. National Archives and Records Administration, Washington, D.C., and Suitland, Md.

Historical File, Tank Section, Ground Combat Weapons Branch. Marine Corps Systems Command, Quantico, Va.

Reference Section. Marine Corps Historical Center. Washington Navy Yard, Washington D.C. (Muster rolls, unit diaries, biography and subject files, etc.)

Official Publications

Bailey, Alfred Dunlop. *Alligators, Buffaloes, and Bushmasters: The History of the Development of the LVT through World War II*. Washington, D.C.: History and Museum Division, HQMC, 1986.

Battlefield Assessment Team. "Armor/AntiArmor Operations in Southwest Asia." Research paper 92-0002. Quantico, Va.: Marine Corps Research Center, July 1991.

Clifford, Kenneth J. *Progress and Purpose: A Developmental History of the United States Marine Corps, 1900–1970*. Washington, D.C.: HQMC, 1973.

FMF Manual 9-3. *Antimechanized Operations*. Washington, D.C.: HQMC, 1965.

Frank, Benis M. *Marines in Lebanon, 1982–84*. Washington, D.C.: History and Museums Division, HQMC, 1987.

Frank, Benis M., and Henry I. Shaw. *Victory and Occupation*. Vol. 5 of *History of U.S. Marine Corps Operations in World War II*. Washington, D.C.: Historical Division, HQMC, 1968.

Garand, George W., and Truman R. Strobridge. *Western Pacific Operations*. Vol. 4 of *History of U.S. Marine Corps Operations in World War II*. Washington, D.C.: Historical Division, HQMC, 1971.

Green, Constance M., Harry C. Thomson, and Peter C. Roots. *The Ordnance Department: Planning Munitions for War*. Washington, D.C.: Chief of Military History, Department of the Army, 1955.

Hough, Frank O., Verle E. Ludwig, and Henry I. Shaw Jr. *Pearl Harbor to Guadalcanal*. Vol. 1 of *History of U.S. Marine Corps Operations in World War II*. Washington, D.C.: Historical Division, HQMC, 1958.

LFB-16. *Employment of the Rifle, Multiple, 106mm, Self-propelled M50-(T165E2)(Ontos)*. Washington, D.C.: HQMC, 5 Nov. 1955.

LFB-23. *Employment of the Antitank Battalion*. 23 Dec. 1959

Marine Corps Equipment Policy 1950. Quantico, Va. Copy 1745 in Archives, Marine Corps Research Center, Marine Corps University, Copy 1, in RG 127/8113/Box 21.

MCS 3-91. *Tanks*. NAVMC 4880. Quantico, Va.: Marine Corps University, 1951.

Meid, Pat, and James M. Yingling. *Operations in West Korea*. Vol. 5 of *U.S. Marine Operations in Korea, 1950–1953*. Washington, D.C.: Marine Corps Historical Center, 1972.

Montross, Lynn, and Nicholas A. Canzona. *The Inchon Seoul Operation*. Vol. 2 of *U.S. Marine Operations in Korea, 1950–1953*. Washington, D.C.: Marine Corps Historical Center, 1955.

———. *The Pusan Perimeter*. Vol. 1 of *U.S. Marine Operations in Korea, 1950–1953*. Washington, D.C.: Marine Corps Historical Center, 1954.

Montross, Lynn, Hubard D. Kuokka, and Norman W. Hicks. *The East-Central Front*. Vol. 4 of *U.S. Marine Operations in Korea, 1950–1953*. Washington, D.C.: Marine Corps Historical Center, 1962.

Osborne, Robert E. "Sand and Steel: Lessons Learned on U.S. Marine Corps Armor and Anti-Armor Operations from the Gulf War." Marine Corps Lessons Learned Data Base Section. Quantico, Va.: Marine Corps Combat Development Command, [1992].

PHIB-18. *Amphibious Operations: Employment of Tanks*. NAVMC 4059. Quantico, Va.: Marine Corps Schools, 1948.

PHIB-23. *Amphibious Operations: The LVT and LVT(A)*. NAVMC 4576. Quantico, Va.: Marine Corps Schools, 1948.

Quilter, Charles J., II. *With the I Marine Expeditionary Force in Desert Storm and Desert Shield*. Washington, D.C.: Marine Corps Historical Center, 1993.

Reynolds, Nicholas E. *Just Cause: Marine Operations in Panama, 1988–1990*. Washington, D.C.: History and Museums Division, HQMC, 1996.

Ringler, Jack K., and Henry I. Shaw Jr. *U.S. Marine Corps Operations in the Dominican Republic, April–June 1965*. Washington, D.C.: Historical Division, HQMC, 1970.

Shaw, Henry I., Jr., and Douglas T. Kane. *Isolation of Rabaul*. Vol. 2 of *The History of U.S. Marine Corps Operations in World War II*. Washington, D.C.: Historical Division, HQMC, 1963.

Shaw, Henry I., Bernard C. Nalty, and Edwin T. Turnbladh. *Central Pacific Drive*. Vol. 3 of *History of U.S. Marine Corps Operations in World War II*. Washington, D.C.: Historical Division, HQMC, 1966.

Shulimson, Jack. *Marines in Lebanon, 1958*. Washington, D.C.: History and Museums Division, 1966; reprint, 1983.

Shulimson, Jack, Leonard A. Blasiol, Charles R. Smith, and David A. Dawson. *U.S. Marines in Vietnam: The Defining Year, 1968*. Washington, D.C.: History and Museums Division, HQMC, 1997.

Shulimson, Jack, and Charles M. Johnson. *U.S. Marines in Vietnam: The Landing and the Buildup, 1965.* Washington, D.C.: History and Museums Division, HQMC, 1978.

Spector, Ronald H. *U.S. Marines in Grenada, 1983.* Washington, D.C.: History and Museums Division, HQMC, 1987.

Telfer, Gary L., Lane Rogers, and V. Keith Fleming. *U.S. Marines in Vietnam: Fighting the North Vietnamese, 1967.* Washington, D.C.: History and Museums Division, HQMC, 1984.

U.S. Marines in Vietnam. 10 vols. Washington, D.C.: History and Museums Division, HQMC, 1977–97.

Books

Alexander, Joseph H. *Storm Landings: Epic Amphibious Battles in the Central Pacific.* Annapolis, Md.: Naval Institute Press, 1997.

———. *Utmost Savagery: The Three Days of Tarawa.* Annapolis, Md.: Naval Institute Press, 1995.

Appleman, Roy E., James M. Burns, Russell A. Gugeler, and John Stevens. *Okinawa: The Last Battle.* Rutland, Vt.: Charles E. Tuttle, 1960.

Chamberlain, Peter, and Chris Ellis. *Pictorial History of Tanks of the World, 1915–45.* Harrisburg, Pa.: Stackpole, 1972.

Crismon, Fred. *U.S. Military Tracked Vehicles.* Osceola, Wis.: Motorbooks International, 1992.

Croizat, Victor J. *Across the Reef: The Amphibious Tracked Vehicle at War.* London: Blandford Press, 1989.

Frank, Richard B. *Guadalcanal: The Definitive Account of the Landmark Battle.* New York: Random House, 1990.

Friedman, Norman. *Desert Victory: The War for Kuwait.* Annapolis, Md.: Naval Institute Press, 1991.

Hammel, Eric. *Chosin: Heroic Ordeal of the Korean War.* New York: Vanguard, 1981.

Harries, Meirion, and Susie Harries. *Soldiers of the Sun.* New York: Random House, 1991.

Hofman, George F., and Donn A. Starry, eds. *From Camp Colt to Desert Storm: A History of U.S. Armored Forces.* Lexington: University of Kentucky Press, 1999.

Hunnicutt, Richard P. *Firepower: A History of the American Heavy Tank.* Novato, Calif.: Presidio, 1988.

———. *Patton: A History of the American Main Battle Tank.* Novato, Calif.: Presidio, 1984.

———. *Pershing: A History of the Medium Tank T20 Series.* Berkeley, Calif.: Feist Publications, 1971.

———. *Sherman: A History of the American Medium Tank.* Belmont, Calif.: Taurus Enterprises, 1978.

———. *Stuart: A History of the American Light Tank.* Novato, Calif.: Presidio, 1992.

Icks, Robert J. *AFV Profile 16: Landing Vehicles Tracked.* Windsor, England: Profile Publications, n.d.

——. *AFV Profile 24: The M48M60 Series of Main Battle Tanks.* Windsor, England: Profile Publications, n.d.

——. *AFV Profile 32: The M6 Heavy and M26 Pershing.* Windsor, England: Profile Publications, n.d.

Michaels, Greg L. *Tip of the Spear: U.S. Marine Light Armor in the Gulf War.* Annapolis, Md.: Naval Institute Press, 1998.

Millett, Allan R. *Semper Fidelis: The History of the United States Marine Corps.* New York: Macmillan, 1980.

Ross, Steven T. *American War Plans, 1945–1950.* London: Frank Cass, 1996.

Yaffe, Bertram A. *Fragments of War: A Marine's Personal Journey.* Annapolis, Md.: Naval Institute Press, 1999.

Zaloga, Steve. *Armour of the Pacific War.* London: Osprey, 1983.

——. *U.S. Amphibious Assault Vehicles.* London: Osprey, 1987.

Articles

Allmon, William B. "The Ontos." *Vietnam* (Aug. 1994): 12–16.

Bale, Edward L., Jr. "Ontos." *Marine Corps Gazette* (Oct. 1957): 48–50.

Cameron, Robert. "American Tank Development during the Cold War." *Armor* (July–Aug. 1998): 30–36.

Croizat, Victor J. "Fifty Years of Amphibian Tractors." *Marine Corps Gazette* (March 1986): 69–76.

Estes, Kenneth W. "Force of Choice." *Armed Forces Journal International* (Sept. 1995): 46–50.

——. "Implications of STOM for Armored Forces." *Marine Corps Gazette* (March 1999): 53–57.

——. "LAVQuo Vadis." *Marine Corps Gazette* (Dec. 1981): 18–19.

——. "A New Day May Be Dawning for the Nation's '911' Force." *The Almanac of Seapower* (1995): 13–21.

——. "A Well-Led Corps . . ." *The Almanac of Seapower* (1994): 14–23.

Klabough, Francis T. "Mobile Protected Weapons System May Be a Substitute for Tanks." *Marine Corps Gazette* (March 1978): 31–34.

Metzger, Louis. "Duty Beyond the Seas." *Marine Corps Gazette* (Jan. 1982): 28–37.

Ogorkiewicz, Richard M. "LVTP7A1—Latest Tracked Landing Vehicle." *Tracked Armoured Vehicles (Special Series 13), International Defense Review.* Geneva: Interavia, S.A., 1982.

Owen, Stan. "Marine Corps M1A1 Tanks in Operation Desert Storm." *Amphibious Warfare Review* (Summer/Fall 1992): 50–54.

Parrish, Stephen L. "A Light Tap with a Strong Arm: Doctrine and Employment of Marine Corps Armor from 1965 to 1975." *Armor* (Sept.–Oct. 1992): 16–21.

Stuart, Arthur J. "The Beach Minefield." *Marine Corps Gazette* (Oct. 1950): 58–64.

——. "Mechanization of the Amphibious Attack." *Marine Corps Gazette* (July and Aug. 1949) (two parts).

——. "Strengthen the Beach Assault." *Marine Corps Gazette* (Aug. 1948): 10–19.

——. "We Must Learn to Stop Tanks." *Marine Corps Gazette* (Oct. 1947): 18–25.

Thompson, Kris P. "Trends in Mounted Warfare." *Armor* (May–June 1998): 43–45.

Zumwalt, James G. "Tanks! Tanks! Direct Front!" USNI *Proceedings* (July 1992): 73–80.

Unpublished Manuscripts

Alphin, Arthur P. "A Bigger Hammer." Instructional manuscript. The Armor School, Fort Knox, n.d.

Burns, Arthur E., III. "The Origin and Development of U.S. Marine Corps Tank Units: 1923–1945." Student paper, Marine Corps Command and Staff College, Quantico, Va., 1977.

Davis, James Ralph. "From the Sea: The Tactical Development of Marine Corps Tracked Amphibian Vehicles." M.A. thesis, University of San Diego, 1995.

Mundy, J. R. "The Future of Tanks in the Marine Corps." Marine Corps Development and Education Center, student paper, Marine Corps University Archives, Quantico, Va., 1953.

Scroggs, Stephen K. "M1A1 Tank Transfer." In *Congress and Military Policy, Course 231, Readings, vol. 1, 58–115. Carlisle, Pa.: U.S. Army War College, 1998.

Stephanson, David R., and Maurice A. Roesch III. "The Selection of a Light Armored Vehicle for the Marine Corps." Research paper, Industrial College of the Armed Forces, Washington, D.C., 1982.

Interviews

Barone, Charles J. (in S-3 staff of 2dTkBn for Operation Steel Pike), 8 Oct. 1998.

Baughman, Prentiss (Korean War service in 2d and 1stTkBns), 8 Oct. 1998.

Beal, Don (Colonel, USMC [Ret.]; service in 1950s and 1960s in tanks, including development of M103), 29 Dec. 1997.

Brown, Doug (service in World War II in M-H, M2A4, M3, M4 tanks, and LVT4 amtrac), 8 Oct. 1998.

Chapman, Fred D. (Colonel, USMC [Ret.]; from M3 tanks on Samoa with 8thDefBn, went on to command B Co, 1stTkBn in Korea and 3dTkBn in Vietnam), 23 April 1999.

Colebaugh, Brian C. (Major, USMC; Operations Officer in Program Manager's Office Light Armored Vehicles, U.S. Army, TACOM), 22 July 1999.

Dial, Everett D. (service in A Co, 1stTkBn, 1950–51), 10 Oct. 1998.

English, Gearl M. (Max) (Major, USMC [Ret.]; Sergeant in M2A4 on Iceland, 1941; Plt Cdr, 4thTkBn, 1944–45; CO, Co A, 1stTkBn, 1950–51), 7 Oct. 1998.

Fullerton, Cecil R. (in A Co, 1stTkBn, 1950–51; tank commander credited with killing first T-34), 10 Oct. 1998.

Gagnon, Donald (Master Sergeant, USMC [Ret.], with service 1946–76, including A Co, 1stTkBn, 1950; secretary of USMC Tankers' Assn.), 18 March 1999.

Haynes, Fred (Major General, USMC [Ret.]; landed at Iwo Jima with 28th Marines; headed 1975–76 force structure board), 29 June 1999.

Klabough, Francis T. (Colonel, USMC [Ret.]; served in tanks, 1960s–80s, project officer for MPWS), 5 May 1998.

Litchult, Russell J. (service in 8thTkBn, 1950s), 9 Oct. 1998.

McInteer, Robert C. (Colonel, USMC [Ret.]; served in tanks 1960s–80s), 7 Oct. 1998.

Metzger, Louis (Lieutenant General, USMC [Ret.]; tank and pioneer armored amphibian officer, 1941–51), 19 March 1999.

Morell, Philip (Colonel, USMCR [Ret.]; commanded A Co, 3dTkBn, becoming Tk Co, 4th Marines; A Co, 6thTkBn, 1943–45. Later commanded 4thTkBn, USMCR), 29 Sept. 1999.

Neiman, Robert M. (Colonel, USMCR [Ret.]; served in USMC tanks, 1941–46), Jan. 99–Oct. 99.

Rowe, Arthur V. (former TSgt., 1940–45; radio NCO in tank units), 13 May 1999.

Steele, Martin R. (Lieutenant General, USMC [Ret.]; tank and pioneer light armored vehicle officer, 1960–99; project officer for M-1 acquisition by USMC), 1 May 1997.

Stewart, Frank R. (Colonel, USMC [Ret.]; commanded Co B, 2dTkBn, at Tarawa, Saipan, Tinian), 27 July 1999.

Swackhamer, Robert E. (service with 4thTkCo, 3dTkBn, World War II), 10 Oct. 1998.

Swartz, Robert D. (USMC tanker, 1953–54; ret. Army warrant officer), 26 April 1999.

Yaffe, Bertram A. (officer in 3dTkBn, 1942–45), 16 July 1999.

Index

AAAV. *See* advanced amphibious assault vehicle

AAV. *See* assault amphibious vehicle

Aberdeen Proving Ground (APG), 14, 21, 24, 29, 151

Abrams tanks. *See* M1 series (Abrams main battle tank)

A Company, 1st Tank Battalion, in Korean War, 114, 135–40, 163

ACVT. *See* Advanced Combat Vehicle Technology Program

add-on stabilization. *See* stabilization

advanced amphibious assault vehicle (AAAV), 190, 191, 194, 196

Advanced Antiarmored Vehicle Evaluation (ARMVAL), 180

Advanced Base Operations in Micronesia, 4

Advanced Combat Vehicle Technology Program (ACVT), 180

"Alligator." *See* LVT1

Allis-Chalmers Corporation, 155

ammunition, 136; armor-piercing, 92, 113, 137–38, 149, 151–52, 160, 161, 174; canister, 49, 50–52, 69, 74; caseless, 193; high-explosive, 90, 170; tanks landing without, 159, 182, 192

Amphibian Vehicle Test Branch (AVTB) (Camp Pendleton, Calif.), 176

amphibious assault: doctrine, 1, 11, 20, 22, 24, 26, 28, 33, 50, 67, 77–78, 107, 115, 121–26, 128, 195; modern, 121–26, 191, 195

amphibious landing craft, high-speed, 161

amphibious landing techniques, development of, 33–34, 50, 77–78, 82, 121–26

amphibious operations, manuals on, 8–9, 115

Amphibious Operations, The: The LVT and LVT(A) (Phib-23), 115.

Amphibious Operations: Employment of Tanks (Phib-18), 115.

amphibious tanks, 6, 9, 15, 34, 65, 108, 195

amphibious tractor (amtrac). *See* landing vehicle, tracked

amtrac (amphibious tractor). *See* landing vehicle, tracked

amtrac training, 33–34, 66, 91, 112

Anderson, C. E., 25

antitank units: battalions, 31–32, 156, 163, 172, 198; companies, 31, 32, 117–18, 142, 145, 148, 156, 166, 175, 190; platoons, 31, 160, 182–83

antitank weapons, U.S.: guns and rifles, 31, 50, 92, 108, 117–18, 120, 137–41, 145, 155–56, 158; missiles, 158, 175, 183, 188, 190, 201, 204; rockets, 83, 84, 87, 92, 137–38, 140, 180, 182, 190

APC. *See* armored personnel carrier

APG. *See* Aberdeen Proving Ground

Arawe, New Britain, assault on, 69

armor, vehicle: 34, 65; add-on, 70, 81, 103, 108, 184, 185; laminate, 193; testing, 14, 22, 23. *See also specific vehicle*

armor doctrine: in A. J. Stuart's theories, 119–27; for armored amphibians 66; of Armor Policy Board, 130–31; based upon the Pacific War, 115; for corps tank battalions, 54; current, 189–90, 202; early concepts of, 26, 28; post-Vietnam, 174–79

About the Author

Kenneth W. Estes, a native of Seattle, is a 1969 graduate of the U.S. Naval Academy. Trained as tank officer, he served as a company grade officer in the 2d and 3d Marine Divisions, interspersed with academic tours of duty. Promoted to major, he continued his service in the Fleet Marine Force with the 2d Marine Division, and, as a lieutenant colonel, with Headquarters, III Marine Amphibious Force. He then joined the operations staff of Headquarters, Marine Corps in Washington, where he remained until ordered to Madrid with the Office of Defense Cooperation, where he performed various duties, culminating in that of chief of international affairs.

Colonel Estes earned his M.A. from Duke University and Ph.D. from the University of Maryland, all while serving as a Marine Corps officer. He also completed the Army Advanced Armor Officer Course and attended the Marine Corps Command and Staff College. The recipient of two U.S. Meritorious Service Medals and the Navy Cross of Merit, First Class, from the the kingdom of Spain, Colonel Estes is the editor of the *Marine Officer's Guide* and *Handbook for Marine NCOs,* both published by the Naval Institute Press.

Retired from the Marine Corps since 1993, Colonel Estes is a professor of history in the United States and Spain.

The Naval Institute Press is the book-publishing arm of the U.S. Naval Institute, a private, nonprofit, membership society for sea service professionals and others who share an interest in naval and maritime affairs. Established in 1873 at the U.S. Naval Academy in Annapolis, Maryland, where its offices remain today, the Naval Institute has members worldwide.

Members of the Naval Institute support the education programs of the society and receive the influential monthly magazine *Proceedings* and discounts on fine nautical prints and on ship and aircraft photos. They also have access to the transcripts of the Institute's Oral History Program and get discounted admission to any of the Institute-sponsored seminars offered around the country.

The Naval Institute also publishes *Naval History* magazine. This colorful bimonthly is filled with entertaining and thought-provoking articles, first-person reminiscences, and dramatic art and photography. Members receive a discount on *Naval History* subscriptions.

The Naval Institute's book-publishing program, begun in 1898 with basic guides to naval practices, has broadened its scope in recent years to include books of more general interest. Now the Naval Institute Press publishes about one hundred titles each year, ranging from how-to books on boating and navigation to battle histories, biographies, ship and aircraft guides, and novels. Institute members receive discounts of 20 to 50 percent on the Press's more than eight hundred books in print.

Full-time students are eligible for special half-price membership rates. Life memberships are also available.

For a free catalog describing Naval Institute Press books currently available, and for further information about subscribing to *Naval History* magazine or about joining the U.S. Naval Institute, please write to:

Membership Department
U.S. Naval Institute
291 Wood Road
Annapolis, MD 21402-5034
Telephone: (800) 233-8764
Fax: (410) 269-7940
Web address: www.usni.org